Essays on Fiscal Sociology

Finanzsoziologie

Herausgegeben von Jürgen G. Backhaus

Band 1

PETER LANG

Frankfurt am Main · Berlin · Bern · Bruxelles · New York · Oxford · Wien

Jürgen G. Backhaus (ed.)

Essays on Fiscal Sociology

PETER LANG
Europäischer Verlag der Wissenschaften

Bibliographic Information published by Die Deutsche Bibliothek
Die Deutsche Bibliothek lists this publication in the Deutsche Nationalbibliografie; detailed bibliographic data is available in the internet at <http://dnb.ddb.de>.

ISSN 1610-059X
ISBN 3-631-39967-7
US-ISBN 0-8204-6036-2

www.peterlang.de

Content

Introduction

Jürgen G. Backhaus
Professor in Public Finance and Fiscal Sociology
Krupp Chair in Public Finance and Fiscal Sociology
University of Erfurt
Nordhäuser Str. 63
99089 Erfurt
Germany
Fon: ++49-361-737-4551
Fax: ++49-361-737-4559
juergen.backhaus@uni-erfurt.de

Fiscal sociology is a field which deals with the wider ramifications of a state's fiscal activities which can either not readily be captured by micro- or macroeconomic analysis or by financial institutional description. Take a simple example. A tax is levied on a particular good or service, there is a revenue, and there is an excess burden. In conventional analysis, the excess burden is considered a welfare loss. If the tax appears in the guise of a regulation, there may even be the additional monopoly loss, since the state does not receive any revenue. In mainstream analysis, the revenue that the state receives can be construed as being welfare-enhancing, one Euro to one, to the general citizenry, however it might be distributed in any particular case. Overall distributional effects could even out. We know, of course, and most citizens know the same, that this is not true. In fact, it is not a rough guess to say that for every Euro taken in by the state, two are taken out of the economy.

The question that now cannot be avoided is: what happened to the other Euro? It is patently not true that the second Euro can be represented in the second or shadow economy. The shadow economy is an interesting subject in itself, also part of fiscal sociology, but not the main focus of our analysis in these essays. The second economy, in many ways, is a clear case and can be analysed along the same lines as mainstream microeconomic analysis. The macroeconomic implications are also fairly easy to deal with. The second economy is like a cushion to the vicissitudes of the business cycle, and in this sense it helps the Minister of Economic Affairs (people are unemployed, but they spend), and they somehow hurt the Minister of Finance (people do not pay taxes on wages, but since they spend they spend taxes on whatever they spend, and hence politicians push for higher and higher taxes on consumption goods).

It cannot be denied that such a situation turns on a different development that further increases the second economy. If you suddenly have to live on subsistence payments, and perhaps a garden and some other activity, you will spend what you earn on what your household needs, if it does not break down in the process, but consumption patterns will also have to change. In the best of events, more of the necessities will come from the garden. But your car repair can also be gotten from your friend, who is equally unemployed.[1] It is, of course, true that the apples produced in the garden and given in exchange for, let's say car-repair or baby-sitting, do not help the Minister of Finance immediately. But they do in this sense that the mother who was released from baby-sitting and could pursue her job, ends up paying somewhere close to 2/3 of her earnings in various forms. If she is more in the executive range of employment, she may either have a husband who is doing the household work: a rare species to find[2], or she will simply pay, whatever she pays, even if she skirts social insurance payments out of her net, i.e. post-tax income. If she pays the lady from White Russia, who takes care of her children and perhaps takes on other chores, out of her cash income, she has already paid half of her income in taxes before she can even get to the cash nexus. Should she find a benign financial regime, she might be able to deduct documented household expenses from her income, if the nanny's pay were to be deducted, thereby endowing her White-Russian nanny with a certain, but in a way also uncertain claim on retirement benefits, this would bring the entire relationship back into the white economy.

Yet we would still be left with the question, where the other Euro went. Take for example the simplest of cases. A particular good is taxed, the supply curve shifts accordingly downward, and the demand curve is supposed to remain the same. The resources that are designed as the welfare loss have not somehow disappeared into thin air. They have been used for other pursuits, and we have moved from the production possibility frontier inwards into an unknown direction. We do not know how big the upsetting effect has been, we do not even know where the move has gone except for knowing that it has gone inwards. This unexplored drain is the area of fiscal sociology. In this book you find examples in this field. After my own attempt at outlining the intellectual landscape of fiscal sociology, Richard E. Wagner explores the structural issues and Michael McLure gives a general impression of the field. Giuseppe Eusepi takes up the central notion of fiscal illusion and effectively applies this concept to an analysis of the welfare

[1] There is a book in my library which details no-cash goods and services (hotel, garage service, computer help and the like included) for the entire original 15 European Union-states. I am looking forward to seeing the version for the 25.

[2] See "Prinzipalin oder Agentin: Die Organisation als ein Ort ökonomischer Austauschbeziehungen", in Gertraude Krell und Margit Osterloh (Hrsg.), Personalpolitik aus der Sicht der Frauen: Was kann die Personalforschung von der Frauenforschung lernen?, München/Mering: Rainer Hamp Verlag, 1993, S. 206-229.

state. Alexander Ebner deals with Schumpeter's fiscal sociology[3] and Richard E. Wagner harps back to Pareto's *Mind and Society*[4] in a modern application. Francesco Forte, a former Italian senator particularly renowned for his role in the Senate Finance Committee, goes into European finance issues. Issues of equity in taxation and government services are discussed by myself respectively. Norio Sasaki discusses the reception of fiscal sociological theory in Japan in general and Goldscheid's anthropocentric economics in particular. Enrico Schöbel goes into the history of thought, and Helge Peukert deals with two leading authors in fiscal sociology. He shows that Johann Heinrich Gottlob von Justi (1717 – 1771), in many ways the founder of public finance as an academic discipline, already dealt with notions of fiscal sociology as well. Fritz Karl Mann's (1883 – 1979) work is rarely discussed in English, although the author taught in Washington, DC as an exile. Here, Helge Peukert fills a void. Finally, he discusses the new edition of Stiglitz' influential text from the point of view of fiscal sociology.

These essays were originally prepared for and read at the Erfurt Conferences on Fiscal Sociology. Please note that this conference is open to all researchers in this field internationally and it is taking place in the second week of October, before the semester starts.

Jürgen Backhaus

Erfurt, November 2004

3 See also Jürgen Backhaus, "Joseph A. Schumpeter's Contributions in the Area of Fiscal Sociology: A First Approximation", *Journal of Evolutionary Economics* (2004) 14, pp. 143-151.

4 Vilfredo Pareto, *The Mind and Society,* edited by Arthur Livingston, 2 Vols. New York: Dover, 1963.

Fiscal Sociology: What For?

Jürgen G. Backhaus
Professor in Public Finance and Fiscal Sociology
Krupp Chair in Public Finance and Fiscal Sociology
University of Erfurt
Nordhäuser Str. 63
99089 Erfurt
Germany
Fon: ++49-361-737-4551
Fax: ++49-361-737-4559
juergen.backhaus@uni-erfurt.de

Abstract: In discussing the question: fiscal sociology: what for, I shall first give a short sketch of the history of thought of the field. Secondly, main issues are identified. First in discussing the concept of the tax state, we emphasize issues in constitutional public finance. Secondly, one of the fields in which fiscal sociology has been most important is the issue of taxation, and notably income taxation. Thirdly, in citing applications and issues, an entire alphabet of fiscal sociological issues is being identified. The third paragraph deals with the future of the field in both instruction and research.

Keywords: Rudolf Goldscheid, Vilfredo Pareto, Joseph Alois Schumpeter.

JEL codes: B1, B2, H0, Z0.

1 A Short History of Fiscal Sociology

Fiscal sociology as a separate field makes sense only once economics and sociology have parted ways, leaving a void in between. Originally, when economics started as a separate field of instruction and research on the European continent, there was no need for a specialty in fiscal sociology. In repeating a perhaps familiar story, economics in an institutional sense started on the European continent when King Frederick William of Prussia, being dissatisfied with the state of the instruction of his future civil servants, founded two chairs in cameral sciences at the universities of Halle (Saale) and Frankfurt (Oder) in 1723. Cameral sciences meant, in essence, public finance. Hence, on the European continent, economics as a separate discipline started with public finance as the core subject area, since the purpose of economic thinking and teaching was to develop institutions so as to foster the wealth and happiness (*Wohlstand und Glückseligkeit*) of the states and thereby the people living in the house of the state. Hence, the wealth of a nation was seen as the result of prudent state economic policy. It would take another 99 years before at Oxford the first chair in political economy was founded in Britain. Here, the question of the nature and causes of the wealth of nations (1786) had been posed rather differently by Adam Smith. He saw the causes as lying in the division of labour as a precondition for extensive trade; the state would be reduced to taxation and upholding the public order, but was not seen as an active participator in economic activity. These two views of economics prevail to this very day, and they are often seen in different positions taken with respect to economic policy undertaken by the European Union.

While on the European continent, ever-larger numbers of students had been trained in economics, the instruction in the field was late to come in Britain and the United States. In Britain, the introduction of the tripos by Alfred Marshall brought a very small number of students indeed. In the United States, it was notably the emerging activity of Washington-based agencies in matters of social policy which required a larger number of well-trained economists and statisticians, i.e. a development of the 20th century. When from 1723 onwards, economics was taught on the European continent, it was done in the context of cameral and policy sciences and the law. Cameral sciences were essentially economics and public finance, all this embedded in a broad social policy approach with the state and its institutions as the main source of initiative. Next to this, the student would be instructed in public administration (*Policeywissenschaften*) and law, with a strong element of technology-related issues covered as well. These might have to do with mining, agriculture, forestry or manufacturing. This entire field of related areas was called *Staatswissenschaften*, and many universities therefore had their own faculties of *Staatswissenschaften*, binding these fields of what today is law, economics, public administration, political science, sociology and contemporary history and policy together. This organization of instruction and research explains why the literature in economics and public finance all through the 19th century has a strong multi-disciplinary and interdisciplinary character, certainly as seen from today's point of view. Even in the 20th century, this is still true for the work of such authors as Werner Sombart, Joseph Alois Schumpeter or Max Weber who, while pioneering in sociology, did not consider themselves primarily sociologists. They all embody the fusion of economics and sociology: in Sombart's case, with economic history in addition, in Schumpeter's case with his strong push for economic analysis and econometrics and in Weber's case with the additional integration of law, his original field of expertise. However, with the pioneering work of Emile Durkheim, Vilfredo Pareto, Georg Simmel and Ferdinand Tönnies, the separate field of sociology had emerged.[1]

[1] The *Deutsche Gesellschaft für Soziologie* was founded in 1909 as an expression of specific research questions and paradigms not generally pursued by economists. For instance, Durkheim and later Franz Oppenheimer explored the connections between economic conditions

These separate developments in sociology had the effect that the two disciplines, economics on the one hand and sociology on the other, parted ways. With the rapid development of the social sciences in the 20th century, economics including public finance, business economics, public administration, sociology, political science and policy science all came to exist side-by-side with separate research programs, and the links between all of them on the one hand and law on the other became more and more severed.[2]

The differentiation of separate disciplines within what formerly had been *Staatswissenschaften* left lacunae or gaps in between. While methodological eclecticism had reigned within the *Staatswissenschaften* with very few exceptions[3], now the different disciplines within the social sciences also differentiated themselves by the methods used and, from a methodological point of view, became more homogeneous internally, but heterogeneous in distinguishing one from the other. The logical consequence was a formation of clusters linking subjects with the appropriate methods. While some subjects remain amenable to an analysis by different methods, others became neglected. As we compare, for instance, the tables of contents of two Chicago-based journals, the *Journal of Political Economy* and the *American Journal of Sociology*, we notice that many topics recur in both publications, such as issues relating to the family, issues relating to behaviour in the workplace or issues relating to the organization of firms and enterprises. Remarkably different are, of course, the questions asked and the methods of analysis used, although both journals emphasize empirical work. On the other hand, the large comprehensive studies leading to ambitious projects of legislation, which characterized the activities of leading social scientists towards the end of the 19th and the beginning of the 20th century by the end of 20th century, have become de-emphasized. The reason is easy to see. Such large legislative enterprises as the launching of a welfare state, the codification of the civil code, a commercial code or the formation of a system of public law

---

and people's health states; Durkheim's were the pioneering studies on suicide. Pareto, having completed the Manual of Political Economy, saw a need to push beyond economics proper and constructed a generalized social system in his treatise translated as "The Mind and Society" by Livingston. Simmel presented in Schmoller's seminar a socio-philosophical study of money, exploring all those aspects of money that are not economic. See also: Backhaus and Stadermann (2000a) and (2000b). Sombart was interested in the conditions which led to the development of modern capitalism and in his historical studies had to go beyond economic causes, emphasizing social, political and legal preconditions for the development of capitalist institutions. Tönnies emphasized community and society, while Weber left us the gigantic attempt at Economy and Society.

[2] The last instance of a close cooperation between economists and lawyers may have been the critique at the first draft of the German civil code mounted by Schmoller and Gierke, which had led to the second draft that was signed into law in 1896 and became effective - to this very day - from 1900 on. See also Backhaus (1999a) and (1999b).

[3] One of them may have been the early attempt by Christian Wolff, who tried to put the entire system within his edifice of natural law. See Backhaus (1998a).

or variously the construction of a workable comprehensive national system of health care all require carefully combined eclectic methods synchronized with respect to the questions asked, the empirical data generated and used, and the policy advice generated so as to be fit for legislation and implementation.

That the differentiation in the social sciences had led to a gap which needed to be filled with a fresh approach became clear towards the end of World War I, when the system of war finance had not only destroyed the state institutions of the allied powers of Germany and Austria to the core; next to the immense human and material losses, the defeated states could not continue their operation after the war in the way they had done before. This was first pointed out by Rudolf Goldscheid, who is also the father of the term fiscal sociology (*Finanzsoziologie*) and therefore one of the first classical authors in the field. His contribution has to be seen next to that of Joseph Schumpeter, since Schumpeter in his classic piece "The Crisis of the Tax State" responded to Goldscheid's analysis and thereby contributed the second classical piece to the field. To this debate, we should now turn.

2 Main Issues

2.1 The Debate on the Crisis of the Tax State

The roots of contractarian or constitutional reasoning are to be found in the tradition of liberalism. The doctrines of liberalism, insofar quite different from the present Leviathan approaches centred around two related sets of civil rights for which constitutional guarantees were sought as a means of protection against the discretion of the king or sovereign: this is because as far as the absolute ruler is concerned, property end the domain of individual liberties are substitutes; in principle, for each infringement on individual liberties imposed by a ruler to further some of his interests, there is a functional tax equivalent with which these interests can be equally served, and *vice versa*. This broader view is also taken into account by Goldscheid, who accordingly advanced an evolutionary theory of the state where, in the beginning, the state as personified by the prince could seek either revenues or services in kind.

Goldscheid's theory systematically relies on this dualism, upon which a second dichotomy is constructed. There are two classes of citizens in the population, the owners of labour and the owners of capital. While the state is able to tax the former and, beyond the point of optimal tax extraction, demand services in kind, capital, which is more flexible and powerful in his model, is only borrowed, and the state incurs the public debt. Where the first group actually contributes to the state's expenses through taxes or (mostly military) services, the second receives a claim in return, a claim which has to be satisfied later out of the general tax revenue or by services in kind.

These services, in particular the draft, play a crucial role in Goldscheid's politico-economic analysis, which is also designed to explain the extraordinary length of duration of World War I. Both Goldscheid[5] and Schumpeter[6] agreed that some state activities, such as the war, could never have been carried out had the enormous cost immediately and visibly been shifted to an identifiable public through ex-propriative taxes. While Schumpeter, however, argued more technically in terms of the maximum exhaustibility of the tax base, Goldscheid put forward his interest group perspective, where the creditors to the public (capital owners) had no interest to end the war, never expecting to be required to foot the bill, rather receiving reliable promises to be repaid.

In either case, the war debt contributed to **fiscal illusion** in that it covered up the destruction of real resources and property and so helped carry out policies which, had their true costs been obvious to the citizens, would never have been accepted. When honouring the war debt, in Goldscheid's model, the labour class would end up with the entire bill as the creditors to the public demanded their interest and repayment out of the national dividend.

It is here where Goldscheid's peculiar approach to the notion of human capital (*Menschenökonomie*) becomes relevant. Whereas the contributions of the labour class to the expenses of the state represent real goods and services, either taxes which represent part of the national product, services in kind or other infringements on individual liberty, the capital class contributes only credits, which are to be repaid. Thus, even when real capital, human and material, is used up or destroyed, only the owners of material capital continue to present claims. These claims constitute political leverage, which, still according to Goldscheid, the creditors use to have the state governed in their own interest.

Whereas this model was obviously constructed under the impression of politico-economic interaction during the First World War in Austria and Germany, Goldscheid's proposal for fiscal reform was based more broadly on his unorthodox interpretation of the fiscal history of the state, from the middle Ages to his days. This story begins with a strong state, independent and relatively rich, relying on large property holdings. Only after the Thirty Years' War, however, the rising demands of the budget exercised by war finance and the desolation of the country give rise to a new approach to economic policy: cameralism, where the state, gradually transforming itself into the tax state, follows policies of economic development in order to strengthen the tax base, notwithstanding engagement in traditional and new forms of public entrepreneurship; both types of policies

[5] Goldscheid (1919).
[6] Schumpeter (1954, 1976).

aiming at long run revenue maximization. This dual policy is constrained by the two relationships governing fiscal technology as discussed above: first, the Cameralist relationship as the interdependence between public spending and the productivity of the tax base; and second the experience of rising marginal costs of tax extraction, which leads to the definition of a point of optimal extraction (Laffer curve).

The issue of defining a tax constitution has re-emerged on the political agenda with the European Union beginning to take shape and with elements of an emerging European constitution becoming visible. These tasks, which we face today, cannot be solved in a technical manner based on simple models. The fiscal constitution of the European Union will have to meet on the one hand the classical criteria developed in political doctrine, it has, on the other hand, to be in line with the requirements of a modern global economy, and thirdly it has to, not only accommodate member states with very different constitutions, economic and political systems, including different systems of taxation and political decision-making, but also different histories, cultures and socio-political visions. In order to meet this challenge, the different disciplines of public finance, law, public administration, political science and sociology will have to join forces as they had in the tradition of *Staatswissenschaften*. In order for such a joint venture to be successful, integrative paradigms such as those of the tax state may very well be useful in the future as they have been in the past.

2.2 *Income Taxation*

At a conference of the international Schumpeter Society in Kyoto (Japan)[7], Richard A. Musgrave, a student of Schumpeter's surprised his audience by insisting that Schumpeter's contribution to public finance had been minimal. He only emphasized, and actually overemphasized the distortions caused by income taxation. In fact, Schumpeter's name rarely appears in current textbooks on public finance.[8] Indeed, Schumpeter's extensive contributions to public finance[9] tend to be collected in his sociological or political writings.[10]

---

[7] Shionoya and Perlman (1994).

[8] The only exception seems to be Richard E. Wagner's public finance textbook.

[9] He taught public finance at the University of Bonn from 1925 to 1932 and contributed fiscal analyses extensively to Wolfgang Stolper's "Der deutsche Volkswirt".

[10] Schumpeter, Joseph A. (1928), *Das deutsche Finanzproblem*, Berlin: Der deutsche Volkswirt.

Schumpeter, Joseph A. (1939), *Business Cycles*, New York: McGraw Hill, 1964.

Schumpeter, Joseph A. (1943), *Capitalism, Socialism and Democracy*, London: Unwin.

Schumpeter, Joseph A. (1954), *A History of Economic Analysis*, New York: Oxford University Press.

In this sense, Musgrave is perhaps correct that most of these writings do not fit within his three-winged cathedral of public finance dealing with allocation, distribution, and stabilization. Schumpeter stood firmly in the continental European tradition of public finance, from Puviani with his emphasis on fiscal illusions to Wicksell[11] with his emphasis on taxation and political decision-making and Da Empoli's[12] emphasis on the multiple economic and social distortions caused by all manner of taxation. In this sense, Schumpeter never severed the ties between public finance and the neighbouring disciplines and can therefore be properly claimed as one of the fathers of fiscal sociology. Indeed, Musgrave's hint may service to offer a simple explanation of what fiscal sociology is about.

2.3 *Applications and Issues*

In the simplest of cases, consider a product (bagels) and an excise tax levy on this product.

Schumpeter, Joseph A. (1954), *Dogmenhistorische und biographische Aufsätze*, Tübingen: Mohr Siebeck.
Schumpeter, Joseph A. (1961), *A Theory of Economic Development*, New York: Oxford University Press.
Schumpeter, Joseph A. (1965), *Ten Great Economists: From Marx to Keynes*, New York: Oxford University Press.
Schumpeter, Joseph A. (1967), *Economic Doctrine and Method*, New York: Oxford University Press.
Schumpeter, Joseph A. (1970), *Das Wesen des Geldes*, Göttingen: Vandenbroeck & Ruprecht
Schumpeter, Joseph A. (1985), *Aufsätze zur Wirtschaftspolitik*, Chr. Seidl and W.F. Stolper (eds.), Tübingen: Mohr Siebeck.
Schumpeter, Joseph A. (1992), *Politische Reden*, with comments by Chr. Seidl and W.F. Stolper (eds.), Tübingen: Mohr Siebeck.
Schumpeter, Joseph A. (1993), *Aufsätze zur Tagespolitik*, with comments by Chr. Seidl and W.F. Stolper (eds.), Tübingen: Mohr Siebeck.
Schumpeter, Joseph A. (2000), *Briefe/Letters*, U. Hetke and R. Swedberg (eds.), Tübingen: Mohr Siebeck.

[11] Wicksell (1896).

[12] Da Empoli (1931).

Figure 1: Standard Example for Tax Burden Analysis

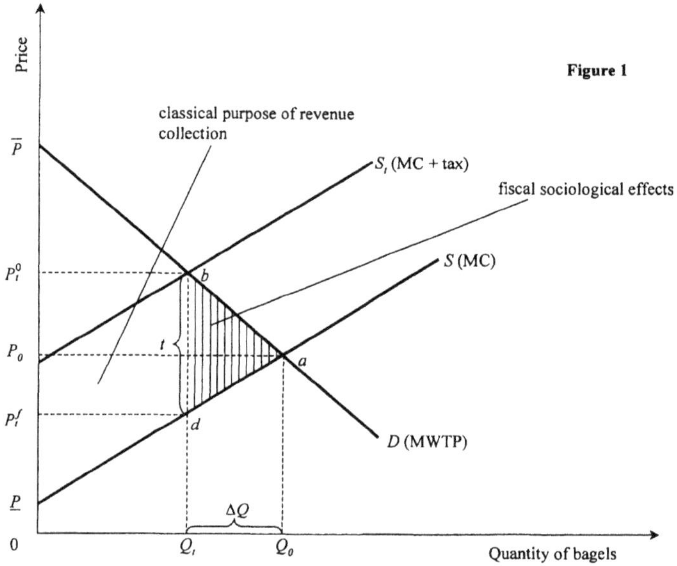

The excise tax increases the demand price, it decreases the supply price and the equilibrium quantity decreases from Q_0 to Q_t. The excess burden is the shaded triangle *bad*, which is equal to the excess burden of the marginal willingness to pay (for bagels) over the marginal costs (of bagels) for those bagels not produced and consumed because of the tax. Here, the textbook treatment ends. Yet the questions remain: What did the people eat who did not eat those bagels that have not been produced and consumed? What did the baker do while not producing the bagels? What, in fact, did consumers and bakers hatch as new ideas so as to be able to avoid the tax? Shall we see new products on the markets to which the tax does not apply? Can we discern new forms of distribution to which the tax would not apply? Under what circumstances can those forms of tax avoidance arise? Where do they thrive and what further consequences do they entail? All these questions can not be asked within the traditional concept of tax burden analysis, but all these questions are indeed those we are interested in when thinking about levying, increasing or decreasing a particular tax.

This standard example of excess burden analysis in the partial and static form just presented falls far short of what Schumpeter tried to attempt in the seventh chapter of his "Theory of Economic Development", which is not contained in the English translation nor in the subsequent editions of the German text.[13] Building on the distinction between static and dynamic analysis, partial and total (in the sense of comprehensive) modelling and introducing entrepreneurial change (defined as new compositions) which affects technology (i.e. the production function) and through this all the other factors involved, Schumpeter tries to describe (verbally) the enormous complexity that would face the economic modeller in the Lausanne tradition. For good reason, he did not try to write such models, but rather tried to use his considerable rhetorical talent to argue a case for a complex analysis, where, indeed, the argument is always on two levels, a simple and a complex one within the same language structure. Even today, with computer-supported modelling strategies we have not been able to come up with credible alternatives to Schumpeter's flowering language on various levels, akin to the suspended gardens of Semiramis. Both instruction and research in fiscal sociology will have to take heed from Schumpeter's attempt, both where he succeeded and where he obviously failed. Before addressing such strategies of instruction and research, however, let us turn to a subjective list of issues interesting in the field of fiscal sociology, and let us try to exhaust the Western alphabet.

2.4 An Alphabet of Fiscal Sociology

The existence of *alternatives* or different opportunities to choose from is at the heart of the possibility of doing economics as a science.[14] Only if there are alternatives to choose from can there be any reaction to an action of the government facing a taxpayer. From the point of view of public policy, the difficulty consists in a central authority's inability to know the full extent of the choices from which a citizen can choose who is intent on minimizing the impact of a governmental action on his own income or wealth. This knowledge about the alternative ways of avoiding harm, such as the burden of taxation (including both the tax itself and the excess burden) is available only in the decentralized form of knowledge and households, firms and other economic entities. It cannot be systematically collected by any central authority.[15] It is for this reason that knowledge about the excess burden will be systematically underestimated by any conceivable attempt at measurement.

The *burden* of taxation can be properly identified as the focus of research in fiscal sociology. The difficulty with this subject consists in its elusiveness. As citizens try to minimize the impact of the burden of taxation (and regulation),

[13] Both the original and the translation can be found at our website: www.uni-erfurt.de.
[14] Buchanan (1979).
[15] Hayek (1945).

they invent ever-new forms of legal avoidance. Once this interaction is properly understood, the anticipation of such avoidance behaviour can be the cornerstone of public policy itself. By explicitly including loopholes into tax codes and regulations, citizens or firms can be made into agents of public policy.

For instance by granting tax *credits* for certain favoured investments such as ecologically preferred technologies, a shift in technological development into a desired direction may be accomplished.[16]

Depreciations, in particular accelerated depreciations can be used to a similar effect. Reginald Hansen[17] has documented extensively how (through the exemptions introduced into the income tax code under section 7) German authorities were able to rebuild the stock of German housing after World War II, rebuild a commercial fleet and essentially rebuild Eastern Germany after reunification. Instead of enacting all these directly, use is made of the initiative of private individuals and their desire to reduce the burden of taxation. This approach has two redeeming consequences. On the one hand, the financial resources spent on, for instance, rebuilding the historical core of a destroyed city according to municipal zoning guidelines do not have to be raised through taxation, hence there is no excess burden. Secondly, opportunities for realizing these preferred investments will be found by private entrepreneurs who can use knowledge that would not be available to a government authority either in the quality or to the extent as it is available privately. Although the method looks roundabout, it is more direct than a tax-financed government programme, which would be its alternative.

The *elasticity* of a particular activity, such as the demand for bagels in the illustration given above, determines the extent or size of the excess burden and, by implication, the realm of the fiscal sociological dimensions of a particular policy measure. Only if a particular activity, such as the demand for heating oil, is completely inelastic, will there be no excess burden, no opportunity to reduce or avoid the burden of the tax. Such cases of inelastic demand or supply functions are very rare indeed. And this implies, again, that the opportunities for avoiding the burden of taxation (or regulation) are manifold and hard to anticipate by a government agent.

Fiscal illusion is the extent to which the burden of a tax (or regulation) is underestimated by a citizenry or, conversely, the benefits of a particular government programme are overestimated. It is in the interest of a government to try to achieve fiscal illusion, and this is true both for democratic governments that are in need to win re-elections, as for non-democratic regimes that likewise need to

---

[16] Backhaus (1998b).

[17] Hansen (1966).

maintain their grip on power.[18] According to the canons of taxation, fiscal illusion should, of course, be avoided. However, given the incentives on the part of taxing and regulatory authorities, this rule is certainly not self-enforcing. If we do not make a special effort at discovering fiscal illusion, it will remain undetected and uncorrected, with the consequence of inefficiency in the public sector: too many projects that do not fit the demand of the citizenry, and too high a burden of taxation with the concomitant high excess burden, i.e. welfare loss. In this sense, research into fiscal illusion can be welfare enhancing in uncovering government caused inefficiencies.

Government bonds can be equivalent to taxation when the strict conditions of the Ricardian equivalence theorem holds. In that case, the anticipated future burden of taxation needed to service and redeem the bond will be factored into the decisions of current taxpayers who rationally perceive their wealth as being reduced by the future burden of taxation. However, these strict conditions only rarely hold.[19] A conceivably extreme case may illustrate the point. Starting in the 80s of the last century, an extensive net of charitable foundations had been set up in Germany, many serving to finance scholarly work, even entire universities such as the University of Frankfurt (Main). These foundations had to hold their wealth in government bonds. As a consequence, after World War I these foundations had lost their wealth. Imperial government bonds could no longer be redeemed, including those issued during the war. The hyperinflation resorted to after the *coup d'état* completed the financial destruction of these foundations. In this case, the consequences, i.e. the harm done in terms of opportunities foregone for this charitable and scientific work that would otherwise have taken place through these foundations is extremely difficult to be accurately established. It can probably only be described, it may not be possible even to attempt a measurement. We thus realize that the limiting conditions of the Ricardian equivalence theorem point to a vast area of research for fiscal sociologists into the burden of government bond issue.[20]

Health effects of taxation can be manifold and surprising. In an effort at harmonizing European excise taxes, Spain departed from its traditional tobacco monopoly which distributed tobacco products through licensed shops and introduced an excise tax along with a liberalization of tobacco sales. In particular the international producers of low-tar brands had pushed for this reform, which was also in line with European harmonization efforts. The surprising result, however, was the disappearance of the traditional local tobacco shops (*estancas*) and the appearance of contraband tobacco sales in bars and restaurants. Obviously, this resulted in heavy losses in public revenue; but it also resulted in an increase in

[18] Tullock (1987).
[19] Backhaus, Holcombe and Zardkoohi (1987).
[20] Backhaus (1993).

the consumption of high-tar tobacco products, which have more adverse health effects than low-tar tobacco products. Without understanding the precise consequences, an established system of taxation (through monopolization) and containment of consumption had been displaced, with the resulting loss in public revenue and an increase in the consumption of the product for which a temperance policy had been envisaged.

Income in kind programmes can likewise have surprising consequences. The socialist Allende administration (1970-1973) in Chile had promised to deliver a litre of milk to every child. It started introducing price controls on dairy products, which, along with the heavy inflation that set in shortly after the administration had taken over, first led to a glut in meat and consequently to a disappearance of dairy products. The administration then bought milk powder in international markets, and distributed bags of milk powder to parents of children under the programme. Due to the enormous shortage of dairy products, these milk powder bags had a substantial resale value and helped the families suffering under the inflationary devaluation of their wage income to support this income through sales in the black market. The outcome, of course, was that the milk did not end up feeding the children targeted by the programme. Such a scenario is, perhaps, extreme, but it follows a strict economic logic and is clearly predictable. Whenever aid is granted in kind, one has to look at both the income and substitution effects.[21]

Jointness of investment and returns is an important principle in ensuring that a particular economic activity is seen in its entirety and taxed accordingly. This principle is often violated when income is taxed according to the source principle without consideration of the expenses it affords. Schmoller had insisted that income be measured as that amount that can be consumed without reducing wealth. Hence, if a household consumes € 100,000 and its wealth had been € 10 million in period 1 and € 10 million in period 2, this consumption is the income that has to be taxed. However, if you disjoin consumption and expenditure behaviour from income and revenue behaviour, interesting effects can occur. The case has been documented of the owner of a landed estate who lived lavishly but never realized any income whatsoever. Hence, he never paid any income tax. In a suggestive way, this can work as follows. Imagine you own a resource which is valued at € 10 million. It should increase in value at some rate, and you can therefore increase your borrowing against the asset at the same rate, discounting for interest. If the asset, for instance, is attractive land that benefits from development of bordering tracts of land, the (speculative) increase in value will be much more than the normal market return on bonds, and you can borrow against this asset accordingly. This may again support this lavish lifestyle, while no

[21] A classical paper is by Bruno S. Frey who showed that increases in development aid may increase weapons imports by the recipient countries. See Frey (1975).

income is generated, rather further and further debt, when the asset that increases in value serves as collateral. If you insist on defining income in terms of its source instead of what it allows in supporting your lifestyle, that is, if you insist in disjoining assets and returns, you will end up with the paradoxical result that the lavishly maintained lifestyle nevertheless is not subject to income taxation. Only by studying the reality of taxpayer response to particular rules of taxation can we establish a realistic picture of the impact of taxation on the behaviour of people and the economic effects of these dual causes.

Kiddy tax is a phenomenon which penalizes households having children under the tax code. It can take many forms.[22] To start with, a woman having a child necessarily has to leave the workplace for a while, and it depends on the cultural environment how long this 'while' will actually take. It may be three months, it may be three years, there are cultures where the process takes longer. This means, however, that the mother may lose not only her proficiency in her job, but also the regular salary increments going along with normal performance. She will thus start at where she stopped, and carry the entire loss forward over the expected duration of her labour experience. From the point of view of the employer, this cannot be otherwise, since the wage has to reflect marginal productivity. From the point of view of taxation, however, it is quite possible to compensate for this necessary effect of having children while being employed. This compensation will have to be the higher, the more the mother earns - an awkward result when equity in taxation is emphasized in terms of equalizing incomes and wealth. In addition, raising children brings about lots of additional expenses, which, if they are not deductible, in fact weigh in as a kiddy tax. Some recent programmes allow mothers to establish home offices.[23] Instead of granting subsidies to some mothers for such home offices, it would be more effective to grant tax deductions for home offices actually established. That would allow for mothers who see an opportunity to combine the work with childhood at home develop entrepreneurship and establish the proper working environment. It is difficult for a state agency to identify such able home working entrepreneurial mothers and tailoring a grant to the needs that actually exist.

Liability for false returns. No market can work without the institution of liability in contract and wrongdoing (violating property rights). Yet in taxation, very little is there in the way of liability for false returns. Tax returns may be used for all manner of ends, not only assessing the tax code, but also different social policy objectives. After all, tax returns are a goldmine of information, and this information, if it is correct, can be effectively used in order to tailor government programmes to citizens' needs. However, if rules of taxation are not self-

[22] Backhaus (1991).
[23] Thüringer Ministerium für Wissenschaft, Forschung und Kunst, Thüringer Landeshaushalt, Kapitel 1524 Titelgruppe 84: Förderung von Frauen in Forschung und Lehre, 2000.

enforcing, the information will be totally misleading and it will not be useful for any ulterior government purpose. Since liability for false returns is difficult to be made actionable (without reversing burdens of proofs), the self-enforcing mechanism practiced in some Swiss cantons is instructive. Here, the method of self-declaration of income is being practiced, but the returns are made public and banks are prudent in using them for their crediting decisions, lest they be critisized in public themselves. This means that a local entrepreneur cheats on his taxes only at the expense of losing his credit line. Banks will deal only with local customers, and the system is closed.

Monitoring compliance is not only important with respect to honesty in taxation. It is particularly difficult for the tax authority when a tax is used as a policy instrument so as to achieve a particular purpose, such as the use of an ecologically preferred technology, production process or resource. The information required to monitor compliance may become very complex in such cases, and it is important to create a system of self-enforcement. Often, the necessary expertise cannot be assumed to lie with a taxing authority, certification may be required from a different agency. In such cases, the extensive use of tax credits reverses the burden of providing the information from the taxing authority to the taxpayer, who thereby has to prove compliance. This reversal of the burden of proof expedites the tax administration and offers a flexible instrument to achieve many and diverse policy objectives.[24]

Norminal gains or losses (or even fictitious or forfeited incomes) are sometimes used for assessing taxes. In principle, only real entities will affect economic behaviour. However, when used for purposes of assessing taxes, fictitious values do indeed become real ones. In this sense, they can affect behaviour and by consequence have an influence on real wealth and welfare. Consider the case of the fictitious value of using one's own home. Under the Dutch tax code, for instance, the forfeited benefit of living in one's own home is calculated not on the basis of rents for equivalent leases, but on the basis of the value of the real estate. This figure is then added to the taxable income, adding to the progressive burden of the income tax. In principle, from a social policy point of view, the objective is to have as much homeownership as possible. This has to do with provisions for old age or other vicissitudes of life, with the stability of neighbourhoods, with health considerations and with the general experience that privately owned housing stock is better and more efficiently maintained than publicly or institutionally owned one. Now consider a family with a modest income that has inherited a valuable house. The fictitious rental value of the house will be added to the income of that family, but the costs of maintaining the house, the opportunity costs of capital contained in the real estate and the opportunity costs of work upon the house are all not deducted from this forfeited

[24] Backhaus (1998b).

income. Consequently, the deck is stacked against private homeownership, thereby frustrating attainment of the traditional social policy objective. It is unlikely that this result is based on a conscious decision of parliament.

Off-shore activities are a clear indication of a weak tax administration as they document opportunities of taxation forgone. The remedy lies in creating a climate in which the business can thrive on-shore and simultaneously serve as a basis for taxation.

Public works intended to overcome chronic unemployment or other forms of economic depressions are often funded from tax revenues, thereby adding to the burden of taxation and to the welfare loss of taxation. Even if the measures are effective in creating opportunities for employment, they at the same time through the method of funding chosen decrease similarly opportunities in the sector subject to taxation and dampen demand for investment and consumption. For these reasons, self-financing forms of public works are preferable such as those designed by Wilhelm Lautenbach and implemented between 1932 and 1935. In relying on the Keynesian multiplier and accelerator effects, the funds spent wisely yield a return that constitutes the original fund.[25]

Quality of service can be tied to taxation through the benefit principle. Wicksell suggested the benefit principle, which has been a core element of the cannons of taxation ever since Justi and Adam Smith in a specific institutionalised form. By insisting on consensual taxation (near unanimity rule) and simultaneity of decisions on taxation and expenditure, taxes are tied to the benefits indeed received, and institutional provisions have to be taken to ensure that tax yields decline *in tandem* with benefits and *vice versa*. This can be accomplished by tying the taxes owned to the receipt and approval of specific services, implying the expression of disapproval and opting out of the bundle of taxes and services.

The *Ricardian equivalence theorem* holding the equivalence between taxation and bond issue has to be taken as one of the typical theorems of limitation which form the basis of economic analysis. Similar theorems are those by Modigliani-Miller and Coase. In emphasizing the specific conditions under which the theorem holds, our attention is pointed to those cases where the conditions are not met. Hence, the equivalence theorem cannot be taken at face value. It serves to emphasize the distortions that occur when the future burden of the bond issue is not accurately perceived by the present generation or cannot adequately be compensated for in the present decisions of future taxpayers.[26]

Surprises are the focus of much work in fiscal sociology, as we try to detect and predict the unanticipated consequences of regulation and taxation. For instance,

[25] Backhaus (1985).

[26] On these limitational theorems see Backhaus (1986).

Laband[27] has recently shown that regulation designed to protect the habitat of endangered species in its effects is likely to endanger those very species. For instance, birds which nest in particular trees, if the habitat is being protected and such trees cannot be cut for logging purposes, logging firms will eliminate those trees from their forests before they attain the required age and will thereby eliminate the habitat intended to be protected. If an entire area is targeted for protection, logging firms will relinquish their activities in these areas, whereby forestry activity will stop and land will revert to other uses. In all these cases, the intended effect of the regulation is completely subverted, since the regulation is written against the interests of the regulated instead of tying the interests of the regulated and the beneficiary of the regulation together.

Time is an important element in determining the intended and unintended effects of taxation and regulation. The simple diagram shown above is completely static. In the long run, the effects of regulation and taxation cumulate and citizens learn to reduce the burden of taxation, thereby increasing the welfare loss, as the economy moves successively away from the production possibility frontier, and a similar effect occurs in polity and society.

Utility is distinguished by Pareto from ophelimity in order to distinguish between those effects which occur in the economy and those further repercussions which affect society in different ways. In principle, Pareto thought that ophelimity could be measured, while utility is in the eye of the beholder. Utility can be experienced in terms of oneself, other members of society as well as society's situation and development as such. About the latter very little can be done by an individual, and individuals may disagree strongly among each other. Further, an individual's ability to influence the utility he ascribes to the well-being of another is equally constrained. What can be objectively observed is how individuals try to improve their own well-being, and hence the ophelimity can, in principle, be inferred, at least in an ordinal way. As we move beyond the economic sphere into the political and social effects of regulation and taxation, we need to work with both the notion of ophelimity and the different notions of utility as Pareto had suggested.

Value and votes are closely connected, as in the polity voting is used to determine the outcome of public policy, including the welfare effects of taxation and regulation. While in their individual behaviour, voters try to reduce the burden of taxation and regulation, this may not necessarily be the case in their political behaviour as the benefits from a particular programme may be concentrated on some, while the burden can be spread over many and in such a way that it is not worth their while to mount an effort at defeating the burdensome programme. Votes are the currency of the political process, and it takes real resources to

---

[27] See Laband (2000).

muster the political strength as expressed in votes to launch or defeat particular programmes.

Wealth, its production, enhancement and preservation depend critically on very specific aspects of the tax system. This has already been noted in the context of the taxation of fictitious incomes. In fact, in the example chosen the tax structure affects the architectural heritage of the people. Likewise, in assessing wealth, human capital and its formation needs to be included along with all manifestations of the cultural heritage, such as libraries, musea, institutions of higher learning, architectural landscapes and the like. All these depend crucially on specific provisions in the tax code, such as education credits, deductions for charitable activities, deductions for maintaining national monuments, encouragement to endow foundations or chairs at universities and the like. We note that there are countless ramifications and interconnections between the tax structure and all aspects of society, which can be ascertained through a wide definition of wealth, as it has been chosen here so as to capture all manner of sociological effects of taxation and regulation.

X-inefficiency is the difference between the ability of an organization to perform and its actual performance. As an organization, a firm, a household, a family and the like tries to minimize the burden it has to bear through taxation and regulation, it moves away from its efficient allocation of resources and thereby creates X-inefficiency. Hence, to the extent that we can demonstrate these effects, we can point to strategies of reducing X-inefficiency that do not lie within the organization, but are at the disposal of policy makers as they decide on issues of regulation and taxation establishing the environment in which the organizations have to operate. While organizational theory has emphasized X-inefficiency in the context of intra-organizational strategies of improving performance, a fiscal sociological approach can emphasize extra-organizational strategies to reduce X-inefficiency.

The *yield* of taxation tends to be entirely overestimated, as the cost of taxation can never be completely established, since tax payers and agents under regulation have no desire to cheaply provide information about their avoidance behaviour. From this point of view, it is advisable to use forms of revenue generation which strictly follow the benefit principle, as the *quid pro quo* between taxes and services provided tends to leave no excess burden and creates incentives to generate information about the transactions between the government and the private sector.

Zero-based budgeting has often been suggested as a strategy to make budgets manageable and contain the growth of government. However, as citizens learn to deal with taxation and regulation just as well as expenditure programmes, they are able to decrease distortions over time. When entire programmes or tax systems are questioned abruptly, the learning done by individuals and organizations is being undone and additional costs of transactions are being imposed on economy and society. What is required instead are budgetary procedures that incorporate as much decentralized information as possible. In using the insights from Hayek's piece on the use of knowledge in society, this can be a plea to organize as much governmental activity as possible in a market context so as to make an optimal use of knowledge in society by both public and private market participants.

3 Fiscal Sociology as a Field of Instruction and Research

3.1 Instruction

In emphasizing opportunities for research and instruction in fiscal sociology, a good start is Humboldt's principle[28] of a unity of research and teaching at the university level. Although this principle seems to fly in the face of the economic principle of the division of labour, a closer look shows that it actually reinforces this principle. Universities as institutions for basic research and high-level instruction have to maintain, increase and communicate that type of knowledge which is not readily canonized into mass education. It is necessarily the role of a research university to be small in the sense of having many small centres of learning where scholars and students can interact directly. In this sense, teaching and research opportunities can very well overlap.

As a field of teaching, fiscal sociology offers fascinating opportunities at all levels of instruction.

At the bachelor's level, elements of fiscal practice can be integrated into the course of study. Consider the bargaining situation between a regulator and a regulated activity, such as the process of applying for a building permit; or alternatively, consider negotiations after filing a tax return. These cases can be realistically simulated in the curriculum and students can be introduced into the breezing climate of adversary negotiations. Through such a method, the technical concepts such as the rectangles and the triangles shown above can be imbued with life and may be readily grasped by students who favour rather non-technical disciplines otherwise and therefore might shy away from taking an economics course.

At the master level, this experience can be built upon. Now, the expertise would have to be raised to the professional level, since fiscal sociology includes a study

[28] Incidentally, this forceful reformer of cultural institutions closed the old (1392) University of Erfurt for not being willing to go with the time.

of the unintended impact of taxation as well as regulation, it has implications for almost every activity of government that somehow affects the private sector. And with this, there is a wide field of professional activities in both government and the respective governmental counterpart where a proper understanding of these effects is of great use. Hence, the supply of interesting topics for master theses is inexhaustible.

Under current conditions of widespread underfunding of universities and the iron cartel of public universities with few private initiatives that can have a chance under such circumstances, it is difficult to encourage PhD students to pursue an academic career. Fiscal sociology, however, is to such an extent an under-researched field that a wealth of research opportunities exists with tangible benefits to both governmental and private agents. And this should, if sufficient effort at convincing sponsors of the use of this work is undertaken, provide for research opportunities that are appealing, even to the most frugal budget administrator.

3.2 Research

As we noted previously, before the dissolution of the unity of *Staatswissenschaften*, scholarly activity was able to centre on legislative projects, such as the civil code, the welfare state and the like. These concerted efforts can, with difficulty, be accomplished again in the context of focused niche subdisciplines. We have recently seen the emergence of health economics, which is such a niche subdiscipline in combining every conceivable economic method to analyse health related issues and institutions. Another such instance is the recent emergence of the subdiscipline of law & economics. Fiscal sociology can be positioned in a similar way. These niche subdisciplines which bridge otherwise separate scholarly pursuits can play a pivotal role in facilitating focused research on major legislative endeavours.[29]

Example 1: With the further integration of the European Union, a repetition of the large legislative project of the civil code will now have to be made for Europe. A framework legislation for a common civil code in the European Union, including harmonization and union access will have to be forthcoming and it will have to address issues of taxation and regulation while helping to integrate diverse legal institutions and cultures. Research into unintended side effects of regulation and taxation will be of immense importance for facilitating such a project.

[29] The leading journal in economics in the German language area during the time of these large legislative endeavours was notably called *Annals of Legislation, Administration and Economics (Jahrbücher für Gesetzgebung, Verwaltung und Volkswirtschaft).*

Example 2: The key concept of public finance is Wicksell's principle of just taxation, which entails a simultaneous process of deciding on taxes and expenditures. With the further integration of the European Union, a framework legislation will have to be forthcoming which satisfies this principle and also allows for popular decisions to be efficiently and effectively made by acknowledging, at the same time, the different histories, cultures and institutions of the different member states. Frey's[30] suggestion of functionally overlapping competing jurisdictions is one such attempt. Research into unintended consequences of such decision-making will have to be a necessary companion of launching such initiatives.

Example 3: With further integration of the European Union, some framework legislation for customs and excise taxes will have to be forthcoming that allows for the different member states and their subdivisions to remain sovereign and democratically constituted while at the same time allowing for harmonization and a minimization of the burden of those custom duties and excise taxes. Again, research into the side effects of legislation on excise taxes and customs duties will have to be necessary in order to help design efficient legislative proposals.

Conclusion

In conclusion, fiscal sociology offers ample opportunities for research and instruction that can be said to be truly helpful in reducing the adverse effects of government activity and thereby enhancing the welfare and wealth of nations.

References

Backhaus, Jürgen G. (1985), "An Essay on Keynesianism in German", in: T. Lawson, M.H. Pesaran (eds. for the Cambridge Journal of Economics), *Keynes' Economics: Methodological Issues*, London: Croom Helm - Armonk, NY: Sharpe, pp. 209-253.

Backhaus, Jürgen, G. (1986), "An Impossible Economist", in: Phil. J. Davis, David Park (eds.), *No Way: On the Nature of the Impossible*, New York: W.R. Freeman, pp. 226-238.

Backhaus, Jürgen G., Randall G. Holcombe and Asghar Zardkoohi (1987), "Public Investments and its Effects on the Burden of the Public Debt", *Southern Economic Journal*, vol. 54, nr. 1, pp. 145-158.

Backhaus, Jürgen G. (ed.) (1991), "The Economic Emancipation of Women and the Tax System", *Journal of Economic Studies*, vol. 18, nrs. 5/6. Also as book: (ed.), *The Tax System and Female Emancipation*, Bradford: MCB University Press.

Backhaus, Jürgen G. (ed.) (1993), "The Economics of Science Policy: An Analysis of the Althoff System", *Journal of Economic Studies*, vol. 20, nrs. 3/4.

[30] Frey and Eichenberger (1999).

Backhaus, Jürgen G. (ed.) (1998a), *Christian Wolff and Law & Economics*, Hildesheim/Zürich/New York: Georg Olms Verlag.

Backhaus, Jürgen G. (1998b), "When Should the Ecotax Kick In? A Cost and Choice Approach", *Kyklos*, vol. 51, nr. 4, pp. 565-575.

Backhaus Jürgen G. (ed.) (1999a), "The German Civil Code of 1896", *European Journal of Law and Economics*, vol. 7, nr. 1, 94 pp.

Backhaus, Jürgen G. (1999b), "Otto von Gierke", in: Jürgen G. Backhaus (ed.), *Elgar Companion to Law and Economics*, Cheltenham: Edward Elgar Publishing Ltd., pp. 313-315.

Backhaus, Jürgen G. and Hans-Joachim Stadermann (eds.) (2000a), *Georg Simmels Philosophie des Geldes: Einhundert Jahre danach*, Marburg: Metropolis Verlag

Backhaus, Jürgen G. and Hans-Joachim Stadermann (eds.) (2000b), *Georg Simmel's Philosophy of Money: A Centenary Appraisal*, Marburg: Metropolis Verlag.

Backhaus, Jürgen G. (2001), *Schumpeter (1884-1950): His German Contributions: The European Heritage*, Boston: Kluwer, forthcoming.

Buchanan, James M. (1979), *Cost and Choice: An Inquiry in Economic Theory*, Chicago: University of Chicago Press.

Da Empoli, Attilio (1931), *Theory of Economic Equilibrium (A study of marginal and ultramarginal phenomena)*, Chicago: Christiani & Catenacci Publishing Co.

Frey, Bruno S. (1975), "Weapons, Exports and Aid to Developing Countries", *Journal of Conflict Resolution*, vol. 1, nr. 2, Spring.

Frey, Bruno S. and Reiner Eichenberger (1999), *The New Democratic Federalism for Europe: Functional, Overlapping and Competing Jurisdictions*, Cheltenham: Edward Elgar Publishing Ltd.

Goldscheid, Rudolf (1919), *Grundfragen des Menschenschicksals: Gesammelte Aufsätze*, Leipzig & Vienna: E.P. Tal.

Goldscheid, Rudolf (1919), *Sozialisierung der Wirtschaft oder Staatsbankrott: Ein Sanierungsprogramm*, Leipzig & Vienna: Anzengruber Verlag: Brüder Suschitzky.

Hansen, Reginald (1996), *Die praktischen Konsequenzen des Methodenstreits*, Berlin: Duncker & Humblot.

Hayek, Friedrich von (1945), "The Use of Knowledge in Society", *American Economic Review*, vol. 35, nr. 4, pp. 519-530.

Laband, David N. (2000), "The Impact of Unfunded Environmental Mandates When Environmental Quality and Timber are Produced Jointly", *European Journal of Law and Economics*, vol. 10, nr. 3, pp. 199-216.

Schumpeter, Joseph Alois (1918, 1953), "Die Krise des Steuerstaates", Graz-Leipzig: Leuschner & Lubensky; reprinted as pp. 1-71 in: J.A. Schumpeter, "Aufsätze zur Soziologie", English translation by W.F. Stolper and R.A. Musgrave in: *International Economic Papers*, vol. IV, London: Macmillan, 1954.

Schumpeter, Joseph Alois (1942, 1976), *Capitalism, Socialism and Democracy*, 5th ed., London: Unwin University Books.

Shionoya, Yuichi and Mark Perlman (eds.) (1994), *Schumpeter in the History of Ideas*, Ann Arbor: University of Michigan Press.

Tullock, Gordon (1987), *Autocracy*, Dordrecht: Kluwer Academic Publishers.

Wicksell, Johann Gustav Knut (1896), *Finanztheoretische Untersuchungen nebst Darstellung und Kritik des Steuerwesens Schwedens*, Jena: Gustav Fischer.

States and the Crafting of Souls: Mind, Society, and Fiscal Sociology

Richard E. Wagner
Harris Professor in Economics
Department of Economics, 3G4
George Mason University
Fairfax, VA 22030
USA
rwagner@gmu.edu
http://mason.gmu.edu/~rwagner

Abstract: For the most part, the theory of public finance follows economic theory in taking individual preferences as given. The resulting analytical agenda revolves around the ability of different fiscal institutions to reflect and aggregate those preferences into collective outcomes. This paper explores the possibility that to some extent fiscal institutions can influence and shape what are commonly referred to as preferences. Statecraft thus becomes necessarily a branch of soulcraft, in that the state is inescapably involved in shaping preferences through its impact on the moral imagination, and not just in reflecting or representing them. This paper first explores some general conceptual issues and then examines some particular illustrations.

Keywords: Endogenous preferences, fiscal institutions, constitutional economics, public enterprise.

JEL codes: D6, D7, H1.

For the most part, the theory of public finance follows economic theory in taking individual preferences as given. The resulting analytical agenda revolves around the ability of different fiscal institutions to reflect and aggregate those preferences into collective outcomes. This paper explores the possibility that to some extent fiscal institutions, and the fiscal practice that those institutions generate, can influence and shape what are commonly referred to as preferences. In standard public finance, the activities of the state simply represent offerings by alternative vendors to those that exist in private markets. Hence, shoppers buy some things from public goods stores and other things from private goods stores. In contrast, this paper explores the possibility that fiscal institutions can shape preferences through the impact of fiscal practice on the moral imagination. This paper first explores in a general way how fiscal institutions might influence preferences through their impact on practice and the moral imagination. Subsequently, it explores some specific illustrations of this possibility, and concludes with an examination of some possible constitutional implications.

Harmonious Fiscal Politics on Smooth Surfaces

For the most part fiscal scholars have developed their formulations under a presumption that there exists a deep homogeneity or harmony within the citizenry. The fiscal process is modeled as taking place on a smooth, twice differentiable surface. This leads to the easy and ready development of propositions about welfare and equilibria. People are characterized as having utility functions whose arguments, in a two commodity space, are a public good and a private good. Generalization of this setting to an n-good space simply converts two singulars into two plurals.

The optimal allocation of resources between public and private goods is conceptually simple and straightforward, even if there might be institutional difficulties in reaching this allocation, as Paul Samuelson (1954, 1955) noted. People receive some of the things they want from public goods stores and other things from private goods stores. The taxation of private activities, in one form or another, is the instrument that stocks the public goods stores and determines the relative sizes of the two categories of store. People may differ among themselves in their preferred public-private allocations, either because of differences in their utility functions or because of differences in their budget constraints.

The extent of those differences, moreover, will be influenced by the fiscal and political rules in place, a point that was made particularly strongly by James Buchanan (1967). People who have identical utility functions and incomes may still prefer different public-private mixes if they face different tax-price tradeoffs. Likewise, people who have different utility functions may nonetheless prefer the same public-private mix in the presence of particular tax-price tradeoffs. For instance, Buchanan (1964) presents a model where the income and price elasticities of demand for a public good is unitary and where the public good is financed by a proportional tax on income. The result is that everyone desires the same amount of the public good. As income rises, people would desire proportionately more of the public good. However, the tax-price they pay also rises proportionately with income, so everyone ends up preferring the same quantity of the public good regardless of their income.

Buchanan's model is highly particular, other models will lead to people differing in their desired public-private mix. Those differences, however, may also be fully consistent with Pareto efficiency. The median voter outcome, for instance, is Pareto efficient provided that the distribution of preferred outcomes is symmetrical around the median. All of these various models represent fiscal politics as a process that operates on a smooth, twice differentiable surface. The political process proceeds peacefully and calmly, as people's minds all possess the same structure when it comes to the evaluation of public and private activity. The differences among people are only of secondary importance, and even these can often be eliminated through appropriate fiscal institutions, as illustrated by Wicksell's (1896) formulation.

These formulations all treat the fiscal process as revolving around the use of private property. Economic life is ordered through private property as envisaged by a model of competitive markets, and the use of property to support public goods stores is categorically indistinct from the use of property to support particular private goods stores. To be sure, it is only in some institutional settings, with the Wicksellian setting being a prominent illustration that the marginal conditions for Pareto efficiency will apply to each person in the society. Otherwise, aggregate conditions for Pareto efficiency may be satisfied while the individual conditions are violated for most people, possibly all but the median voter. Even these violations of individual conditions would generally be treated as small in the sense that the gain from attaining the individual conditions would be less than the added cost of collective effort to satisfy those conditions, as exemplified by Buchanan and Tullock's (1962) formulation of a tradeoff between external costs and decision costs.

Discordant Fiscal Politics on Tectonic Surfaces

It is noteworthy that fiscal scholarship mostly treats property relationships identically regardless of the institutional arrangements that govern public-private relationships. This is surely not satisfactory in light of the flowering of scholarship on the economics of institutions and organizations, where it would be readily recognized that economic organizations that possess residual claimacy and alienable ownership would differ in important ways from cooperative organizations where ownership was inalienable. While a profit seeking firm can be generally assimilated to governance through private property, a cooperative takes on features of common property governance. To be sure, the governance of cooperative or common property relationships can in some cases proceed relatively harmoniously and efficiently, as noted in Elinor Ostrom (1990). In any case, though, the differences in institutional relationships and the arrangements for governance would be presumed to be economically significant, both with respect to the *ex ante* creation of different organizational forms and to the *ex post* conduct of those different organizations.

There are vast and significant differences among the institutional arrangements by which public-private relationships might be generated and governed. Some of those differences were central to the famous debate between Joseph Schumpeter and Rudolf Goldscheid, as collected in Rudolf Hickel (1976) and as elaborated in Jürgen Backhaus (1992). They also recall the huge difference between Adam Smith (1776) and Johann Heinrich Gottlob von Justi (1771) in their approaches to public finance. Smith argued that public activities should be financed by taxes and not through net revenues generated from state enterprises. Justi argued the reverse, and pretty much claimed that a prince who required taxes to support his activities had failed in his princely duties because he should have been able to raise sufficient revenue from his enterprise activities.

Smith and Justi, and Schumpeter and Goldscheid, were arguing that the institutional arrangements of property and governance were of great significance for the economic vitality of the citizenry. There is much merit in this proposition, which is explained and explored below. As a first-order simplification, private economic organization will be treated as governed by a simple framework of private property while public economic organization is treated as governed by a simple framework of common property. This is, of course, a simplification, and more elaborate and nuanced lines of analysis could be developed. Wicksell and Justi conceptualized a public sector that operated within the same institutional framework as private organizations, whereas Schumpeter and Smith treated the public institutional framework as categorically distinct from the framework that governed private enterprises.

What is of central interest here is to illustrate how the incorporation of property and governance arrangements into the theory of public finance generates an alternative orientation toward public-private relationships. In particular, what we call preferences can no longer be taken as independent of the private-public mix, for these are themselves influenced by that mix, and are even the objects of fiscal politics. Statecraft is necessarily soulcraft, to appropriate the title of a book by George Will (1983). If soulcraft is generated in part through institutionalized practice, we confront a significant difference of approaches. The line of thought represented by Justi and Wicksell looks to some institutional congruency between public and private, but the line of thought represented by Smith, Schumpeter, and Samuelson looks to institutional disharmony. This disharmony, however, generates discordant fiscal politics on tectonic surfaces, and not harmonious fiscal politics on smooth surfaces.

Some issues relating to the development of urban transportation in the United States offers good illustration of these points, particularly as illustrated by E-ckert and Hilton (1972) and Klein (1997). Early in the 20th century, urban transportation was organized overwhelmingly through private enterprise. Jitney service formed a significant share of the market. Jitneys were operated by private automobile owners who contracted to carry people downtown in the morning and back out in the evening. Jitney service reduced traffic congestion without requiring large investments in busses or other forms of public transportation. Moreover, there was no need to recruit a staff of full time employees to operate capital equipment for which there was relatively little demand most of the day. Jitneys were organized within the market framework of private property and freedom of contract. People who did not want to drive their automobiles downtown and back could catch a ride with a jitney operator. This was a purchase from a private goods store.

Now consider the injection of a public goods store into the picture, in the form of a public transit enterprise. That public enterprise could be organized within the same institutional framework as private enterprises. This would be an institutional arrangement that would be more or less consistent with that envisioned by Wicksell and Justi. The fate of this public enterprise would depend on its ability to be successful in competing for patronage with privately organized enterprises. Such competitive success might arise through technical efficiency in the provision of the service. While there is good reason for doubting this possibility over a wide variety of activities as a general case, in comparison with enterprises organized under private property, we also know that a wide variety of cooperative organizations do thrive within a market setting. Hence, the possibility that a state-organized transit enterprise could survive with open market competition cannot be rejected out of hand.

Competitive success for the state-organized enterprise could also arise because private competition was restricted. Indeed, if the public enterprise does not possess equal or superior technical efficiency, its survival will require that it restrict the competitive ability of private enterprises. The state has many ways it can restrict privately organized enterprises that otherwise would be competitive with it, short of outright abolition. The problem the public enterprise faces is that its costs must be higher than private enterprises, so long as the public enterprise is technically less efficient than private enterprises. Charging higher prices to cover higher costs, however, is no way to expand patronage.

Under these circumstances, a public enterprise can offer competitive prices to customers only by imposing higher prices on some subset of the citizenry. Even if private enterprises charged a single price for their service, a public enterprise would have to charge multiple prices. It would have to practice some form of price discrimination, where price reductions to a desired clientele were made possible through charging higher prices to others, people who would be forced riders with respect to the public transit enterprise.

There are two paths along which such forced ridership may be created. One is through taxation, as Pantaleoni (1911) explains and Wagner (1997) elaborates. Taxation creates a form of political pricing system that is parasitical upon the set of market prices. For instance, a proportional tax on income to subsidize public transportation would charge prices that varied across people in proportion to their incomes. People who pay taxes but do not use the services of the public enterprise are forced riders, paying for rides they don't take. The other form of forced ridership is through regulatory restrictions on the ability of people to patronize privately organized enterprises that compete with the public enterprise. For instance, a regulation that prohibited people from carrying other people for a fee without a taxi license would make private options more costly, thereby increasing the demand for public transit services. This increased demand for publicly provided services would really be a form of forced ridership that was generated through the restriction on market competition.

This extended illustration illustrates a problem that arises when public and private enterprises operate within the same neighborhood, commercially speaking, and yet are organized and supported under incongruent institutional arrangements. So long as technical inefficiency characterizes publicly organized enterprises, those enterprises will not be competitive with privately organized enterprises in their neighborhood. One possible public response to this inefficiency is to restore a semblance of competitiveness through price discrimination via taxation. Another possible response is to restrict the scope for private competition. The greater the restrictions on private competition, the higher the induced demand for the service offered by the public enterprise. This increased demand, moreover, is likely to increase the use of price discrimination through direct prices, as distinct from tax prices. This use of direct price discrimination simultaneously creates "cream" for private enterprises to try to skim, which generates still further efforts at regulation to restrict the cream skimming, the opportunities for which were set in motion by the relative inefficiency of the public enterprise, and which thereby generate the peculiar but understandable dynamics of the mixed economy (Ikeda 1997).

Institutional Practice and the Moral Imagination

Robert Frank (1987) asks "If Homo Economicus Could Choose His Own Utility Function, Would He Want One with a Conscience?" The point of Frank's paper was to argue that a conscience could be a valuable means of pre-commitment, which in turn suggests the value of an affirmative answer. In this formulation, it is taken for granted that conscience, or morality generally, is an object of choice. One can choose among moral precepts just as one can choose among books or shoes. This formulation treats the mind as a tabula rasa, onto which morality can be placed or erased as the author chooses.

In sharp contrast, the classical approach to moral education approached the moral imagination quite differently. Morality was not an object of choice on the same plane as ordinary consumer goods. An adult did not have the option to choose a morality because that morality had been implanted during childhood, for better or for worse. Morality was instilled through practice until the moral sentiments became habits outside the realm of conscious thought or reflection. The existence of a conscience, or the substantive structure of that conscience, was not an object of choice but rather was something that had been generated through practice during childhood.

This is not to say that morality remains invariant after leaving childhood. It is only to assert the primacy of practice as the means by which the substantive conduct that constitutes morality is acquired or extinguished. A system of bourgeois commercial relationships rests upon a legal order of property, contract, and liability. These legal institutions create the central governing framework for a market economy. These institutions also reflect a particular form of moral imagination. These legal institutions can be given a reasonably accurate representation as moral injunctions. The legal principle of property maps reasonably well into a moral injunction to refrain from taking what is not yours. The legal principle of contract maps reasonably well into a moral injunction to keep your promises (or to secure the permission of the aggrieved party before breaking a promise). The legal principle of liability maps reasonably well into a moral injunction to make good the wrongs you do onto others.

A market order operates more effectively in the presence of people who possess such moral imaginations. At the same time, a market order tends to reward practice that conforms to that morality. For the most part, commercial activity that is consistent with the moral order that, in turn, is complementary with the legal order will yield higher commercial returns than will conduct that violates that moral order. Such traits as being reliable, energetic, and trustworthy will tend to bring larger commercial value than such traits as being unreliable, lazy, and dishonest. Hence, commercial practice tends to reinforce its supporting morality.

What happens when a state and its economic activities enter the picture? To address this question, it is necessary to look first of all to the kinds of practice that the state sponsors. This is because the crucible within which the moral ima-

imagination is shaped and reshaped is primarily the world of practice and not the world of conscious reflection. To pose the question in this fashion is to ask whether the state calls forth the same, or at least complementary, kinds of practice as do commercial enterprises.

Constitutive Policy: Statecraft as Soulcraft

The classical approach to moral education recognized that it is through practice that right conduct moves from becoming an object of conscious deliberation to becoming a central default setting of the soul or psyche. Wrong practice would, in turn, promote wrong conduct through its ability to generate an ill-ordered soul. In any case, the focus of classical moral education was upon the creation of individual souls, with society being built up through interaction among individuals whose souls might have possessed varying degrees of order or disorder.

It is also reasonable to ask how various institutional arrangements promote or extinguish notions of normativity though the kinds of collective practice they encourage or discourage. To go down this path is not to embrace a pure moral conventionalism. One can believe that our natures limit the range of moral belief while nonetheless recognizing that those natures can accommodate a wide variety of conventional practice, a point that is articulated nicely in Ekkehart Schlicht (1998).

It is a common textbook illustration to show the equivalence of a tariff and a quota. For any tariff that increases the price and reduces the amount imported, there will be a quota that can achieve the same outcome. There is an equivalence between a tariff and a quota as these are drawn on the blackboard. They are not, however, equivalent in practice. A tariff and a quota generally involve different institutional frameworks that generate different forms of institutionalized practice and, hence, promote the formation of different beliefs about normativity. A tariff, so long as it is relatively low, is compatible with the market framework of properthy, contract, and liability, as noted in Eucken (1952) and as further exemplified in the essays collected in Liepold and Pies (2000). A tariff makes a product more expensive, but otherwise does not disrupt ordinary market processes. How much of that product is sold in the aggregate, and how that aggregate is distributed among different vendors, are governed in decentralized fashion through open competition and interaction among buyers and sellers. With a tariff, people are still free to work out commercial arrangements among themselves through private ordering, subject only to the surcharge that the tariff represents. A tariff disrupts ordinary market relationships only when it becomes so high as to encourage smuggling.

A quota disrupts ordinary market relationships from the start. As compared with a tariff, a quota creates a qualitatively different regime of human governance, as do what are called "voluntary restraints" on trade. With the quota, the distribution of sales across vendors and the specific types of products sold are not determined through ordinary commercial arrangements. Rather, they are determined through a political process where those who hold offices of political power are able to award allotments to the particular vendors that those holders of power choose. A quota necessarily injects venality, inequality, and hierarchy into political practice and changes the character of effective commercial conduct. What economists refer to as rent seeking (Tullock 1967)(Rowley, Tollison, and Tullock, eds. 1988) and rent extraction (McChesney (1997) will flourish under quotas, and such activities may eventually come to comprise new norms for commercial conduct.

A low tariff maintains the legal principles of property, contract, and liability, along with their supporting normative sentiments. With market conformable institutional arrangements, commercial practice reinforces the normative complements to the private ordering principles of property, contract, and liability. In contrast, the quota generates a different form of practice, one that is part of a hierarchical, status, or caste society and the values that support it. For no longer is everyone free to enter the competition for market share. Only those who receive a quota allotment can do so. Those in a position to award allotments hold a position of privileged status, as do those who receive allotments. Furthermore, a quota will generate incentives for people to evade the quota. State officials know that quotas have this effect, and to curb this evasion they will employ undercover agents to spy on people and to entrap them into evasion. Where the ordinary liberal institutions of property and contract spread trust and friendship throughout a society, the quota, and all policy measures of its type, promote suspicion and distrust, thereby generating a structured hierarchy of relationships within society.

A quota is, of course, but one particular outcome of a democratic process. Many similar outcomes can emerge, as illustrated by the vast and expanding literature on rent seeking and rent extraction. Democracy may clash severely with market conformability. Among other things, there is a fundamental clash among democracy, property, and an open society. Consider a small town with only three residents. Primo and Secunda like to play tennis, Terzo does not. Within the market framework of private property and freedom of contract, Primo and Secunda could readily finance from their own funds the building of a court on which to play tennis. However, they also comprise a voting majority, and could play tennis more cheaply if they to declare the provision of tennis courts to be a town activity. Democracy allows Primo and Secunda to rob Terzo to subsidize their tennis matches, only it is called democratic policy and not robbery (Epstein 1985).

There is a potentially deep cleavage between democratic ideology and democratic practice. The ideology treats government as an institution of common benefit that people create to promote their common interests. The practice, however, seems often to clash with the ideology. There are two approaches to limiting the clash. One looks to the cultivation of virtue within the populace, so that majorities would not exploit their voting power. The other looks to auxiliary measures that would limit the domain of democratic governance, as illustrated by a variety of constitutional provisions to limit and structure the exercise of governmental power. To the extent such constitutional limits are imposed, the governing regime becomes something other than purely democratic.

Valuation, Cognition, and the Constitution of Governance

Alexander Hamilton opened Federalist No. 1 by asking "whether societies of men are really capable or not of establishing good government from reflection and choice, or whether they are forever destined to depend for their political constitutions on accident and force." The task of securing good governance through reflection and choice requires the exercise of both the cognitive faculties and the moral imagination. The task can be likened to a form of social agriculture. Good social agriculture involves both appropriate valuation and accurate cognition.

With respect to valuation, one might dedicate some land to growing squash, and have no desire to support squash bugs or various forms of rust or blight. How to achieve these desired ends requires the exercise of the cognitive faculties across a variety of domains, including such things as soil chemistry and plant genetics. Normative desires about food will generally amount to little without the application of the cognitive faculties. Furthermore, the exercise of the cognitive faculties may in some cases influence the content of what is thought to be normative. For instance, the growth of knowledge may lead to a realization that squash bugs contain some enzyme that, when processed, offers protection against some dreaded disease.

What holds for agriculture holds as well for the social agriculture with which Hamilton was concerned in *Federalist* No. 1. Government necessarily involves a form of Faustian bargain, as Vincent Ostrom (1994) notes. Government injects an instrument of evil, force and violence, into human relationships, under the presumption or hope that the weight of the evil forestalled or prevented is even heavier. Whether this hope is born out is a different matter that involves both cognition and valuation.

Valuation refers to desired principles for governing human relationships. Cognition refers to the scientific appraisal of the compatibility between those normative principles and the prudential imperatives that exist within a particular regime. Liberal values may lead to the selection of a particular governing regime. That regime, however, may promote practice that undermines those liberal values. The prevention of such regime drift requires particular institutional arrangements that promote practice that reinforces the founding values. Cognition must be enlisted in the service of valuation, much as Hamilton recognized in *Federalist* #1.

In a very generic sense, liberal values will lead to institutional arrangements where human relationships are governed through the principles of property, contract, and voluntary association. These abstract principles, however, are always instantiated through specific institutionalized practice. That practice may, in turn, conflict with the governing principles, perhaps leading to a revision of the underlying values, at least to the extent that normative belief adapts to conventional practice. For instance, a quota may be imposed in place of a low tariff, and with similar replacement occurring across a broad range of activities.

For a people who generally embrace the liberal values of a free and open society, the organization of human governance is both a limited and a tricky matter because of cognitive types of matters, as well as because of the interaction between cognition and valuation. Just as success in growing squash is constrained by such things as soil and climate, so is success in liberal governance constrained by the constitutional system of governance that we adopt. Liberal governance may flourish under some constitutional frameworks while morphing into various forms of illiberal governance under other constitutional frameworks. This conflict between what is held desirable and what is promoted through institutionalized practice is redolent with themes that have been central in the development of ordnungspolitik and ordnungstheorie (in addition to some of the works cited above, see the interesting comparison of Walter Eucken and Max Weber in Rath (1998)). Such themes, moreover, would surely occupy an important position in any reinvigoration of fiscal sociology.

References

Backhaus, J. (1992), "The State as a Club: A Perspective for Public Finance in a Prosperous Democracy." *Journal of Public Finance and Public Choice* 10: 3-16.

Buchanan, J. M. (1964), "Fiscal Institutions and Efficiency in Collective Outlay." *American Economic Review*, Proceedings: 54: 227-35.

Buchanan, J. M. (1967), *Public Finance in Democratic Process*. Chapel Hill: University of North Carolina Press.

Buchanan, J. M. and Tullock, G. (1962), *The Calculus of Consent*. Ann Arbor: University of Michigan Press.

Eckert, R. D. and Hilton, G. W. (1972), "The Jitneys." *Journal of Law and Economics* 15: 293-325.

Epstein, R. A. (1985), *Takings: Private Property and the Power of Eminent Domain*. Cambridge, MA: Harvard University Press.

Eucken, W. (1952), *Grundsätze der Wirtschaftpolitik*, 6th ed. with "Forward" by Ernst-Joachim Mestmäker. Tübingen: J. C. B. Mohr, 1990.

Frank, R. H. (1987), "If Homo Economicus Could Choose His Own Utility Function, Would He Want One with a Conscience?" *American Economic Review* 77: 593-604.

Hickel, R., ed. (1976), *Die Finanzkrise der Steuerstaates*. Frankfurt: Suhrkamp.

Ikeda, S. (1997), *Dynamics of the Mixed Economy*. London: Routledge.

Justi, Johann Heinrich Gottlob von. (1771), *Natur und Wesen der Staaten*. Darmstadt: Scientia Verlag Aalen, 1969.

Klein, D. B. (1997), *Curb Rights: A Foundation for Free Enterprise in Urban Transit*. Washington: American Enterprise Institute.

Leipold, H. and Pies, I., eds. (2000), *Ordnungstheorie und Ordnungspolitik: Konzeptionen und Entwicklungsperspektiven*. Stuttgart: Lucius & Lucius.

McChesney, F. (1997), *Money for Nothing: Politicians, Rent Extraction, and Political Extortion*. Cambridge: Harvard University Press.

Ostrom, E. (1990), *Governing the Commons*. Cambridge: Cambridge University Press.

Ostrom, V. (1984), "Why Governments Fail: An Inquiry into the Use of Instruments of Evil to do Good." In J. M. Buchanan and R. D. Tollison, eds. *Theory of Public Choice II* (Ann Arbor: University of Michigan Press), pp. 422-35.

Pantaleoni, M. (1911), "Considerazioni sulle proprieta di un sistema di prezzi politici." *Giornale degli Economisti* 42: 9-29, 114-33.

Rath, C. (1998), *Staat, Gesellschaft, und Wirtschaft bei Max Weber und bei Walter Eucken*. Egelsbach: Hänsel-Hohenhausen.

Rowley, C. K., Tollison, R. D., and Tullock, G. eds. (1988), *The Political Economy of Rent Seeking*. Dordrecht: Kluwer Academic Publishers.

Samuelson, P. A. (1954), "The Pure Theory of Public Expenditure." *Review of Economics and Statistics* 36: 387-89.

Samuelson, P. A. (1955), "Diagrammatic Exposition of a Theory of Public Expenditure." *Review of Economics and Statistics* 37: 350-56.

Schlicht, E. (1998), *On Custom and the Economy*. Oxford: Clarendon Press.

Smith. A. (1776), *An Inquiry into the Nature and Causes of the Wealth of Nations*. New York: Modern Library, 1937.

Tullock, G. (1967), "The Welfare Cost of Tariffs, Monopolies, and Theft." *Economic Inquiry* 5: 224-32.

Wagner, R. E. (1997), "Parasitical Political Pricing, Economic Calculation, and the Size of Government: Variations on a Theme by Maffeo Pantaleoni." *Journal of Public Finance and Public Choice* 15: 135-46.

Wicksell, K. (1896), "A New Principle of Just Taxation." In R. A. Musgrave and A. T. Peacock, eds. *Classics in the Theory of Public Finance* (London: Macmillan, 1958), pp. 72-118.

Will, George F. (1983), *Statecraft as Soulcraft: What Government Does*. New York: Simon and Schuster.

Approaches to Fiscal Sociology*

Michael McLure
School of Economics and Commerce M251
The University of Western Australia
35 Stirling Highway, CRAWLEY WA 6009
Australia
Michael.McLure@uwa.edu.au

Abstract: This paper reviews developments in Fiscal Sociology, commencing with the seminal Austrian studies by Rudolf Goldscheid and Joseph Schumpeter and the classic Italian studies by Gino Borgatta and Guido Sensini, and ending with a review of new approaches to fiscal sociology. It is suggested that a received view on the methodological and analytical framework of new fiscal sociology has not yet emerged. Although developments have been noteworthy, the challenge ahead is to define the sociological dimension in theoretical fiscal studies, so it can be clearly differentiated from more descriptive notions of fiscal 'politics'.

Keywords: Fiscal sociology, Goldscheid, Pareto, Public Finance, Schumpeter, social equilibrium, taxation.

JEL codes: B0, H0.

1 Introduction

Fiscal sociology analyses public finances in the context of the social, political and economic environment in which fiscal decisions are made. It may consider: the influence of the social, political and economic environment on fiscal phenomena; and/or the influence of the fiscal phenomenon on the social, political and economic environment.

American fiscal sociology is largely a legacy of pioneering investigations, undertaken towards the end of World War I, by Rudolph Goldscheid and Joseph Schumpeter in Austria on the question of whether states that rely on general taxes to fund the provision of public services (i.e. 'tax states') will necessarily

* This is a modified and extended paper based on the author's 'fiscal sociology' entry in the *International Encyclopedia of Public Policy* (O'Hara, forthcoming).

fall into fiscal crisis. Nevertheless, the origin of fiscal sociology is not limited to Austria, with the relationship between social equilibrium and the fiscal phenomenon being closely scrutinized in Italy in the first half of the Twentieth Century (Boccaccio and De Bonis, 2003). The scope of new studies in this field has now expanded beyond the issue of fiscal crisis, with theoretical fiscal sociologies considering constitutional, legal and institutional influences on fiscal policy. Applied fiscal sociologies are also emerging.

The purpose of this paper is to briefly review the development of the main approaches to fiscal sociology and to note the major issues that still need to be addressed in this field. The emergence of European fiscal sociology is reviewed in Section 2, focusing on the well know Austrian, and less well known Italian, approaches. The post World War II development of American fiscal sociology is presented in Section 3 as a response to the classic Austrian contributions. Some new fiscal sociologies are reviewed in Section 4, with particular attention given to the notion of 'sociological intolerances', methodological and policy issues (such as the relationship between fiscal sociology and other fiscal disciplines), Paretian themes and applied studies of taxation. The outlook for fiscal sociology is discussed in Section 5, suggesting that the emergence of a commonly accepted new fiscal sociology is contingent upon clarifying the 'sociological' (as distinct from the narrower, and more particular, 'political') dimension of research into fiscal events.

2 Emergence of European Fiscal Sociology

Fiscal sociology emerged as a field of study in Europe, with two distinct traditions developing, an Austrian tradition and an Italian tradition. In Austria, seminal contributions were made by Rudolph Goldscheid, such as in his 1917 Staatssozialismus oder Statkapitalismus and 1925 "Staat, öffentlicher Haushalt und Gesellschaft, Wesen und Aufgaben der Finanzwissenschaften vom Standpunkte der Soziologie", ([1925] 1967), and by Joseph Schumpeter, especially in his influential "Die Krise des Steuerstaats" ([1918] 1954). In Italy, formative contributions along Paretian lines were made by Gino Borgatta, in works such as "I problemi fondamentali della scienza finanziaria" (1913) and "Lo studio scientifico dei fenomeni finanziari" (1920) and Guido Sensini in his "Cenni di finanza teorica" (1929) and "La Finanza Sociologica" (1932). Aspects of the Paretian approach were also developed by Etore Lolini (1928) Roberto Murray (1913, 1915) and Stanislaw Scalfati (1928, 1932). While leading scholars from the Italian fiscal tradition, like Mauro Fasiani (1932-33 [1980], 1950) and Benvenuto Griziotti (1950, 1953), were not to embrace the Paretian form of fiscal sociology, they nevertheless generally recognized the importance of considering the sociological context of fiscal events.

The Austrian approach recognised that the 'sociology' of public finances, developed from an historical investigation of fiscal information, provides considerable insight into both the fiscal activities of government and the prevailing social structures and arrangements. Goldscheid, and subsequently Schumpeter, placed the notion of the 'tax state' as the subject of their analysis, with financial history and the consequent development of public debt and fiscal crisis central to their critical assessments. Notwithstanding their agreement on applying sociology to the study of fiscal matters, the differences between these two approaches were significant, with Goldscheid and Schumpeter ultimately reaching quite different conclusions on the nature and sustainability of the tax state.

Goldscheid was influenced by Karl Marx, and relied on class analysis to investigate the exploitative features of fiscal outcomes. From fiscal history, Goldscheid found that states progressively disposed of public property in response to increased enfranchisement, and provided the opportunity for public creditors – whose interests he equated with capitalists and the ruling class – to exploit the state as it came to progressively rely more and more on public debt. In this circumstance, tax pressure to service debt was presented as a manifestation of social struggle, with the fiscal exploitation of workers by the tax state (for the benefit of public creditors) being interdependent with, and complementary to, capitalist exploitation of workers throughout the private economy. A tendency to fiscal crisis became a consequence of the relationship between the fiscal system and capitalism.

In contrast, Schumpeter analysed the nature of the tax state in terms of an evolution in the complexity of the relationship between individual and collective needs. He reserved use of the term 'the state' to circumstances where a 'public purpose', as opposed to an individual's purpose, was pursued on behalf of the collective. While "Goldscheid saw the emergence of the tax state as leading to State impoverishment, Schumpeter heralded it as the very creation of the State" (Musgrave 1992, p.33). Furthermore, while Goldscheid relied extensively on class analysis, Schumpeter tended to emphasize groups and the role of interests in shaping the activities of the state: "It is always important to recognize who or whose interest it is that sets the machine of state in motion and speaks through it." (Schumpeter [1918] 1954, p.19). Consequently, Schumpeter's notion of 'common' need was not naive or simplistic, but was considered as something that emerged within the general context of the relationships of social power that exist within and between groups.

Goldscheid's solution to the twin issues of fiscal crisis and fiscal exploitation was for the working class to conquer the bourgeois classes by creating a wealthy state (a 'state capitalism'), with the state acquiring property to use for economic purposes and for the associated 'surplus value' to be expended in the interests of society. For Schumpeter, however, the case for fiscal crisis had not been demonstrated. His interest was not in periodic or avoidable crises, but the fundamental question of whether the tax state must descend into fiscal crisis as a result of funding the state provision of services in response to a mixture of common need and private purpose. By complementing his sociological explanation of the growing demand for public expenditures with an economic explanation of the relative stagnation in tax receipts (Seidl 1984, p91), Schumpeter was able to conclude "there is no 'crisis in the tax state'" (Schumpeter [1918] 1954, p37). That is, while tax states can collapse, a collapse is not a logical necessity of the tax state, at least not in the particular historical moment under consideration.

The Italian approach to fiscal sociology has at least one common factor – its main proponents were ex-students or associates of Vilfredo Pareto (McLure 2005). A change in fiscal settings modifies the existing combination of revenue raising, expenditure and debt which, according to Pareto, cannot be considered in isolation. Instead, the variation in economic and social equilibrium resulting from each aspect of a new fiscal setting must first be established before arriving at any judgement on the welfare implications of the new fiscal settings. In a letter written in September 1917 to Benvenuto Griziotti, Pareto complained that "... the 'science' of finance knows little of economic equilibrium and nothing of social equilibrium" (Pareto 1975 p.984), but confessed that he was unsure of how fiscal studies should be progressed, contenting himself with the observation that "... at least I have the merit, like Socrates had, of knowing my own ignorance" (Pareto 1975 p.984).

Gino Borgatta and Guido Sensini were the most prominent of Pareto's followers to have contributed to the development of Italian fiscal sociology. The importance of these authors is that they developed an analytical framework to accommodate an economics and sociology of public finance that focused on social equilibrium. They criticized the reliance on analytical hedonism within the dominant stream of the Italian tradition in public finance, as this 'benefit' approach tended to treat the fiscal phenomena as if it were the product of voluntary exchange rather than a coercive process to pursue group interests through patron-client relationships. Their vision is predicated on the view that the public phenomenon represents a conduit for redistributing economic goods among individuals and groups, altering economic activity in the process, and that this redistribution is socially determined and politically implemented. Consequently, Italian fiscal sociology treated fiscal redistribution as the primary issue in fiscal theory and examined the consequences for this for the form of a society and its social equilibrium, the main attributes of social utility within a given society. The economic and social characteristics of the governing class and its relationship to the governed is also as central issue, including the impact of different types economies on relationships with the governing class, as is the role of fiscal phenomenon in influencing general sociological regularities.

Such investigations evolved from a Paretian general sociology into a genuine fiscal sociology, because Borgatta and Sensini recognized that public finances play an integral role in realizing the general regularities associated with a particular social equilibrium. In this regard, while the main attributes of social utility within a given society may be identified through an applied sociology, the fiscal dimension emerges as significant when considering the type of economy within a particular society, the economic and social characteristics of the governing class, the stability of the relationship between the governing class and the governed and the stability of the relationship between the governing class and the economy. Borgatta's contribution is also noteworthy for extending Pareto's work on *rentiers* and *speculators* to provide a fiscal explanation for economic growth (McLure, forthcoming). Based on extensive induction, Borgatta noted a correlation between the rapid growth in European economic prosperity observed in the Nineteenth and early Twentieth Centuries, and the redistribution of economic goods through the fiscal phenomenon. As fiscal policy had actually imposed a more than proportionate tax burden on low risk-taking *rentiers* (partly because they were easier to tax and less likely to pursue avoidance activities), Borgatta suggested that capital had been effectively transferred to higher risk-taking investors, whose more speculative use of capital lead to increased economic prosperity in the collective.

In the 1930s and 1940s, the fiscal sociology critique of public finance associated with Borgatta, Sensini and others moderated, with fiscal sociology becoming less a substitute for, and more of a complement to, the science of public finance. Borgatta came to the view that considering public finances in the context of social equilibrium (the central point of reference in Paretian fiscal sociology) is important because it accounts for the most general aspect of the fiscal phenomenon (Borgatta 1933, p59), but there is no suggestion that it is the only perspective. When reflecting on developments in Italian fiscal studies to the middle of the Twentieth Century, Benvenuto Griziotti (1950) concluded that the renewal of fiscal studies sought by Pareto was largely complete, with fiscal research in Italy developing along three related but distinct lines: the science of public finance; the macroeconomics of public finance; and the sociology of public finance. However, within this general scheme, the sociology of public finance was largely stripped of its original Paretian foundation, evolving into an essentially ad hoc treatment of political influences on fiscal decisions.

Somewhat surprisingly, the Italian approach has had little influence on modern fiscal sociology. No doubt language barriers have contributed to this unfortunate neglect, although it is possible that the concurrent developments of fascism and fiscal sociology in Italy may have also contributed the lack of enthusiasm for the subject.

3 American Fiscal Sociology of Crisis

While fiscal sociology initially found its way to English-speaking scholars through the essays of Fritz Karl Mann (1943, 1947), an exile from Nazi Germany, it was not until the translation and publication of Schumpeter's "Crisis of the Tax State" (Schumpeter 1954) and Goldscheid's "A Sociological Approach to Problems of Public Finance" (Goldscheid 1967) that the subject took a reasonably firm hold within America. Perhaps not surprisingly then, the classic issue of fiscal crisis became the first major theme in American fiscal sociology.

The American reprise in the sociology of fiscal crisis is primarily associated with James O'Connor's influential *The Fiscal Crisis of the State* (O'Connor 1973), which developed from within a Marxist intellectual tradition, and Richard Musgrave's important "Theories of Fiscal Crisis: An Essay in Fiscal Sociology" (Musgrave 1980), which largely followed Schumpeterian lines of analysis.

O'Connor observed that unproductive state 'social expenses', such as welfare payments, redress the 'contradictions of capitalism' and contended that tax systems under advanced capitalism are designed to effectively quarantine 'monopoly capital' from having to fund such unproductive state expenses. Under this analysis, the concurrent growth in monopoly capital and public sector outlays, and the associated privatization of surplus and socialization of 'social expenses', were presented as interrelated but internally contradictory, leading to a tendency towards fiscal crisis in advanced capitalism. In contrast to Goldscheid, who assigned a primary role to public creditors in his analysis of exploitation, O'Connor emphasised the contradiction of advanced capitalism itself and the inability of the state to correct this contradiction. Consequently, instead of following Goldscheid's prescription favoring the development of state capitalism, O'Connor advocated a reduction in the need for unproductive social expenses, probably though the replacement of advanced capitalism with a socialist system.

The response to O'Connor's work was mainly from authors writing within Marxist traditions, with critiques generally being favorable, although concerns were raised over the presentation of class struggle in the competitive and monopolistic sectors as incidental to market determined wage outcomes (Loxley 1982) and the difficulty of empirically testing O'Connor's thesis due to the abstract classification of public expenditures (Block 1981).

Richard Musgrave (1980) provided the definitive non-Marxist response to O'Connor, and to the general proposition that structural imbalances in the budget result in a general tendency to fiscal crisis. From a conceptual perspective, Musgrave emphasized that fiscal benefits and costs cut across class divisions and link better to group interests. For example, taxation activity is often stratified by income source, tastes or the pattern of household expenditure and age. Consequently, not only is the net incidence of fiscal activity too complex and multidirectional to be analysed in terms of the labour-capital dichotomy, but monopoly capital is also unlikely to be quarantined from the economic consequences of fiscal policy. From the empirical perspective, Musgrave noted that the growth in social expenses (as a share of gross national product) has been negligible – which is also contrary to O'Connor's thesis. He also suggested that much of the observed increase in growth in other public expenditures could be accounted for by a particular factor; the growth in population from the post World War II baby boom.

4 New Fiscal Sociologies

In addition to the perennial issue of fiscal crisis, other important issues to emerge in new theoretical approaches to fiscal sociologies over the last two decades include investigation of: sociological intolerances to tax policy; the relationship between macro and micro considerations; the methodological relationship between cameral sciences and fiscal sociology for studies of economic integration and regulation; the relevance of constitutional themes to fiscal sociology; and endogenous preferences where statecraft becomes soul-craft. The contemporary relevance of Paretian themes to the methodology and method of fiscal sociology has also been under consideration.

The Schumpeterian approach to fiscal sociology was extended in the 1980s to investigate the sociological 'intolerances' associated with the tax structure (Christian Seidl's 1984). When public perceptions of the distribution of the tax burden do not reflect evolutionary change in social values, sociological intolerances begin to emerge over the tax system. Within this context, relevant considerations for tax policy include the evolution of social perceptions in regard to: the relative incidence of taxation on consumer and producer sovereignty; the extent of tax related income redistribution; the degree of privacy relative to the degree of avoidance associated with the tax system; and the extent of non-political power enjoyed by private sector benefactors whose actions influence the need for taxation.

Recent investigations have emphasized the importance of micro considerations to fiscal policy, concluding that an enhanced understanding of the flexibility and subtlety of fiscal arrangements in mixed economies requires investigators to be cognoscente of both macro and micro issues (Musgrave 1991). The importance of this approach is that it suggests that Schumpeter cannot be followed in taking public expenditures as largely given or in ignoring public finance insights into factors such as 'externalities'. The inference here is that, when investigating the fiscal phenomenon, the insights of both public finance theory and fiscal sociology are complementary - a position that is consistent with the Italian approach to fiscal studies adopted in Borgatta (1935).

More recently, the methodological foundations of the European tradition in the cameral sciences and *Staatswissenschaften* have been proposed as a sound basis for casting fiscal sociology as a policy study, particularly for the investigation of issues in economic regulation and integration between jurisdictions, such as in the European Union (Backhaus 2002). In this context, fiscal sociology effectively provides the synthetic unification of economic, sociological, political and legal approaches to public policy issues.

Another promising recent development is the attempt to introduce the principles of constitutional political economy to fiscal sociology (Wagner 2002). This approach contrasts the reliance of exogenous preferences in traditional public finance with a reinvigorated fiscal sociology where statecraft and fiscal activity are recognized as preference altering activities. Within this framework, rules and procedures of human governance, including the rules governing the operation of fiscal institutions, play an important role in shaping preferences, with statecraft treated as a form of 'soul-craft'. Like the normative basis of constitutional political economy, the constitutional approach to fiscal sociology is directed towards establishing rules where constitutional frameworks support liberal governance. The constitutional approach to political economy, like its Schumpeterian predecessor, also has the capacity to consider the development of fiscal institutions and their impact on fiscal programs.

A new approach to fiscal sociology, inspired by Pareto and the Italian approach to fiscal studies, is also at a formative stage in the work of McLure (2003). This approach derives from: the attempt by Borgatta and Sensini to link fiscal phenomena to social equilibrium; Pareto's suggestion that the substantive aspects of social equilibrium concern the forces for stability or instability in equilibrium, in a given period; the cyclical, albeit irregular, movement of social equilibrium in the long term; and the association of substantive social change with a variation in the degree of decentralization, or centralization, associated with social equilibrium (McLure 2001). This new Paretian approach considers the relationship between the degree of decentralization in fiscal programs (defined in relation to:

the distribution of revenue raising powers across the tiers of government in a sovereign nation; and the inverse of the nation's vertical fiscal imbalance) and the degree of decentralization in each of the three aspects of Paretian social equilibrium; namely the economic, political and socio-psychological balances. This is predicated on the view that, within certain upper and lower bounds, fiscal decentralization is positively correlated with decentralization of each of the three elements of social equilibrium, which interact and determine the forces for social continuity or change. By definition, an increase in the decentralization of the social equilibrium is revealed when: (i) the economic balance reveals an increase in the incidence of high risk-taking economic activity relative to low risk-taking economic activity; (ii) the political balance reveals an increase in the incidence of individuals' rights prevailing over states' rights; and (iii) the socio-psychological balance reveals an increased incidence of observed non-conformist conduct in periods of stable equilibrium. This approach also builds on Borgatta's linkage between fiscal activity and growth in economic prosperity, by hypothesizing that the rate of growth and stability of fiscal activity correlate with the trend, and shorter term cyclical movement, for each of the three aspects of social equilibrium.

In addition to the theoretical and methodological work undertaken as part of a modern renewal of interest fiscal sociology, there have also been a number of applied studies. These have focused primarily on the sociology of taxation. John Campbell (1993) surveyed fiscal research literature to summarize the identified social attributes of taxation. The survey found that the main social determinants of taxation are broad, ranging from war, macroeconomic circumstances and crisis, to classes, interest groups and the centralization of the state. Similarly, the main identified consequences of taxation were also found to be broad, extending from political rebellion and state building to economic organization, labor force participation and philanthropy.

Perhaps the most notable and recent applied fiscal sociology of taxation is the study of Japan's property tax revolt in the 1990s by Jinno and DeWit (1998), who point to the aggressive re-centralization of taxing powers in the 1940s and the relatively decentralized distribution of public spending responsibilities as outcomes of American reforms. The consequential constitutional arrangements are characterized as a 'centralized-deconcentrated' system, with the power to tax being largely centralized while the responsibility for expenditure not being fully concentrated in the central government. The key fiscal institutions considered are the Ministry for Finance, an institutional force for the centralization of taxation, and the Ministry for Home Affairs, an institutional force that acts in opposition to tax centralization, because it has authority over local taxation. In tracking the relative successes (and failures) of these bureaucracies in influencing taxation policy in the late bubble, and early post-bubble, economy of Japan in the 1990s, Jinno and DeWit conclude that institutions with fiscal responsibilities may have long term 'memories' (or policy agendas) which can prove important role in the development of fiscal policy.

> The (implicit) four step approach employed by Jinno and DeWit (1998) is worthy of note, as it has general relevance for applied fiscal sociologies of taxation outside Japan. The first step is to establish, through historical observation, the key defining elements of the fiscal system under consideration. The second step is to establish, again through historical observation, the taxation policy agendas pursued by the key public sector bureaucracies. The third step is to examine the incidence and outcome of institutional competition to influence the government's taxation policy agenda. The final step is to re-examine the fundamentals of the fiscal system in light of the new tax policy, after accounting for the impact of the measure on economy, the community and political parties.

Finally, it should be noted that fiscal sociology has influenced historical studies. In this regard, John Hobson (1997) investigated the relationship between taxation, the fiscal system and foreign policy, supported by empirical case studies of Britain, Russia and Germany. This approach suggests that the cost of militarism during the free trade period, between 1860 and 1879, represented a constant force on states to increase their indirect taxes, culminating in higher tariffs and ultimately shifting states into a protectionist period, subsequent to 1879. This effectively highlights links between the State and the national and international economy, including the mode of taxation employed by the state and the social relations that shape taxation policy. In this context, the state is effectively presented as an institutional ensemble, with the authority of the state only deriving from the group elements that comprise the ensemble. Although Hobson's work is essentially historical, the forces he identifies are of some contemporary relevance.

5 The Outlook

The development of fiscal sociology in the Twentieth Century has not been continuous, and the re-emergence of fiscal sociology in the last twenty years remains largely formative, and in some instances provisional. Notwithstanding this, development of fiscal sociology remains a significant international episode in the social sciences.

It is clear that the scope of issues being addressed in new fiscal sociologies has widened and the approaches proposed are: novel; often complementary; and appear to have methodological relevance and scientific potential. However, it is also clear that no unequivocal consensus has emerged on the defining characteristics of new fiscal sociology. For these approaches to develop into a new fiscal sociology, it would appear necessary to reach a received view on the actual sociological dimension to fiscal sociology. Moreover, fiscal 'sociology' should be differentiated from the more particular, and less profound, notion of fiscal 'politics', which tends to be the basis for (often *ad hoc* and *ex post*) rationalizations of governments' failure to introduce policies derived from public finance theory.

In summary, the current consensus on the likely benefits from complementing public finance theory with fiscal sociology should prove even more fruitful once a clear, and general, accord has emerged concerning the theoretical foundations on which fiscal sociology is based.

References

Backhaus, J. (2002), Fiscal Sociology: What For? *American Journal of Economics and Sociology*, vol. 61, no. 1, 55-78.

Block, F. (1981), The Fiscal Crisis of the Capitalist State, *Annual Review of Sociology*, vol. 7, 1-27.

Boccaccio, M and De Bonis, V. (2003), Political Sociological Theories in the Italian Tradition of Public Finance, *Pensiero Economico Italiano*, vol. 11, no. 1.

Borgatta, G. (1913), I Problemi Fondamentali della Scienza Finanziaria, *Atti Reale Accademia delle Scienze di Torino*, vol.48, 985-1007

Borgatta, G. (1920), Lo Studio Scientifico dei Fenomeni Finanziari, *Giornale degli Economisti*, vol.lv, 1- 24 and 81-116.

Borgatta, G. (1933), *Principi Generali di Scienza delle Finanze: Appunti di Scienza della Finanze a Diritto Finanziario*, Milano, Giuffrè.

Campbell, J. (1993), The State and Fiscal Sociology, *Annual Review of Sociology*, vol. 19, 193-185.

Fasiani, M. [1932-33] (1980) "La Teoria della Finanza Pubblica in Italia ["Der Gegenwärtige Stand der Reinen Theorie der Finanzwissenschaft in Italien"], in *Il Pensiero Economico Italiano 1850-1950*, Bologna: Cappelli, 117-202.

Fasiani, M. (1950) "Contributi di Pareto alla Scienza delle Finanze", in *Vilfredo Pareto: l'Economista e il Sociologo*, Università Bocconi (ed), Milano, Malfasi: 262-307.

Goldscheid, R. [1925] (1967), A Sociological Approach to Problems of Public Finance" ("Staat, öffentlicher Haushalt und Gasellschaft, Wesen und Aufgaben der Finanzwissenschaften vom Standpunkte der Soziologie") translated by Elizabeth Henderson, in *Classics in the Theory of Public Finance*, Musgrave, R. A. and A. T Peacock, eds.Macmillan, London, 202-213.

Griziotti, B. (1950), Alla Scuola di Vilfredo Pareto e Maffeo Pantaleoni, *in Vilfredo Pareto: l'Economista e il Sociologo*, Università Bocconi (ed), Malfasi, Milano, 340-346.

Griziotti, B. (1953) "L'Evoluzione della Teoria Generale della Finanza nelle Opere di Gino Borgatta", in *Studi in Memoria di Gino Borgatta, vol.2* Bologna: Istituto di Cultura Bancaria di Milano, Arte Grafiche, 1-13.

Jinno, N. and DeWit, A. (1998), Japan's Taxing Bureaucrats: Fiscal Sociology and the Property-tax Revolt, *Social Science Japan Journal*, Vol. 1, Issue 2, 233-246.

Hobson, J. (1997), *The Wealth of States: A Comparative Sociology of International Economic and Political Change*, Cambridge University Press, Cambridge.

Lolini, E. (1928), Il Caratere Sociologico della Scienza delle Finanze e lo Studio Scientifico dei Fenomeni Finanziari, *La Vita Italiana*, vol. xvi, gennaio-febbraio, 11-47.

Loxley, J. (1982), Fiscal Sociology and the Fiscal Crisis of the State – A Review of Goldscheid and O'Connor", *Contemporary Crisis*, vol. 6, .285-301.

Mann, F. K. (1943), The Sociology of Taxation, *Review of Politics*, vol. 5, 225-235.

Mann, F. K. (1947), The Fiscal Component of Revolution: An Essay in Fiscal Sociology, *Review of Politics*, vol. 9, 331-349.

McLure, M. (2001), *Pareto, Economics and Society: the Mechanical Analogy*, Routledge, London.

McLure, M. (2003), *An Italian Foundation for New Fiscal Sociology: A Reflection on the Pareto-Griziotti and Pareto-Sensini letters on Ricardian Equivalence and Fiscal Theory*, University of Western Australia, Economics Discussion Paper No. 03.11.

McLure, M. (2005) "Italian Fiscal Sociology: a Reflection of the Pareto-Griziotti and Pareto-Sensini Letters on Fiscal Theory", *European Journal of the History of Economic Thought*, 12(4).

McLure, M. (forthcoming) "La Sociologia Finanziaria di Gino Borgatta", *Pensiero Economico Italiano,* Atti dei Convegni: La scuola di economia di Torino: da Cognetti de Martiis a Einaudi, University of Turin, 5-8 May 2004.

Murray, R. (1913) "Intorno alla Nozione dei Bisogni Pubblici" *Giornale degli Economisti e Rivista di Statistica*, 46, 27-37.

Murray, R. (1915) "La Scienza delle Finanze, Il Diritto Finanziario e la Nozione di Stato" *Giornale degli Economisti e Rivista di Statistica*, 51(3), 27-37.

Musgrave, R. (1980), Theories of Fiscal Crises: An Essay in Fiscal Sociology, in Henry J Aaron and Michael J Boskins (eds), *The Economics of Taxation*, Brookings Institution, Washington, 316-390.

Musgrave, R. (1992), Schumpeter's Crisis of the Tax State: An Essay in Fiscal Sociology, *Journal of Evolutionary Economics*, vol. 2, no.2, 23-47.

O'Connor, J. (1973), *The Fiscal Crisis of the State*, St. Martin's Press, New York.

O'Hara, P. A. (forthcoming) *International Encyclopedia of Public Policy,* Routledge, London.

Pareto, V. (1975), A Benvenuto Griziotti, letter of 2 September 1917, in Giovanni Busino (ed) *Correspondance, vol 19/2, Vilfredo Pareto Œuvres Complètes*, Droz, Geneva, 983-985.

Scalfati, S. (1928) "Studii di Scienza e di Legislazione Finanziarie", Roma: Libreria Internazonale F.lli Treves Dell'Ali.

Scalfati, S. (1932) "L'Ecole du Lausanne et l'Étude des Phénomènes Financiers", in Scalfati, S (1932) *Studi Paretiani*, Roma: Il Giornale Economico, pp136-176.

Schumpeter, J. A. [1918] (1954), The Crisis of the Tax State [Die Krise des Steuerstaats], in Alan T. Peacock, ed., *International Economic Papers*, no. 4., MacMillan. 1954, 5-38.

Seidl, C. (1984), The Tax State in Crisis: Can Schumpeterian Public Finance Claim Modern Relevance in Christain Seidl (ed) *Lectures on Schumpeterian Economics*, Springer-Verlag, Berlin, 89-109.

Sensini, G. (1920), Classificazione Generale dei Problemi Principali della Finanza, *Giornale degli Economisti*, vol.ix, 209-283.

Sensini, G. (1929), Cenni di finanza teorica, *Giornale degli Economisti*, vol.xliv, 373-384.

Sensini, G. (1932) "La Finanza Sociologica", in *Studi di Scienze Sociali*, P Maglione, Rome (a revised version of "Prime Linee di Finanza Teorica", in *In Onore di Tullio Martello*, 1917, Bari).

Wagner, R.E. (forthcoming) "States and the Crafting of Souls: Mind, Society and Fiscal Sociology", *Journal of Economic Behavior and Organization.*

Public Finance and Welfare: From the Ignorance of the Veil to the Veil of Ignorance

Giuseppe Eusepi
Università degli Studi di Roma "La Sapienza"
Facoltà di Economia, Dipartimento di Economia
Pubblica, Via del Castro Laurenziano 9,
00161 ROMA
Italy

Abstract: The unconstitutional or present day welfare state, which is a blend of Organicism and Keynesianism, may survive as long as bureaucracies and governments can create "optimistic" illusions among taxpayers-voters. It is no wonder, therefore, that illusion creation has contributed to soaring public expenditure. Illusion creation involves increasing costs, and this paper shows that the present welfare state is necessarily destined to fail, and indirectly to open up the pathway for a constitutional welfare state. Mazzola and Wicksell first offered a theory of both public choice and public goods which, in a sense, was constitutional, but the intellectual godfathers of the genuine alternative to the present welfare state are Buchanan and Tullock in the early sixties and Rawls a decade later. The virtuous circuit obligations-entitlements-rights, which the institutions of present welfare states helped to make it crumble, may be restored behind the veil of ignorance.

Keywords: Welfare, fiscal illusion, constitution.

JEL code: H30.

It would seem to be a blatant injustice
if someone should be forced to contribute
toward the cost of some activity which
does not further his interests or may even
be diametrically opposed to them.

Knut Wicksell, *A New Principle of just Taxation,*
English translation in R.A. Musgrave, A.T. Peacock (1958).

Introduction

Seeking the "roots" of the welfare state to see whether this "tree" has overgrown - (as I believe) or has simply grown in a disorganic way (as Musgrave[1] believes), is of cardinal importance in any consideration of public economics. The first thing to be stressed is that an enormous number of branches have intertwined over the roots and trunk of welfare economics so that they could hardly be separated, unless a time perspective is introduced. This paper tries to shed light on the alternatives to the present day or unconstitutional welfare states.

The focal point of section 1 is a review of the historical developments of public finance theory, which have led to the post-war II welfare state. Specifically, it outlines the debate among the various continental schools (German, Italian and Swedish), and their opposition to the Anglo-Saxon tradition. The historical perspective allows me to move from the simple to the complex, and to separate theories from ideologies more easily. Since value judgements are inherent in this kind of analysis, I examine the welfare state of the "real" world from the perspective of methodological individualism in the light of the Wicksell-Buchanan constitutional logic[2].

Section 2, which is the innovative part of the paper, extends Puviani's theory of fiscal illusion, which was intended to explain government behaviour in a non-democratic polity, to a democratic context such as that of the welfare state. This is done in two ways: (1) by showing the active role that bureaucracies of the present welfare states play in creating illusions; and (2) by showing that a centralised tax system allows local governments and bureaucracies to exploit voters' illusion through a mechanism that entitles them to spend without being accountable for the future revenues needed to exploit voters' illusion. The constitutionalization of the welfare state is suggested in sections 3 and 4 as the only alternative to the failures of the real welfare states. It would be unwise here to deal with the passage from welfare state to the constitutional welfare state because such an analysis would involve a general theory of constitutional revision indicating the path to reforms. The aim here is simply that of suggesting how to supplement customary democratic constitutions of the welfare state with a fiscal constitution. On this basis, section 4 explores the obligations which have to be incurred to cover the entitlements-rights circle and then analyses the role that transfers may play at a constitutional level by distinguishing between a weak and a robust version of Rawls's difference principle. The paper ends with a critical discussion

---

[1] See R.A. Musgrave (1966).

[2] See K. Wicksell (1958), J.M. Buchanan, G. Tullock (1962), L. Jonung (1996), R.E. Wagner (1988).

of some possible ambiguities coming from a robust version of the difference principle. Some concluding remarks are offered in section 5.

1 Classical Schools on the Welfare State: An Overview

The welfarist component appeared explicitly for the first time in A. Wagner[3]. Believing that taxation has two distinct though complementary objectives, he thought, following the traditional Anglo-Saxon scheme, that taxation is on the one hand a covering instrument of service costs; and on the other, it is the instrument through which government modifies distribution with the aim of increasing social welfare[4].

Although with the serious implications underlined by Musgrave and Peacock[5], and especially by Buchanan[6], the assumption that public expenditures are neutral, might have found a justification in some way in the Anglo-Saxon tradition, which assigned the state a very restricted role. In that setting, in fact, where individual advantages from expenditures were marginally equal, the ability-to-pay principle appeared to be as a reasonable criterion for imputing the costs of public economy. But the ability-to-pay logic loses its legitimacy when transplanted into the Welfarist German tradition, which takes an explicitly organicist turn from Wagner onwards. The reason which could explain why the expenditure side was left out of the analysis lies in Wagner's way of designating expenditures as politically motivated, external, then, to the science of public finance and its connected principle of the ability-to-pay. Because the budget ends up by concealing future obligations, it is separate and independent of the expenditure side. Although the limits of this reasoning will be covered at length further on, it should be mentioned here that this approach has at least the merit of making explicit that the political aim of transfers was that of correcting the existing distribution for welfare purposes. Hence, if public finance derives from an organic point of view as in Wagner as well as in von Stein[7], the introduction of a maximising welfare scheme cannot but have bureaucrats and politicians as executors. This is why utilities to be maximised do not hinge on someone's rights, which in

---

[3] See A. Wagner (1958).
[4] The statement in the text on the distinctiveness-complementarity argument can be clarified by recalling that Wagner used two distinct instruments to fulfil the two objectives (proportional taxation to cover expenditures, progressive taxation to increase social welfare). As long as the expenditure side is supposed to be neutral, progressive taxation appears to be the only redistributive tool.
[5] See R.A. Musgrave, A.T. Peacock (1958), pp. IX- XIX.
[6] See J.M. Buchanan (1960).
[7] See L. Von Stein (1958).

turn imply someone else's obligations, but are simply rights created by rules without covering entitlements: there is no way to link fiscal rights with fiscal obligations, unless we abandon the organic perspective and move towards an individualistic perspective.

We might say that Mazzola[8] was the first to strike a novel note by introducing the individualistic perspective, soon followed by Wicksell. Unfortunately, the Mazzola-Wicksell approach has had little impact for a period of about sixty years, and in fact the dominant school in public finance continued to be the Anglo-Saxon one, initially interested only in taxation and then with the Keynesians in expenditures. The 1980s developments[9] on optimal taxation go back to considering only the tax side with the aim of minimizing both distortions and collection costs. Hence, we may say that the optimal taxation theory might solve public finance problems in a satisfactory way only under condition that the role of public spending is supposed to be unimportant. In this sense, the theory of optimal taxation could well serve as an efficiency test of the ability-to-pay principle[10] typical of the Anglo-Saxon tradition. Wicksell's statement in the epigraph, according to which no one can be forced to pay a tax that would not yield to him an at least equal benefit, assumes the individual as acting in a voluntary exchange relationship. This implies, of course, that the benefit principle or Value and Countervalue principle be the choosing criterion. The benefit principle is not only "compatible" with the theory of social contract, as Sóderstrom puts it, but it is at the root of all contractarian paradigms[11].

From the nineteen century onwards, the ability to pay principle has become generally accepted both in England and Germany. Although the political settings in the two countries were different - Liberal in the English case, Organicist in the German one - the ability-to-pay principle has been related solely to liberalism, at least in the political debate. And it has remained such also after the introduction of the theory of the minimisation of the aggregate marginal sacrifice. Clearly, such theory adopts a logic that is hardly consistent with liberalism.

It was Pigou[12] who first introduced the expenditure side into the Anglo-Saxon tradition, although his perspective was completely different from that of Mazzola-Wicksell. Pigou, in fact, mimicked the sacrifice theory by distributing the tax so as to equalise the marginal sacrifice. By extending the same logic to the expenditure side he assumed the equality between aggregate marginal sacrifice

[8] See U. Mazzola (1890), especially chapter 9, also (1958).
[9] See A.B. Atkinson, J.E. Stiglitz (1980).
[10] See L. Soderstrom (1986) and J. S. Mill (1970).
[11] This explains why it has been adopted by Locke, Pufendorf as well as by Smith. See E. R. Seligman (1908) and E. Lindahl (1919).
[12] See A. C. Pigou (1920), (1928).

and aggregate marginal benefits as the maximising criterion.

With this Pigouvian trick a *two-sided* budget was formally introduced also into the Anglo-Saxon tradition. What can, then, ensure that the marginal evaluation of public expenditures be related to the marginal evaluation of taxation so that the equality makes a sense? Absolutely nothing, unless a subjectivist approach and the related opportunity cost theory is adopted.

The opportunity cost theory, being based on the benefit principle, makes marginal costs and benefits comparable and as a consequence meaningful in terms of individual tax/expenditure alternatives. As seen, the first economist deliberately to introduce this perspective was Mazzola whose work developed a system of equilibrium between private and public or complementary goods starting from the most radical form of the subjectivist or individualist approach[13].

On this basis, it is clear that individual satisfaction or utility is maximised when the "final utility" that an individual receives from private expenditures is equal to the "final utility" he receives from public expenditures[14]. Mazzola's analysis is correct but the scenario he has in mind is absolutely unrealistic. Where does the drawback of his theory lie? Not in the logical construction, but in his method. Since the equilibrium between demand and supply of complementary goods is attained in the absence of a political or voting market, it is as if it were possible that each single individual *per se* could choose his own equilibrium directly, and not as a member of real institutions[15]. This evaluation of mine would be still valid even in the case of direct democracy. If Mazzola had been aware of this, he would have realised that in the political market with non-excludible or complementary goods, the individual behaves differently from the market. In fact, while in the latter the payment of a price is unavoidable, in the political market with "consolidated" or non excludible goods, the individual would maximise his own satisfaction only if he paid a zero tax price or, in other words, if he were a free-rider. This, of course, would bear theoretical consequences, even in the absence of pressure groups, because bureaucracy would be eager to catch potential fiscal rents. Hence, even in a democratic political system with a reasonably efficient tax system, if *i* is a free-rider his maximising function could not be explained in terms of his opportunity costs (that is *i*'s tax price), but in terms of *j*'s opportunity costs. This amounts to saying that if we leave aside

---

[13] See U. Mazzola (1980) especially chapter 9.

[14] In any economy, the tendency towards maximizing utility causes available resources to be so distributed among various uses that the degrees of final utility of all the goods allocated are, after the distribution, equal. See U. Mazzola (1958), section 15, p.46.

[15] Mazzola's references to Parliamentary decisions in the same chapter 9, and his knowledge of Pantaleoni's analysis suggests an interpretation which is less strong than that of the text. At the moment of this writing, however, I see no reasons to modify it.

the cost that the dodger incurs to evade the tax, *i* does not suffer any cost, and hence the maximisation of his equilibrium would involve that he pays a zero tax-bill. This, in turn, means that *i*'s maximisation does not depend on his own opportunity costs, but on *j*'s opportunity costs. In this case, however, his equilibrium is necessarily non-optimal in terms of *j*'s opportunity costs.

This critique, which goes back to Wicksell, is undoubtedly meaningful and it explains why the ability to pay logic should be abandoned in a fiscal system which mimics price formation. One should move instead to an individual choice framework based on the willingness to pay by introducing a decision making process where individual wills would emerge as approximating unanimity. The Wicksellian scheme hinges on the following basic elements: (1) the Value-Countervalue principle as a criterion of Parliamentary approval of an expenditure-taxation bill; (2) the proportional sacrifice theory applied to revenues covering expenditures which do not give specific benefits; (3) limits to the fiscal power of redistributing. Ostensibly, the Value-Countervalue theory is the very core of just taxation because it is exactly this principle that allows to set an insurmountable limit to fiscal obligations or fiscal pressure.

On this point Wicksell's analysis is particularly convincing. The ability to pay principle, which is still present in Wicksell's work, although in a residual position, is grounded on an organicistic perspective, because the state is the one who has to establish the evaluating criteria concerning individuals' ability-to-pay.

Since the ability-to-pay principle is a criterion used to distribute taxation only, and does not fix an aggregate upper limit, it becomes impossible to determine the upper individual tax bill as a share of the aggregate one. It is thus arbitrary to fix limits to fiscal pressure. Clearly, when we speak of "just taxation" within a democratic framework, the benefit principle becomes its logical foundation with the exception, though partial, of interest payments on public debt, which can be viewed as a simple *ex post* settlement of a previous negotiation which has led to a clearance account[16].

By imposing constraints on the amount which can be redistributed through the political market, the unanimous consent as a constitutional device is the only guarantee taxpayers have against whatever type of welfare state, where distribution is contingent on politicians' and bureaucrats' expected gains[17]. Moreover, since in real institutions, especially those characterised by a huge public sector, bureaucracy plays a pressure group role *par excellence*, the resulting equilibrium is more or less far from the Mazzola-Wicksell or Lindahl equilibria[18]. This, in no

[16] On this see J. M. Buchanan (1969).
[17] See K. Wicksell (1958), pp.90
[18] See E. Lindahl (1919).

way, means that their perspectives have lost either their theoretical value or explanatory power! It is rather revealing that the decision-making institutions of the real welfare states do not hinge on voters and taxpayers' interests, but on the politico-bureaucratic power that seeks advantages through bureaucratic and fiscal illusion.

Not only have existing welfare states exerted their legitimate fiscal power grounded on the ability to pay of *present* taxpayers, but they have even illegitimately presumed as to have fiscal power on future taxpayers through debt creation. It is exactly to this particular dangerous perspective - lacking a theoretical basis, but winning in the voting market - that Keynesianism has provided the necessary ethical framework even before giving a theoretical or political justification.

In my opinion, even the Wicksellian unanimity theory itself, and a fortiori, the less than unanimity versions do not guarantee that the decisions which individuals take in t is taken without harming individuals living in $t+1$, unless such decisions are constrained by a constitutional logic. This explains why in sections 3 and 4 I shall maintain that only the existence of a fiscal constitution could have prevented the governments of the real welfare states from pursuing *ex post* adjustments through budget deficits. The constitutional perspective, however, would convert the real or bureaucratic welfare state into an *ex ante* welfare state, a state which becomes conceivable behind the veil of ignorance.

2 The Role of Illusion-Creating Institutions in Present-Day Welfare State Settings: A Simplified Graphic Scheme

As surprising as this may appear, the most interesting interpretation of both the origin and the development of the real welfare state can be traced back to Puviani's theory of fiscal illusion. By considering the ruling class as the decision-making body both for taxation and expenditures, Puviani introduced a third option between an abstract individualism *à la* Mazzola and a pure organicism *à la* Wagner. My interpretation of Puviani's analysis as a third option - which by looking at the state as non-organic allows to identify individuals and institutions[19] as its elementary components - legitimates the extension of his approach also to democratic conditions, including those of the real welfare states.

In a democratic context, in fact, politico-bureaucratic institutions still maintain

[19] This may also explain why, even in the basic ambiguities, Puviani was so interested in extending Marginalism to the just taxation-expenditure analysis. See A. Puviani (1896), especially p. 303.

both political and fiscal illusion as a means to gain power over the citizen-taxpayer, especially if the bureaucratic organisation is of the "long chain" model, and the fiscal system centralised. Having dealt with this topic elsewhere[20], I shall develop here the fiscal illusion perspective by separating the active promotion of fiscal illusion by bureaucracy and the rents bureaucracy enjoys from a centralised tax system.

Though the graphic analysis which follows may appear to be a polar case, it well depicts a stylised functioning of the real welfare state settings. This especially the case with those countries characterised by a clear cut separation between the spending side and the taxing side, and a centralised tax system as well. This is the most favourable terrain for an illusion-creating bureaucracy[21].

Assuming (1) a unifunctional local government providing a given good at constant marginal costs; (2) the degree of its publicness; (3) the number of users in the jurisdiction, and (4) the number of voters/taxpayers, it is possible to choose a quantitative measure unit of the good such that the tax price of each unit the average taxpayer has to pay is equal to one.

In other words, if the quantity of the good that the average taxpayer perceives as average user is X, the corresponding tax price which this individual has to pay must be always X. Moreover, let us assume that individual preferences for the good to be provided by the local government is known. If in such a setting the majority rule is used as the decision-making criterion, the result which will prevail is determined by the median voter. If P denotes the average price of the public good, the tax price the median voter has to pay is P multiplied by an adjusting factor, say θ which incorporates the differences between the median voter and the average taxpayer in terms of their property or income depending on the type of taxation used (property tax, or income tax). Concluding, the tax price that the median voter pays for each unit of a local public good he perceives is:

$$P_m = \theta \qquad (1)$$

If the local government receives transfers from the central government the setting changes as follows: let m denote the quota of local expenditures covered by a proportional grant from the central government; suppose moreover that the central government adds a lump sum transfer to cover that expenditure, if G

---

[20] See on this in detail G. Eusepi (1998).

[21] This is exactly what happens in Italy with local expenditures local governments having no obligations to cover their bureaucracies' costs. One might say that the Italian version of welfare state is the one which maximizes the role of bureaucracy and, as such, represents the alternative polar case to the constitutional welfare state discussed below.

denotes the amount of transfer which goes to the voter taxpayer then the average price to the median voter becomes:

$$P_m = \theta\,(1-m) - \frac{\theta G}{q} \qquad (2)$$

Figure 1: Tax Price Perceived by the Median Voter

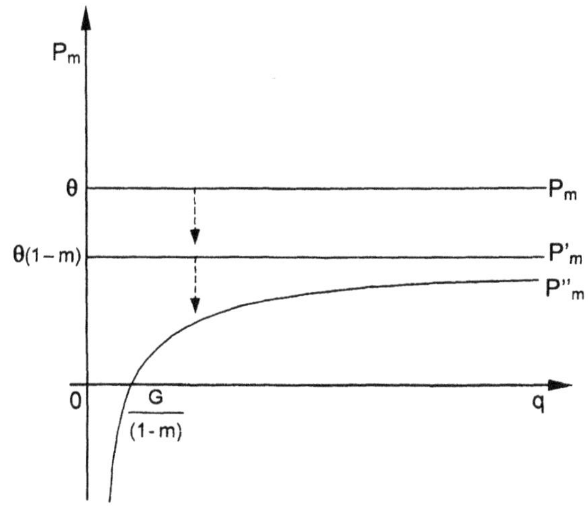

The reduction in the average price as a consequence of transfers can be visualised in Figure 1 by shifting the line of the average price P_m downward that becomes a curve under a lump-sum transfer whose effect decreases with increasing production. Given his own budget constraint, the median voter chooses in such a way as to maximise his own utility, Hence, let us determine now the median voter budget constraint. Let y represent the net increase for the median voter, R his income net of the central taxes only, and T_m his local tax bill which, of course, depends on the quantity of the public good provided and the related price. The budget constraint of the median voter is given by:

$$y = R - T_m$$

that is

$$y = R - P_m q \qquad (3)$$

If (2), which represents the average price for the median voter, is inserted into

(3) we have the classical case of neutral lump sum transfers: They would be perceived by the median voter as an increase in disposable income that can be visualized in Figure3 along the line $R'B'$.

$$y = R + \theta \cdot G - \theta \cdot (1 - m) \cdot q \qquad \text{(3 a)}$$

Where $\theta \cdot G$ represents the effect of a lump-sum transfer and $\theta \cdot (1 - m)$ the effect of a proportional transfer.

But in my view, for this to be true bureaucratic behaviour has to be neutral and the median voter should have precise information at low costs. If these conditions are not satisfied, an event which is plausible in real world settings, the median voter may mix up the average price with the marginal cost. The politician (agent) supports this misperception of the voter (principal) as the pivot around which bureaucracy centres its active search for illusion. The perception of the average price as it were a marginal cost has a quantity q that, given G, implies an average price P_m^* to be inserted in (3) hence:

$$y = R - P_m^* \cdot q \qquad \text{(3 b)}$$

Due to (1) the difficulty in having precise information at low costs about the way of the local expenditures are financed and to (3) the easiness in concealing the real cost of the public good provided, the median voter budget constraint coincides with that of the local government. The local government gains this result by disguising a lump sum transfer as a conditional grant destined to reduce the tax price of the locally provided good. In fact, this is the only effect the local taxpayer perceives.

Figure 2 illustrates how a lump-sum transfer can result in a price effect. Part (b) of the figure draws on the graphic representation of Figure 1 concerning the reduction in average price due to the introduction of a lump-sum transfer (a proportional transfer has been omitted here). If a budget constraint, based on the average price rather than on the marginal cost, is introduced in this setting we have to add the average price Pm after the transfer in (3). It is soon evident that as the average price function has taken the shape of a curve, it is impossible to determine the exact slope of the budget constraint, since it varies according to the quantity provided. In other terms, it happens what is described in part (a) of Figure 2: Each chosen level of q will modify the slope of the budget constraint such that the new constraint be valid only and exclusively in correspondence with q. By increasing the number of observations, there emerges a map of budget constraints with R as origin, which depicts a sort of *compound* budget constraint through its relevant points (one point for each budget constraint). By increasing the number of observations, there emerges a map of budget constraints with *R* as origin, which depicts a sort of *compound* budget constraint through its relevant points (one point for each budget constraint).

Figure 2: Price Effect Induced by a Lump-Sum Transfer

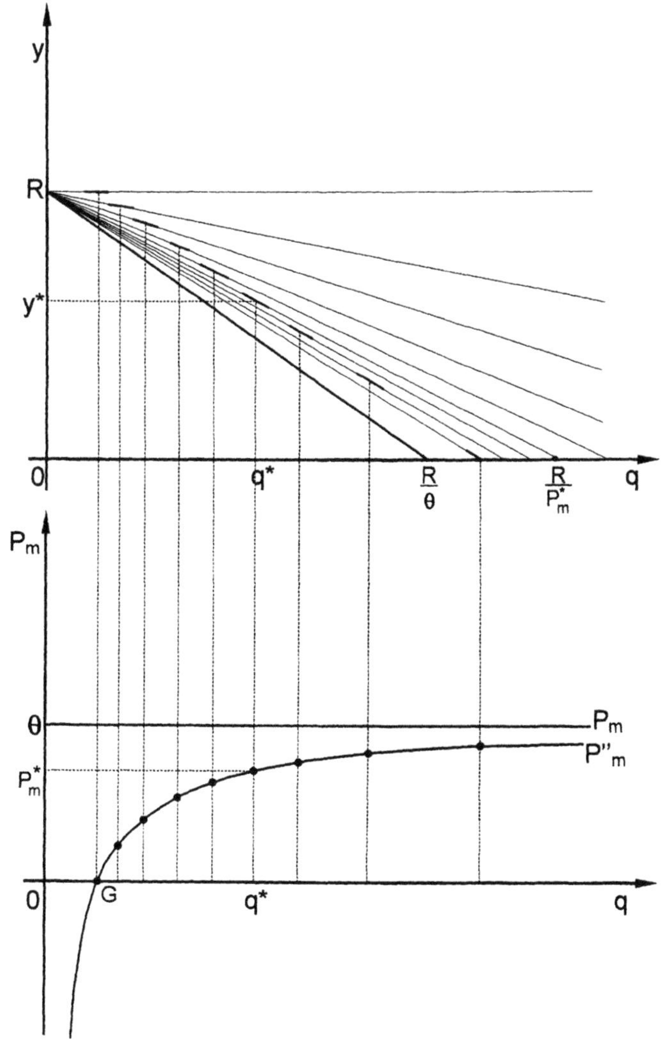

This *compound* constraint, although a line, has a different slope in every point, namely, it increases with the increase of the quantity provided due to the inverse relation in (3) linking P_m, and q.

Figure 3 shows how this effect might be exploited to increase the level of local public expenditures.

Figure 3: Median Voter's Budget Constraint with Illusion

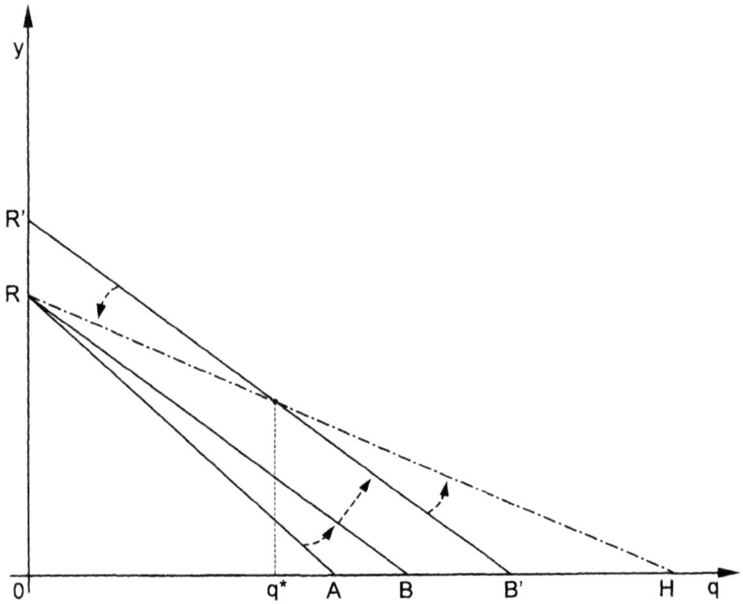

RH = Equation 4 (with illusion)
$R'B'$ = equation 3 bis.

The constraint *RA* depicts a situation where the local expenditure is financed only through local taxation. The well known effects due to the introduction of both a proportional transfer and a lump sum transfer are obtained by pivoting the budget constraint about point *R* to *RB* and by *shifting* the line into $R'B'$ which represents both the budget constraint of the local government and that of the median voter. As mentioned above, the median voter perceives a lump-sum transfer as a simple reduction in price. In other words, once the quantity to be provided is q *, the tax price the median voter is requested to pay is such that the budget constraint shifts to *RH*, so that the median voter's choice will be q *.

The equation of the *RH* constraint, including also the proportional transfer, is as follows:

$$y = R - \theta \cdot \left(1 - m - \frac{G}{q^*}\right) \cdot q \qquad (4)$$

The choice mechanism can be better visualised in Figure 4 through the introduction of the utility function of the median voter.

Figure 4:Local Expenditures Increase under an Active Illusion-seeking Bureaucracy

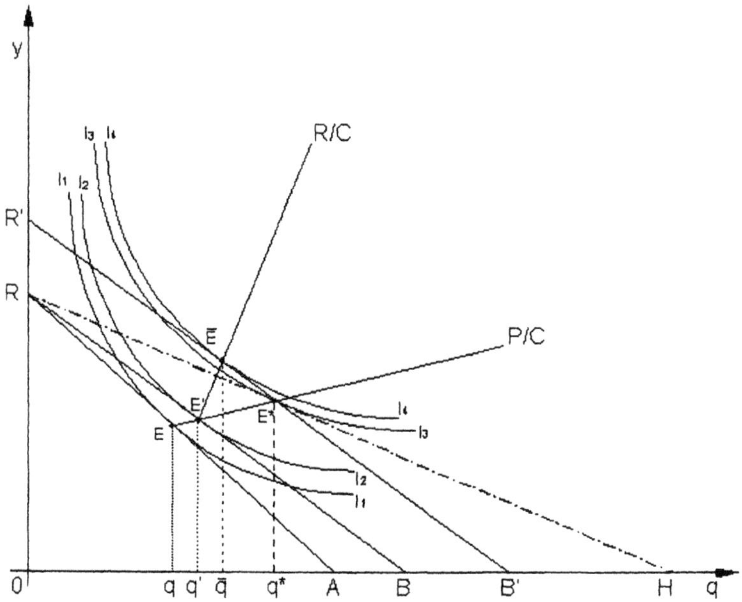

y = disposable income after taxes; q = perceived level of a locally provided service.
$R'B'$ = budget constraint including a general lump-sum transfer as well as a specific proportional transfer.
RH = budget constraint perceived by the voter.
R/C = income consumption path.
P/C = price-consumption path.
$\bar{E}$ = equilibrium with both illusion created by a centralized tax-system and an illusion created by an actively seeking bureaucracy.
$\bar{q}q*$ = increase in demand as a consequence of an active illusion-seeking bureaucracy.

Given the level of income R, the voter's choice changes with the changing in price, along the Price-Consumption function denoted as P/C in the graph. It is exactly along the P/C function that the level of equilibrium of an illusion-seeking bureaucracy lies; the introduction of a lump-sum transfer is not perceived as an increase in disposable income - which would have had $\overline{E}$ as an equilibrium point - but as a reduction in price so as to induce to choose E *.

Concluding, we can say that due to the two mentioned equilibrium points, the illusion-creating effect can be easily identified in the segment $\overline{q}q*$ that represents the increase in the perceived level of production.

Let us look now at the second type of illusion, the one due to a centralised taxing power that also leads to an increase in local expenditure. Taking out the distorting effect which has led to E*, we notice that the proportional transfer from central government to local government is equal to the quantity produced multiplied by the tax ratio m. In other words, as appears crops out from Figure 5, the subsidy that the local government manages on behalf of the median voter is equal to

$$UC = \theta \cdot m \cdot \overline{q} \qquad (5)$$

To understand the effect of this second kind of illusion, one wonders what the level of local expenditure would have been if the central government had chosen *ad personam* transfers instead of a proportional transfer managed by the local government. Assuming that redistribution equals zero, *ad personam* transfers may be seen as an unconditional reimbursement of central taxes.

In this case, the median voter perceives what before was concealed to him, namely that he is not only *directly* but also *indirectly* financing the local expenditure, if the central government decided not to levy the amount of taxes which it gives back as transfers, the median voter's budget constraint would coincide with the line $R''\ D$ in Figure 5. The average price of the local public good for the median voter would be θ once again and the budget constraint would be the following:

$$y = [R + \theta \cdot (G + m \cdot \overline{q})] - \theta \cdot q \qquad (6)$$

Figure 5: Local Choice Free from an Illusion-Creating Centralized Tax-System

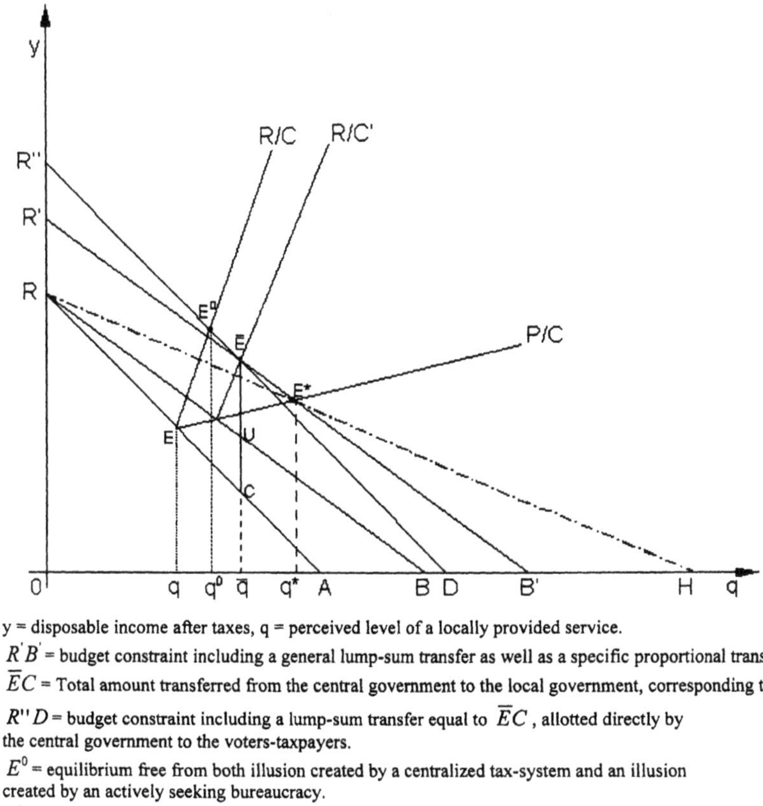

y = disposable income after taxes, q = perceived level of a locally provided service.

$R'B'$ = budget constraint including a general lump-sum transfer as well as a specific proportional transfer.

$\overline{E}C$ = Total amount transferred from the central government to the local government, corresponding to $\overline{q}$.

$R''D$ = budget constraint including a lump-sum transfer equal to $\overline{E}C$, allotted directly by the central government to the voters-taxpayers.

E^0 = equilibrium free from both illusion created by a centralized tax-system and an illusion created by an actively seeking bureaucracy.

$q^0\overline{q}$ = increase in demand as a consequence of an illusion created by a centralized tax-system.

In conclusion, under this budget constraint the equilibrium point E^0 is unaffected by the two kinds of illusion. Consequently, in E^0 the production of the local public good is not only lower, but as is shown in Figure 6, which reproduces to the details the equilibrium points $E^0, \overline{E}, E^*$ seen in Figure 5, implies also the highest level of utility.

Figure 6: The Optimal Choice Free from the two Kinds of Illusion

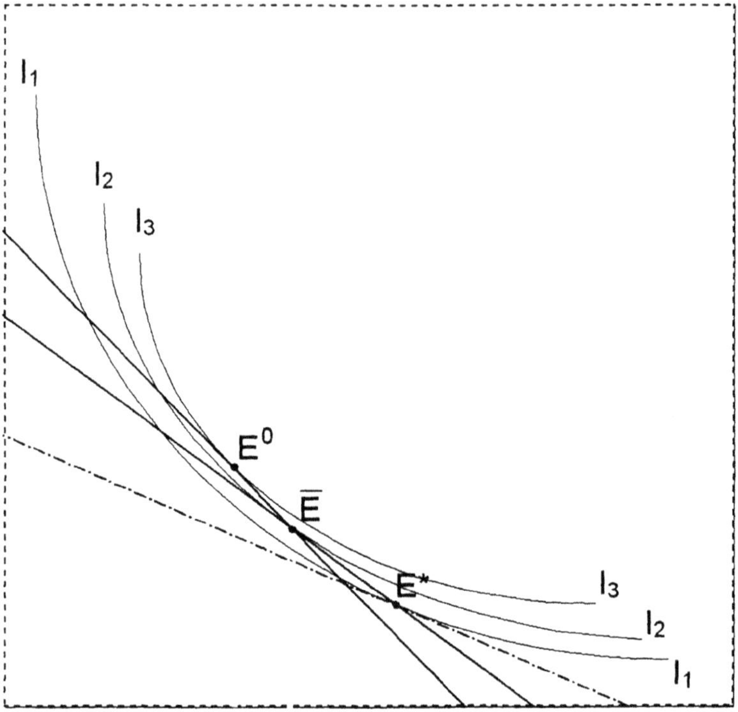

$E*$ = equilibrium with both an active illusion-seeking bureaucracy and a centralized tax-system.
$\bar{E}$ = equilibrium free from the effects of an active illusion-seeking bureaucracy.
E^0 = equilibrium free from fiscal illusion.

In reality, the concept of equilibrium free from both types of illusion is incompatible with that of the real welfare state characterised, as it is, by *ex post* adjustments. One can deduce from it that this illusion free equilibrium can only be brought about within a contractarian constitutional framework where illusion creating bureaucratic/ political institutions are drastically reduced if not cancelled.

Conversely, the illusion component in the welfare state has the consequence that individuals perceive a political bureaucratic coercive act as it were Lindahl's prices. It should be added, on the other hand, that the political-bureaucratic regime has to invest directly in illusion-creating activities to win consent in order to precommit the demand for bureaucratic services. Moreover, it is *noteworthy* to underline that with regard to *illusion creation*, the salient linkage is that between top level bureaucrats and the majority if the latter prefers an expansionary budget; it becomes instead one between top level bureaucrats and the minority if the majority offers a budget that top level bureaucrats consider too restrictive. Since in the real welfare state the government has no budget constraints and is characterised by a "long chain" or Niskanenian model, the decisive linkage is that between bureaucracy and majority, unless the minority behaves strategically by promising even larger budgets, and has a high probability of becoming a majority[22].

If public opinion were well informed and acted rationally in its own interest towards its representatives and bureaucrats, the illusion creating activity would probably have decreasing returns, and bureaucrats' and politicians' advantages would be lowered. Since, as has been shown, the welfare state lacks stringent fiscal institutions, the creation of fiscal illusion is complementary to and coexists with the presuppositions of the *ex post* adjustment theory.

The theoretical analysis and the stylised graphic schemes may give an answer also to Musgrave's question concerning the optimal size of the public sector in a "good society". On this issue, Musgrave gave unsatisfactory answers. This is not, in fact, as Musgrave[23] seems to maintain, a matter of defining the "normal" dimension of the public sector so as to contrast it with an oversized-undersized one. (Deviations in both cases!) As this paper suggests, the real welfare state necessarily involves an oversized public sector due to its illusion-creating bureaucratic and fiscal institutions. Musgrave argues that Lindahl's fiscal prices are not at the basis of the decisions of the majorities, which, in fact, might approve proposals not able to pass the efficiency test, and by contrast reject others able to pass it. Such reasoning does not prove at all that Lindahl's test is erroneous; it simply shows that the efficiency criterion is not at the basis of the welfare states. My scheme, based on the two kinds of *illusion*, visualises the deviations from Lindahl's equilibrium of the real welfare state. This, however, does not amount to say that the value-countervalue or benefit principle is unimportant *per se*; it only means that in the real welfare states decisions are not taken on an efficiency basis. This conclusion would be impossible to derive under Musgrave's reasoning. My analysis suggests that an oversized bureaucracy is wholly compatible with a shortage in the provision of public services because it favours both inefficiencies and misallocation of resources.

---

[22] In a proportional voting system, this would not require a new election, so that the likelihood of the text is not a pure abstraction.

[23] See R.A. Musgrave (1983).

This situation reveals the existence of a conflict between an oversized bureaucracy, which provides bureaucratic goods, and citizens who demand genuinely public goods. Yet, the conflict is hidden since bureaucracy has an illusion-creating power. If my analysis actually seizes the essential determinants of the real welfare state, what seems to be certain is that the real welfare state is destined to disregard taxpayers and citizens' preferences, and what follows from them. Yet, if some sort of welfare state is to fulfil its purpose a new setting free from political and bureaucratic illusions has to be created. The first question in many people's minds when confronted with this issue is how to set limits. To put the question differently, can we prefigure a welfare state which working under uncertainty guarantees that there is no room for illusion-creating institutions? This calls for an explanation of the different role uncertainty and illusion play in economics. While uncertainty simply involves incomplete information, and is inborn in democratic choices, illusion necessarily involves the systematic distortion of information. This does, of course, end up by being a deceitful limit to a democratic public choice. Perhaps the key to the survival of some kind of welfare state is in the introduction of constitutional limitations.

3 Towards a Constitutional Welfare State

In the logic of contractarian constitutionalism, Wicksell's theory of just taxation is the most outstanding antecedent of fiscal justice. As is well-known, the peculiar character of a democratic fiscal system s determined by the fact that it fixes a method or decision-making procedure based on the individual *willingness-to-pay principle* which is the opposite of the *ability-to-pay* one.

This conflict solution gives an answer also to the problem adumbrated in the previous section as to which elements of the real welfare state should be kept, and which should be rejected. The following consideration may explicitate this point. If government were to pass an expenditure exceeding the individuals' willingness to pay, that government would be *ipso facto* the advocate of a welfare state. But this event is intrinsically incompatible with the contractarian constitutionalism. In no case, this could mean that in the contractarian fiscal constitution, grounded on the benefit principle, there is no room for redistribution. As is well known, the traditional welfare state theorists, following the Marshallian logic, justify subsidies that create either positive externalities, or stop negative ones.

But they fail to see that also in this case such a decision would be taken behind the veil of ignorance precisely because the subsidy would benefit all consumers in the polity. It would thus pass the constitutional efficiency test based on the unanimity rule. It is also worth keeping in mind that the issue of redistribution/no redistribution should not cause divisiveness between the supporters of the welfare state and those of the contractarian constitutional welfare state. The distinctive element lies, in fact, in the kind of maximisation. At a constitutional level transfers are genuine and general so that there is no reason why the expenditures should not meet the constitutional efficiency test, while in the real welfare state the maximising function does not take into account individual preferences and discriminates against future generations[24].

Again, this is a different way of saying that the real welfare state can be seen as congenial to the flourishing of politicians and bureaucrats' welfare function. By contrast, what could a constitutional welfare state really maximise? The fact that the Constitution fixes budget rules can be seen as a force that might enhance individuals or their representatives to make choices on the political market by confronting alternative expenditure-taxation proposals. This choosing procedure would no doubt be in the direction of ensuring fiscal justice, which passes the efficiency test based on unanimity or approximate unanimity. As the real welfare states shun the constitutional test and adopt *ex post* adjustments, the results determined by the government are unavoidably assessed as being optimal by the government itself[25]. This optimality, however, may at the most, reflect citizens' evaluations as manipulated by the two kinds of illusion, and never their genuine opportunity costs[26]. To state the matter shortly, the distinction between real welfare states and constitutional welfare states can be synthesised with the passage or path going from the optimal taxation to the optimal rule in public choices.

Although this topic would be completely out of place in the benevolent despot hypothesis which is behind the real welfare state, let us nevertheless suppose that a benevolent despot is in power, say, by God's will but he were to be reconfirmed through elections. Would this benevolent despot be willing to maintain his behaviour unaltered in both alternatives[27] and would it really be the same welfare functions to be maximised in either case? The answer is unequivocally in the negative. The contractarian logic, seen as an agency relationship, involves that the principal sets limits to his agent[28]. Namely, should the principal-taxpayer evaluate that the benefits he receives as Counter value of his tax bill are lower than those he would receive from the alternative private use, the taxpayer would give the government an amount of his income corresponding to a certain

[24] See J.M. Buchanan (1993), (1997).

[25] The text overlooks the extreme case of an organic state in which the omniscient benevolent despot unduly claims to be entitled to know all his subjects' unrevealed preferences.

[26] See R.E. Wagner (1988).

[27] For the debate between Wicksell and Kuylistierna, which is within the logic of the text, see L. Jonung (1996).

[28] On the delegation limits see C.B. Blankart (1994).

quota of GNP. Hence, the government would be *entitled* to levy only within those limits[29].

Needless to say, if the government levied higher taxes it would *ipso facto* disregard the limits imposed by the constitution and would violate the agency relationship. (Although both the taxpayer and the government could accuse each other of rule breaking[30])

In a non-constitutional welfare logic, decisions are led by the politico-bureaucratic power that plays a major part in taming the decision power of the governed. The key issue is whether there can be institutions that authoritatively fix redistribution while meeting the equal treatment criterion that underlies the constitutional state. In answering in the affirmative, I shall define the body of those institutions as an *ex ante* welfare state or, simply, a constitutional welfare state. From this point of view, it is possible to define some rights as inalienable, and I mean by this that all individuals have the guarantee to be "entitled to", e. g. the lexicographical priority of the equal liberty principle as well as of the difference principle in Rawls's terms.

It follows that only in the event that a welfare state assigned obligations to meet those rights, one could say that the constitutional logic is met. This, in no way, means, however, that all rights created by the rules of the real welfare states may find their justification behind this concealment. When we move to the institutions of real welfare states, there emerges dramatically the problem of rights-creation. Rights created by the law violate the equality principle, which is the skeleton upon which the welfare state should be based in order to be defined as constitutional. One effect of this is that in the non-constitutional welfare state the coercive power is not used in defence of the individual entitled to receive transfers because of the difference principle, and against the violation of this right by other individuals[31]. (In this context, in fact, the coercive power would be wholly legitimate.) It is used, instead, as a rent-seeking device by pressure groups, especially bureaucracy, as shown in section 2.

---

[29] The reader will note that I am simply adopting here Mazzola's criterion which is wholly coincident with that of Wicksell, at least as far as the discourse in the text is conceived. See Mazzola (1890), chapter IX, especially sections 6, 7, 9 and 10. See also the English translation in R. A. Musgrave, A.T. Peacock (1958).

[30] This may be imputed to an abuse by the governors, an error by the governed, finally defects of representativeness. Though important these arguments may be, I cannot dwell upon them here.

[31] On this point see H. Kliemt (1993) created rights and contract.

4 Rights and Obligations: Behind the Veil of Ignorance

It is hardly surprising that in real welfare states there is a systematic conflict between right and duties. The reason for this is embodied in the particular way of assigning rights or titles to receive transfers. The analysis carried out up to this point has tried to show that, with the exception of the Mazzola-Wicksell approach, the two sides of the fiscal account have been kept separate[32]. Only under the heroic assumption that all property is at the disposal of the fiscal authority, can a rights-creating law omit to designate the obligations. But in this case, the taxpayer is left without any valid obligations to finance the growing needs of the fiscal authority. And this fact raises the question: where does democracy lead us?

Hence, the real welfare state should be crafted to include the obligations-entitlements-rights circuit as constitutional boundary. The constitutional analysis, however, due to the manner it has been introduced, has evidenced that the equal opportunities of the liberal theory are not an outcome spontaneously achievable, and that the equal opportunity principle is a *built* or *artificial* dimension. From this perspective, the distributive component, especially in terms of *ad personam* transfers, is an explicit part of the constitutional contract as is clear in Buchanan and Tullock,[33] as well as in Rawls.[34]

So even limiting my analysis to transfers, it does need to be emphasized that also on this point the constitutional approach drastically differs from that used in real welfare states. In fact, the supply of goods and services is handled by bureaucracy as an alternative to *ad personam* transfers. Adopting this latter state of things should be an instrument for preventing fiscal obligations from being directed to the maintenance of an oversized bureaucracy as a high powered pressure group[35]

From this we might reasonably be led to expect that there might be so even neglecting that in the presence of a "bribe market" the demand by bureaucracy could increase. Yet though this public attitude to bribery is not justified by welfare states, it is nevertheless the point round which they eddy, as demonstrated in the graphic scheme.

The analysis developed here suggests also that the political sponsor's neutrality

[32] A. de Jasay (1991) has clarified the fundamental difference between law-created rights and contract-created rights. In the latter case, no discrimination between rights and obligations is possible.
[33] See J.M. Buchanan, G.Tullock (1962) and LM.Buchanan (1975).
[34] See J.Rawls (1971).
[35] On this point see T. E. Borcherding, W. C. Bush, R. M. Spann, (1977).

towards his bureaucratic agent is not convincing at all. And, in fact, politicians and bureaucrats together make up a single pressure group with the power of creating both political and "optimistic-like" fiscal illusion[36] among taxpayers-voters. Clearly, fiscal limits to the welfare state, like the classical equal opportunity principle or the newer Rawlsian principle, should be put at constitutional level. The Rawlsian difference principle seems to have a more marked redistributive impact than the liberal postulate of equality in the initial position that was requested, more or less explicitly by the theory of the minimal state[37].

In the remaining part of this work much light is thrown on the difference principle, and it is shown that it is covered by the constitution so long as the principle is weak, but it may lose such a coverage if it is robust. Rawls's difference principle is, of course, weak and does not hinge on a liberal logic *stricto sensu*. The justice it refers to is one of the procedural or *ex ante* kind, and as such, cannot be discriminatory. Wicksell had brilliantly noticed that if the *real status quo* were unjust, the correct procedure would give rise to a result that should be defined still unjust[38].

Thus an unjust *status quo* is not compatible with the contractarian constitutional logic, no matter whether in the unanimity version or in that of the veil of ignorance, at least in the version I call *weak*. Clearly, no one would be interested in approving rules that could systematically harm someone else. Behind the veil of ignorance or within an *ex ante* logic, in fact, the individual cannot know whom the "anyone" will correspond to.

The welfare state based on a constitutional perspective cannot legitimate an unjust *status quo*, since this could be equal to empowering a rule which would never pass the conceptual unanimity test required for entering the Constitution.

The reading of the difference principle in terms of equality in results may originate, however bizarre this may appear, just from its being a constitutional principle that cannot be circumvented. This change in the meaning of the difference principle stems from the creation of *robust* distributive rights.

When the compulsoriness of the difference principle is combined with a quanti-

[36] See A. Puviani (1897), (1903). Due to the role fiscal illusion plays in the real welfare states of Western democracies, Puviani's contribution has an explanatory power which goes well beyond that of the ruling class, and should rather represent the litmus paper to separate errors from imperfect information - which are unavoidable - from errors coming from systematically falsified information, which, instead, would be inconsistent with the constitutional welfare state sketched here.

[37] This is a different manner of maintaining that Kliemt thesis, on the grounds of which the minimal state included a redistributive component, is correct. See H. Kliemt (1993).

[38] See L. Jonung (1996).

tatively large redistribution, the difference principle is as it were a device to determine a just result rather than a just procedure. In this light, the difference principle would generate equality in results, the individuals being endowed with *primary goods* quite independently of their individual merit.

The hypothesis of a quantitatevely *robust* difference principle may lead to a lower growth path than the potential one due to the fall in incentives to invest. Results would, in fact, be *politicised*, while risks would remain with *privates*.

In a sense, a *robust* version of the difference principle finds its upper limit precisely in the relation obligations/rights. In this way, legitimating redistributive entitlements may arise on condition that an agreement on fiscal obligations has been reached in advance. Even so the coercive element is not the legitimating procedure of fiscal obligations here; such legitimating procedure, in fact, is a *voluntary* choice behind the veil of uncertainty; the coercive element appears only at a post-constitutional level to restrain people from free-riding. The coercive element, then, emerges only with the implementation, while the choice is free, although within the Wicksellian version of a conceptual agreement.

There is, however, an important consideration still left. The difference principle can be explained with the concept of negative liberty, and automatically ceases with the end of the motivation that originated it. Hence, the individual's entitlement to the difference principle lies in his being a *disadvantaged guiltless* individual. Yet, the difference principle cannot cover all future disadvantages of individuals, since behind the veil of ignorance constituents necessarily reason within a scarcity context. That is why the problem of fiscal justice arises at a constitutional level.

If, instead, the law creates rights to receive transfers independently of fiscal obligations as is the case of the real welfare state, conflicts between fiscal obligations and fiscal rights become blatant and do not emerge only because an impression of abundance is surreptitiously created through debt illusion and money creation. And by definition, abundance is "beyond distributive justice".

Clearly, in this context, the Rawlsian difference principle would violate intergenerational equality before the law, because through debt financing government precommits unjustified constraints to the choice set available to future individuals, including those who would benefit from the difference principle. One can't say that this would be the result of the difference principle *per se*. It is just a consequence of its incorrect use, as happens in the real welfare states.

6 Conclusions

The purpose of this paper was neither that of sketching some alternative profiles of welfare offered by different national doctrines of public finance, nor that of supplying the recipe or a corrective to the creation of a constitutional welfare state. Main emphasis has been rather placed on the contemporary welfare state outlining the differences among the various schools, namely Italian, German, Swedish and English. This may have induced me to overemphasise differences rather than underline similarities. Yet different as these schools are, a paternalistic element is ever present in all the versions with the only exception of Mazzola and Wicksell.

The core of the paper is an extension of Puviani's theory of fiscal illusion that was designed for non-democratic institutions to the democratic institutions such as those of the welfare state. It is fairly evident that the related illusion mechanism allows the welfare state to have discriminatory powers. The overcoming of these discriminatory powers, suggested in the paper, leads almost by necessity towards constitutional political economy.

In particular, the work has emphasised the linkage between fiscal rights and fiscal obligations. The last part of the paper has suggested a solution to some possible ambiguities which may be *prima facie* improperly ascribed to the Rawlsian difference principle.

References

Atkonson, A.B., Stiglitz, L.E. (1980), *Lectures on Public Economics*, (Maidenhead: McGraw Hill).

Blankart, C.B. (1994), "Club Governments versus Representative Governments", Constitutional Political Economy", Vol. 5, n. 3, pp. 273-283.

Borcherding, T.E., Bush, W.C., Spann, R.M. (1977), "The Effects on Public Spending of the Divisibility of Public Outputs in Consumption, Bureaucratic Power, and the Size of the Tax Sharing Group", in BORCHERDING T.E. (eds.), Budgets and Bureaucrats: The Sources of Government Growth, (Durham,N.C.: Duke University Press).

Buchanan, J.M. (1960), "La Scienza delle Finanze': The Italian Tradition in Fiscal Theory", in Fiscal Theory and Political Economy, (Chapel Hill: North Carolina University Press).

Buchanan, J.M. (1967), *Public Finance in Democratic Process*, (Chapel Hill: North Carolina University Press).

Buchanan, J.M. (1969), *Cost and Choice. An Inquiry in Economic Theory*, (Chicago: Markham Publishing Company).

Buchanan, J. M. (1975), *The Limits of Liberty: Between Anarchy and Leviathan*, (Chicago: University of Chicago Press).

Buchanan, J. M., Tullock, G. (1962), *The Calculus of Consent*, (Ann Arbour: University of Michigan Press).

Buchanan, J.M. (1993), "How Can Constitutions Be Designed So That Politicians Who Seek

To Serve 'Public Interest' Can Survive and Prosper", *Constitutional Political Economy*, Vol.4, no.1, pp.1-6.
Buchanan, J. M. (1997), "Le crisi nelle democrazie del 'welfare'", in Arcelli, M. (ed.) Globalizzazione dei mercati e orizzonti del Capitalismo, (Bari, Roma: Laterza).
De Jasay, A. (1991), *Choice, Contract, Consent: A Restatement of Liberalism*, Institute of Economic Affairs.
Eusepi, G. (1998), "Mercati istituzionali alternativi: un modello burocratico 'a catena breve' come superamento dei modelli 'a catena lunga'", *Rivista di Politica Economica*, Anno LXXXVIII, Serie III, Febbraio 1998, Fascicolo II.
Jonung, L. (1996), "Knut Wicksell: The Principles of Just Taxation an Unpublished Manuscript by Knut Wicksell", translated into English for the Liberty Fund Colloquium "Public Finance in a Free Society" celebrating the centennial of Finanztheoretische Untersuchungen, Potsdam, September 5-8, 1996.
Kliemt, H. (1993), "On Justifying a Minimum Welfare State", Constitutional Political Economy, vol. 4, n. 2, Spring/Summer, pp. 159-172.
Lindahl, E. (1919), *Die Gerechtigkeit der Besteuerung. Eine Analyse der Steuerprinzipen auf Grundlage der Grentznutzentheorie*, Gleerups, Lund.
Mazzola, U. (1890), *I dati scientifici della finanza pubblica*, (Roma: Loescher).
Mazzola, U. (1958), "The formation of the Prices of public Goods", in R.A. Musgrave, A. T. Peacock (eds.) (1958), Classics in the Theory of Public Finance, (London: Macmillan).
Mill, J. S. (1970), *Principles of Political Economy, with Some of Their Applications to Social Philosophy*, (Alesburg, Bucks: Penguin books).
Musgrave, R. A. (1939), "The Voluntary Exchange Theory of Public Economy", *Quarterly Journal of Economics*, 53, February, pp.213-237.
Musgrave, R.A. (1966), "Principles of Budget Determination", in J. Scherer, J.A. Papke (eds.), Public Finance and Fiscal Policy, (Boston: Houghton Mifflin Company).
Musgrave, R.A. (1983), "When Is the Public Sector Too Large?", in Why Governments Grow. Measuring Public Sector Size, (Beverly Hills: Sage Publications).
Musgrave, R.A., Peacock A.T. (1958), *Classics in the Theory of Public Finance*, (London: Macmillan).
Pigou, A. C. (1920), *The Economics of Welfare*, (London: Macmillan).
Pigou, A.C. (1928), *A Study in Public Finance*, (London: Macmillan).
Puviani, A. (1896), "Il problema edonistico nella scienza delle finanze", in Riforma Sociale, Anno III, Vol. VI, fasc. 5, Il semestre.
Puviani, A. (1897), *Teoria della illusione nelle entrate pubbliche*, Annali dell'Università di Perugia, Vol. VII, fascicoli 2-3.
Puviani, A. (1903), *Teoria della illusione finanziaria*, (Palermo: Sandron).
Rawls, J. (1971), *A Theory of Justice*, (Harvard: Harvard University Press).
Seligman, E.R. (1908), *Progressive Taxation in Theory and Practice*, (New York: Princeton University Press).
Soderstrom, L. (1986), "The Wicksellian Alternative", Skandinaviska Enskilda Banken Quartely Review, 3, pp. 88-96.
Von Stein, L. (1958), "On Taxation", in R.A. Musgrave, A.T. Peacock (eds.) (1958), *Classics in the Theory of Public Finance*, (London: Macmillan).
Wagner, A. (1958), "Three Extracts on Public Finance", in R.A. Musgrave, A.T. Peacock (eds.) (1958), *Classics in the Theory of Public Finance*, (London: Macmillan).
Wagner, R.E. (1988), "The Calculus of Consent: A Wicksellian Retrospective", *Public Choice*, 56, pp. 153-166.

Wicksell, K. (1958), "A New Principle of Just Taxation", in R.A. Musgrave, A.T. Peacock (eds.) (1958), *Classics in the Theory of Public Finance*, (London: Macrnillan).

Institutions, Entrepreneurship, and the Rationale of Government: An Outline of the Schumpeterian Theory of the State

Alexander Ebner
Assistant Professor
Krupp-Chair of Public Finance and Fiscal Sociology
Faculty of Economics, Law and the Social Sciences
University of Erfurt
Nordhäuserstrasse 63
D-99089 Erfurt
Germany
alexander.ebner@uni-erfurt.de

Abstract: The Schumpeterian theory of the state, based on the conceptual framework of fiscal sociology, parallels the theory of entrepreneurship in its concern with the institutional dynamism of capitalist development. Schumpeterian entrepreneurship denotes the capability for carrying out innovations by means of leadership. It may be executed by diverse agents, whose capabilities are embedded in a variety of institutional forms. This institutional variety is an indispensable condition of capitalist development, due to its role in the behavioural articulation of entrepreneurship which is basically driven by atavistic motives. These are also relevant in other domains of socio-cultural evolution, even affecting the genesis of the modern state which is perceived as an equivalent to the entrepreneurial features of competitive capitalism. Its rationale mirrors the emergence of a distinct sphere of self-interested economic activity in a private sector. While the state is concerned with the provision of common goods, its economic impact needs to be assessed with regard to the social interests that mark its relationship with the private sector. This holds for the evolution of the fiscal system as well as for other domains of government activity. Indeed, Schumpeter pointed out that the state could temporarily carry out the entrepreneurial function in capitalist development, quite in accordance with the notion of entrepreneurship as institutional leadership.

Keywords: Schumpeter, institutional variety, entrepreneurship, theory of the state, entrepreneurial state.

JEL codes: B15, B25, B52, P16.

1 Introduction

The Schumpeterian theory of the state has been largely neglected in recent discussions on the analytical relevance of Schumpeter's thought for current theorising on the economic role of the state. Indeed, it is rather the matter of entrepreneurship and innovation that seems to have dominated the ongoing reassessment of Schumpeter's theorising – perhaps apart from scattered references to Schumpeter's notion of democratic competition. However, it is argued in the following essay that the Schumpeterian theory of the state provides quite valuable analytical insights for an institutional perspective on the rationale of government, the formation of fiscal systems and the related orientation of economic policy. In particular, it is proposed that the Schumpeterian theory of the state parallels the theory of entrepreneurship in its concern with the institutional dynamism of capitalist development. This is in accordance with Schumpeter's suggestions on the methodological role of economic sociology as an analytical device for the institutional analysis of modern capitalism, pinpointing the matter of entrepreneurship as a key concern, with fiscal sociology identified as a sub-discipline. Indeed, it is argued in the following essay that fiscal sociology provides those conceptual foundations for the Schumpeterian theory of the state that parallel the analytical impact of the sociology of leadership in the Schumpeterian theory of entrepreneurship, as both conceptual frameworks account for the developmental impact of institutional variety.

According to the Schumpeterian approach, entrepreneurship denotes the capability for carrying out innovations by means of leadership. It constitutes the decisive internal source of capitalist development. The entrepreneurial function may be executed by diverse agents, whose capabilities are embedded in a variety of institutional forms. The underlying institutional dynamism, characterised by a tendency of rationalisation, is basically derived from the persistence of pre-capitalist institutions. This institutional variety is an indispensable condition of capitalist development, due to its role in the behavioural articulation of entrepreneurship which is basically driven by atavistic motives. These specific motives are also relevant in other domains of socio-cultural evolution, such as competition, imperialism and parliamentary democracy. Even the genesis of the modern state, interpreted as a tax state, is associated with an aristocratic influence that is transformed in the course of capitalist development. The tax state is actually perceived as an equivalent to those entrepreneurial features of competitive capitalism which shape the bourgeois epoch, for its rationale mirrors the emergence of a distinct sphere of self-interested economic activity in a private sector. While the state is concerned with the provision of common goods, its actual economic impact needs to be assessed with regard to the underlying social interests that mark its relationship with the private sector. This holds for the evolution of the fiscal system as well as for other domains of government activity. Indeed, Schumpeter pointed out that the state could temporarily carry out the entrepreneurial function in the setting of capitalist development, quite in accordance with the notion of entrepreneurship as institutional leadership.

In outlining the Schumpeterian theory of the state, the essay proceeds with three sections. First, the matter of institutional variety in the course of economic development is taken to the fore. Following a discussion of fiscal sociology as a framework for theorising the state, the Schumpeterian notion of modern capitalism is explored with regard to its institutional underpinnings, resulting in a presentation of the behavioural aspects of the development process. Second, the matter of Schumpeterian entrepreneurship is reconsidered, highlighting the aspects of institutional embeddedness and historical specificity. Third, the Schumpeterian theory of the state is discussed in more detail. Based on a presentation of the decisive arguments in Schumpeter's work on the tax state, then, the related problems of an entrepreneurial state are examined, which leads to an assessment of related policy conclusions.

2 Institutional Variety in Economic Systems: Schumpeterian Perspectives

2.1 Fiscal Sociology and the Theory of the State

Schumpeter's research program was characterised by an orientation toward the integration of historical and theoretical concerns, thus promoting a perspective of methodological pluralism.[1] Accordingly, in the "History of Economic Analysis", Schumpeter identified the particular fields of economic history, statistics, theory, and economic sociology as techniques of economic analysis. Economic sociology, in particular, should deal with an institutional analysis of economic development, highlighting a reasoned type of economic history. It would transcend the assumption of given behaviour as the guiding principle of methodological individualism, exploring instead the diversity of behavioural patterns and their motivational foundations (Schumpeter 1954: 21). The matter of government belongs to that domain of economic sociology:

"By 'economic sociology' (the German *Wirtschaftssoziologie*) we denote the description and interpretation of – or "interpretative description" – of economically relevant institutions, including habits and forms of behaviour in general,

[1] Schumpeter's assessment of the methodological controversy between the Austrian School and the German Historical as ill-conceived and futile was of particular importance for the related account of theorising on economic development (Ebner 2000a: 361n).

such as government, property, private enterprise, customary or 'rational' behaviour (Schumpeter 1949a: 203).

In other words, economic sociology is concerned with the institutional framework of the economic processes, yet it needs to be combined with theoretical, historical and statistical instruments in order to grasp the dynamism of economic development (Swedberg 1989: 508n). In this context, then, the Schumpeterian approach to fiscal sociology would constitute a sub-discipline of the more comprehensive domain of economic sociology, based on a focused concern with the fiscal patterns of government as an institutional expression of socio-economic evolution. Expressed in current terms, fiscal sociology differs from the rational actor perspective of public finance by allowing for an interdisciplinary approach to the variety of economic as well as non-economic aspects of government activities, budget structures and fiscal policies that integrates the specific positions of economics, law and social sciences (Backhaus 2002: 73n). Therefore, fiscal sociology promotes the recognition and analytical exploration of complex social interactions that are embedded in a historically specific institutional context (Campbell 1993: 164n). Thus, the institutional perspective of economic sociology, with fiscal sociology as a sub-discipline, provides the analytical foundations for Schumpeter's theory of the state. In accordance with Schumpeter's concept of sociology as an analytical approach that deals with the variety of institutional forms in society, this implies that non-rational patterns of behaviour and extra-capitalist institutions are taken to the fore. Based on these considerations, which hint at the behavioural impact of atavistic motives, economic sociology accounts for the matter of leadership in socio-cultural affairs (Schumpeter 1954: 25n). Entrepreneurship, perceived as industrial leadership, is also viewed from the perspective of economic sociology, that is, it involves a specific sociology of leadership which contributes to the institutional core of Schumpeter's theory of economic development.[2] As this scheme applies basically to the capitalist process, it follows that the analytical framework of economic sociology is set to grasp the institutional characteristics of modern capitalism, thus underlining the historical specificity of the Schumpeterian approach.

---

[2] Schumpeter referred most explicitly to the inspiration provided by Friedrich von Wieser's "sociology of leadership" (Schumpeter 1926: XVIII). Indeed, Wieser, well in addition to his value and price theory of imputation, excelled regarding his sociological theses on leadership and the problems of mass behaviour which exercised a persistent influence on Schumpeter's theory of entrepreneurship (Streissler 1981: 66n).

2.2 Institutional Variety in Modern Capitalism

Among Schumpeter's most pointed definitions of capitalism, the focus is on the monetary means of introducing novelty to the circular flow of the economic process, perceived in institutional terms: "capitalism is that form of private property economy in which innovations are carried out by means of borrowed money, which in general, though not by logical necessity, implies credit creation" (Schumpeter 1939: 223). In agreement with that focus on institutional aspects, Schumpeter argued that rising capitalism would promote the evolution of the specific institutional dimension of rationality. Money becomes a unit account and thus serves the practice of cost calculation, whereas progress in science and technology becomes a systematic result of capitalist development. Even cultural spheres are subjugated to that type of hegemonic rationality, which finally extends its reach to the domains of art and life styles, as well as to related segments of government and politics. This leads to the point of view that the institutional substance of modern capitalism transcends the narrow margins of the economic process, as it contributes to the gradual emergence of a specific civilisation, representing historically-specific social and institutional patterns that reflect a drive for quantification and rationalisation (Schumpeter 1942: 123n).

Schumpeter rejected the notion of an acquisitive spirit as the decisive factor behind the historical genesis of capitalism, while emphasising the gradual character of changes in institutional settings:

> So soon as we realize that pure Feudalism and pure Capitalism are equally unrealistic creations of our own mind, the problem of what it was that turned the one into the other vanishes completely. The society of the feudal ages contained all the germs of the society of the capitalist age. These germs developed by slow degrees, each step teaching its lesson and producing another increment of capitalist methods and of capitalist 'spirit' (Schumpeter 1954: 80n).

Capitalism therefore evolved from the socio-cultural substance of preceding forms of economic organisation, based on institutional elements that were cumulatively growing in economic and social influence. Thus, Schumpeter accentuated the notion of institutional variety as a basic feature in the dynamism of economic development (Schumpeter 1928a: 477). Indeed, the thesis of the constitutive role of institutional variety in actually existing socio-economic systems was also applied to feudalism and other historical formations, implying that "every society contains, at any given time, elements that are the products of different social systems" (Schumpeter 1943: 114n). This resembled a "principle of continuity", also prominent with the eminent Austrian economist Friedrich von Wieser, perceived as a macroscopic position on the continuity of historical processes that could impede the accurate delineation of economic epochs (Schumpeter 1939: 227).

This constitutive role of variety was also prevalent in Schumpeter's conceptualisation of differences in the institutional set-up of nation-states and national economies. While Schumpeter held sympathy for the idea of historically rooted national regularities in habits and thoughts, subsumed under the term "*Volksgeist*" which had been prominent in idealist strands of German political philosophy, he argued that these would result from social values set up by dominant groups and classes in a certain historical context, exhibiting a high degree of inertia. National economies would accordingly differ in terms of their inherent variety of production modes, accompanied by an equivalent variety of social, institutional and organisational ensembles (Schumpeter 1929a/1953: 214n). Schumpeter then concluded on the matter of variety and changes in institutional settings:

> Social structures, types and attitudes are coins that do not readily melt. Once they are formed they persist, possibly for centuries, and since different structures and types display different degrees of this ability to survive, we almost always find that actual group and national behaviour more or less departs from what we should expect it to be if we tried to infer it from the dominant forms of the productive process (Schumpeter 1942: 12).

In current discussions on the evolution of economic systems, these developmental aspects raised by Schumpeter have been reiterated in terms of an impurity principle that has become prominent with systems theory. In this context, the impurity principle maintains that each functional system contains impurities which are not typical of the whole, but which are nevertheless necessary for the reproduction of that particular system. The related principle of dominance then suggests that every system exhibits a dominant functional structure. It follows that economic systems represent diversified pluralities which exhibit a dominant economic structure by which they may be classified, yet based on multi-facetted and inter-penetrating components (Hodgson 1988: 167n). For instance, the institutional dynamism of modern capitalism may be portrayed as the combination of a system of contractual commodity exchange that is embedded in distinct segments of the institutional setting apart from the domain of the contract-based market mechanism, highlighting community-based trust and family-oriented values (Fukuyama 1995: 3n).[3]

[3] In related terms of economic anthropology, Karl Polanyi suggested that sustainable economic processes were embedded both in economic and non-economic institutions. Hence, the seemingly self-regulating market mechanism would be necessarily framed by non-economic institutions like religious beliefs, kinship-related custom, as well as government activities (Polanyi 1977: 55n).

Moreover, it is a decisive point in Schumpeter's argumentation that these historically persistent institutional segments, which seem to be alien to the rationale of capitalist market economies, exhibit a dynamising role in the development process. Thus, it is not only the adaptive potential with regard to changes in the data environment that constitutes an advantage of institutional variety, as suggested by the impurity principle of systems theory, but it is primarily the embedded capability for creative responses by innovative activities. Thus, countering Marxist positions on the materialist determination of institutional change, which would imply an assessment of historically-rooted institutional constellations as a potential impediment to the development of the productive forces, Schumpeter claimed that pre-capitalist institutions would contribute decisively to economic evolution in modern capitalism by providing institutional incentives as well as by shaping modes of economic behaviour that could be conducive to the carrying out of innovation (Ebner 1999: 148n). More specifically, Schumpeter pointed to the role of family sentiment as a motivating force of economic activity in general, and of entrepreneurship in particular. Indeed, as discussed subsequently, the figure of the entrepreneur belongs to the outstanding representations of Schumpeterian ideas on institutional variety in economic development. This is expressed implicitly in Schumpeter's proposal that "the capitalist order not only rests on props made of extra-capitalist material but also derives its energy from extra-capitalist patterns of behaviour which at the same time it is bound to destroy" (Schumpeter 1942: 162).

2.3 *Behavioural Aspects of Development*

Accordingly, the developmental tendency of rationalisation, which is an outcome of the distinct type of rationality that characterizes capitalist civilisation, also affects non-capitalist institutions. As technological and organisational innovations drive the competitive restructuring of firms and industries, a decomposition of established institutional and social configurations is taking place, at last fuelling a tendency of capitalist decline, while heralding the possibility of socialist transformation (Schumpeter 1942: 131n). Again, the institutional devaluation of the family provided a most important illustration of that argument, for it seemed to promote the adoption of short-run philosophies and anti-saving attitudes in the economic domain, thus obstructing the developmental dynamism of the capitalist system (Schumpeter 1942: 160n). Schumpeter's conclusion then followed rather provocatively:

> In breaking down the pre-capitalist framework of society, capitalism thus broke not barriers that impeded its progress but also flying buttresses that prevented its collapse. That process, (...) was not merely a matter of removing institutional deadwood, but of removing partners of the institutional stratum, symbiosis with whom was an essential

> element of the capitalist schema. Having discovered this fact (...) we might well wonder whether it is quite correct to look upon capitalism as a social form sui generis or, in fact, as anything else but the latest stage of the decomposition of what we have called feudalism (Schumpeter 1942: 139).

In this context, it needs to be underlined that the Schumpeterian notion of feudalism allows for an extended role of atavistic value schemes which are reflected by allegedly aristocratic characteristics of heroic leadership. This hints at another decisive facet of Schumpeter's thought, namely the intellectual impact of *fin de siécle* philosophy, mirroring the crisis of beliefs in a rationality-based automatism of socio-cultural progress. Schumpeter pointed to Nietzsche, Bergson and Sorel as the most prominent representatives of that strand of philosophical thought with its anti-rationalist stance and "anti-intellectualist" orientation (Schumpeter 1954: 774n). In particular, vitalist philosophy informed the Schumpeterian argumentation on the developmental dynamism that would be promoted through institutional variety, for extra-capitalist institutions would allow for a non-rational orientation that was perceived as indispensable in proceeding with the type of discontinuous economic change that characterised modern capitalism. Atavistic values regarding power and conquest were said to motivate those types of entrepreneurs who were identified as the internal force of the development process in the setting of capitalist market competition, for they would carry out innovations by means of their leadership capabilities. In other words, Schumpeter associated rationality with adaptive routine behaviour in an established setting, while non-rational behaviour was associated with a radical mode of change, reflecting the impact of novelty and leadership (Ebner 2000b: 82n).

This distinction was derived from a conceptual framework that should highlight the relationship between novelty, leadership and endogenous change. Indeed, Schumpeter applied the underlying mode of argumentation also to other domains of socio-economic life. Concerning the sphere of competition, he suggested that industrial concentration and trustification were not based on efficiency considerations, but resulted from the impact of instinctive rivalry, rooted in "nationalist, militarist, imperialist instincts of struggle" (Schumpeter 1920-21: 313). Furthermore, the motives of leadership, authority and power were also traced in the political system of representative democracy, which was interpreted as a selection procedure of political leadership. Democracy as a method for the selection of leaders would imply political competition for the vote of the electorate. In this context, the capability for political leadership was introduced as a charismatic feature of aristocracy that would contrast with bourgeois rationalism. Hence, in accordance with the proposition that a pure system of capitalism could not exist, Schumpeter rejected the idea of a pure democracy, which would be based solely on the principles of people's sovereignty and parliamentary order (Schumpeter 1942: 137n). At last, the ongoing process of social rationalisation would also affect the political domain, leading to the rise of political parties as electoral machineries whose activities tend to parallel economic rationalisation (Schumpeter 1942: 282n).

Additionally, Schumpeter used these arguments in his analysis of imperialism. He maintained that imperialism was neither an outcome of concrete economic interests, including class interests in Marxian terms, nor a structural feature of modern capitalism, but rather the manifestation of atavistic motives like "expansion for the sake of expanding, struggle for the sake of struggling, win for the sake of winning, rule for the sake of ruling", as the leitmotif of an ongoing "plus ultra" led to the brief definition: "Imperialism is the objectless disposition of a state to violent expansion without statable limits" (Schumpeter 1918-19: 3n). Again, aggressive nationalism and national rivalry were said to be rooted in instincts of dominance and warfare. Thus, imperialism should be understood as a historical atavism, that is, a persisting element of pre-capitalist institutional patterns. In this context, Schumpeter explicitly noted with regard to the non-hedonistic behaviour of the "captains of industry", that this portrayal of imperialist motives paralleled the matter of entrepreneurial motives (Schumpeter 1918-19: 21). Indeed, the evolution of modern capitalism should imply a reduction of imperialist leanings, reflecting an inherently pacifist rationale of capitalism; just like instinctive modes of entrepreneurial behaviour were gradually replaced by rational calculation and bureaucratisation. The conflict between free-trade regimes and neo-mercantilist policies then denoted varieties of capitalist performance. Mercantilism with its instinct of domination was set against free trade as an equivalent of peaceful and mutually beneficial exchange (Schumpeter 1918-19: 119n). Again, this points to the perception of entrepreneurial leadership, rooted in atavistic motives, as a basic theme in Schumpeter's theory of economic development. An outline of the institutional substance of entrepreneurship in the capitalist process thus evolves as an indispensable condition for approaching the Schumpeterian theory of the state.

3 Schumpeterian Entrepreneurship as Institutional Leadership

3.1 Theorising Entrepreneurial Leadership

The Schumpeterian approach to economic development deals with innovation as the internal force of discontinuous change, carried out by the means of entrepreneurial leadership. This argument is framed by the idea that novelty does not evolve harmoniously from within an established economic setting, but places itself alongside established patterns and competes them down (Schumpeter 1939: 241). More specifically, entrepreneurs fulfil their developmental function by introducing innovations as new combinations of productive means, basically new goods and new methods of production, new markets and supply sources, as well as new organisational constellations in an industrial sector (Schumpeter 1926: 100n). The entrepreneur is modelled as a specific type of economic agent who carries out innovations by setting up a firm as the organisational terrain for the new combination of productive means. This venture is credit-financed by capitalists who represent the rationally calculating element in capitalism. The cost-related advantages of innovations generate an entrepreneurial profit, perceived as the material incentive for related business activities. However, quite in accordance with the exposed role of atavistic motives in the development process, entrepreneurial profits are viewed as means to achieve further ends.[4] These seemed to exhibit an aristocratic atmosphere, reflecting extra-capitalist habits and values, as highlighted by the drive for building a family-empire or dynasty, accompanied by an impulse for conquering and fighting, as well as the joy of creating (Schumpeter 1926: 138n). Thus, Schumpeterian entrepreneurship is driven by motivations which are alien to the rationalist foundations of capitalist civilization.[5] Still, regarding the actual implementation of innovations, entrepreneurs were said to be void of traditional relationships, yet oriented towards individualist rationalism in the carrying out of the entrepreneurial function (Schumpeter 1926: 134).

The Schumpeterian notion of entrepreneurship should reflect the impact of leadership, based on an interplay of imagination and creation, which was identified as a most relevant source of socio-cultural change, whereas it had emerged specifically as the internal driving force of economic development in modern capitalism (Schumpeter 1912: 124n). Acts of creative leadership, which were traced in diverse areas like industry, politics, the arts, and science, were said to be based on a temporary reservoir of vitality and energy, underlining the impulsive character of innovation (Schumpeter 1912: 147). Leadership constitutes the decisive component of entrepreneurship: "The carrying out of new combination is form and content of development, just like the activity of the leader is its driving force" (Schumpeter 1912: 162).[6] The original Schumpeterian position then

[4] Thus the profit incentive does not represent the ultimate cause for entrepreneurial activity (Santarelli and Pesciarelli 1990: 685).

[5] This position has raised the critical question, whether Schumpeterian entrepreneurship is really an internal force of capitalist development, as entrepreneurial motives seem to remain exogenous to the economic process (Shionoya 1997: 170). Yet this criticism misrepresents Schumpeter's notion of institutional variety as a characteristic of modern capitalism, which allows for non-capitalist components as an indispensable requirement of its evolutionary dynamism.

[6] Hints at the theory of entrepreneurship are to be observed even in Schumpeter's early works on static theory. Already in "*Wesen*", certain "energetic" elements are sorted out, which represent the internal source of economic change (Schumpeter 1908: 596n). Schumpeter also suggested that phenomena like the "will to power" could serve as fundamental arguments for

highlighted static and dynamic types of behaviour, paralleled by hedonistic and energetic motives (Schumpeter 1912: 128). Schumpeter claimed that the motives of ordinary economic agents in the circular flow were not based on rational choice and egoistic hedonism, but on habits that were meant to satisfy given wants that are also shaped by the social environment (Schumpeter 1926: 132n). That is why Schumpeter claimed the motto "plus ultra" as the characteristic device of entrepreneurial ventures (Schumpeter 1926: 137).

More specifically, the role of entrepreneurial leadership was derived from an institutional reorientation after the introduction of novelty, due to the disruption of the routines of the circular flow. The radical change of data that had been used as guideposts for calculation would lead to a decomposition of habitual attitudes and experience-based rationality. Autonomous adaptation would be impossible for ordinary economic agents who face radical uncertain. It follows that novelty needs to be forced upon the majority of economic agents, as progress in general is basically a result of force and confrontation (Schumpeter 1912: 185n). Corresponding entrepreneurial tasks contain breaking the inertia of traditions and routines, finding strategic partners for the carrying out of innovations, and gaining the acceptance of consumers (Schumpeter 1926: 125n). The clustering of innovations, meant as a fundamental aspect of Schumpeter's business cycle theory, was derived from these effects of entrepreneurial leadership, as pioneering innovations would enlarge opportunities for further ventures that could be carried out by less entrepreneurial agents (Schumpeter 1939: 100n).

3.2 Schumpeterian Types of Economic Agents

This differentiation points to the modelling of distinct types of economic agents by comparing spontaneous-creative and habitual-adaptive types of behaviour (Schumpeter 1926: 119). According to this argument, the entrepreneurial function is characterised by the capability for creative response – a notion, which, like the phrase of creative destruction, hints once more at the vitalist dimension of Schumpeter's theorising.[7] In contrast to an adaptive attitude, denoting adapta-

---

elaborating on a general approach for dealing with major economic changes from a historical perspective (Schumpeter 1908: 618). Moreover, in a subsequent review of advances in economic theory, published in 1910, Schumpeter claimed in delineation against established neoclassical theorists like Clark that the "herd of consumers" needed to be "mastered and guided" by the "leading personalities" of the production sphere (Schumpeter 1910b: 51).

[7] For instance, Schumpeter explained in a private comment on Marschak's criticism of "Business Cycles" as published in 1940, pointing to a lack of formal theory, that enterprise should represent a "source of energy" internal to the system and related to the Bergsonian notion of "*evolution créatrice*". Hence, a useful theory of economic development would not deal with

tions to gradual changes in the set of economic data, creative response is neither predictable nor determined, for it implies activities outside of the range of existing practice (Schumpeter 1947a: 150). With creative response present, the evolution of modern capitalism would remain undetermined. It therefore characterises the quality of entrepreneurship as a historical factor in economic development (Schumpeter 1947b: 8). These essential features of the Schumpeterian modelling of economic agents are outlined in Figure 1.

Figure 1: Schumpeterian Types of Economic Agents

	Ordinary Type ***"Wirte"***	**Entrepreneurial Type** ***"Unternehmer"***
Type of Response	*Predictably Adaptive*	*Unpredictably Creative*
Type of Behaviour	*Experience-Based Habitual*	*Novelty-Embracing Spontaneous*
Type of Motivation	*Hedonistic Calculation*	*Visionary Imagination*
Mode of Action	*Uncertainty-Absorbing Routine*	*Uncertainty-Spreading Innovation*
Mode of Change	*Slowly Gradual by Administering Structures*	*Rapidly Discontinuous by Creating Structures*

However, the logic of Schumpeterian entrepreneurship is not associated exclusively with the institutional setting of capitalist market economies, as it represents a general principle which is also of utmost relevance for other historical formations, and in different areas of social life. This universal nexus between novelty and leadership was underlined as follows:

> Social leadership means deciding, ordering, carrying out, forging ahead. As such it is special, both within the actions of the individual, and within the social whole always a distinguishable function. It is to be considered only when confronting novel individual and social situations, and it would not exist if the life of the individual and the peoples would run steadily in the tracks of always the same routine (Schumpeter 1927: 64).

Its historicity is described by the proposition that the universal nexus of novelty and leadership would manifest itself through diverse carriers, historically conditioned in institutional and organisational shape. Hence, Schumpeter claimed that the entrepreneurial function could be fulfilled by the organs of a socialist commonwealth or by the chief of a primitive horde, that is by those agents who

"surface mechanical relations" but with an unpredictable evolutionary process. This would impede its formalisation (Stolper 1994: 375).

would hold the leading and commanding position in their particular social and institutional environment, enabling them to enforce the dynamism of change by introducing novelty (Schumpeter 1926: 111).

3.3 Entrepreneurship and the Phases of Capitalist Development

This aspect of the historicity of entrepreneurship was also applied to capitalist development. Underlining the historical specificity of institutional patterns, Schumpeter combined business cycle analysis with the delineation of specific phases of capitalist development (Ebner 2003: 117n).[8] Yet the elaboration on these phases abstracted from the statistical framework of the business cycle scheme. Instead, the perspective of a rationalisation of the capitalist process was taken to the fore. The reconsideration of this perspective needs to be assessed with respect to one of Schumpeter's basic research motives, namely the question whether modern capitalism would evolve towards socialism, driven by rationalisation and bureaucratisation.[9] Most arguments on the institutional transformation of capitalism had already been formulated in an essay on the "possibilities of socialism", published in 1920. First, industrial concentration and the emergence of corporations and trusts would lead to the dominance of bureaucratic organisations. Second, the rationalisation of economic life, as indicated by the automatisation of technological change, would imply the obsolescence of the entrepreneurial function, with leadership replaced by administration. Third, rationalisation would cut loose the economic sphere from pre-capitalist and non-economic sentiments and ties, illustrated by the decreasing role of family values as a motive for the private accumulation of wealth (Schumpeter 1920-21: 312n). The conclusion pointed to rationalisation as a step towards socialism: "The principle of efficiency can assert oneself much purer in the economy, when all the persons involved are merely calculating, instead of ruling, serving and being guided by other than purely economic considerations" (Schumpeter 1920-21: 319).

---

[8] Kondratieff cycles as "historical individuals" were accordingly outlined. The first Kondratieff cycle from the 1780s to 1842 should mirror the impact of the industrial revolution in Western Europe. The second Kondratieff cycle from 1842 to 1897 should represent a so-called bourgeois age of steam and steel, that is the industrial process of developed capitalist economies. The third Kondratieff from 1898 onwards should reflect the economic and institutional setting of a neo-mercantilist period (Schumpeter 1939: 170).

[9] Recognising these aspects, shifts in the analytical emphasis of Schumpeter's approach to entrepreneurship become accessible. It has been suggested that a conceptual continuity in Schumpeter's argumentation is to be observed as soon as a historical perspective is taken into consideration, combining the characterisation of the carriers of the entrepreneurial function with the development pattern of modern capitalism (Langlois 1998: 57n).

Subsequently, Schumpeter distinguished between "competitive" capitalism during the 19th century, and "trustified" capitalism in the 20th century, derived from institutional patterns that could be identified in Western Europe and the United States (Schumpeter 1928b: 362). The "liberal epoch" of competitive capitalism was dominated by family enterprises. The motivation of the entrepreneurial type of the "industrial bourgeois" was accordingly characterised by a sense of duty as well as an unambiguous family-orientation (Schumpeter 1929b: 308).[10] Trustification during the "neo-mercantilist" period of capitalism would lead to the dominance of large enterprises, based on the capability for organising large-scale technological change as a professional routine (Schumpeter 1929b: 316). Accordingly, different types of entrepreneurs would be selected, as large organisations required capabilities in the domain of organisational coordination and cooperation (Schumpeter 1929b: 317n). Schumpeter even suggested that employees in large corporations could act as entrepreneurs, for they would need to exhibit the entrepreneurial blend of charismatic leadership only temporarily in the context of professional routine tasks. Innovation would become foreseeable, as even consumers got accustomed to a type of predicated economic change. Hence, the leadership function of entrepreneurship would become obsolete in terms of personal leadership (Schumpeter 1942: 132n). In accordance with that developmental tendency, the totality of capitalist institutions becomes the subject of structural decomposition, also involving its extra-capitalist components. The family, for instance, has no particular role to play in the emerging post-capitalist institutional order (Schumpeter 1942: 156n).[11]

Accordingly, Schumpeter acknowledged the perspective of socialist transformation, prepared by the establishment of "state capitalism" as a transition stage, resembling a mixed economy with a strong public sector and extended administrative guidance (Schumpeter 1943: 125). Moreover, this position implied that the state could carry out the entrepreneurial function: as a temporary device in the capitalist setting, yet permanently in a socialist system of administrative planning. Transformation, however, would affect the institutional rationale of government. Indeed, just like entrepreneurial leadership in the private sector is a historically-specific feature of capitalism, so is the modern state an element of the capitalist process. From the Schumpeterian perspective follows that the evolution of the state complements the dynamism of entrepreneurship. Although neglected in the literature on Schumpeterian thought, Schumpeter's conceptual

[10] This entrepreneurial type, also typified as the "merchant" who dominated the competitive epoch, was additionally portrayed as a socially responsible businessman, as a patriarch and master who tended to care for the enterprise in terms of a personal as well as a family concern, implying a rationale beyond pure economic calculation (Schumpeter 1928a: 484n).

[11] This aspect may be related to Schumpeter's proposition that families constitute the basic analytical unit in a theory of social classes, for the family represented the decisive unit of social mobility and group behaviour in the cyclical renewal of elites (Schumpeter 1927: 12n).

range even included the analytical device of an "entrepreneurial state". In order to explore Schumpeter's theory of the state, thus, the following section proceeds with a reconsideration of the concept of the tax state, for it provides a basic institutional approach to the rationale of government.

4 The Tax State and the Rationale of Government

4.1 The Institutional Evolution of the Tax State

In accordance with positions on institutional variety, Schumpeter's approach to the "tax state" explicitly accounted for the modern state in terms of a specifically capitalist institutional form. Its character was said to be shaped by distinct forces of economic and socio-cultural evolution, embedded in an institutional setting that would resemble a specific cultural pattern (Schumpeter 1918/1953: 3). It should be analysed as an ideal typical fiction which does not exist as a pure type, for it was penetrated by "elements of the past" and "shadows of the conditions of the future" (Schumpeter 1918/1953: 23).[12] The modern state evolves from a historical process in which it obtains a role beyond merely representing the underlying material interests of those social classes and groups which promoted most actively its institutional evolution. In particular, the differentiation of private and public domains, endowed with specific legal frameworks in private and public law, reflects the genesis of the modern state as an institutional form.[13] Historically, it is the dissolution of the institutional order of the feudal system that leads to the emergence of a specific private domain as the subject of fiscal efforts, organised by an evolving state apparatus. The rationalising effects of capitalism are the underlying factor in the institutional dissolution of feudalism, as Schumpeter remarks with formulations that echo both Marxian and Weberian thought:

> While the stream of productive revolutions sweeps away this world, the knight forgets the Holy Grail and is reminded of his landed property, thus this order breaks up like a corpse swollen by putrefying gases – and it breaks up into individuals and families with a thousand conflicting interests (Schumpeter 1918/1953: 19).

[12] Schumpeter outlined this conceptual problem as follows: „Each social condition contains remnants of the past and seeds of the future, and the latter are especially noticeable to research looking back through the glasses of a later time. *Natura non facit saltum*, and one can speak of every condition in the sense of a definitely defined type only as an abstraction. Yet such abstractions are necessary in terms of an „economy of thinking". Every concrete condition, in its totality (*not* as an abstraction) gives birth to the succeeding one in its totality" (Schumpeter 1918/1953: 61, emphasis in original).

[13] Thus Schumpeter criticised the functionalist distinction of a private sphere and a sphere of state activity, basically regarded as the public sphere (Schumpeter 1918/1953: 62n).

With individualism and private property as fundamental institutional conditions of its evolution, as expressed by the formation of individuals and families as economic units, the modern state is indeed perceived as a historically-specific institutional form in the capitalist system. Different forms of political leadership govern pre-capitalist systems, like the organisations of primitive hordes, as well as socialist systems with their comprehensive bureaucratic organisation. In these systems, a distinction of private and public domains could not exist, for all individual activities are merged in the social whole (Schumpeter 1918/1953: 18n). The state then serves common purposes that persist despite the societal decomposition of community:

> Therefore the state can never be its own end but only a machine for those common purposes. It belongs to its nature as a representative of the latter that it stands opposite the individual personifications of self-interest. Only then it is a separate, distinguishable social entity (Schumpeter 1918/1953: 20).

Historically, Schumpeter approached the modern state, which is the tax state, as a product of the princely fiscal crisis since the 14th century, following the structural crisis of the demesne economy. The need for financing the rising expenses for warfare and courtly waste was confronted by the dissolution of the institutional order of feudalism with its societal consequences, namely the emergence of market relations with individuals and families as economic units (Schumpeter 1918/1953: 9n). As the prince got into debt, the fiscal crisis induced the development of the modern state as an organisation for raising taxes and governing the tax system. This organisation mirrored not only the concerns of aristocracy, for a bureaucracy of the estates was soon established in order to administer the fiscal system. Still, the princes usually took control of that bureaucratic apparatus – thus shaping the modern state in manner that would persist even in a democratic setting (Schumpeter 1918/1953: 14n).

Given these considerations, Schumpeter's references to Goldscheid's notion of the public budget as "the skeleton of the state stripped of all misleading ideologies" – a notion that should be constitutive for the approach of fiscal sociology – becomes accessible in terms of a theory of the state.[14] Moreover, with regard to the matter of economic development, government activity needs to be reconsidered in terms of the fiscal manipulation of the flow of resources that constitutes the economic process. This aspect is paralleled by the motivational impact on economic agents (Schumpeter 1918/1953: 4n). Indeed, Schumpeter argued:

> Not only has the economic policy of all states been primarily driven by financial motives up to the turn of our century – (…), but the fiscal measures of the state, even

[14] This argument was reiterated in the "History of Economic Analysis", as Schumpeter argued that "nothing shows so clearly the character of a society and of a civilization as does the fiscal policy that its political sector adopts" (Schumpeter 1954: 769).

> where it was not intended at all, have created and destroyed industries, industrial forms and industrial regions, and have thus contributed directly to the construction (and distortion) of the edifice of the modern economy and through it of the modern spirit (Schumpeter 1918/1953: 4n).

Thus, the state is both result and propagator of the rationalisation process underlying the evolution of capitalist civilisation. Taxation is of major importance in this process, as it affects its motivational and behavioural dimension:

> With the tax bill in hand, the state penetrated the private economies, gaining increasing power over them. And the tax brings monetary economy and calculating spirit in corners, where they do not yet dwell, and thus exhibits a formative effect on the organism which has developed it (Schumpeter 1918/1953: 17n).

Still, in the course of capitalist development, the state establishes a distinct nature as an institutional force that moulds the fiscal system in which it is rooted, while penetrating the private sector with its entrepreneurial business ventures (Schumpeter1918/1953: 21).[15]

4.2 States, Markets and the Common Good

The institutional character of the state as well as the rationale of government, however, is not to be assessed independently from a reconsideration of the social foundations.

> Decisive for a realistic understanding of the phenomenon of the state – apart from its character as a machine for some relatively narrow ends, to which machine the whole of the national cultural life with all its essential driving forces is standing opposed to – is the recognition of the importance of that group of persons in whom it is socially materialised and of those factors which gain dominance over it. This explains its real power and the way in which it is used and developed (Schumpeter 1918/1953: 22).

Consequently, in the Schumpeterian theory of the state, the relationship between state and society is interpenetrating, for the societal context shapes government activity, while the latter may influence social patterns:

[15] Various historical cases of the development of fiscal systems hint at a pattern of increasing military expenditures followed by tax increases. This implies that state-building, perceived as nation-building, and the evolution of taxation are closely related, as both the form and level of taxation matter (Campbell 1993: 176n). In the framework of the transaction cost approach to economic history, for instance, North refers to Schumpeter's notion of the fiscal crisis of the state in the context of an institutional analysis of the divergence of development paths of England and Spain in the sixteenth century (North 1990: 113n).

> Really, one should never say: 'the state does this or that.' It is always important to recognise who or whose interest it is that sets the state machine in motion and speaks through it. Such a position must be repulsive to everyone for whom the state is the highest good of the people, the crown of its achievements, the sum of all its ideals and powers. However, only this position is realistic. It also contains, what has been true in the otherwise wrong theory that the state is nothing but a means of exploitation for the ruling class: neither the moment of the class state, nor the idea of the state floating above all parties and classes as an entity which is simply the organised 'totality', is adequate to the nature of the state. Yet neither of the two is taken out of thin air: the state always reflects the social power relations, although it is not a mere reflection of these (Schumpeter 1918/1953: 68).

An implication of that position was the explicit rejection of any "ideological theory of the state that raises the latter into a superhuman agency for the public good"; a position that was also meant as a demarcation from those policy ideals that should become influential with the rise of Keynesianism (Schumpeter 1954: 37).

In historical terms, then, the pioneering social force within the state apparatus is the prince, who establishes it as a system of administrative rule. In the course of the development process, bureaucracy gains influence, representing a shift from ruling to serving personnel, while the state evolves as a distinct social entity that penetrates the behaviour of economic agents, at last even resembling a habit of thought. The limits of the state are thus not to be found in the domain of institutions, but rather in its fiscal potential.[16] Its country-specific features are derived from institutional settings and social structures, as well as from the nature of wealth that reflects the pattern of the development process. Differentiating between old and new forms of wealth, Schumpeter even stylised rentier states and entrepreneurial states, as outlined in Figure 2.

These types reflect a distinction of economic scenarios, involving stagnation versus novelty-based accumulation. Schumpeter even hinted at the impact of further limiting factors, like military expenditures, debt service, the moral spirit of bureaucracy, as well as the degree of etatism in the populace (Schumpeter 1918/1953: 22n).

[16] These considerations have been reiterated in recent transaction-cost approaches. For example, North's "neo-classical theory of the state" provides a definition of the state that emphasises the role of property rights. The state is approached as an organisation which is endowed with comparative advantages in the execution of violent means, yet limited in its territorial range by the capability for taxation (North 1981: 21).

Figure 2: Rentier State and Entrepreneurial State

	Rentier State	**Entrepreneurial State**
Economic Foundations	*Routine-Based*	*Innovation-Driven*
Nature of Wealth	*Established Wealth*	*New Wealth*
Developmental Tendency	*Stagnation*	*Accumulation*

As the private sector of the capitalist economy provides the dynamising elements of the economic process, the state remains a peripheral and particularly even hostile entity which confronts the self-interested individualism of economic agents in the private sector by means of the fiscal system. As such, Schumpeter claims that the tax state may be viewed as "an economic parasite" in the setting of bourgeois values of competitive capitalism. As the state is in permanent need of the revenue that is generated by private economic agents, then, the promotion of private sector entrepreneurship marks the rationale of government (Schumpeter 1918/1953: 23n).[17] This aspect constitutes a fundamental relationship between entrepreneurship and the rationale of government, as viewed from a Schumpeterian perspective. Therefore, the taxation of entrepreneurial profits would affect the process of industrial evolution in terms of an institutional obstacle that manipulates the material incentives for entrepreneurial activity (Schumpeter 1918/1953: 27n).[18] Even a position of the state as an entrepreneurial owner of the means of production would not alter that situation, for the data and methods of the private sector would prevail as dominant principles (Schumpeter 1918/1953: 30n). Accordingly, Schumpeter argued that no economic structure has been created by the state that would not have evolved in more or less the same manner as a result of initiatives from the private sector in the setting of market competition (Schumpeter 1918/1953: 58).

It may be emphasised that these arguments were meant as contribution to contemporary debates on a solution of the economic problems of the Austrian Republic in the aftermath of the First World War. While Goldscheid's influential essay on the perspectives of state socialism and state capitalism, published in 1917, had proposed a comprehensive socialisation programme, Schumpeter favoured the reconstruction of private sector entrepreneurship through a capital levy. Indeed, a fiscal crisis in Schumpeterian terms would basically occur as a

[17] The tax state thus appears as a "fiscal analogue" to the institutional setting of the market system (Musgrave 1992: 90).

[18] Schumpeter actually portrayed the income tax as the tax of bourgeois liberalism, adapted to the culture of the bourgeois factory and the bourgeois household in the competitive market system, and administered by a liberal state that would follow an anti-interventionist orientation (Schumpeter 1929-30/1985: 127n).

result of irreversible social changes, as exemplified by the decline of feudalism.[19] Capitalism, however, was far from over – its dynamism would instead contribute most promisingly to the reconstruction of the Austrian economy. Thus, according to the Schumpeterian position, published right before his ill-fated intermezzo as an Austrian Minister of Finance, there was no inherent crisis of the Austrian tax state, but a need for a revival of entrepreneurial activities in the face of a political crisis of capitalism (Schumpeter 1918/1953: 56n).

4.3 Policy Implications for the Entrepreneurial State

Along the lines of the preceding arguments, more recent discussions on the role of economic policy, as viewed from the Schumpeterian perspective, have emphasised the facilitation of change through innovations as well as the mitigation of the social costs that arise from that change (Stolper 1991: 203n). In the institutional framework of the market process, this broad perspective has been interpreted as if Schumpeterian policies should primarily highlight the public sector as an intermediary in providing credit facilities to entrepreneurs who are in need of these funds in order to proceed with their innovative ventures (Jackson 1988: 299n). The Schumpeterian theory of the state, however, allows for policy implications that pinpoint the problems of selective government interventions, associated with the concept of an entrepreneurial state that rests its economic position on the accumulation of wealth through novelty. Indeed, the matter of rationalisation and socialist transformation, implicit in the Schumpeterian perspective on economic development, leads to the controversial thesis that even government may carry out the entrepreneurial function – temporarily in the institutional context of the capitalism, yet permanently in a socialist system. At first glance, it seems to be rather difficult to reconcile this concept of an entrepreneurial state with Schumpeter's general theoretical framework of market competition and personal entrepreneurship (Freeman 1992: 75). Nonetheless, in assessing this concept of the entrepreneurial state, the historical specificity of the institutional order of modern capitalism needs to be taken into consideration. According to Schumpeter, an administrative enforcement of innovation as the dominant type of entrepreneurship would already signal the socialist transformation of trustified capitalism. Capital, credit and interest would lose their function as monetary levers of change, for innovation would result from administrative command.

[19] This implies that the evolution of the tax state addresses three specific dimensions of long-term change, namely a change in the source of revenue, a change of social structures and a change of the political system (Schmidt 2003: 343).

Thus, in a socialist system, the state could carry out the entrepreneurial function directly by exercising economic leadership (Schumpeter 1912: 173).[20]

The Schumpeterian perspective on government agencies as entrepreneurial agents was of course perceived as historically conditioned. Schumpeter illustrated it by invoking agricultural policies in the United States which had been revolutionising the practice of farmers through the introduction and dissemination of novel methods; a process that was primarily based on extensive efforts in training and education (Schumpeter 1949b/1951: 255). Moreover, an articulation of the entrepreneurial function by organs of the state would point to an entrepreneurial intervention in certain industries by setting up public enterprises that could proceed with the introduction of innovations. Another domain of entrepreneurial states was associated with the conditioning of the economic process through institutional and physical infrastructures. Thus, Schumpeter stylised statecraft as a particular kind of entrepreneurship that could temporarily shape the data of capitalist development (Schumpeter 1939: 235).

Yet it is worthy to note that Schumpeter accentuated problems with the sustainability of these policy measures. Recognition of the temporary character of entrepreneurship allowed for a more affirmative assessment of states as entrepreneurs. Indeed, with regard to those policy options that should provide a long-term view on the development process, the aspect of conditioning private sector entrepreneurship by adequate policies seemed to provide the most promising perspectives. Underlining the persistent relevance of this aspect, Schumpeter emphasised that innovation resulted from a distinct type of entrepreneurial behaviour which could be incited by an appropriate institutional environment. The latter would include government involvement in the promotion of entrepreneurial behaviour among economic agents: "This business behaviour may, of course, be moulded not only by general environmental conditions but also by the specific action of other social organs, governments for instance, taken with the intention of calling it forth" (Schumpeter 1939: 86).[21] Therefore, it becomes

---

[20] Indeed, Schumpeter closed his first ever exposition of the theory of economic development with an outlook on the matter of economic crises. There he argued that the impact these crises, perceived as the turning points of business cycles, would diminish in the future due to advances of economic culture. The development process would become a respected fact of economic life, perhaps supported by monetary measures, as opposed to futile attempts of regulation by policy intervention (Schumpeter 1910a: 323n). This argumentation differed from the bureaucratisation perspective that became a prominent topic in Schumpeter's subsequent works, when even the planning of innovations and thus the stabilisation of the economic process seemed to be feasible. In this case, Schumpeter claimed: "(G)iven sufficient power and insight in a central authority, innovation may of course be planned for in such a way as to minimize disturbance" (Schumpeter 1939: 697).

[21] A similar viewpoint has been outlined in recent institutionalist discussions on the theory of the state. The state is approached as an organisation through which collectives may pursue

once again obvious that it is the behavioural dimension of entrepreneurship, embedded in the context of institutional variety, which constitutes a key concern of the Schumpeterian theory of the state – analytically as well as in terms of the policy conclusions. This underlines once more the outstanding role of institutional aspects in Schumpeter's theorising.

6 Conclusion

The institutional dimension of Schumpeter's theory of economic development highlights the systemic impurity of modern capitalism in terms of an institutional variety that contains capitalist as well as extra-capitalist elements. The former represent the process of an ongoing rationalisation of the socio-cultural domain, with economic life as a crucial segment of that domain, whereas the latter point to the diverse patterns of motivation and behaviour which drive entrepreneurial initiative. Schumpeter then pointed to the combination of atavistic values, as represented by pre-capitalist institutions, and the drive for rationalisation which would characterise the capitalist civilisation. According to Schumpeter, this specific combination of diverse institutional components had been indispensable for promoting the dynamism of capitalist development, for it informed the entrepreneurial carrying out of innovations – motivated by atavistic values yet implemented in a most rational manner. In a similar fashion, Schumpeter presented the state as a historically specific institutional phenomenon, associated with the constitution of a private sphere of economic activity that would require the provision of common goods by a basically tax-financed state. The bureaucratic administration of the state, however, exhibits historical roots which reach back to the fiscal needs of the prince, resulting from motives that resemble those pre-capitalist values which drive entrepreneurship in the competitive phase of modern capitalism. Schumpeter thus argued that private sector entrepreneurship and public sector government represent two sides of a comprehensive development process. Therefore it was suggested that the rationalisation of the socio-economic sphere, heralding the emergence of socialism, would result both in the decline of private sector entrepreneurship and the transformation of the tax state.

A reassessment of these considerations on the development tendency of modern capitalism may lead to the conclusion that Schumpeter underestimated the economic potential of an expanding public sector, misjudging it as an indication of capitalist decline, whereas the market system seems to have benefited from

their goals, yet it is also understood as an institutional configuration that influences the meaning and methods of politics, thus shaping society as a relatively autonomous agent (Skocpol 1985: 27n).

some aspects of the welfare state, thus promoting a diversity of institutional forms that corresponds to a persistent variety of capitalist settings (Musgrave 1992: 102). Similar arguments apply to the matter of entrepreneurship, for Schumpeter seemed to have misjudged the capacity for institutional reproduction that characterises the various modes of entrepreneurship, ranging from small business ventures to the initiatives of entrepreneurial states. However, this does not affect the analytical value of Schumpeterian thought, for these developments may be explained by Schumpeterian theorising too. Regarding the Schumpeterian theory of the state, in particular, the impact of ideological factors and social interests remains of utmost importance for the institutional analysis of governance.

References

Backhaus, J. (2002), Fiscal Sociology: What For?, *American Journal of Economics and Sociology*, Vol.61, No.1, pp.55-78.

Campbell, J. (1993), The State and Fiscal Sociology, *Annual Review of Sociology*, Vol.19, pp.163-185.

Ebner, A. (1999), Understanding Varieties in the Structure and Performance of National Innovation Systems: The Concept of Economic Style, in J. Groenewegen and J. Vromen (eds.) *Institutions and the Evolution of Capitalism: Implications of Evolutionary Economics*, Aldershot: Elgar, pp.141-169.

Ebner, A. (2000a), Schumpeter and the "Schmollerprogramm": Integrating Theory and History in the Analysis of Economic Development, *Journal of Evolutionary Economics*, Vol.10, No.1-2, pp.355-372.

Ebner, A. (2000b), Systems of Innovation between Globalisation and Transformation: Policy Implications for the Support of Schumpeterian Entrepreneurship, in A. Kukliński and W.M. Orłowski (eds.) *The Knowledge-Based Economy – The Global Challenges of the 21st Century*, Warsaw: State Committee for Scientific Research of the Republic of Poland, pp.80-99.

Ebner, A. (2003), The Institutional Analysis of Entrepreneurship: Historist Aspects of Schumpeter's Development Theory, in J. Backhaus (ed.) *Joseph Alois Schumpeter: Entrepreneurship, Style and Vision*, Boston: Dordrecht, pp.117-139.

Freeman, C. (1992), *The Economics of Hope: Essays on Technical Change, Economic Growth and the Environment*, London: Pinter.

Fukuyama, F (1995), *Trust: The Social Virtues and the Creation of Prosperity*, New York: Free Press.

Hodgson, G.M. (1988), *Economics and Institutions: A Manifesto for a Modern Institutional Economics*, Oxford: Polity Press.

Jackson, P.M. (1988), The Role of Government in Changing Industrial Societies: A Schumpeter Perspective, in H. Hanusch (ed.) *Evolutionary Economics: Applications of Schumpeter's Ideas*, Cambridge: Cambridge University Press, pp.285-308.

Langlois, R.N. (1998), Personal Capitalism as Charismatic Authority: The Organizational Economics of a Weberian Concept, *Industrial and Corporate Change*, Vol.7, No.1, pp.195-213.

Musgrave, R.A. (1992), Schumpeter's Crisis of the Tax State: An Essay in Fiscal Sociology, *Journal of Evolutionary Economics*, Vol.2, No.2, pp.89-113.

North, D.C. (1981), *Structure and Change in Economic History*, New York: W.W. Norton.
North, D.C. (1990), *Institutions, Institutional Change and Economic Performance*, Cambridge: Cambridge University Press.
Polanyi, K. (1977), *The Livelihood of Man*, ed. by H.W. Pearson, New York: Academic.
Santarelli, E. and Pesciarelli, E. (1990), The Emergence of a Vision: The Development of Schumpeter's Theory of Entrepreneurship, *History of Political Economy*, Vol.22, No.4, pp.677-696.
Schmidt, K.-H. (2003), Schumpeter and the Crisis of the Tax State, in J. Backhaus (ed.) *Joseph Alois Schumpeter: Entrepreneurship, Style and Vision*, Boston: Dordrecht, pp.117-139.
Schumpeter, J.A. (1908), *Das Wesen und der Hauptinhalt der theoretischen Nationalökonomie*, Berlin: Duncker und Humblot.
Schumpeter, J.A. (1910a), Über das Wesen der Wirtschaftskrisen, *Zeitschrift für Volkswirtschaft, Sozialpolitik und Verwaltung*, Vol.19, pp.271-325.
Schumpeter, J.A. (1910b), Die neuere Wirtschaftstheorie in den Vereinigten Staaten, *Schmollers Jahrbuch für Gesetzgebung, Verwaltung und Volkswirtschaft im Deutschen Reiche*, Vol.34, No.1, pp.913-963.
Schumpeter, J.A. (1912), *Theorie der wirtschaftlichen Entwicklung*, Duncker und Humblot, Berlin.
Schumpeter, J.A. (1918/1953), Die Krise des Steuerstaates, *Zeitfragen aus dem Gebiet der Soziologie*, Vol.4, pp.1-71, repr. in J.A. Schumpeter, *Aufsätze zur Soziologie*, ed. by E. Schneider and A. Spiethoff, Tübingen: Mohr, pp.3-74.
Schumpeter, J.A. (1918-19), Zur Soziologie der Imperialismen, *Archiv für Sozialwissenschaft und Sozialpolitik*, Vol.46, pp.1-39 and pp.275-310.
Schumpeter, J.A. (1920-21), Sozialistische Möglichkeiten von heute, *Archiv für Sozialwissenschaft und Sozialpolitik*, Vol.48, pp.305-360.
Schumpeter, J.A. (1926), *Theorie der wirtschaftlichen Entwicklung: Eine Untersuchung über Unternehmergewinn, Kapital, Kredit, Zins und den Konjunkturzyklus*, Second Edition, Berlin: Duncker und Humblot.
Schumpeter, J.A. (1927), Die sozialen Klassen im ethnisch homogenen Milieu, in *Archiv für Sozialwissenschaft und Sozialpolitik*, Vol.57, pp.1-67.
Schumpeter, J.A. (1928a), Unternehmer, in L. Elster (ed.) *Handwörterbuch der Staatswissenschaften*, Fourth Edition, Vol. 8, Jena: Gustav Fischer, pp. 476-487.
Schumpeter, J.A. (1928b), The Instability of Capitalism, *Economic Journal*, Vol.XXXVIII, No.151, pp.361-386.
Schumpeter, J.A. (1929-30/1985), Ökonomie und Soziologie der Einkommenssteuer, Der deutsche Volkswirt, Vol.4, 1929/1930, pp.380-385, repr. in J.A. Schumpeter (1985) *Aufsätze zur Wirtschaftspolitik*, ed. W.F. Stolper and C. Seidl, Tübingen: Mohr, pp.123-132.
Schumpeter, J.A. (1929a/1953), Das soziale Antlitz des Deutschen Reiches, Bonner Mitteilungen, No.1, repr. in J.A. Schumpeter, *Aufsätze zur Soziologie*, ed. by E. Schneider and A. Spiethoff, Tübingen: Mohr, pp.214-225.
Schumpeter, J.A. (1929b), Der Unternehmer in der Volkswirtschaft von heute, in B. Harms (ed.), *Strukturwandlungen der Deutschen Volkswirtschaft*, Second Edition, Vol.1, Berlin: Reimar Hobbing, pp.303-326.
Schumpeter, J.A. (1939), *Business Cycles: A Theoretical, Historical and Statistical Analysis of the Capitalist Process*, Two Volumes, New York: McGraw-Hill.
Schumpeter, J.A. (1942), *Capitalism, Socialism and Democracy*, London: Allen and Unwin.
Schumpeter, J.A. (1943), Capitalism in the Postwar World, in S.E. Harris (ed.) *Postwar Economic Problems*, New York: McGraw-Hill, pp.113-126.

Schumpeter, J.A. (1947a), The Creative Response in Economic History, *Journal of Economic History*, Vol.VII, No.2, pp. 149-159.

Schumpeter, J.A. (1947b), Theoretical Problems of Economic Growth, *Journal of Economic History*, Vol.VII, Supplement, pp. 1-9.

Schumpeter, J.A. (1949a), The Communist Manifesto in Sociology and Economics, *Journal of Political Economy*, Vol.LVII, pp.199-212.

Schumpeter, J.A. (1949b/1951), Economic Theory and Entrepreneurial History, Change and the Entrepreneur, pp.63-84, repr. in R.V. Clemence (ed.) *Essays of J. A. Schumpeter*, Cambridge, Mass.: Addison-Wesley, pp.248-266.

Schumpeter, J.A. (1954), *History of Economic Analysis*, New York: Oxford University Press.

Shionoya, Y. (1997), *Schumpeter and the Idea of Social Science: A Metatheoretical Study*, Cambridge: Cambridge University Press.

Skocpol, T. (1985), Bringing the State Back In: Strategies of Analysis in Current Research, in P.B. Evans, D. Rueschmeyer and T. Skocpol (eds.) *Bringing the State Back In*, Cambridge: Cambridge University Press, pp.3-37.

Stolper, W.F. (1991), The Theoretical Bases of Economic Policy: The Schumpeterian Perspective, *Journal of Evolutionary Economics*, Vol.1, No.3, pp.189-205.

Stolper, W.F. (1994), *Joseph Alois Schumpeter: The Public Life of a Private Man*, Princeton: Princeton University Press.

Streissler, E.W. (1981), Schumpeter's Vienna and the Role of Credit in Innovation, in H. Frisch (ed.) *Schumpeterian Economics*, New York: Praeger, pp.60-83.

Swedberg, R. (1989), Joseph A. Schumpeter and the Tradition of Economic Sociology, *Journal of Institutional and Theoretical Economics*, Vol.145, No.3, pp. 508-524.

Polycentric Public Finance and the Organization of Governance

Richard E. Wagner
Harris Professor in Economics
Department of Economics, 3G4
George Mason University
Fairfax, VA 22030
USA
rwagner@gmu.edu
http://mason.gmu.edu/~rwagner

Abstract: For the most part, the theory of public finance treats government as a unitary being that intervenes into polyarchically organized market processes. While this treatment leads to simple and tractable models, it also misrepresents the tasks of organizing public governance. The situation for governance is not one where a government governs people, but is one where people govern themselves. It is one where people participate in the governance of their own activities, and not one where "the state" governs people. Recognition of this distinction leads to a polycentric formulation of governance, where various governmental organizations provide arenas where people participate in the governance of their relationships and activities.

Keywords: Polycentricity, governance, fiscal institutions, constitutional economics, public enterprise, property rights.

JEL Codes: H1, D7, L3.

For the most part, the theory of public finance treats government as a unitary being that intervenes into polyarchically organized market processes. While this treatment leads to simple and tractable models, it also misrepresents the tasks of organizing public governance. The situation for governance is not one where a government governs people, but is one where people govern themselves. It is one where people participate in the governance of their own activities, and not one where "the state" governs people. Recognition of this distinction leads to a polycentric formulation of governance, where various governmental organizations provide arenas where people participate in the governance of their relationships and activities.

My exposition proceeds in four stages. I start by considering some ontological and epistemological presuppositions that that are relevant to human governance. This involves knowledge, belief, and the requisites for good civic practice, and seeks to bring the cognitive faculties to bear on the mitigation of conflict within the public square. In so doing, there is a family resemblance to some of the formulations in the literature on Ordnungstheorie. The second section explains why the public economy should be conceptualized on polycentric and not hierarchical terms: as a nexus of relationships and not as some choosing agent. The third section explores some implications of this polycentric vision of the public economy for the organization of governance within the public square. The fourth section continues in the same vein by treating governance as a process of civic association, in which federalism and not democracy is the primary principle of governance, with democracy subordinated to a procedural status within a federalist framework of civic association.

Some Architectonics for Good Civic Governance

In *Federalist* No. 1, Alexander Hamilton asked "whether societies of men are really capable or not of establishing good government from reflection and choice, or whether they are forever destined to depend for their political constitutions on accident and force." One possibility is that good governance belongs in the realm of the natural, as with such activities as breathing and chewing. The alternative is that good governance is a talent or capacity, which can be learned or forgotten and performed better or worse, as illustrated by such activities as writing poetry or roller-skating. If good governance is a talent or capacity, moreover, it is one that must be exercised in coordinated fashion among a collection of interacting people. Such coordinated interaction is a province of the institutional framework that governs those interactions.

As much as we may speak of things virtual these days, we still all have corporeal existence. We take up space and rub up against one another, sometimes to wonderful effect and other times with nasty brutality. A central concern of fiscal sociology is how to expand the domain of the wonderful while shrinking that of the brutal and nasty. This task is not, however, one of simple choice, but is one of complex patterns of interactions amongst multiple choosers, and with those individual choosers differing in what they know or think they know.

The challenge of achieving good governance is a form of societal agriculture. Mother Nature provides us with opportunities and resources, but also with perils and traps. We supply mutual gain to one another through some forms of social interaction, while we prey upon each other through other forms of interaction.

The challenge of societal agriculture, moreover, is far knottier and tangled than the problem of regular agriculture, and for two reasons. One is that regular agriculture is a relatively simple matter of individual choice, but societal agricultural is interactive. The other involves a fundamental distinction between the natural and the humane sciences. People might differ over whether squash bugs should be fought with pesticides or by some sort of green-friendly approach, and those differences might even become sufficiently intense as to spill into the public square. Nevertheless, the natural world operates independently of what we think about its operation. Squash bugs will act like squash bugs, regardless of whether someone fights them with chemical sprays or drops of vinegar. This is not so with the social world, for there the institutions we generate and the patterns of conduct we form can influence our activities and practices, which in turn can influence conventional norms about the governance of human relationships (Wagner [in this volume]).

The mental maps that we bring to bear on our activities can influence those activities. The challenge of securing good governance involves both the moral imagination and analytical reasoning about the performance characteristics of the institutional arrangements we create. Institutional arrangements can affect the content of practice, which in turn can affect the content of the moral imagination. To achieve good governance requires both knowledge and will on the one hand, and supporting and consistent institutional arrangements on the other hand.

It is consistent with this analytical orientation to imagine a society of people whose members believe that their individual and common flourishing is best promoted through the liberal arrangement of private property, freedom of contract, and the like. Governance occurs through the network of associations that people form as they act within the framework provided by those liberal arrangements. Such a simple framework can accommodate immense organizational complexity in the arrangements of governance, as Richard Epstein (1995) explains. Suppose that a parliamentary assembly, to articulate and deal with some problems of general interest and concern, is also part of that institutional framework.

Consider a small town with only three residents, all landowners: Prima, Secundo, and Terza. Prima's land contains a marshy area that birds like, and on which she would like to drain, fill, and build a swimming pool. Secundo and Terza, though, like hearing the birds sing and watching them fly by, and would like to see that land maintained as a bird sanctuary. This would be easy for them to accomplish within the legal framework of a market economy. But they would also have to pay for their bird sanctuary. In contrast to any of several possible market solutions, there are also many particular political solutions that would place much if not all of the cost on Prima. Such democratic solutions would seem to allow Secundo and Terza effectively to rob Prima, only it is called public policy and not robbery, as has been observed in the on-going debate over takings, as surveyed in Richard Epstein (1985). The injection of such takings into an otherwise market economy can set in motion a process of institutional drift.

Just as success in the regular agriculture of growing squash is constrained by such things as soil, climate, and bugs, so is success in the societal agriculture of liberal governance constrained by the constitutional system of governance that we adopt, as well as by our understanding about the working properties of institutional arrangements. Liberal governance may flourish under some constitutional frameworks while morphing into various forms of illiberal governance under other constitutional frameworks. This conflict between what is held desirable and what is promoted through institutionalized practice lies at the center of the emphasis on market-conformability that was central to the analysis of order policy that was articulated initially in Walter Eucken (1952), and which has been carried forward in such places as Helmut Liepold and Ingo Pies (2000), Wolfgang Kasper and Manfred Streit (1998), Corinna Rath (1998), Manfred Streit (1992), and Viktor Vanberg (1988).

The treatment of market conformability in that literature reflects a recognition that societies could contain incongruent institutions, with this incongruence creating internally generated sources of conflict and practice. This point has been noted as well by Maffeo Pantaleoni (1911) in his theory of parasitical political pricing, as elaborated in Richard Wagner (1997a). It is easy enough to think of an urban transit industry that contains many different participants. To start, suppose the consensual framework of a market economy governs the relationships among all participants. Accordingly, some people might drive their own cars each day, while other people might create taxi or limousine companies. Still others might establish bus service, others might try monorails, and yet others might try to establish a subway service. All of these enterprises might be operated privately by profit-seeking companies, but if so this would be an emergent feature of the process and not something dictated in advance. There might be some cooperative enterprises that participate in this industry, and there could even be some municipally owned operations.

With the prospect of municipal operation comes the Faustian bargain that Vincent Ostrom (1984) explains crisply. It is one thing for government agencies to participate within polycentric societal processes on the same terms as other participants. In this case, municipally sponsored transit enterprises would have to compete for customers on the same basis as all other enterprises. Governments, though, have the possibility of subsidizing enterprises that might otherwise fail in open competition with private transit enterprises. They can also impose disabilities on competitive enterprises through regulation, as discussed in Daniel Klein (1997). The competitive ability of a privately organized bus company might be degraded by requiring it to maintain routes and schedules that are not profitable. The competitive ability of a municipal transit company might be strengthened by restricting the numbers of parking spaces that can be created within buildings located downtown. There are an indefinitely large number of ways by which a government can use taxation and regulation to secure advantages for the enterprises it sponsors relative to other enterprises within a society.

The various formulations of Ordnungstheorie sought to develop a conceptual test to distinguish between government ordinances that were compatible with the basic ordering principles of a market economy and those that were not. A concern with governance in relation to the curbing or the promoting of conflict reflects a similar orientation, as do the examination of the working properties of so-called mixed economies in Stephen Littlechild (1978) and Sanford Ikeda (1997). The practice of self-governance requires a proper mental orientation among the participants. Subsequent practice may reinforce that orientation, but it might also weaken it.

The Polycentric Public Economy

Within the contemporary theory of public finance, government is almost universally construed as a unitary being that intervenes into society both to correct and to complete. One the one had, government is construed as that agent which corrects what the analyst regards as the failures of market processes to generate Pareto efficient allocations of resources. On the other hand, government is construed as completing the productive structure of hypothesized allocative efficiency by providing public goods that the analyst presumes would not be organized efficiently otherwise. This hierarchical and unitary vision of government and its public economy is clearly simple and elegant, as all hierarchical and unitary visions must be.

A polycentric vision necessarily is more complex and less elegant. It also removes government as a locus of ultimate knowledge and final authority within the analyst's model. With this removal, moreover, analytical closure or a point of invariance is removed as well. For instance, in the customary formulations of welfare economics and the theory of public finance, market participants are treated as writing the first draft of the manuscript of economic and social life, so to speak, with government then revising and correcting the manuscript so as to attain various necessary conditions for Pareto efficiency.

A polycentric approach to the public economy fits well, of course, with the Wicksellian approach, particularly Knut Wicksell's (1958, p. 82) observation that the theory of public finance "seems to have retained the assumptions of its infancy, in the seventeenth and eighteenth centuries, when absolute power ruled almost all Europe." A good deal of contemporary public finance has maintained the choice-theoretic orientation toward public finance, as if fiscal phenomena are still generated through the same processes that were in place in absolutist times. In democratic regimes, however, fiscal phenomena do not arise out of some ruler's optimizing choices. They arise through interaction among fiscal participants. What results is an interactive or catallactic approach to public finance, which leads often to quite different implications for public finance than does the choice-theoretic approach, as illustrated, for instance by James Buchanan (1967), as well as by Jürgen Backhaus (1992)(2002). Fiscal interaction, moreover, need not be voluntary and agreeable for everyone. Duress and force are as much phenomena of interaction as is agreement, and all are encompassed within a catallactic approach to public finance (Wagner 1997b).

The object of study in the catallactical orientation is not how government can intervene into the economy to promote some fiscal philosopher's objective function, but rather is how people participate through government to achieve their various ends. The state does not stand above the market economy and its participants. The same people who participate in the market economy participate in state governance as well. Fiscal phenomena are not the product of some ruler's maximizing choices, but rather emerge through interaction among people (Wagner 2002). This interaction might be beneficial for everyone or nearly everyone, or it might be beneficial for only a few, and costly for many others. The state is treated not as a person, but as a nexus of contractual and exploitive relationships in which everyone participates to varying degrees. The extent to which those relationships are contractual or exploitive depends on the constitutive structure of governance that is in place.

As a matter of general principle, political relationships are both contractual and exploitive. It is fine to say that taxes are the prices we pay for civilization. This doesn't mean, however, that the relationship between citizens and state is the same as the relationship between customers and the retail outlets they frequent. A customer can refuse to buy and, moreover, generally can return merchandise that turns out to be defective or otherwise unsatisfactory. There is no option to do this in politics. To say that civilization is being priced too highly and to withhold payment will only land the protester in prison. And there is certainly no point in asking for a refund by claiming that the state's offerings weren't as good as its advertisements claimed them to be.

To speak of a catallactical approach to public finance is not to claim that the phenomena of public finance arise through voluntary interaction among people. It is only to say that those phenomena arise through interaction among people, the very same people as who interact with one another within the market economy. Much of the phenomena of public finance surely arise through duress and not through genuine agreement. This aspect of duress was given particular stress in a good deal of the Italian scholarship on public finance, and which is surveyed in James Buchanan (1960), as well as in Richard Wagner (forthcoming b). A catallactical approach toward the organization of the public economy leads directly into a conceptualization of polycentric public finance. Within that conceptualization, there is open competition within the public square for the organization and operation of enterprises that provide services to clients and offer returns to sponsors, all mediated within an institutional framework of civic governance within the public square.

Public Administration and Polycentric Public Finance

A general treatment of a polycentric public economy leads to a recognition that many different enterprises are involved with the provision of services within the public square. As Vincent Ostrom (1962) explains, it is not the case that water is supplied either by market-based organizations or by governments. Rather, it is that myriad different enterprises participate in the provision of water, and these enterprises operate under a variety of organizational frameworks. It is a straightforward matter to conceptualize a municipal services industry, as this was articulated by Vincent Ostrom, Charles Tiebout, and Robert Warren (1961), and elaborated further in Vincent Ostrom (1973).

It is necessary to replace the standard hierarchical orientation toward government with one of polycentric and competitive organization and administration of enterprises within the public square. In theories of decentralization, it is common to speak of some assignment of tasks among jurisdictions. These formulations lead to neat mappings where different units of government provide different services, depending on the geographical range over which those services extend. A city police department might police city streets and issue parking tickets, but it would take a larger jurisdiction to track down arsonists.

Within an orientation that treats municipal services as being organized hierarchically through assignment, the key questions revolve around the exploitation of economies of scale and the internalization of externalities. With respect to economies of scale, the size of jurisdictions is taken to depend on cost conditions. If jurisdictions are so small as to be on the declining portion of some average cost function, consolidation into larger jurisdictions would be warranted. Similarly, if the choices made by one jurisdiction impose external costs or benefits on other jurisdictions, some type of intervention by higher levels of government could be warranted to internalize those externalities.

Neither of these types of concern is relevant to some definition of jurisdictional boundaries. So what if 20 towns of 10,000 residents each exist when the least cost manner of securing general police service requires that it is supplied for 100,000 residents? Even if we began with each jurisdiction providing its own police force, we would expect to find some jurisdictions dropping their police services and buying them from other jurisdictions. There is a clear distinction between the jurisdictional units through which demand are articulated and the jurisdictional units within which production is organized. In terms of the arithmetic described above, it is easy enough to envision two producers of police services, each of which offers services to nine of the other jurisdictions, a theme that is developed clearly in Robert Bish and Vincent Ostrom (1973).

To be sure, this simple arithmetic doesn't speak to the variety of possible story lines that this simple scenario contains. Among other things, it does not speak to the operation of the actual processes of governance by which some jurisdictions stop providing their own police services and buy them from some other jurisdiction instead. The simple arithmetic says that there is an opportunity for people to receive police services in less costly fashion through organizational restructuring. But there are other considerations that might also come into play. For instance, 20 police chiefs will be reduced to two. Even if salaries remain the same, social standing of those ex-chiefs might fall, which in turn might galvanize some resistance to such organizational rearrangement. Regardless of the outcome in particular settings, the material emerges out of a setting of polycentric public finance.

What holds for economies of scale holds for externalities as well. Several adjacent cities might be connected by a highway that carries much traffic among the cities. If each city sets traffic signals along the stretch of highway within its boundaries, overall traffic flow could be slowed through a resulting non-synchronization of traffic signals. This would be an illustration of an external diseconomy stemming from the signal timing choices by individual jurisdictions. The hierarchical solution to this problem is to invoke some higher level of government to take over the setting of traffic signals. An alternative resolution would be as simple as a conference call or an exchange of emails, as the postulated setting is one where there are clear advantages to all participants from securing a more effective coordination of traffic flows.

Once again, the simplicity of this alternative resolution doesn't speak to the variety of possible story lines that this scenario can hold. For instance, everyone might not be of the same mind in thinking that faster movement along the highway is invariably better. People who seek to move twenty miles down the road may think that faster travel is better than slower travel. In contrast, people who might use only a two or three mile stretch of the highway, stopping several times in the process to shop, may be more concerned with the ease of entering and exiting the highway. The interest of such people might be better served by an increased density of traffic signals that slow down the average rate of movement. Moreover, the actual operation of the polycentric processes by which signals are erected and their timing established will be polycentric and not unitary in its nature.

The standard formulations, in any case, are focused on the assignment of functions and the allocation of resources. One major problem with this approach is that resources cannot allocate themselves, nor can functions assign themselves. Only people can do these things, and how they do so is governed both by what they know and how the institutional arrangements within which they operate channel and constrain their actions. In the allocationist-centered approach to public economics, government is construed as an instrument of intervention to correct what would otherwise be misallocations. In an alternative, institutionalist-centered approach, government is simply a subset of the myriad arenas for human interaction within the public square.

The effort to treat governments as arenas of human governance within a polycentric system of liberal governance recalls the cameralist approach to civic governance, with the cameralists being perhaps the first theorists of public administration, though they were also practitioners. To be sure, the cameralists arose within the absolutist regimes of central Europe in the 15th century, and they operated suitably with models of hierarchy. Wicksell did not voice his lament in their direction, however, but directed it at his contemporaries. While the cameralists operated within the context of absolutist regimes, their central orientation, which is elaborated variously in Jürgen Backhaus and Richard Wagner (1987), Erhard Dittrich (1974), Albion Small (1909), and KeithTribe (1984), was one where those princes operated as participants in similar fashion to all other participants within the on-going processes and institutions of society. It is a short step to adapt this orientation to an enterprise-based public finance within a polycentric public economy where numerous enterprises participate within the public square.

Compound Republics, Civic Association, and Federal Liberty

Federalism is often used as a synonym for decentralization and at the same time is often thought to be a way of achieving decentralization democratically. Most work on federalism treats it as a matter of decentralization, with the problem of federalism being one of solving a type of assignment problem whereby public activities are assigned to those jurisdictions that can deal with them most effectively (Oates (1972)(1999)). To solve an assignment problem is to invoke notions of hierarchical ordering. There will be some process or person that assigns neighborhood parks to cities, regional parks to special districts that encompass several counties, and so on.

This is a hierarchical and not polyarchical vision of federalism, but it is problematic to equate federalism with decentralization. Federalism seems widely to be construed as a pro-liberty form of governance. At first glance, however, this is a puzzling construction. At the purely formal level, compare societies operating with unitary polities with those operating with federal polities. With unitary polities, people face but a single government that taxes them and regulates them. In contrast, with federal polities, people face at least two such governments, and perhaps more, each of which is able independently to tax and to regulate. On the surface, federalism would seem to be a move away from liberal arrangements of governance, through its ability to multiply the number of governments that can act directly upon individual citizens. If the *sine qua non* of government is coercion as part of the Faustian bargain, how is it that the multiplication of the sources of coercion is a good thing, when appraised against the downside of the Faustian bargain?

The answer must reside in the ability of federalism to limit the despotic possibilities of democracy, possibilities that were illustrated by the earlier discussion of Prima, Secundo, and Terza. For this limit to be realized, it is necessary to treat federalism as prior to or more foundational than democracy. It is not that a democratic government decentralizes and thereby becomes federal. To be sure, this is the presumption of most contemporary thought on the relationship between federalism and democracy, with federalism being a subset of democracy. At base, federalism is a principle of association in a context where people participate in many forms and types of association, a theme developed with particular cogency in Vincent Ostrom. The arrangements of governance that a free people might develop can plausibly be thought of as involving both fragmentation and overlapping among jurisdictions, and with the various boundaries being an emergent feature of openly competitive processes. To the extent that civic association serves relatively accurately for a synonym for free association, expansion and contraction in the domains of various jurisdictions will reflect a general consensus among the participants. Such a model of federal governance could thus be regarded as an extension of the Wicksellian orientation, only allowing for fragmented and overlapping jurisdictions.

Vincent Ostrom (1987) argues that the original American constitutional system, both as formally established and informally practiced, reflected a polycentric approach to governance. To be sure, this polycentric orientation was pursued incompletely, and in the ensuing years has been corrupted in many ways. For instance, Ostrom (1991) argues that a good concept of federalism can make it possible to escape the trap offered by concepts of sovereignty. At least this is some idealized notion of federalism; the actual practice of federalism may fall short of that ideal.

The American system of federalism, for instance, contains a basic constitutional asymmetry that threatens to elevate the democratic over the federal principle, as William Niskanen (1978) notes with particular clarity. If people are able to use a national forum to challenge state action, so should they be able to use a state forum to challenge the constitutionality of national action. Indeed, this was pretty much how it worked in the early years of the American republic, for the republic was founded on a principle of subsidiarity even if it was not articulated in this manner. The 9th and 10th amendments are clear expressions of subsidiarity. So was the doctrine of interposition, which was alive through the first half-century or so of the American national existence. The 11th Amendment, moreover, arose largely through interposition, in response to the resistance of a number of states to edicts promulgated by judicial offices of the national government.

Interposition was a state's assertion of its sovereignty against invasion by the national government. With assertions of state sovereignty negating assertions of federal sovereignty, the very notion of sovereignty as a locus of final domination evaporates. Something like nullification would seem to be required by elementary principles of symmetry. If people are to use a federal forum to challenge state actions, they must be able to use a state forum to challenge federal actions. Short of some such organizational arrangement as this, offices and agencies of the federal government are in danger of becoming judges in their own cause. To be sure, the general direction of movement for more than a century has been one of moving away from federalist governance toward democratic governance.

In Closing

Good government is not a destination or final resting point. It is a continual, never ending process. There are two basic though complementary tasks involved in securing good government. One involves the moral imagination, and concerns the principles by which we are to live together. History and our imaginations can present us with many options in this respect. This essay starts from an affirmation of the values of a liberal and open society, where human relationships are governed by mutual respect among equals.

Ideals are at best realized only imperfectly in practice, of course, and the Faustian character of the bargain that government represents assures us that this will be the case. The second task requires us to undertake the cognitive work of relating our institutional arrangements to the types of practice that those arrangements promote or block. This will lead in several directions, and can generate a number of general associations. For instance, it is inconsistent to support an open society and simple democracy, because democratic practice will undermine the values of the open society. It is, however, possible to maintain democratic polities in a federal form of governance, provided that that form of governance operates according to polyarchical and not hierarchical principles. Most fundamentally, governance in a liberal order must be construed in a bottom-up type of manner. With respect to valuation, democracy is a derivative value, with governance grounded in relationships of mutual respect among equals being primary, and with fragmented and overlapping civic association emerging out of the extension of those relationships. With respect to cognition, the actual institutional arrangements of governance must be conformable with those principles of value, otherwise contrary practice can set in motion a process of regime drift, a beautiful example of which was portrayed brilliantly in Charles Warren's (1932) masterful little book *Congress as Santa Claus*.

References

Backhaus, J. G. (1992), The State as a Club: A Perspective for Public Finance in a Prosperous Democracy, *Journal of Public Finance and Public Choice* 10: 3-16.

Backhaus, J. G. (2002), Old or New Public Finance? A Plea for the Tried and True, *Public Finance Review* 30: 612-45.

Backhaus, J. G. and R. E. Wagner (1987), The Cameralists: A Public Choice Perspective, *Public Choice* 53: 3-20.

Bish, R. L. and V. Ostrom (1973), *Understanding Urban Government: Metropolitan Reform Reconsidered,* Washington: American Enterprise Institute.

Buchanan, J. M. (1960), The Italian Tradition in Fiscal Theory. 24-74 of his *Fiscal Theory and Political Economy,* Chapel Hill: University of North Carolina Press.

Buchanan, J. M. (1967), *Public Finance in Democratic Process,* Chapel Hill: University of North Carolina Press.

Dittrich, E. (1974), *Die deutschen und österreichischen Kameralisten,* Darmstadt: Wissenschaftliche Buchgessellschaft.

Epstein, R. A. (1985), *Taking: Private Property and the Power of Eminent Domain,* Cambridge: Harvard University Press.

Epstein, R. A. (1995), *Simple Rules for a Complex World,* Cambridge: Harvard University Press.

Eucken, W. (1952), *Grundsätze der Wirtschaftpolitik,* 6th ed. with "Forward" by Ernst-Joachim Mestmäker. Tübingen: J. C. B. Mohr, 1990.

Ikeda, S. (1997), *Dynamics of the Mixed Economy,* London: Routledge.

Klein, D. B. (1997), *Curb Rights: A Foundation for Free Enterprise in Urban Transit,* Washington: American Enterprise Institute.

Leipold, H. and Pies, I., eds. (2000), *Ordnungstheorie und Ordnungspolitik: Konzeptionen und Entwicklungsperspektiven,* Stuttgart: Lucius & Lucius.

Littlechild, S. C. (1978), *The Fallacy of the Mixed Economy,* London: Institute of Economic Affairs.

Niskanen, W. A. (1978). The Prospect for Liberal Democracy, in Buchanan, J. M. and R. E. Wagner, eds. *Fiscal Responsibility in Constitutional Democracy,* 168-74, Leiden: Martinus Nijhoff.

Oates, W. E. (1972), *Fiscal Federalism,* New York: Harcourt Brace Jovanovich.

Oates, W. E. (1999), An Essay on Fiscal Federalism, *Journal of Economic Literature* 37: 1120-49.

Ostrom, V. (1962), The Water Economy and Its Organization, *Natural Resources Journal* 2: 55-73.

Ostrom, V. (1973), *The Intellectual Crisis in American Public Administration,* University AL: University of Alabama Press.

Ostrom, V. (1984), Why Governments Fail: An Inquiry into the Use of Instruments of Evil to do Good, in Buchanan, J. M. and R. D. Tollison, eds. *Theory of Public Choice II,* Ann Arbor: University of Michigan Press, 422-35.

Ostrom, V. (1987), *The Political Theory of a Compound Republic,* 2nd ed. Lincoln: University of Nebraska Press.

Ostrom, V. (1991), *The Meaning of American Federalism,* San Francisco: ICS Press.

Ostrom, V. (1997), *The Meaning of Democracy and the Vulnerability of Societies: A Response to Tocqueville's Challenge,* Ann Arbor: University of Michigan Press.

Ostrom, V., Tiebout, C. M. and R. Warren (1961), The Organization of Government in Metropolitan Areas: A Theoretical Inquiry, *American Political Science Review* 55: 831-42.

Pantaleoni, M. (1911), Considerazioni sulle proprieta di un sistema di prezzi politici. *Giornale degli Economisti* 42: 9-29, 114-33.

Rath, C. (1998), *Staat, Gesellschaft, und Wirtschaft bei Max Weber und bei Walter Eucken,* Egelsbach: Hänsel-Hohenhausen.

Small, A. (1909), *The Cameralists: The Pioneers of German Social Polity,* New York: Burt Franklin.

Streit, M. (1992), Economic Order, Private Law, and Public Policy: The Freiberg School of Law and Economics in Perspective, *Journal of Institutional and Theoretical Economics* 148: 675-704.

Tribe, K. (1984), Cameralism and the Science of Government, *Journal of Modern History* 56: 263-84.

Vanberg, V. (1988), Ordnungstheorie as Constitutional Economics: The German Conception of a 'Social Market Economy', *ORDO* 39: 17-31.

Wagner, R. E. (1997a), Parasitical Political Pricing, Economic Calculation, and the Size of Government: Variations on a Theme by Maffeo Pantaleoni, *Journal of Public Finance and Public Choice* 15: 135-46.

Wagner, Richard E. (1997b), Choice, Exchange, and Public Finance, *American Economic Review*, Proceedings 87: 160-63.

Wagner, R. E. (2002), Some Institutional Problematics of Excess Burden Analytics, *Public FinanceReview* 30: 531-45.

Wagner, R. E. (2003), Public Choice and the Diffusion of Classic Italian Public Finance, *Il Pensiero Economico*, 11: 271-82.

Warren, C. (1932), *Congress as Santa Claus: National Donations and the General Welfare Clause of the Constitution*. Charlottesville, VA: Michie.

Wicksell, K. (1896), A New Principle of Just Taxation, In *Classics in the Theory of Public Finance*, Musgrave, R. A. and A. T. Peacock, eds. London:Macmillan, (1958), 72-118.

Fiscal and Monetary Illusion and the Maastricht Rules

Francesco Forte
Professor of Economics
Department of Economics
School of Economics
Università di Roma, La Sapienza
forte@dep.eco.uniroma1.it

Abstract: Fiscal and monetary illusion, as theorized by Amilcare Puviani and subsequent scholars consist in the wrong perception of some phenomenon, by given subjects either as a consequence of an intentional action or because of some endogenous inability of having the correct perception. In Paretian analytics, fiscal and monetary illusions are a sub class of the non logical actions as contrasted to the logical ones. Both in areas of fiscal illusion, of monetary illusion and of monetary-fiscal illusion the focus generally is on the wrong perceptions of economic phenomena by the *citizens* and related distortion of their judgements. The *politicians and bureaucrats* whether intentionally or unintentionally, on the other side of the causal nexus. However there may be other kinds of illusions originating unintentionally or intentionally by the politicians and bureaucrats with the effect of causing a wrong perception among the public authorities themselves and originating "non logical actions". In this paper I deal with the monetary-fiscal illusion created by the authorities of the EU and of the member countries about the impact of the Maastricht rule of a maximum 3 per cent deficit on GDP, normally considered from the point of view of the nominal deficit. Never has been considered the real deficit, which differs from the real one, when the depreciation of public debt, due to the increase in the prices level of the considered fiscal year, is taken into account and one can see the creditors of public capital loss, i.e. their Pigou-Patinkin negative effect. I work out, for the period 1997-2003 the real deficit or surplus of the General Government budgets of the 15 EU states, of the European Union and of the 12 Euro area states and compare them with the nominal deficits or surplus. One can see that, after the correction ice, generally several countries, in several years, were in surplus and no country as ever violated the 3 per cent deficit threshold. And in 2000, among the big countries, Germany, now, shows a sizable surplus of the General Government's *real* budget of 1,9 per cent of GDP, Spain exhibits a *real* surplus of 1,3 per cent of GDP , Italy of 2,2 per cent of GDP, UK has a *real* surplus of 4,2 of GDP. But also in 2001, after the correction for the Pigou-Patinkin negative effect, the general impression, as for the EU and Emu countries, is not that of a "Keynesian democracies in deficit". The aggregate of the General Governments' budgets of the 15 EU member states, in the two years 2000 and 2001 has a *real* surplus of 2 per cent and then of about 0,5 per cent of GDP while in 2002 has a small real deficit of 0,57.If the budgetary figures are divested of the subjective monetary-fiscal illusion, on balance, in the considered period the EU member countries did not adopt an expansive, bur rather a restrictive fiscal particularly considering the *objectively* counter cyclical fiscal policy of 2002. The monetary-fiscal illusion works to make more restrictive, the Maastricht deficit rule, for countries with an higher Debt/GDP ratio and a greater propensity to inflation like Italy or Greece or higher propensity to inflation as Spain and Portugal.One can say that, under the illusion thus created , the EU authorities and those of the member states would works more effectively to the end of the Amsterdam pact inventors, at the expense of the pursuance of others, as economic growth and employment. The two ends seem to *enter in sharp conflict.* Thus politicians are led to suggest changes in the deficit rule, as the exclusion of some expenditures from the 3 per cent threshold which they would not suggest if an objective view of the phenomena under discussion was adopted.

Keywords: Fiscal illusion, Maastricht, deficit, non logic actions, Pigou effect.

JEL codes: E24, E27, E62, H27.

I.

The Nature and Relevance of Fiscal and Monetary Illusions

1. Fiscal illusion and monetary illusion have a well recognized place both in public economics and in fiscal sociology. They consist in the wrong perception of some phenomenon, by given subjects either as a consequence of an intentional action by somebody to let them have that illusion or because of some endogenous inability of having the correct perception or for both reasons. In Paretian analytics, fiscal and monetary illusions are a sub class of the non logical actions as contrasted to the logical ones. [1] And the distinctive tract of the non logical actions *in general* as compared with the logical ones it is that that in the last the subjective view, coincides by and large, with the objective view, while in the first the subjective view differs from the objective one It should be noted that, according to Pareto, the distinction between the two classes of action may be made clearly only at the abstract level. In real life as sharp distinction it is often impossible. For instance, he observes, there are individual who, in the stock exchange, more easily speculate upward than downward and other individuals who have the opposite (non logical) attitude and , within this general bias, act logically[2]. In his work Pareto generally did not labelled as fiscal and

[1] See Pareto V.(1906),*Manuale di Economia politica, con una introduzione alla scienza sociale*, Milano, Società Editrice libraria, Chapter II, "Introduzione alla scienza sociale",§ 3 ss.
[2] See *Manuale*, Chapter II, §3.

monetary illusions his examples of "non logical actions" that could deserve this label[3]. Thus Pareto writes that the actions of a taxpayer' "who does not know the many effects of taxes, or more generally and better, of the many financial transactions" have "the nature of non logical actions, of which the theory is much more difficult" than the standard economic theory. But it is clear, that most of these non logical actions, because done under a false perception of the reality, would fit the list to which the label of "fiscal illusion" can be applied, after the seminal works of Amilcare Puviani's[4]. And, any way, as we shall see, later[5], in a short writing, Pareto explicitly labelled as "fiscal illusion" the deception of the owners of public debt, arising by creeping inflation and manipulations as debt conversions.

As for fiscal illusions, the most important authors which, after Puviani, have explicitly dealt with it, from the theoretical economic point of view or from the economic-sociological perspective - as Fasiani (1941,1951), Schmolders (1960), Buchanan (1964), Wagner (1976), Cavaco Silva (1977) Pommerhene and Schneider (1978), Peacock and Rizzo (1978)[6] and Peacock (1992) and Giardina (1992)[7] - generally consider the *deliberate* actions by political and bureaucratic actors, to deceive taxpayers, perceivers of public expenditure benefits and, most of all, the ordinary citizens, as for the effects of governments deficits and debts. Even if the results are, some time, controversial, the bulk of the literature pointing to the relevance of these fiscal illusions has achieved a solid reputation.

2. More controversial is the case as for the monetary illusion, arising from the changes in value of currencies, in terms of purchasing power or of some other yard stick as other currencies or precious metals, in the market transactions in the market and in business accounting. Here one should distinguish the illusion caused in the public by sovereign powers through a deliberate devaluation of the domestic currency from the illusion that may be caused by an ongoing inflation. It is well known, since the ancient times, that currencies may be altered. And indeed they have been often altered by the Sovereign powers to capture a benefit deriving from the deception of creditors and holders of these currencies. However the benefit thus obtained by the Sovereign powers needs not derive from the intent of deceiving the owners of that currency about its real value; may simply arise from a violation of their "bona fide" expectations. The illusion then,

---

[3] See the Letter to G. Sensini, quoted by J. Buchanan, in *The Effects of Institutions on Fiscal Choices*, Ch.10, "The Fiscal Illusion", p.126, footnote 2, Vol. 4 of the *Collected works* of J. Buchanan.

[4] Puviani A. (1903), *Teoria dell'illusione finanziaria,* Palermo. A good edition by F. VOLPI (1973), Milan, Isedi it is currently available.

[5] 1917 in the last of three letters addressed to B. Griziotti.

[6] And the "reply" of H. Shibata and Y. Kimura (1978) in the same Journal, same issue.

[7] A. T. Peacock, (1992), "Fourth Lecture", 3. "The case of a Balanced Budget Constraint, and the discussion by E. GIARDINA in his "Commentary 4", p. 160-163.

in Paretian terms, is not a wrong perception of the value of the currency but a wrong trust of the public authorities. Pareto maintains that Governments *deliberately* cause currency depreciations (eventually causing inflations) to spoil creditors of the state[8]. One may object that more than often Governments and monetary authorities are *forced* to do so by factors overriding their will of respecting their commitments. Still, one may observe that this is a typical case of monetary illusion arising from the naive belief that fiscal and monetary Sovereign powers are really able to pursue their declared commitments: a belief that, in spite of the contrary evidence, has a multi secular persistence[9].

In the case of *an ongoing* inflationary process, originated from a combination of factors, rather that a deliberate act of a given authority, which the economic operators expect to persist, monetary illusions is much more doubtful phenomenon, unless under wined with other factors of difficult perception. Thus it seems quite doubtful the old theorem of the asymmetric behaviour of the workers and Unions in relation to changes in real wages due changes of prices under invariant nominal wages and to changes in real wages due to changes in nominal wages with invariant prices. It may be true that workers and Unions would strongly oppose a wage cut even if real wages would be invariant because prices went down but does not appear true that they do not react with the same strength when real wages are reduced by a price increase. Nor it is true that savers would buy bonds overlooking the ongoing inflation rate and the likelihood of its persistence in future times. On these phenomena, perhaps, one may recall the old sentence that somebody may deceive one person several times or several person one time but not several persons several times.

3. The above seen kinds of fiscal and the monetary illusions, caused by deliberate actions by politicians and bureaucrats, are *separate* phenomena caused by respectively by the confusion between *nominal* and *real* value of t money and with the *understatemen*t or *overstatement* of the (real) effects of fiscal actions on individuals. But the most intriguing illusions, i.e. those more difficult to detect

---

[8] See W: Pareto (1917), "Sugli effetti dei prestiti e delle imposte", letter to B. Griziotti, reprinted B. Griziotti (1956). Vol. II, pp. 263-67 and W. PARETO (1920) "Imposte, debito, carta moneta". Pareto, as fiscal illusions, mentions the conversions short term public debt certificates in long term bonds at a reduced interest rate in (not so long lasting) periods of low inflation. See Giardina (1992) quoted above p. 163.

[9] A characteristic recent case of this type of monetary illusion deriving from the wrong belief that public monetary and fiscal authorities are capable of respecting their commitments has been that of the pesos of Argentina whose value was warranted by a "currency board system" in which the issuance of an unit of pesos had to be backed by the ownership of a dollar by the Central Bank. It is still a mystery why the international community was under the illusion that the currency board system could not collapse (as actually did) through an huge gap in the balance of payment due to the unrealistic rate of exchange of the pesos accompanied by bankrupts caused by the automatic credit restraint relating to the dollars outflow.

and to get rid of, are those characterized by a combination of fiscal and monetary factors. An important fiscal illusion of monetary nature it is the "fiscal drag" due to the automatic increase of real tax rates and to the loss of real value of the lump sum deductions, in progressive income and property taxes, due to the price increase. When the annual rate of price rise is low the fiscal drag may go unnoticed, at least for a number of years. And politicians who announce and carry on a reduction in the rates of the progressive income tax are often acclaimed as if they did reduce them *really* rather than simply adjusting to the change in the real value of money. Less known is another kind of fiscal-monetary illusion: i.e. that of taxing the revenues of interests on capital at their face value, without deduction of the share that balances the loss of value of the credit. With an inflation of 3 per cent an a nominal revenue from capital of 5 per cent, the net revenue is 2 ; and a rate of 44 per cent, as the Italian top rate of the personal income tax, would take 2,2, i.e. 0,2 more than the effective revenue!. No wonder that in several countries, as in the case of Italy, revenues from capital are subject to a final withholding tax at a flat rate ranging between 12 and 20 per cent. Finally, a fiscal monetary illusion of crucial importance arises in profits taxation, due to the fact that depreciations allowances are based on the book value of the assets, which in most cases is the historical value. Here again one may find the *true* economic reason why so often special deduction are "granted" to "stimulate" business investments: indeed, in many cases, they are not "tax expenditures", but merely a remedy for the over taxation of income deriving from investments.

As the above review shows, both in areas of fiscal illusion, of monetary illusion and of fiscal-monetary illusion the focus generally, is on the wrong perceptions of economic phenomena by the *citizens*, in market operations. The illusion distorts their choices in the market place and as electors. *Politicians and bureaucrats i.e. the public authorities* are on the other side of the causal nexus, acting as intentional or unintentional deceivers.

4. However there may be other kinds of illusions -originating unintentionally or intentionally by the politicians and bureaucrats – that cause not only a wrong perception among the citizens and possibly distort their choices, but also, *and primarily*, a wrong perception among the public authorities themselves. And often heavily distort their choices.

A macro case, that I have presented in Forte (1997), it is how national product and per capita product or income are evaluated, by official statistics of developed and under developed countries. Rather than considering aggregate and per capita national product at factor cost, the figure of GDP, aggregate and per capita have been considered: which include, depreciations and indirect taxes, hardly endowed of intrinsic economic utility to the individuals. A curious result of this illusory way of inflating the value of product of the countries and of their individuals it is that an increase of taxes classified as indirect taxation, accompanied by an equivalent reduction of taxes which are not classified as indirect, as, for instance profit taxes, increase the aggregate and per capita product of the nation, via the increase of its GDP. One might object that generally the introduction of indirect taxes increases prices, and that therefore even if they inflate nominal GDP, real GDP adjusted for inflation remains invariant. However it is not always true that the substitution of taxes classified as indirect to taxes to profit taxes cause an increase of prices. For instance in Italy, in 1997, a new regional value added tax on business and independent workers, has been introduced to replace national health social security contributions and taxes on income of these taxpayers. That new value tax in spite of its nature of value added tax of income type, has been classified as indirect tax. And, there fore, has been added to the product at factor costs, while the social security contributions and business taxes replaced where not added to it. But there was no evidence of a differential shifting of the new tax, nor a reason to expect that it would take place. The result has been an artificial increase of GDP. At any rate, countries with higher depreciations and higher indirect taxes have, ceteris paribus, a greater GDP, than countries with the same income at factor cost; and there is no reason to assume that this artificial effect is reflected in the rate of exchange of their currencies: if not for other reasons, because domestic indirect taxes are rebated on exports and equivalent taxes are applied on imports.

This singular methodology of inflating national and per capita product, by which indirect taxes and depreciations enter in the measure of national product, creates a underassessment of the effective tax burden, of the public debt burden and of the size of the public sector in the aggregate economic process. It seems that this illusion not only deceives the citizens, but also political and bureaucratic actors distorting their understanding of the effects of their choices and their behaviours.

One may argue that relying on GDP rather than to less misgiving measures of the domestic product or income may not create illusions, as for monetary policy, in relation to the quantity of money to be issued: but this may not be the case when new indirect taxes do not add to prices and there fore to the volume of market transactions. Furthermore a reference to the domestic product at market prices really sold on the market, i. e. net of value added produced by the public administration would appear more proper[10].

To my knowledge the area of illusions exogenously or endogenously created, affecting politicians and influencing their choices in different ways, has not been systematically explored, except in a seminal sociological work, about ninety

[10] See on this issue F. Forte and J. M. Buchanan (1961).

years ago, by Wilfred Pareto, in his already mentioned "monstrous"[11] *Treaties of general Sociology*, where they are extensively dealt under the label of "non logical actions".

II.

The Monetary-fiscal Illusion built in the Maastricht Deficit Rule

1. In this paper I deal with a big instance of monetary-fiscal illusion exogenously created by the monetary and fiscal authorities of the EU and of their member countries and affecting their very perception of the fiscal and monetary phenomena on which they must tune their fiscal and monetary policies: i.e. the rules on deficit set for the countries of the European Monetary Union, by the Maastricht Treaty and by the Stability and Growth Pact of Amsterdam. As it will appear, in this case, monetary and fiscal illusion are interlaced and cause a great disturbance in the discussion and decision making about the proper choices between the various European fiscal and monetary authorities.

As it is well known, according to these rules EU states member of the European Monetary Union - and particularly those belonging to the Euro area (Ea), constrained by the Amsterdam pact- as for the General Government Budget, should never trespass the threshold of a deficit of 3 per cent of GDP. And in period of depression Government would be allowed to do this only by drawing on a budgetary surplus accumulated in previous years. On the other hand, the States member of EU should never trespass the threshold of 60 per cent. The rationale of these rules has been under fire, with several arguments relating to the logic of fiscal policy in periods of depression. To them one might add arguments about the need of countervailing by a more permissive fiscal policy an excessive increase of the rate of exchange of the Euro with other currencies, due to a divergence between the rate of interest set by the European Central Bank and the rate set by the Federal Reserve of U.S. for the dollar. As for the budgetary deficits of specific countries as France and Germany that rose above the 3 per cent fatidic threshold, has been objected that they are only temporary, because structural reforms of the welfare state have been introduced, with beneficial effects in the long run on the General Government budget. And in a sense, the deficits exceeding the 3 per cent rule represent the price to buy a social consensus for these heavy structural changes. But, discussing these topics, in principle or referring to specific European countries, whether arguing pro or cons the relaxation of this Maastricht-Amsterdam rule, to my knowledge, every body has dealt with the

[11] The definition belongs to Raymond Aron, quoted by N. Bobbio in his "Introduction" to the 1964 Italian edition of the work which extends in two volumes of nearly two thousand pages. "Non logical actions" together with the "residuals", which are permanent non logical beliefs, occupy about 800 hundred pages of the first volume.

strictures of the Maastricht-Amsterdam deficit rule, from the point of view of the nominal deficits, never has been considered the real deficit. And real deficit may be (much) lower than the real one, when the depreciation of public debt, due to the increase in the prices level of the considered fiscal year, is taken in to account.

2. Let us now work out how the monetary-fiscal illusion operates in concealing the real deficit or surplus of General Governments of the EU countries, under the Maastricht rule according to which deficits of General Governments should never trespass the threshold of 3 per cent of GDP and under the stability pact of Amsterdam by which the long run objective of General Governments of the 12 Euro area member countries should be the balanced budget, *supposedly as an end of neutral fiscal policy.*

Let us now calculate, for the seven fiscal years 1997-2003, the real deficit or surplus of the General Government budgets of the 15 EU states and of the 12 Euro area states, by multiplying the inflation rate of each state and area as given by the Official European Index Harmonized Index of Consumer Prices (HICP) given in Table 1 for its debt/GDP ratio given in Table2, thus obtaining the correctors presented Table 3.

They shall be subtracted to the nominal deficit or surplus/GDP ratios of each state and area, given in Table 4, in order to get their real deficit or surplus/GDP ratios presented in Table 5 and compare them with the nominal deficits or surplus ratios.

The real deficit or surplus/GDP ratios, in Paretian methodology, give the *objective view* of the balance of the budgets of General Governments of the 15 EU countries, and therefore show their *objective* macro economic effects as contrasted with the *subjective* view, arising by considering the nominal deficits, considered by the Maastricht-Amsterdam rules.

The loss of value of the outstanding debt stock of the General Government, for each country, at the end of each of the seven years, given by Table 3, is a capital gain of its General Government which, logically, in a correct accounting methodology, has to be added algebraically to the balance of its budget in the same year, as we did. And since , according to the Maastricht-Amsterdam fiscal rules, one does not considers the absolute values of public debts and budgetary balances, but their ratio to GDP, also the correction for the capital gains in the outstanding debt stock has to be done by ratios to GDP.

3. The results of Table 5 are rather startling.

Table 1: Inflation Rate (HCPI)

COUNTRY	1997	1998	1999	2000	2001	2002	2003
Belgium	1.53	0.94	1.18	2.85	2.64	1.77	1.58
Germany	1.54	0.62	0.66	2.16	2.55	1.75	1.50
Greece	5.87	5.14	2.54	3.51	4.75	4.92	4.38
Spain	1.94	1.86	2.40	3.82	3.21	4.13	3.63
France	1.31	0.69	0.59	1.91	1.90	2,09	1.96
Ireland	1.27	2.22	2.60	5.70	4.53	5.58	5.33
Italy	1.98	2.09	1.78	2.85	2.63	2.90	2.78
Luxemburg	1.40	1.00	1.05	3.96	2.61	2.35	1.93
Netherland	1.89	1.83	2.14	2.51	5.61	4.62	3.30
Austria	1.18	0.85	0.53	2.04	2.44	1.83	1.80
Portugal	1.95	2.32	2.33	3.07	4.97	4.07	3.46
Finland	1.23	1.38	1.36	3.10	2.88	1.89	2.26
Denmark	1.97	1.37	2.17	2.94	2.50	2.26	2.54
Sweden	1.86	1.03	0.57	1.37	2.84	2.00	2.03
United Kingdom	2.8	2.7	2.3	2.1	2.1	2.2	2.8
Euro Area	1.68	1.21	1.19	2.51	2.77	2.73	2.53
EuropeanUnion	1.9	1.5	1.4	2.2	2.4	2.3	2.2

Source OECD and EUROSTAT

Table 2: DEBT/GDP

COUNTRY	1997	1998	1999	2000	2001	2002	2003
Belgium	124.7	119.6	114.8	109.1	108.1	106.8	100.5
Germany	61.0	60.9	61.2	60.2	59.4	60.8	64.2
Greece	108.2	106.8	106.2	106.2	106.9	104.7	103.0
Spain	66.6	64.6	63.1	61.2	57.5	54.6	50.8
France	59.3	59.5	58.5	57.2	56.9	58.6	63.
Ireland	65.1	54.9	48.6	38.4	36.1	32.3	34
Italy	1202	116.3	115.5	111.2	110.6	108.0	106.2
Luxemburg	6.0	6.3	6.0	5.5	5.5	5.7	4.9
Netherland	69.9	66.8	63.1	55.9	52.9	52.6	54.8
Austria	64.7	63.7	67.5	67.0	67.1	66.6	65.0
Portugal	58.9	55.0	54.3	53.3	55.6	58.1	59.4
Finland	54.1	48.6	47.0	44.6	43.9	42.6	45.3
Denmark	61.2	56.2	53.0	50.1	47.8	47.2	45.0
Sweden	73.1	68.0	62.8	52.8	54.4	52.6	51.9
United Kingdom	50.8	47.7	54.0	42.1	38.9	38.5	39.9
Euro Area	75.3	73.7	72.8	70.4	69.4	69.2	70.4
EuropeanUnion	71.0	68.8	67.8	64.0	63.2	62.5	64.0

Table 3: Nominal Deficit' Corrector (Inflation Rate DEBT/PIL=Depreciation of DEBT/PI)

COUNTRY	1997	1998	1999	2000	2001	2002	2003
Belgium	1.91%	1.12%	1.35%	3.11%	2.85%	1.89%	1.59%
Germany	0.94%	0.38%	0.40%	1.30%	1.51%	1.06%	0.96%
Greece	6.35%	5.49%	2.70%	3.73%	5.08%	5.15%	4.51%
Spain	1.29%	1.20%	1.51%	2.34%	1.85%	2.26%	1.84%
France	0.78%	0.41%	0.35%	1.09%	1.08%	1.22%	1.23%
Ireland	0.83%	1.22%	1.26%	2.19%	1.64%	1.80%	1.81%
Italy	2.38%	2.43%	2.06%	3.17%	2.91%	3.13%	2.95%
Luxemburg	0.08%	0.06%	0.06%	0.22%	0.14%	0.13%	0.09%
Netherland	1.32%	1.22%	1.35%	1.40%	2.97%	2.43%	1.81%
Austria	0.76%	0.54%	0.36%	1.37%	1.64%	1.22%	1.17%
Portugal	1.15%	1.28%	1.27%	1.64%	2.76%	2.36%	2.06%
Finland	0.67%	0.67%	0.64%	1.38%	1.26%	0.81%	1.02%
Denmark	1.21%	0.77%	1.15%	1.47%	1.20%	1.07%	1.14%
Sweden	1.36%	0.70%	0.36%	0.72%	1.55%	1.05%	1.05%
United Kingdom	1.42%	1.29%	1.24%	0.88%	0.82%	0.85%	1.12%
Euro Area	1.27%	0.89%	0.87%	1.77%	1.92%	1.89%	1.78%
EuropeanUnion	1.35%	1.03%	0.95%	1.41%	1.52%	1.44%	1.41%

Table 4: Nominal Deficit or Surplus/GDP

COUNTRY	1997	1998	1999	2000	2001	2002	2003
Belgium	-2.0	-0.7	0,4	0.2	0.5	0.1	0.2
Germany	-2.7	-2.2	-1.5	1.3	-2.8	-3.5	-3.9
Greece	-4.7	-2.5	-1.8	-2.0	-1.4	-1.4	-1.7
Spain	-3.2	-3.0	-1.2	-0.9	-0.4	-0.0	0.3
France	-3.0	-2.7	-1.8	-1.4	-1.5	-3.2	-4.1
Ireland	1.2	2.3	2.4	4.4	1.1	-0.2	0.2
Italy	-2.7	-2.8	-1.7	-0.6	-2.6	-2.3	-2.4
Luxemburg	2.8	3.0	3.7	6.3	6.3	2.7	0.1
Netherland	-1.1	-0.8	0.7	2.2	0.0	-1.9	-3.2
Austria	-2.0	-2.5	-2.3	-1.5	0.2	0.2	-1.1
Portugal	-2.6	-3.2	-2.8	-2.8	-4.4	-2.7	-2.8
Finland	-1.5	1.5	2.2	7.1	5.2	4.3	2.3
Denmark	0.4	1.1	3.3	2.6	3.1	1.7	1.5
Sweden	-1.6	2.3	2.5	5.1	2.8	0.0	0.7
United Kingdom	-2.2	0.2	1.1	3.9	0.7	-1.6	-2.2
Euro Area	-2.6	-2.3	-1.3	0.1	-1.6	-2.3	-2.7
EuropeanUnion	-2.5	-1.7	-0.7	1.0	-1.0	-2.0	-2.6

Table 5: Real Deficit or Surplus/GDP

COUNTRY	1997	1998	1999	2000	2001	2002	2003
Belgium	-0.09%	0.42%	1.75%	3.31%	3.35%	1.99%	1.79%
Germany	-1.76%	-1.82%	-1.10%	2.60%	-1.29%	-2.44%	-2.94%
Greece	1.65%	2.99%	0.90%	1.73%	3.68%	3.75%	2.81%
Spain	-1.91%	-1.80%	0.31%	1.44%	1.45%	2.25%	2.14%
France	-2.22%	-2.29%	-1.45%	-0.31%	-0.42%	-1.98%	-2.87%
Ireland	2.03%	3.52%	3.66%	6.59%	2.74%	1.60%	2.01%
Italy	-0.32%	-0.37%	0.36%	2.57%	0.31%	0.83%	0.55%
Luxemburg	2.88%	3.06%	3.76%	6.52%	6.44%	2.83%	0.19%
Netherland	0.22%	0.42%	2.05%	3.60%	2.97%	0.53%	-1.39%
Austria	-1.24%	-1.96%	-1.94%	-0.13%	1.84%	1.42%	0.07%
Portugal	-1.45%	-1.92%	-1.53%	-1.16%	-1.64%	-0.34%	-0.74%
Finland	-0.83%	2.17%	2.84%	8.48%	6.46%	5.11%	3.32%
Denmark	1.61%	1.87%	4.45%	4.07%	4.30%	2.77%	2.64%
Sweden	-0.24%	3.00%	2.86%	5.82%	4.34%	1.05%	1.75%
United Kingdom	-0.78%	1.49%	2.34%	4.78%	1.52%	-0.75%	-1.08%
Euro Area	-1.33%	-1.41%	-0.43%	1.87%	0.32%	-0.41%	-0.92%
EuropeanUnion	-1.15%	-0.67%	0.25%	2.41%	0.52%	-0.56%	-1.19%

EU was in deficit all the years except in 2200 in which had a surplus of 1 per cent of GDP. After the correction, Euro area has a surplus both in 2000 and 2001 and EU in the entire period 1999-2001. It should be noted that 2001 was a terrible year, with a very poor rate of growth of GDP due to the deflation of the stock exchanges international bubble and to the Twin Towers shock. Germany and Italy, in 2000 have a surplus of about 2,6 per cent of GDP, Belgium of 3,3, Netherland of 3,6: the core of the old European Community had a huge surplus, with the only exception of France with a budget with a small deficit of 0,3. Outside the Euro area, U.K. had a surplus of 4,78, Sweden of 5,82 and Denmark of 4 per cent. But also in 2001, fiscal policy, in the Euro area, and even more at the EU level, in real terms, was restrictive.

No wonder if the EU, and the Euro area entered, then, in a period of sluggish growth and subsequently of semi-recession. But even in the subsequent years, if one considers the real and not the nominal balances of the budgets of the General Governments, the general impression, as for the EU and Euro area countries, is not that of a "Keynesian democracies in deficit". Indeed, Germany and France, the two big countries which, in the nominal deficit perspective have trespassed the 3 per cent of GDP threshold, appear to have been within the 3 per cent parameter in both years. 2002, has a *real* deficit higher 1 per cent of GDP, France has a *real* deficit of less than half point of GDP. Italy has a *real* surplus higher or close to 0,5 while Spain a *real* surplus higher than 2 per cent. Outside the EU, UK has a *real* deficit lower than 1 per cent while Sweden and Denmark have a substantial *real* surplus. In spite of the socio-political events, that caused, at the world wide level and particularly in US, a dramatic deterioration of the economic perspective, the European countries did not undertake a relaxed fiscal policy. So that one, perhaps, can better understand why in 2002 Germany and France had a *nominal* deficit trespassing 3 per cent and Italy was I difficulty in keeping it below the 3 per cent threshold.

4. Let me deal with the likely objections to my claim that the deficits in the official balances of these budgets are illusory subjective views while the correct objective view is the one obtained by my methodology

To begin with, one may ask why to apply this procedure, to budgets that, as those of General Governments, ordinarily are only conceived in terms of flows and do not take in to account the variations in the assets of the same Governments. A first answer it is in terms of accounting principles. One has to remind that General Governments budgets, under the methodology of Eurostat '95 accounting rules, are conceived as debts and credits budget, in accord to the general statistical principles of national economic accounting. Therefore in order to ascertain their balance one has to add to the difference between the credits and debt that have been liquidated in a given year the difference between those formed in that year (in Pigouvian terminology their announcement effects arose that year), even if not paid. And a loss of value of the outstanding debt it is relevant for this difference. Indeed, since the budget of General Government at the end of the year must comprehend any change of obligations during the year, even if born off budget, there is no reason to exclude this change.

Furthermore the *absolute* money value of the balance of a (General) Government's budget or of the outstanding debt of a given year cannot be compared with that of a different year, in meaningful economic terms, unless adjusted for the change in real value. And if one wants to compare the General Government budgets and debts of EU countries over the years, must take in to account the change of the value of the money in which they are expressed.

Maastricht rules elegantly bypass but not overlook the question of change of value of money in assessing the balances of the budgets and the outstanding of the various years of the General Governments of the various EU countries, by not considering their absolute values, but their ratio to GDP. And, when the prices level increases during the year, the GDP at the end of the year has an increased value in nominal terms over the GDP at the beginning of the year, given by the ratio of that price change. The GDP of the EU countries, over the years, increase in money terms by the rate of increase of the prices of the items forming them. And given nominal stocks of debt of the General Governments of the considered countries, existing at the beginning of the year, represent, at the end of the year, a lower ratio to the GDP existing at the beginning of the year: the reduction being given by the ratio of prices increase multiplied by the ratio of that debt stock to GDP. Thus, what we are doing, adding algebraically to the nominal balance of the budgets of the General Governments of the EU countries, the capital gain arising in the stock of debt of General Government , by the inflation rate , it is noting but an application of the accounting principles underlying the Maastricht rules.

But one may object that even if this may be true, I have not yet demonstrated that the procedure that I have adopted is the correct one to have an *objective view* without fiscal and monetary illusion.

5. Between the balance of the budget of the General Government and the change in value of its debt stock, outstanding at the end of every fiscal year, there isn't a mere accounting relation. There is an objective macro economic relation. If a nominal deficit of the General Government equal to the depreciation of the real value of the outstanding public debt does not increase (non decreases) the ratio Debt/PIL, there must a deflationary stock effect on the assets side that compensate the inflationary effect on the flow side represent by the budget' balance. Actually what I do by adding algebraically the capital gain on the debt of the General Government to the balance of its budget, implies a subtraction from the market economy of an equivalent capital loss, due to the devaluation of the public debt in the hands of the savers, creditors of the Government. This "capital loss" is nothing but the Pigou-Patinkin effect[12]: considered not *as a positive effect* as - in the *theoretically* more familiar – case of reduction of the general price level but *as a negative effect*, caused by the - *empirically* more familiar-case of an increase of the general price level. If one looks to inflation as a "off budget tax" on creditors to the benefit of the debtors, one may say that the current value of the public debt in the hands of the private debtors of the General

[12] For the seminal works See G. Haberler (1937 and 1958) *Prosperity and depression*, Cambridge Harvard (the 1958 ed. Includes, as Appendix the paper "On the Pigou effect once more", originally published in the *Journal of Political Economy*), and the "classics" A. C. Pigou (1941) and D. Patinkin, (1957).

Government every year is reduced by the rate of inflation. And this "off budget tax" must be added to the revenue side of the General Government' budget, to have its true aggregate deficit or surplus[13].

It may appear odd that this negative Pigou- Patinkin it is so much overlooked by the current theory of fiscal policy, to the point that it is possible to consider realistic the "expansionary effects of a balanced budget", on the mere basis of the Haavelmo theorem macro economic nominal accounting, overlooking the fact without that normally price do rise and there is a public debt.

But clearly there is, in this case, a fiscal-monetary illusion of the economists as well as of the fiscal and monetary authorities.

On the other hand, one cannot argue that normally savers, as for the value of their public debt stock, are under a monetary illusion, in relation to the changes in price level. Indeed, it is easy to observe that the nominal rate of interest on public debt (and bank deposits and bonds in general) it is systematically affected by the existing rate of inflation and by the expectations on the future rates. For this reasons, in periods of high inflation, short term bonds have a better market than long term ones. If savers ask for a premium to take account of the inflation, when buying and keeping public debt, it follows that they, normally, are not under a monetary illusion about the effective value of their savings invested in public debt. And, by the same reasoning, it follows that they, normally, consider, as their true income, the interest rates perceived minus the depreciation of their credit due to the change in prices.

From a monetary point of view, one may infer that the money flow outgoing from the General Government's budget, in so far as there is an equivalent Pigou-Patinkin negative effect on the holder of public debt, it is sterilised by them, to keep their financial investment intact. Notice that I am not arguing that the share of the deficit of the General Government due to the expenditure on interests on public debt, as premium for inflation, in a given year, corresponds to the capital loss on the debt stock incurred by the savers in that year, because of the increase of price level of that year. The share of interests paid be the General Government as premium for inflation on in its public debt may be lower or greater than the share of interests that the savers must keep to avoid a reduction of the real value of their stock of public debt, in relation to the price increase of that year, depending from the average interest rate due by the Government on the stock of medium long term debt issued in previous year and still outstanding in that year.

---

[13] I owe to Giorgio Brosio the observation that the burden of inflation on public debt is similar to the burden of the "Ricardo's" extraordinary tax falling proportionally on the wealth owners, in his "equivalence theorem". For the critic of the supposed equivalence see F. Modigliani.

5. There is only one possible objection to this line of reasoning, about the true effects of a given deficit of the budget of the General Government: i.e. that, in an open economy, while the General Government may get a capital gain, due to the loss o value of public debt not necessarily there is an equivalent capital loss i.e. an equivalent Pigou-Patinkin negative effect on domestic savers, because a share of the domestic public debt may be well owned by foreign investors. This, *in principle,* is certainly a relevant observation. And it may perhaps help to explain why for some countries as US, whose public debt is, for a substantial share, in the hands of foreign investors, the deflationary effect of the increase in price level on the economy, via the related Pigou-Patinkin negative effect may be less important. But as for the General Governments of the EU 15 countries, the opposite may be true, particularly in relation to the 12 that are member of the European Monetary Union, considered as a whole. Indeed it is reasonable to assume that, because o the creation of the Euro area, the public bonds issued in one member country are considered by the investors of the other member countries, ceteris paribus, as preferable to the public bonds issued by states non belonging to the Euro area. And a similar reasoning may hold as for the investors of EU countries not belonging to the euro area (UK, Sweden and Denmark) as for their portfolio choices, when considering debt issued by non EU states.

An important inference from the above discussion it is that when considering the effects of the balances of the budgets of the General Governments of the EU and Euro area countries, in real terms, the "objective" point of view must take in due consideration the cross effects of these balances from each country to all the others.

One can see that the aggregate of the General Governments' budgets of the 15 EU member states, in years 2000 has a *real* surplus of 2 percentage points of the aggregate GDP. No wonder that the rate of growth of GDP in the next year was only a modest and that the real surplus of the aggregate General Government' budget shrank to a half percentage point of GDP. The rate of growth of GDOP of the EU in 2002 was and a real deficit of half a point of GDP did appear in the aggregate General Government' budgets. As for the Euro area countries the *real* budgetary surplus in 2000 was smaller than in the entire EU. But the rate of growth of GDP in 2001.was also smaller than in the aggregate EU area only 1,55 per cent. In spite of that situation and of the effects of the Twin Towers tragedy, the real surplus of the aggregate General Government of the EU area was kept at more than one and an half point of GDP. The rate of growth of GDP in 2002 resisted at the level of 1,45 per cent, the real surplus of the aggregate General Government budget did disappear, but no expansionary fiscal policy was undertaken. And in 2003, the rate of growth of GDP of the Euro area went down to only an half point. A real deficit did eventually emerge of 1,4 per cent, because the revenue could not follow the natural rate of growth of the social welfare expenditures. If the budgetary figures are divested of the subjective monetary-fiscal illusion and the objective view is adopted, it seems clear that, on balance, in the considered period the EU member countries did not adopt an expansive, bur rather a restrictive fiscal policy. This view is reinforced as for the Euro are particularly considering the *objectively* neutral fiscal policy of 2002, in presence of important factors working in the direction of an economic depression.

A debate on the "stupidity" of the Amsterdam pact did actually develop, particularly from 2003, but no one considered the fact that the stupidity, if any, consisted in overlooking the real balance of the Governments budget, always focusing on the illusory nominal balance.

6. In his "Treatise of general sociology", Pareto distinguishes non logical from logical actions, by the following preliminary double classification

- all logical actions, by definition, have a logical end and the subjective end is identical to the objective one

- non logical actions may have or not a logical end and the subjective end may differ or not from the objective end.

Considering then the non logical actions, the combination between the first couple of possibilities- that they have or not a logical end and the second couple of possibilities, that the subjective end does differ or not from the objective one, one has the following cases[14]:

- non logical actions without a subjective non logical end

- non logical actions with a subjective logical end different from the objective end

- non logical actions with a subjective logical end identical to the objective end

Let us apply this classification to the monetary-fiscal illusion relating to the Maastricht-Amsterdam rules, considering the experts and the Governments that set forth the Maastricht rule on deficit for the European Monetary Union and the Amsterdam pact applying it to the countries that entered the Euro area, the authorities in charge of its surveillance, at the European Commission level and at the European Council level and the Governments that are individually responsi-

---

[14] See PARETO, *Trattato di sociologia generale,* Vol. I, Chapter 2, §151

ble of comply to them. It seem fair to say that perhaps some of the experts and the politicians that draw the Maastricht Treaty and the Amsterdam pact were aware of the real effects of the General Government's deficit rule, but preferred to conceal them under the monetary-fiscal illusion arising from focusing on the deficit/GDP ratio and overlooking the effect of the inflation rate on the Debt/GDP ratio. Indeed, the greater it is this ratio, for a given country, the greater, is the Pigou-Patinkin negative effect of a given inflation rate, for any budgetary deficit of that country. And the Pigou-Patinkin negative effect is also greater, for a given country, with a given Debt/GDP ratio the greater its inflation rate. Therefore the monetary-fiscal illusion works to make more restrictive, the Maastricht deficit rule, for countries with an higher Debt/GDP ratio and a greater propensity to inflation like Italy or Greece, in comparison with countries with a smaller Debt/GDP ratio and a lower propensity to inflation as Germany. The rule is also more restrictive for countries with a higher propensity to inflation as Spain and Portugal, as compared with countries with a similar Debt/GDP ratio as many Nordic countries and Germany. Finally, the rule is severe with countries with a high Deb/ GDP ratio as Belgium as compared with countries at the same (moderate) tendency to inflation but a lower Debt/GDP ratio. There fore one can say that, under the illusion thus created, the EU-authorities and those of the member states would works more effectively to the end that the Maastricht rule and Amsterdam pact inventors were pursuing than if deprived from illusion, provided that they *shared that end,* even at the expense of the pursuance of others, as economic growth and employment.

But while the public authorities in control of the application of the Maastricht rules may share the end of the reduction of the debt/GDP ratio, even at expense of these other objectives, the Governments who are under the same monetary-fiscal illusion, do feel more concerned with their domestic economic growth and with the European growth than with the "orthodoxy" of the fiscal policy at the EU or Euro area level, as the two ends seem to *enter in sharp conflict.*

Thus they were led to suggest changes in the deficit rule, as the exclusion of some expenditures from the 3 per cent threshold as those on (specific) investments, or those for scientific and technological research or those for defence: i.e. respectful objectives, by inconsistent with the macro economic logic and construct of the Maastricht and Amsterdam deficit rules. The (new) European Commissioner of the EU in charge of the fiscal policy rules and behaviours, on the other hand in summer 2004, suggested an undetermined period of fiscal deficit, to be permitted since a slow down in the economy appears. The new wording practically makes the 3 per cent deficit rule a sort of chewing gum, suitable diverse shapes, according to the circumstances. Under an objective view of the phenomena under discussion the recourse to non logical solutions would not be necessary, to achieve the desired objectives.

But, admittedly, it would be very difficult to device a rational deficit rule, based on an objective view that pursues a satisfactory balanced between the end of differential fiscal discipline for countries with different debt/GDP ratios and different inflation rates and the end of differential fiscal policies for all countries in the different economic cycles. The countries in different situations would have different views about the right rule.

Perhaps a consideration of the 3 per cent *real* deficit rule as supplementary to the 3 per cent *nominal* rule would work better, as *a second best* solution. One may quote here what Pareto argued, with his sceptical positive mind, in introducing the theory of non logical actions

> One has to keep in mind that non–logical dose not mean illogical; i.e. a non logical action may be the best that one could find with the observation of the facts and with logic to adapt the means to the end. But this adaptation has been obtained by a way different from the logic.[15]

References

Bobbio N. (1964), "Introduzione" to Pareto V. (1923, 1964).

Buchanan, J-M. (1964), "Public Debt, Cost Theory and Fiscal Illusion", in J.M. Ferguson (1964).

Buchanan J. M., (1967, 1999*), Public Finance in Democratic Process,* reprinted as vol. 4 of the collected works of J. BUCHANAN, Indianapolis, Liberty Fund, 1999

Buchanan J. M. and Wagner (1977), *Democracy in Deficit. The Political Legacy of Lord Keynes,* London Academic Press

Buchanan, J-M. (1999), *The Effects of Institutions on Fiscal Choices*, Vol. 4 of the *Collected works* of James Buchanan, Indianapolis, Liberty Fund.

Cavaco Silva A. (1977), *Economic Effects of Public Debt*, London, Martin Robertson

Fasiani M. (1951), *Principi di Scienza delle Finanze,* Torino, Giappichelli, 2nd ed.

Ferguson J.M. (editor) (1964), *Public Debt and Future Generations*, Chapel Hill, University of North Carolina Press.

Forte, F. (1997), "The Measurement of Fiscal Burden on GDP instead than on National Net Value Added Produced. A Chapter in Fiscal Illusion", Banca Nazionale del Lavoro Quarterly Review, n. 202, September.

Forte F. and J. M. Buchanan, (1961), "The Evaluation of Public Services"*, Journal of Political Economy*, LXIX, n.2.

Giardina E. (1992), "Commentary" to Ch. 4 of Peacock A.T., (1992), in Peacock A.T., (1992).

Griziotti B. (1956), *Studi di scienza delle finanze e diritto finanziario*, Milano, Giuffrè, Vol. II.

Haberler. G. (1937 and 1958), *Prosperity and depression*,. Cambridge Harvard.

Haberler G. "On the Pigou effect once more", *Journal of Political Economy.*

Pigou A.C., (1941), *Employment and Equilibrium*, London, McMillan.

Patinkin D, (1957), *Money, Interests and Prices*, Evanston, Ill. Row and Paterson.

---

[15] Pareto (1906), Chapter II,§ 3

Pareto V. (1906), *Manuale di Economia politica, con una introduzione alla scienza sociale*, Milano, Società Editrice libraria.
Pareto V, (1916), Trattato di Sociologia Generale, 1srt ed, Firenze, Barbera.
Pareto V, (1923), *Trattato di sociologia generale,*2nd, Firenze Barbera, and (1964) edited by N. Bobbio, P. Farneti, F.Frassoldati. Milano, Comunità.
Pareto V. (1917), "Sugli effetti dei prestiti e delle imposte", letter to B. Griziotti, reprinted in B. GRIZIOTTI (1956).
Pareto V. (1920), "Imposte, debito, carta moneta", in L' Economista, March 28, reprinted in *Battaglie liberistiche* Salerno, Casa Editrice Salernitana n. d.
Peacock A.T. (1992), *Public Choice Analysis in Historical Perspective,* Cambridge University Press, New York.
Peacock A.T. and Rizzo I. (1987), "Government Debt and Growth in Public Spending", *Public Finance*, n. 2.
Pommerhene W. and Fritz Schneider (1978), "Fiscal Illusion Political Institutions and local spending", *Kyklos*, n.31.
Puviani A. (1903), *Teoria dell'illusione finanziaria,* Palermo, riedited by F. Volpi (1973), Isedi, Milano.
Puvlani A. (1960), *Die Illusionen in der Oeffentlichen Finanzwirtschaft*, Berlin
Schmolders G. (1960), *Introduction* to A. Puvlani (1960).
Shibata and Y. Kimura (1987), "Reply" to Peacock A.T. Rizzo I. (1987), Public Finance, n. 2
Wagner R.E. (1976), "Revenue Structure. Fiscal Illusion and Budgetary Choices", *Public Choice*, n.25.

The Impact of Equity Driven Policy Measures on the Equity of the State*

Jürgen G. Backhaus
Professor in Public Finance and Fiscal Sociology
Krupp Chair in Public Finance and Fiscal Sociology
University of Erfurt
Nordhäuser Str. 63
99089 Erfurt
Germany
Fon: ++49-361-737-4551
Fax: ++49-361-737-4559
juergen.backhaus@uni-erfurt.de

Abstract: During the last decades, the idea that government can be and should be an effective instrument for the attainment of social justice and other ideals dear to social economists has come under powerful attack. Sometimes the attack is of a doctrinaire kind: designating areas where government should or should not intervene. In economics, this is often done in the tradition of identifying areas of "market-failure". Sometimes, however, the attack is fuelled by serious shortcomings of well-intentioned governmental activities leading to poor results. Some economists have tried to identify these areas of poor government policy in terms of a theory of governmental failure. In this paper, a different route is chosen. Building on traditional public finance theory, the concept of public equity is developed as a measuring rod with which to judge the outcomes of policies guided by considerations of social equity or justice.

This results in an analysis of a curious relationship. The purpose of this paper is to give an analysis of the curious relationship between the two equity concepts such as the one used in the finance (both public- and business-) literature on the one hand and in health economics on the other. The documentation of six equity induced health care measures is followed by a conceptual discussion of the different equity concepts in part I. Their impact on the equity of the state is analyzed in part II by using standard public finance and public choice theory. The paper concludes with an agenda for further research.

Keywords: Equity of the state, theory of taxation.

JEL codes: D31, H11, I118.

---

* I should like to thank John Davis, Justin Harriss and two anonymous referees for helpful comments

Introduction

The equity of a business corporation is generally understood to be the net present value of its assets, allowing for its liabilities, or - in short - its net worth. Equity is a measure of the value of all the means with which goods and services are produced, revenues collected, and obligations met. The equity of the state likewise is the net present value of revenue sources, again allowing for liabilities such as the public debt state equite is largely dependent upon the productive capacity of its citizens, their skills and their health. Curiously, in much of the health economics literature, equity is considered to be achieved if for example:

1. public prices vary according to personal gross income;[1]

2. there is "solidarity" between good risks and bad risks in public insurance schemes;[2]

3. technologies are economically assessed in terms of their "equity', before being introduced into public services;[3]

4. responsibilities are diffused and limited as a matter of course, in order to guarantee "equitable" decisions;[4]

5. access to public supply of health care services is at the same time considered a basic human right and restricted by administrative procedures not subject to judicial review but administered in the name of "equity";[5]

6. the general practitioners serve as entry barriers into the public health care system ensuring "equitable" access to services.[6]

---

[1] 'Ministerie van Welzijn, Volksgezondheid en Cultuur, *Financieel Overzicht van de Gezondheidszorg en Maatschappelijke Dienstverlening, 1986,* 's-Gravenhage: Staatsuitgeverij, 1985. The principle is ubiquitous in the Netherlands not only for the compulsory social security System in its various wings ("volksverzekeringen") but also for pricing public services not remotely related to health, such as nursery schools. Throughout the social security system, a pricing formula is crucial: a contribution is levied on the household according to (gross) income up to a maximum; elder people pay no contribution at all. See H.J.J. Leenen, H.D.C. Roscam-Abbing, *Bestuurliik Gezondheidsrecht.* Alphen ald Rijn, Brussel: Tjeenk Willink, 1986, p. 139.

[2] H.D.C. Roscam-Abbing & F.F.H. Rutten, "Solidariteit versus Equivalentie-beginsel" (hoofdstuk 5). In: H.D.C. Roscam-Abbing & F.F.H. Rutten, *Verleden en Toekomst van het Ziektekostenverzekeringsstelsel in Nederland*, Deventer, 1985.

[3] Ger Haan, *Effecten en Kosten van In-Vitro-Fertilisatie*, Doctoral Dissertation. Rijksuniversiteit Limburg, Maastricht, 1989, p. 166.

[4] Publicly authorized corporate forms are introduced which resemble foundations but lack endowments and are exempt from liability. These institutions implement delicate policy measures.

[5] Ger Haan (1989) p. 163.

Although these cases are exclusively drawn from Dutch sources, this is done for reasons of clarity and ease of exposition only. The principles discussed here resurface to different degrees in decisions on pricing and packaging public services in all the advanced western democracies, from Britain to the United States, Germany to France, with the smaller northern democracies certainly pioneering new applications and variations on basically the same principle. This is also the reason why examples drawn from these sources are better suited for a general discussion of the underlying principles than those from the larger democracies such as the United States, where the institutional realization will never be set forth in the pure forms observed in the smaller politically more homogeneous northern democracies.

During the last decades, the idea that government can be and should be an effective instrument for the attainment of social justice and other ideals dear to social economists has come under powerful attack. Sometimes the attack is of a doctrinaire kind: designating areas where government should or should not intervene. In economics, this is often done in the tradition of identifying areas of "market-failure". Sometimes, however, the attack is fuelled by serious shortcomings of well intentioned governmental activities leading to poor results. Some economists have tried to identify these areas of poor government policy in terms of a theory of governmental failure.[7] In this paper, a different route is chosen. Building on traditional public finance theory, the concept of public equity is developed as a measuring rod with which to judge the outcomes of policies guided by considerations of social equity or justice.

This results in an analysis of a curious relationship. The purpose of this paper is to give an analysis of the curious relationship between the two equity concepts such as the one used in the finance (both public- and business-) literature on the one hand and in health economics on the other.

The purpose of this paper is to give an analysis of the curious relationship between these two concepts of equity. The documentation of six equity induced health care measures is followed by a conceptual discussion of the different equity concepts in part I. Their impact on the equity of the state is analyzed in part II by using standard public finance and public choice theory. The paper concludes with an agenda for further research.

---

[6] M.H.L. van Tits, "An Experiment with Financial Incentives for General Practitioners in the Netherlands". *Research paper* for "The Joint Meeting on the First European Conference on Health Economics" Barcelona, September 1989.

[7] In creating a mirror image to Francis Bator's "The Anatomy of Market Failure" (*Quaterly Journal of Economics*, 1958), Charles Wolf jr. developed his theory of governmental failure, first in an article entitled "A Theory of Non-Market Failure", *Journal of Law and Economics*, 1979 and then in his book *Market or Government: Choosing between imperfect alternatives*. Cambridge, Massachussets: The MIT Press, 1988.

1

Theory: Equity in Business and Public Finance

In business finance, equity is the residual value of a company's assets after all outside liabilities (other than the shareholders') have been allowed for. In public finance, a country's equity is the residual value of its assets after all outside liabilities (other than the internal debt the State owes to its citizens and other institutions inside its jurisdiction) have been allowed for. The assets of modern democratic states consist largely of claims in the form of taxes, of which most are either levied on labour (income taxes, payroll taxes, social security taxes) or consumption. In addition, most states hold land or other natural resources the value of which tends to increase with economic development; an increase that sometimes is more than offset by a larger relative increase of the public debt. In assessing a country's equity position, it is not correct to compare the foreign debt with gross national product. The reason is that the foreign debt cannot be serviced out of the total gross national product, which is not by itself at the disposition of the State. Only that part which can be levied through taxation is available for servicing the foreign debt. The yield of any particular tax tends to be subject to decreasing returns, once a tax rate has reached some level, the precise location of which is heavily dependent on the relationship between benefits received in consideration of the taxes paid.[8]

At this level, further tax increases are to the detainment of the taxing government. Furthermore, the fecundity of the tax base also depends on the size of the internal debt, since the larger the internal debt (given a predetermined expenditure level), the smaller can be the tax financed outlays for public production of goods and services, on which the fecundity of the tax base depends at least in the long run. In estimating the assets of a state, one therefore has to start with the net present value of its future taxes, which has to be adjusted downwards *ceteris paribus*, the higher the public share in gross domestic product, the higher the share of public debt in gross domestic product, and the less attractive the tax/benefit ratio is to the most important groups of taxpayers. The last three aspects seem to be particularly relevant for the small northern democracies *e.g.*, the Netherlands and the Scandinavian countries.

Apart from the three considerations already mentioned as determining the equity of the state by virtue of affecting the net present value of the state's assets, there is a forth important aspect which has always figured prominently in public finance analysis for as long as the discipline has been subject to economic discourse. The population of a state has to be in good health, since the better the health state of a population, the higher the revenues and the lower the outlays

[8] The standard Laffer curve is too simplistic a tool for this analysis, since benefits arc ignored in this relationship.

will be and, conversely, the less healthy a population, the higher the outlays of the state on promoting health and health care, and the smaller the revenues from people who produce or consume.[9] This basic relationship yields the proposition that, in public finance, the better the health state of a population, the better is that state's equity position.

The (explanatory) *benchmark principle* follows that measures to improve the health state of a population should be carried out with tax financed funding to the extent that the marginal outlays are covered by expected marginal tax revenues.

Distributive Equity and Some Theory of Taxation

This simple policy principle, although probably acceptable as a base line to any student of the matter, is not sufficient to *explain* either the extent or the structure of health care provision in contemporary developed economies with western style democracies such as the United States and Canada, Germany, Britain or the northern democracies such as the Scandinavian countries and the Netherlands. The literature discussing these health care systems, which is largely synonymous with the new discipline of health economics, has developed a completely different concept of equity which has originally been taken from public finance analysis but meanwhile has taken on a life of its own. In addition to the standard notions of financial equity discussed above, there is also the notion of distributional equity which, following the classical textbook by the Musgraves, acknowledges three fiscal functions of the State, *viz.* the allocation function, the distribution function, and the stabilization function.[10] Since taxes are determined in a political context, public finance analysis cannot ignore their distributional consequences. Musgrave & Musgrave spell out the relationship between allocation and distribution in public finance in clear terms:

But the theory of efficient factor use by itself is not a theory of distributive justice. For one thing, the proposition that factor allocation should be based on efficient factor pricing does not require that the final distribution of income among individuals be set equal to the proceeds from sales of their factor services to the market. The two can be separated by intervention of the distributive branch of the budget. For another thing, the ultimate concern of justice in distribution is with distribution among individuals or families and not among groups

[9] See Jürgen Backhaus, *Die Finanzierung des Wohlfahrtsstaats* (Inaugural Lecture). Maastricht: Rijksuniversiteit Limburg 1989, p. 7 (Dutch version p. 10). Referring to Christian (Freiherr von) Wolff, *Grundsätze des Natur- und Völckerrechts*. Halle: Renger, 1754, III, § 1022.
[10] See Richard A. Musgrave & Peggy E. Musgrave, *Public Finance in Theory and Practice*, first edition 1973, New York: MacGraw-Hill, 1989 (5), chapter 1.

or factors. Factor shares are only loosely related to the interfamily distribution of income. While it is true that capital income accrues more largely to high income families and wage income more largely to low income families, there are important exceptions to the rule. The problem of distribution among individuals or families must thus be addressed directly. (p. 74).

The cases discussed below are not covered by this exception. Health affects neither capital nor natural resources, but only one factor of production: labour; and it affects persons in both their ability to produce and to consume. The question of justice, then, is *eo ipso* less one of distribution but one of allocation, *i.e.* of the *efficient* use of the available resources in the interest of optimizing the health state of the population.

In the theory of taxation, the concept of equity typically takes this basic form:

a. are taxpayers (individuals, households, or firms) differently burdened according to differences among them, such as differences in their ability to pay, their benefits from the tax financed expenditure or some other relevant criterion? This concept is called *vertical equity*.

b. are taxpayers differently burdened although they are equal? This concept is called *horizontal equity*.

If the question is reduced to the criterion of ability to pay only, the dual concept takes on the form:

a. *vertical equity*: how does the tax burden vary across taxpayers (individuals or households) of different means? and

b. *horizontal equity*: how does the tax burden vary across taxpayers (individuals or households) of identical means?

The oldest equity principle in public finance is the straightforward *benefit principle*, re-emphasized by Knut Wicksell.[11] The dual equity principle then reads:

a. *vertical equity*: does the tax burden vary across taxpayers (individuals or households) according to the different benefits they derive from the expenditure?

b. *horizontal equity:* do taxpayers (individuals or households) have to carry different tax burdens although they derive the same benefit from the expenditure?

[11] See Knut Wicksell, *Finanztheoretische Untersuchungen*, Jena: Gustav Fischer, 1896. James Buchanan follows this tradition.

The measure or policy is equitable if the first question (a) is answered in the affirmative and the second (b) in the negative.

In health economics,[12] we sometimes find that the concept of equity is split into different concepts depending on whether they refer to the expenditure or the revenue side. On the provision side, we find the notion that a vertically equitable provision of goods and services depends on the *need* of the individuals concerned; the more intense (express?) the need, the more services should be provided. On the revenue side, on the other hand, *ability to pay* is often invoked as the principle of vertical equity: the better the ability to pay, the more a particular taxpayer (individual or household) should contribute. In practice, this criterion is translated into something else, equating ability to pay with *gross income.* Since the appropriate definition of income for matters of taxation is important both from an allocative and a distributive point of view, this problem is taken up in the next section.

The Concept of Income in Taxation Theory[13]

In economics, categories and terms are defined with respect to the models in which they fulfil a function. In some disciplines, such as law, terms can be significant as such, independent from their context. They can add significance to a certain context.[14] As it happens therefore in economics, terms are completely dependent upon the context in which they are used. The context is typically a model. Terms such as capital, profit or income take on completely different meanings depending on whether they are used in a macro-economic model, a micro-economic model or, as in the case under consideration, the theory of taxation. In taxation, income is a permanent magnitude on which a permanent charge can be levied. Since we are concerned with permanent sustainable financial streams, the relative proportions (*e.g.* of the tax in relation to the income) have to remain stable. This implies not only that the tax cannot exceed certain bounds beyond which it would reduce the stream of income to be taxed in the future and thereby endanger the sustainable yield; the principle further implies that income as an economic magnitude cannot be seen independent from the sources which generate income and from the economic unit which provides the structure in which income is generated. In simple economic terms, we define income in

[12] See *e.g.* Jeremy Hurst, "Equity in the Delivery of and Payment for Health Services. ch. 7, In: J.W. Hurst, *Financing Health Care in the US., Canada. and Britain.* Kings Fund 1985.

[13] See originally Gustav Schmoller, "Die Lehre vom Einkommen in ihrem Zusammenhang mit dem Grundprinzip der Steuerlehre". In: *Zeitschrift für die gesammte Staatswissenschaft,* 19, 1863, pp. 1-84.

[14] See Jürgen Backhaus, *Mitbestimmung im Unternehmen,* 1986, pp. 145-146, with further references to Ch. Wolff and J. Esser.

terms of a functional relationship such as equation (1) which relates income to its determining variables.

$Y = f(C, S, R, E, H)$ (1)

Y: Income

C: Capital

S: Skills

-

R: Incidental Revenues

-

E: Incidental Expenditures

H: Health

Equation (1) shows the level of income to depend on the capital endowment used, the human capital or level of skills[15] employed, incidental revenues such as bequests, incidental expenditures such as those for accidents and sickness, and the health states of the individual(s) involved in generating the income flow. The permanent stream of income depends only on capital, skills and health, since the incidental revenues and expenditures will affect one of the other variables but not permanently affect the income stream.

$T=f(Y)$ (2)

T: Tax Revenue

Equation (2) is straightforward in simply relating the permanent tax revenue and the permanent income stream. This functional exposition readily yields two general principles.

Principle 1: The unit of taxation is the unit generating the income.

Principle 2: Taxable income is the permanent or sustainable stream of income after allowances for all those expenditures which have been made in order to leave the income generating unit intact.

---

[15] This refers to an output variable; "schooling"as used in van Doorslaer (1987) would be an inappropriate proxy. See Eddy K.A. van Doorslaer, *Health, Knowledge and the Demand for Medical Care,* Assen/Maastricht: Van Gorcum, 1987.

Application

We can now apply the above analysis to the problem of financing a public health care service by means of a tax on income. Let us assume that the unit of taxation is correctly identified as the household which generates a stream of income and maintains its productive assets. Self employed households will typically differ from households whose members are dependently employed with respect to the size of their capital stock. Both types of households invest in maintaining or improving their skill levels and their health states. The taxable income, consequently, has to be corrected for those expenditures on capital maintenance, education and health. This implies that the taxable income is an appropriately defined *net* income variable, and not the *gross* income variable we previously encountered.

Expenditures on public health care provision depend on the demand for health. The household demand for health, in turn, is a negative function of the opportunity costs of treatment. The opportunity costs of treatment are the higher, the larger is the improvement in health expected from the treatment and the smaller are the expected costs of the treatment. In a market environment of health care provision, the household demand for health will be a typical negatively downward sloping curve, with the position of the demand curve largely dependent on the health states of the members of the household, and the quantity of health care services demanded depending on the price charged. In public health care provision, if no price is charged to the household, the position of the demand curve will again be largely dependent upon the health states of the household, but the quantity demanded will depend on those costs of the rationing mechanism employed that fall on the household as a consequence of seeking treatment. If the rationing mechanism is a simple queue requiring time spent in order to receive the treatment, the cost borne by the household will be in terms of income foregone and a suboptimal health state of the member seeking treatment. Both negatively impact on income. If the rationing device does not literally require time spent in waiting for the treatment, but simply lags seeking and receiving treatment, the cost borne by the household is the opportunity cost of the suboptimal health state of the member(s) seeking treatment and has a depressing effect on household income. The circle is closed by noting the following

Proposition 1: The reduction in household income due to gross income based pricing policies in public health services will also reduce the revenue from a tax on income and consequently reduce the equity of the state as defined above.

Income Invariant with Health

The preceding discussion was based on the assumption, expressed in equation (1), that the income a household can generate will depend on the health states of its members. In that case, the stream of sustainable income on which taxes can be levied will decrease if health states remain impaired. There is a class of households for which this assumption does not hold true. Inactive households, whose income is based on some type of claim such as a pension, can maintain their income stream irrespective of capital maintenance and retention of skills provided health states remain above a sustainable minimum. This condition is expressed in equation (3).

$$Y = f(C, R, E, H) \quad (3)$$

Household income now depends only on the fixed claim C which can be expressed as a fixed capital stock, on incidental revenues and incidental expenditures as well as a minimum state of health. Note that incidental revenues will now also count as income, since (and as long as) they are not re-invested into the income generating ability of the household. The household's economic situation is sustainable as long as the sum of permanent consumption and incidental expenditures (such as those on health maintenance) does not exceed the fixed permanent income flow.

The analysis points to an important *source of income taxation*, when inactive households do not re-invest incidental revenues in order to enhance their income generating ability. Curiously, as pointed out above (see footnote 1), this very group of households tends to be exempted from certain income based social security taxes altogether.

Stabilizing and De-stabilizing Pricing and Financing Formulae

If health care services are delivered in a market environment, decisions on how to provide and package services and how to price them simultaneously solve the funding problem. Services which do not generate a sustainable revenue stream will be discontinued. The system is a self-equilibrating one.

In the public sector, decisions on financing and providing services obviously have to be synchronized too. Often, political considerations make it impossible to use a straightforward market based pricing formula. A particular service may be provided publicly for the very reason to operate it differently from a market operation. In this case, a different formula driving decisions on funding and quantity and quality of provision of Services has to be used. The classical formulation of the equity principle as given above provides for such a formula. In the Wicksellian formulation, roughly homogenous groups of beneficiaries subscribe to a particular public service and generate the necessary funding according to their willingness to pay.

Proposition 2: Willingness to pay obviously reflects ability to pay, but it also reflects a judgement on service. This information is of crucial importance in order to maintain quality standards in the public sector, since the public sector service cannot rely on the same signals a market based operation receives.

A benefit principle therefore requires that subscriptions to the service be open to renewal or refusal. Membership in a particular group or fund cannot be compulsory; the state may only impose a duty to join at least one such a group or fund, provided these offer service and funding profiles that are sufficiently different one from the other in order to provide for a meaningful choice. The classical equity principle allows for a self sustaining provision of a public service. If a group becomes smaller as subscriptions dwindle and consequently the sustaining fund starts shrinking, the service either has to be repackaged and improved, or it will gradually loose importance and ultimately disappear, yielding room for a public service better matching subscribers‘ expectations with respect to service profiles and quality and their willingness to pay for these services.

The commonly used funding principle “provision according to need, financing based on gross income” generates a completely different constitutional design. On the supply side, there is no provision whatsoever to filter consumers‘ decisions into responses with respect to the quality and profile of services. On the funding side, as demonstrated in the preceding section, the formula cannot generate a sustainable stream of revenues since it systematically erodes the income generating ability of households by not taking account of the difference between stocks and flows.

The formula then combines at least three destabilizing elements:

1. in the long run, gross income taxation destabilizes its own funding source.

2. since there is no feedback with consumers, service profiles, quantity and quality are likely to match poorly with consumers‘ expectations and willingness to pay.

3. since the formula disjoints decisions on funding and decisions on production, it cuts through the most important self-regulating mechanism to control costs. Permanent cost increases are the likely consequence.

In conclusion we can note:

Proposition 3: Equity considerations in funding the provision of public services, such as health care services, can have important consequences for the quality, the quantity and the profile of services as well as for the costs of their provision. Equity driven funding formulae can either stabilize or destabilize the long term provision of a service. These formulae can provide incentives for cost control and quality maintenance, but they can also do the opposite. Far from being of a purely distributive nature, equity based funding formulae can have important allocative consequences.

2

Social Justice and Provision According to Need

It is sometimes suggested that in such areas as health care, social justice requires provision according to need and, therefore, considerations of allocative efficiency have to be relegated to secondary importance. Such a notion is, however, faulty, since allocative efficiency and justice cannot be juxtaposed as opposites. Consider the following quote from John Rawls‘ *A Theory of Justice*:[16]

> The main problem of distributive justice is the choice of a social system. The principles of justice apply to the basic structure and regulate how its major institutions are combined into one scheme. Now, as we have seen, the idea of justice as fairness is to use the notion of pure procedural justice to handle the contingencies of particular situations. The social system is to be designed so that the resulting distribution is just however things turn out. To achieve this end it is necessary to set the social and economic process within the surroundings of suitable political and legal institutions. Without the proper arrangement of these background institutions the outcome of the distributive process will not be just. Background fairness is lacking. I shall give a brief description of these background institutions as they might exist in a properly organized democratic state that allows private ownership of capital and natural resources (...). This is achieved by policing the conduct of firms and private associations and by preventing the establishment of monopolistic restrictions and barriers to the more desirable positions. Finally, the government guarantees a social minimum either by family allowances and special payments for sickness and employment, or more systematically by such devices as a graded income supplement (a so-called negative income tax)... Since the market is not suited to answer the claims of need, these should be met by a separate arrangement. Whether the principles of justice are satisfied, then, turns on whether the total income of the least advantaged (wages plus transfers) is such as to maximize their long-run expectations (consistent with the constraints of equal liberty and fair equality of opportunity).

In Rawlsian terms, the maximum rule as applied to health care provisions suggests that the system respond in an optimal fashion to the health care demands of

[16] London, Oxford University Press, 1972, Chapter 43.

those most in need to be taken care of. This requires two categorically distinct sets of policies. On the one hand, the health care system has to be structured so as to achieve allocative efficiency. On the other hand, health care demand has to be made effective in the sense of matching willingness to pay with ability to pay. These two results, however, cannot be achieved by the same policy, such as the funding formula "provision according to need, financing based on gross income". The result can only be achieved if the transfer problem (ensuring effective demand) is separately dealt with from the allocation problem (ensuring optimal health care).

3

Six Cases: An Illustration

In looking at the six cases documented in the discussion, the various equity notions can be further illustrated. One should keep in mind that the concept of equity, once we move beyond the benefit principle, can be substantiated with almost any conceivable criterion that comes to mind. The benefit principle captures all the various dimensions of burdens and benefits as they are valued by the individuals or households. Once we move beyond the benefit principle, proxi-indicators have to be chosen. Among these proxies, we can look at the distribution between different age groups and generations, between the public and the private sector, between the gender groups of distribution, according to geographical location, with the contrast between the city and the country on the one hand, but also (often overlooked but important in the context of "1992") the contrast between the citizens living within the jurisdiction and those immediately neighbouring it on the other, the effects on families on the one hand and single household units on the other, the distributive effects between the healthy and the sickly *etc*. The list can be continued indefinitely along the entire spectrum of social indicators.

Case 1

The effects of levies on gross household income with exemptions for inactive households, employed as a means to finance social services, on the overall health state of the population have been discussed extensively in the previous section. The financing formula is deficient for sustaining the financial needs of the service for which it is used, but it also generates adverse effects on the provision side, favouring the inactive households over the active households. The most productive consumers are least well served. The formula is in open violation of the benefit principle. Its additional equity implications are also problematic. Although there is a certain preferential treatment of the elderly who are exempt from the levy, the same is true for other non-active individuals and households who receive some form of public assistance. The intergenerational equity is questionable, as the next generation is likely left with poor health states and a badly functioning system. The system is tilted towards public provision at the expense of private initiative, but the financial burden is also predominantly carried by public sector employees who are least able to avoid the levy. The formula seems to be neutral with respect to gender, but not with respect to geographical location. In particular, it would be interesting to compare the tax/benefit ratio's in a European context.

Health, as an economic good, is a complement to both labour and consumption. Deteriorations in the health state of a population therefore negatively affect the taxing power of the state where it is strongest: income taxes including social security and payroll taxes and consumption taxes such as the value added tax.

Proposition 4: If the gross income funding formula indeed has a negative impact on the health state of the population, it also negatively affects the tax base and thereby the equity of the state.

The question here has been analysed in conjectural terms; it would be important to follow this exploratory analysis up empirically.

Case 2

The concept of solidarity between good and bad risks flies in the face of received insurance theory. The origin of the concepts can best be demonstrated with the following stylized example. Consider a public insurance scheme which is compulsory up to a certain income level. The levies depend on age and gross income, the outlays on health states. In addition, a private insurance market remains. The predictable result has the "good risks" migrate to or remain with the private insurance system, whereas the "bad risks" accumulate in the public sector. From the point of view of allocative efficiency, the correct solution is to adopt the classical benefit principle and try to discriminate as deeply as possible between the different risk groups. If distributional concerns are important, which no doubt they are in the case assumed, public assistance (in the form of subsidies or tax credits) can be attached to the bad risks and left to migrate to whichever insurance pool proves most attractive. Since the public insurance scheme is likely to be exempt from taxation, attaching tax benefits to bad old age insurance risks could prove to be a powerful instrument for keeping them in the private sector. An allocation problem remains, however, as long as the system lacks incentives to contain the costs of bad risks, *i.e.* positive incentives to maintain health in as good a state as possible, granted to both insurees and insurers. The principle of discriminating among risks serves this function, with poor risks facing higher premiums. The principle of solidarity neutralizes this incentive system and creates impediments to reducing costs by pooling appropriately defined risk groups towards which health measures can be more directly pointed.

Proposition 5: The adverse effects of the principle of solidarity between good and bad risks on both health states and costs to the insurance system can be substantial.

Again, these effects can be empirically established either in terms of a long term experiment or in terms of comparing the present system with an international sample where cases can be pooled according to risks and costs.

Case 3

Assessments of medical technologies prior to adoption substitute the medical specialists' and the patient's judgement by that of the economist who undertakes the technology assessment study. Such a study is necessitated by the dissolution of funding and treatment decisions consequent to the split equity criterion (needs/means). The allocative consequences of such equity induced technology assessments can best be demonstrated by taking up a well done study and looking at its major implications. In principle, such a study can at best lead to the exclusion of an advanced technology which amounts to an artificial restriction of the production possibility frontier of the medical specialist who administers a treatment. The restriction is made necessary because the treatment, under the split equity criterion, proceeds without due regard to costs. It should be clear, however, that by imposing an artificial restriction, at least for some groups of patients the optimal treatment (even with regard to costs) is excluded. Consequently, and considered collectively, the group of insurees does not get the maximum return on its compulsory insurance contributions, quite irrespective of income position.

In fact, even well done studies can make a mockery of economic analytical techniques. Consider the case of two treatments for fertility. One treatment has traditionally been available under the state system, the other being new has not. Both treatments complement each other in so far as they yield better results with different groups of patients. This should imply that for equity reasons, both treatments should be made available. But the final conclusion of a technology assessment study on a new fertilization treatment reads otherwise; after referring to the general context of funding the various treatments, the author concludes: "Part of the discussion will concern the question whether fertility treatment - successful or not - increases the couple's health situation. Additional life years for the treated couple are not to be expected and an increase of the couple's quality of life in the long run is questionable." (Haan, 1989, 166). The revealed preferences of couples seeking treatment indicate clearly that improvement in the couple's expected general level of wellbeing, *i.e.* an increase in the couple's quality of life is clearly and unambiguously expressed by those concerned. What is not available is a cost oriented assessment. The author's conclusion, however, is nothing but a third person's super-imposition (in disguise) of his own judgement. Instead of trying to establish the expected benefits from treatment by looking at parents' willingness to pay, if necessary in opportunity cost terms, average life years are used, a measure which does not express utility. In addition, the most important person for which this treatment is undergone, the child to be conceived and to be born, does not figure at all.[17]

Case 4

In market based economies, one of the characteristic features is the synchronization of control and liability in order to contain the damage from harmful decisions. When the harm from a decision could be foreseen and avoided by taking appropriate care, the person who was able to foresee the harm and able to take the appropriate steps, *i.e.* the person who was in control will also be held liable for the consequences of his action or lack of actions.[18] In public health care provision, as we have seen earlier, there is substantial potential for harmful decisions; we also observe at the same time that the extent of liability is minimal and the synchronization of control and liability almost non-existent. From an economic point of view, this situation needs to be remedied. If for instance a patient suffers a serious injury because a doctor did not administer the necessary treatment, which he failed to do because, in order to administer the treatment, according to state regulations, he needed the written consent of two colleagues whom he could not reach because they were tied up in meetings, this doctor cannot be held liable for the injury imposed on the patient; nor can the full damage remain with the patient, if an efficient allocative result is to prevail; rather, the principle of synchronizing control and liability requires to make those jointly

---

[17] An anonymous reader has offered the following criticism at this point: "The case of fatility treatments reveals another weakness in the concept of the states equity. Just as the Hahn quotation ignores benefits reflected by willingness to pay, the state's equity will likely fall if fatility is enhanced and labour force participation, if primary care taken, is reduced. Clearly, consumer't rent (Oster plus) and related welfare concepts should be considered in reevaluating the concept of the state's equity".

If this suggestion were followed, the concept of the state's equity would no longer be empirically relevant. We can clearly measure state revenues but we cannot measure a couple's increased welfare from having a child; in addition, this welfare is privately experienced and should not be related to the state. It is important to avoid the velocity of depicting the state as the maximize of some social welfare functions. The equity consequences of additional (voluntary) conceptions should be straight forward and plausibly assumed to be positive; although there may be a temporary reduction in labour force participation by a parent, the new child will eventually join the labour force and, if healthy and skilled, contribute to the state's net worth.

[18] See also J.H.R. van de Poel, *Judgment and Control: Individual and Organizational Aspects of Performance Evaluation*, Groningen: Wolters-Noordhoff, 1986.

and severally liable who contributed to passing the regulations causing the problem - tying up doctors in meetings and requiring a written consent to engage in professional activities - in the first place.

By law, however, the nexus between control and liability is often weakened in every conceivable form. Consider the case of a treatment program[19] which substitutes a cheap and highly addictive drug for an expensive and (almost) equally addictive drug as a matter of treatment, dispensing the cheap drug for free. Irrespective of medical detail, the practice sounds questionable and might give rise to legal recourse from parents and dependents of addicted patients thus treated. We find the program being administered purely with government funds but through a private "foundation" without endowment, *i.e.* an agent with very shallow pockets, who consequently cannot be held liable. As instances like these multiply in a particular health sector, the adverse consequences of such unchecked treatments can amount to very substantial damage for that economy and society, damage for which nobody will be held liable in any form. The equity of the state and the wellbeing of its citizens can be substantially impaired, with nobody being held liable for such impairments.

By way of example, the "Consultatiebureau voor Alcohol en andere Drugs in Limburg" distributes methadone to about 1500 drug addicts in Limburg. It has no medical doctor on its regular staff. The institution is chartered as a foundation ("stichting") with an endowment of 100 dfl. Its revenues stern exclusively from various public bodies in the form of contract-subsidies.

Case 5

> For several years, Dutch health authorities have been trying to develop a policy of deferred adoption of new techniques in the social insurance package. In the try-out period, the technology is provided only on a limited scale under defined conditions. Simultaneously, a cost effectiveness analysis is carried out. (Haan 1989, p. 163).

The author continues by explaining that the new technique will first be used in a limited number of hospitals, while the study is underway.

From an economic point of view, this case adds an aspect beyond what has already been discussed under case 3 which is relevant to the principle of synchronization of control and liability just discussed. The straightforward results of the practice, namely the artificial slowdown of medical technology adoption is justified on equity grounds; a doubtful justification at best, since the negative consequences are likely to be distributed in a most inequitable way over those covered by the public health insurance system. In addition, however, the implementation

[19] See Edward Jay Epstein, Methadone: The Forlorn Hope. *The Public Interest* 36, 1974, 1-24.

is inequitable in itself, preferring patients in the vicinity of hospitals chosen over those in districts not chosen. Most importantly, however, although a procedure is followed, this procedure cannot be challenged in an appropriate review process by those concerned: doctors and, above all, patients refused the treatment. The absence of such a review procedure further weakens incentives to prevent harm (from lack of treatment offered).

By imposing a cost *effectiveness* study instead of a cost *benefit* analysis, a further step is taken which detracts from the equitability of the procedure. As we have seen in the discussion of case 3, cost effectiveness studies will use proxies for individual valuations and consequently do not take into account the most important aspects which have probably led to the development of the new treatment techniques analyzed. By systematically disregarding consumers' rent, the procedure is already tilted towards the inequitable result of not adopting a new technique. Again, the allocational inefficiency in the public health care system can be substantial consequent to this type of procedure.

Case 6

The idea to strengthen general practitioners' role as gate keepers (to the more costly treatment of specialists and in hospitals) was conceived after it became apparent that in the Netherlands, general practitioners rationally responded to the following financial arrangement. For patients covered under the public insurance fund, the general practitioner received a flat annual recompensation. For patients covered under private insurance programs, remuneration was according to time spent and treatment category. The predictable result, referral of time-consuming patients covered under the public fund to the more expensive care by specialists and hospitals led to the adoption of an experiment in which general practitioners received a financial incentive for making fewer referrals than a general average. The experiment resulted in a selective re-arrangement of the referral practice, with those general practitioners participating in the experiment referring fewer children and engaging in more smaller treatments (like audiograms) and more prescriptions which had previously been left to the specialists.

Again, the experiment was accompanied by a "scientific" study. The root of the problem taken up with this experiment lies in the differentiation of pay schedules. This led general practitioners to take on more treatment of privately insured patients relative to publicly covered patients, opening the "gate" to publicly covered patients to more expensive treatment methods, while tying privately insured patients up for a longer time in the general practitioner's office. In principle, this difference of treatment based not on medical conditions but on medical coverage flies in the face of the principle of equity, however conceived.[20]

A patient appearing in front of a doctor and showing symptoms that could, in principle, reflect different conditions will receive different treatment depending on whether he appears before a general practitioner or a specialist. The general practitioner is more likely to proceed with a cure even if the underlying condition has not been established with certainty than the specialist; therein lays the basic difference in approach. The advantage of the general practitioner is in expediency, the relative advantage of the specialist lies in accuracy. This refers to both decisions about treatments and the delivery of the treatment itself; the specialist will have more expertise in the limited number of treatments rendered than the general practitioner. The trade-off between expediency and accuracy cannot be avoided; it calls for an optimization on the basis of all the available knowledge. Knowledge can come from two sources, the doctor(s) involved and the patient. In appointing the general practitioner as the gate keeper of the system, a source of knowledge is blocked with the foreseeable result that the trade-off cannot be optimally resolved. By additionally offering financial rewards to a general practitioner for non-referral, the decision-making process is further tilted and the patient's position weakened, also because he faces a monopoly provider of medical services with the general practitioner whereas he faces an oligopolistic supply side of medical services if granted access to the specialist immediately. The likely consequence of such an approach, again, is a suboptimal provision of medical services, lower quality of medical services rendered than is possible with the amount of resources claimed by the system. Again, the allocative consequences of this equity driven pricing formula can be substantial. Interestingly enough, the doctors involved in the experiment tried to contain the possible damage by absorbing more routine tasks into their practices and relying to a larger extent on medication than on further tests and on the more focussed drug treatment the specialist can provide. The inter-generational equity impact of absorbing more pediatric cases into the general practitioner's office are worthy of further scrutiny. In conclusion a detailed discussion of the six cases selected gives us still more reason to expect that equity driven measures in public health care provision, far from being purely of a distributive nature, can have important allocative consequences.

[20] Most likely, the practice is also incompatible with the Hippocratic oath.

4

An Agenda for Further Research

The considerable mismatch between the results derived from standard public finance analysis and those found in the six cases discussed above raises the question of whether received public finance analysis is at all adequate for understanding the operation of the health sector in modern democracies of the small northern European type. One of the classics in the theory of taxation, Emil Sax (1924) offered this word of caution in applying his tax theory:

> Our theory is based on normal taxation. Quite a different matter are confiscatory taxes aiming at a modification of the income and wealth of certain population groups. The reasons for such interference with the existing property distribution are exogenous to the theory. Nor has the question of absolute and relative amount of such taxes any relevance, since it is subject to *a priori* decisions in the light of political purposes and political power. (Sax 1924, cited from the transiation p. 187).

Is the set-up of the public health care provision to be explained, not in terms of equity but in terms of redistributing income and wealth through the deep regulation and monopolization of health services in the public domain? If this were so, one would have to show that the design of the public health service in a country such as the Netherlands is conducive to organizing a rent-seeking game, and that rents can be claimed by identifiable interest groups at the expense of the quantity and quality of health care provision in general. Such a conjecture is conceivable. Hurst *e.g.* finds in conclusion, "that health services are not an agent of income redistribution to such a degree in the U.S. as in the U.K. and Canada." (p. 120).

References

Backhaus, Jürgen (1989), *Die Finanzierung des Wohlfahrtsstaats,* (Inaugural Lecture). Maastricht: Rijksuniversiteit Limburg.

Doorslaer, Eddy K.A. (1987), *Health, Knowledge, and the Demand for Medical Care,* Assen/Maastricht: Van Gorcum.

Epstein, Edward Jay (1974), "Methadone: The Forlorn Hope", *The Public Interest* 36, 1-24.

Haan,Ger (1989), *Effecten en Kosten van In-Vitro-Fertilisatie,* Doctoral Dissertation, Rijksuniversiteit Limburg, Maastricht, 1989.

Hurst, Jeremy (1985), "Equity in the Delivery of and Payment for Health Services". In: J.W. Hurst, *Financing Health Care in the U.S., Canada, and Britain,* Kings Fund.

Leenen, H.J.J. and H.D.C. Roscam-Abbing (1986), *Bestuurlijk Gezondheidsrecht*, Alphen a/d Rijn, Brussel: Tjeenk Willink.

Ministerie van Welzijn, Volksgezondheid en Cultuur (1985), *Financieel Overzicht van de Gezondheidszorg en Maatschappelijke Dienstverlening,* 1986, 's-Gravenhage: Staatsuitgeverij.

Musgrave, Richard A. and Peggy E. Musgrave (1989), *Public Finance in Theory and Practice*, first edition 1973, New York: MacGraw-Hill.
Poel, J.H.R. van de (1986), *Tudgment and Control: Individual and Organization Aspects of Performance Evaluation,* Groningen: Wolters-Noordhoff.
Roscam-Abbing, H.D.C. and F.F.H. Rutten (1985), "Solidariteit versus Equivalentiebeginsel". In: H.D.C. Roscam-Abbing & F.F.H. Rutten, *Verleden en Toekomst van het Ziektekostenverzekeringsstelsel in Nederland,* Deventer.
Rawis, John (1972), *A Theory of Justice*, London: Oxford University Press.
Sax, Emil (1958), "The Valuation Theory of Taxation". In: Richard A. Musgrave & Allen T. Peacock (eds.) *Classics in the Theory of Public Finance,* London: MacMillan, pp. 177-189; originally published as "Die Wertungstheorie der Steuer". *Zeitschrift für Volkswirtschaft und Sozialpolitik*, new series, volume 4, 1924.
Schmoller, Gustav (1863), "Die Lehre vom Einkommen in ihrem Zusammenhang mit dem Grundprinzip der Steuerlehre". In: *Zeitschrift für die gesamte Staatswissenschaft,* 19.
Tits, M.H.L. (1989), "An Experiment with Financial Incentives for General Practitioners in the Netherlands". *Research paper* for "The Joint Meeting on the First European Conference on Health Economics" Barcelona, September 1989.
Wicksell, Knut (1896), *Finanztheoretische Untersuchungen.* Jena: Gustav Fischer.
Wolff, Christian Freiherr von (1754), *Grundsätze des Natur- und Völckerrechts.* Halle: Renger.

German Fiscal Sociology's Influence on Japan

Norio Sasaki
Associate Professor of Public Finance
Graduate School of Economics and Management
Tohoku University
Kawauchi, Aobaku,
Sendai 980-8576
Japan
Fon: ++81-22-217-6276
sasaki@econ.tohoku.ac.jp

Abstract: It is meaningful to know how fiscal sociology has been taken up in Japan, which confronts with economic and fiscal crisis. Because of strong influence of German public finance, some literature about fiscal sociology appeared in Japan. But it received less attention than in Germany. The fundamental reasons are a strong influence of Marxism and the fact that there have not been serious fiscal crisis in Japan until recently. However, nowadays Japanese government has large public debt. Thus, some Japanese scholars pay attention to fiscal sociology. However it is not established social science. In order to develop persuasive discussion, it is necessary to arrange it theoretically.

Keywords: Fiscal sociology, Germany, Japan, public finance, public debt.

JEL codes: B1, B2, H0, H1, H6.

1 Meaning of Reconsidering Fiscal Sociology

Nowadays we can see a distinct relationship between economics and public finance, in which the former provides abstract theories and the latter applies it to concrete fiscal problems. This fixed relationship seems to have been established since World War II, that is to say, since the American and English "public economics" became dominant. But seemingly, recent economics has been subdivided into many branches and each branch has gradually lost academic exchanges each other, and only looked for theoretical completeness, paying little attention to reality.[1] However, I think that the confidence of any science depends

[1] As for this problem of modern economics, see Hodgson (1999).

on how exact it explains events in real world. Therefore, there seems no dominant theory in contemporary economics.

On the other hand, watching Japanese economic situation in recent ten years, the economic and fiscal policy by Japanese government seems no longer effective to push up Japanese economy. Indeed until now, Japanese government has spent much money from its budget into fiscal policy every year, abolished many regulations to be seen as obstacles to activity of firms, and privatized or decided to privatise some important governmental firms, which has been said to be representative of inefficient activities of Japanese government.[2] But the bulk of these efforts were in vain, and an enormous amount of governmental debt remains.[3]

The above- mentioned two facts points out that public finance which has long time depended on modern economic theory is unreliable to solve current economic or fiscal problems. Of course it could also be said that the bad adjustment of economics to Japan is only a special case occurring in one of oriental countries where history, culture and way of thinking are very different from western ones. But if it is so, we must be all the more doubtful about effectiveness of such public finance as to be useful only under restricted social conditions.

Therefore, it should be time to reconsider fiscal sociology, which has been paid little attention for a long time under the prevalence of modern public finance based on neoclassical or Keynesian economics. Fiscal Sociology has dynamic and politico-economic view on fiscal systems, the development of which was in parallel to its national economy. Recently there appeared some new important contributions in this field. One remarkable example is reconsideration of tax theory by J. G. Backhaus,[4] where the concept "tax state", being made by Schumpeter, but long time neglected, is analyzed from the viewpoint that this concept offers important base for dynamically social effect of taxation. Another example in relation to the subject of this paper, are some recent studies and proposal on Japanese fiscal problems, as referred later. Most works of that theme were written by Japanese economists. However, the fact is very important that

[2] Of course there are opinions by many economists that recent Japanese deregulation or privatization is not yet enough to be so called "structural reform". But I will emphasis the fact that in recent years Japanese economic situation has become worse contrary to the progress of economic reforms by Japanese government.

[3] To indicate, from 1995-2000 among 7 developed countries (United States, Japan, Germany, France, Italy, United Kingdom and Canada), only Japan marked minus growth rate of GDP per year (in 1998). As for inflation rate per year during same period, in all year except for 1997 recorded minus rate in Japan. Fiscal indicator seems more serious. During same period Japanese general government balance in each year became worse. In 2000, it was –7.5 per cent of GDP. The worst number except for Japan in 2000 was –2.4 per cent (France). The data mentioned above is from International Monetary Fund (2001).

[4] See Backhaus (1994), Backhaus (1997).

they took up fiscal sociology in order to solve those current problems in Japan, confronting with the worst economic and fiscal situation among developed countries.

Originally fiscal sociology has been a seminal field where many social sciences, e. g. economics, politics, jurisprudence and sociology etc interact. Therefore in this field we can find a lot of new knowledge and meaningful suggestions on theoretical and real problems.

In fiscal sociology, however, there has not been established standard and firm approach yet. Maybe those are still "in lap of the gods", as Schumpeter said. Therefore, it seems duty not only for me, but also for all scholars who concerns about fiscal sociology, to absorb essence of representative works of fiscal sociology, and to refine it for the purpose of applying to current economic or fiscal problems. For this theme, it would also make sense to know the influence of fiscal sociology on countries except for Germany and Austria[5].

However, before doing so, the definition of fiscal sociology, that is to say, how far the term of fiscal sociology could be extended in German fiscal literature must be decided. If we suppose the fiscal sociology to be a social science that explains fiscal phenomenon by not only taking economic factors into accounts, but political and social factors as well, its origin could be extended to *Kameralistische Wissenschaft* (cameralistics) in 18th or 19th centuries. I think this way is right. But in this paper, in order to make the subject clear, I will restrict to the scholar who consciously used the term "Fiscal Sociology" and promoted this method.

Here at first, I explain how original fiscal sociology's works were introduced and evaluated in Japan. Second, the influence on Japanese economics and public

---

[5] As is well known, some scholars concerning fiscal sociology are not German, but Austrian, as Goldscheid, the creator of the name "fiscal sociology", and Schumpeter. Therefore, it might seem inaccurate to use the phrase "German fiscal sociology" in the title of this paper. But because of two reasons, this naming seems suitable. First, the Austrian proponents of fiscal sociology surely criticized German public finance up in that time. But, they had same view as Historical School in the sense that they regard history very important, and admit each country to have different economic or political institutions and to pursue independent economic or fiscal policy subject to their own histories. Exactly, Goldscheid also contributed to the *Handbuch der Finanazwissenschaft* (1. Aufl.) and made up the lack of reality in German public finance which had too much emphasized explanation of fiscal institutions and could not offer adequate perspective for changing economic, political and social environments. Second, I took up some recent works by mainly American political scientists, which are categorized into fiscal sociology too. But these approaches seems to be different from original German works in some senses, as we see later. Therefore, in order to distinguish this works from original ones, I name the latter "German fiscal sociology".

finance is detailed, and the reason of this response is discussed from the viewpoint of the economic and social situation at that time. In conclusion, I refer recent changes in academic condition, concerning about fiscal sociology, and express my view.

2 Academic Background of Introducing Fiscal Sociology in Japan

In order to understand Japanese economist's response to German fiscal sociology, we should know the situation of economics in Japan shortly after the end of World War I. After the Meiji-revolution in the latter half of 19th century, in which Japan changed from feudal state to modern state, many universities and colleges were established by national government, in order that they introduce foreign advanced knowledge and technique, including economics, to Japanese people. Of course the classical economics, made in Great Britain, was imported in that time. However, because of weakness of Japanese economy in those days, the classical economics, which insisted the merit of free trade, did not received more attention in Japan than German historical school, which in contrast insisted protective trade and promotion of main domestic industries by government. That is to say, most Japanese economists at that time eagerly tried to absorb the knowledge of the economics which was seemed to be useful to strengthen Japanese political and economic power.

Concerning public finance, German study naturally became a model because it endowed in governments transcendent power to arrange economic or social problems. In Japanese universities, typical in University of Tokyo, German Public finance was taught in order to educate prospective bureaucrat of government, with no adding theoretical or positive examination.

In summation, many Japanese economists at that time made efforts only to import foreign achievements, mainly made in Germany, and did not create their own theory. Therefore, as might be easily expected, Japanese economics lost its backbone and fell into confusion along with declining the prestige of German economics after World War I. A typical example is the life of "Japanese Association for the Study of Social Policy".[6]

During Sino-Japanese War and Russo-Japanese War, Japan rapidly became industrialised. But along with economic development, inequality of wealth spread wider, and labour problem became more serious. For that reason, in 1896

[6] About the details of its foundation, its contribution to Japanese social policy and the reason of its disappearance, see Fujii (1998).

it was established, in imitation of German one, by large number of scholars, managers, bureaucrats and politicians. For a while after it was founded, this association played an important role in legislation of Factory Acts in Japan, enacted in 1911, insisting early introduction of it and appealing to public with some large scale conferences and many reports about the situation of Japanese workers. But afterwards a serious conflict escalated between socialist group, having H. Kawakami as central figure, and anti-socialist group, with T. Fukuda, a representative classical economist at that time and strong opponent against Marxism, being one of the leaders. At last, after World War I, the association disappeared in 1924.

During this time, in the field of public finance, reflecting its academic character to need detailed explanation or analysis of fiscal institutions, critical conflict of thoughts as the case of economics, did not occurred. On the contrary, textbooks of German public finance written by famous scholars A. Wagner etc, seemingly most effective in latter half of nineteenth century in its homeland, had been taught dogmatically at Japanese universities even after World War I.

That is the very character of Japanese environment of economics and public finance, where the academy had split into two main groups, classical and socialist, and no leading theory for public finance existed. In addition, the fact must be noted that at that time the thought that placed governmental activity in the market based economic theory had not been recognised by most Japanese economists yet. The "marginal revolution" in public finance theory had already been started in 1920's by the pioneer, K. Wicksell, F. von Wieser and English welfare economists, A. Pigou and F. Y. Edgeworth etc. However, in those days, there were few works which only introduced marginal approach of taxation e.g. the "least sacrifice theory" by E. Sax, with H. Ito (1935) a representative.

Therefore, the lack of advanced knowledge in public finance theory of Japanese scholars seems to have been enormous obstruction for Japanese economists to accept and analyse fiscal sociology accurately. It was after World War II that the mathematically elegant method, mainly made in United States, was introduced in Japanese economics and public finance theory.

3 Acceptance and Criticism of Fiscal Sociology in Japan

Now, we can proceed to concrete explanation on the introduction of fiscal sociology in Japan. First, in table 1, literatures of fiscal sociology written by Japanese economists are listed chronologically. Looking at this table, it seems strange that in Japan one of the most important literature, *The Crisis of Tax*

State, written by Schumpeter in 1918, was much later translated and explained than other literature of fiscal sociology. This fact shows that Japanese public finance scholars before World War II had put comparably low value on Schumpeter. But if we consider that his book was written as an opposition to Goldscheid's work, which was most frequently taken up and cited in Japan, it was definitely unfortunate that the study of Schumpeter was delayed in Japanese public finance. In this section, some remarkable studies in Japan were taken up by each author.

Table 1: Literature of Fiscal Sociology by Japanese Economists[a]

1921 -1930	Ito, H. "Zaisei Gakuha" (The Schools of Public Finance) (1927) Ouchi, H. "Zaisei Shakaigaku–Goldscheid no Zaiseigaku Hihan" (Fiscal Sociology: Goldscheid's Critique on Public Finance) (1928) Abe, K. "Zaisei Gakuchi" (History of Public Finance) (1929) Ohata, B. *Shakaiteki Zaiseigaku* (Social Public Finance) (1930)
1931 -1940	Yonehara, S. "Goldscheid no Zaisei Gakusetsu to Sono Hihan" (Goldscheid's Fiscal Thought and Critique) (1932) Yonehara, S. "Zaisei Shakaigaku no Saikin no Keiko" (Recent Tendency of Fiscal Sociology) (1933) Ohata, B. *Sozei Kokkaron* (Tax State) (1934) Yamashita, K."'Zaisei Shakaigaku' no Igi oyobi Hoho" (The Meaning and Way of 'Fiscal Sociology') (1933-34) Nagata, K. *Gendai Zaiseigaku no Riron: Kisei Taikei no Hihan to Hansei* (Modern Theory of Public Finance: Criticism and Review of Exisiting System) (1937) Ohata, B. *Zaiseigaku Josetsu* (Introduction of Public Finance) (1939)
1941 -1950	Kanbe, S"Atarashii Zaiseigaku to Furui Zaiseigaku" (The New Public Finance and the Old Public Finance) (1940) Nagata, K *Zaiseigaku no Tenkai* (Extensive Public Finance), Tokyo: Nihon Hyoronsha. (1942)
1951 -(1962)	Kimura, M. "Kaisetsu " (A Statement) (1951) Takagi, H"Showa Nendai Shiki niokeru Zaisei Gakusetsu no Tenkan Katei" (The Changing Process of Fiscal Theory at the beginning of Showa era) (1959) Yamashita, K "*Zaiseishakaigaku*" *Kenkyu* (Study of "Fiscal Sociology") (1962)

a. In this table, literature to be seen important concerning the history of public finance in Japan is listed.

It was in 1927, that the literature of fiscal sociology was at first introduced into Japan. After this, "Staat, öffentlicher Haushalt und Gesellschaft. Wesen und Aufgabe der Finanzwissenschaft vom Standpunkte der Soziologie" written by Rudolf Goldscheid in *Handbuch der Finanzwissenschaft*, 1st ed., 1926, was partly translated and was explained in detail by Hyoe Ouchi, who was a Marxist and an authority of economics and public finance in those days of Japan. In this article he admitted Goldscheid's contribution to German public finance as regards he criticised it because of its unreality and created new approach which emphasises that real political, economic and social environment, and fiscal activity regulate each other. But from the standpoint of Marxism, Ouchi criticised Goldscheid's thoughts severely as follows.

First, Ouchi says that Goldscheid's criticism of German public finance had been already done by socilalist:

> This criticism, which regards public finance as incapable, is the same criticism as of *Begriffsjurisprudenz*(conceptual jurisprudence) or former conceptual German *Staatswissenschaft*(state science), which have already brought by many people. Especially thoughts of socialist have strongly pointed out this weakness (1927, 667).

Second, Ouchi points out that the property tax, expected to play very important role in Goldscheid's proposal, was not effective. This one time tax is extracted through transfer of stocks from firms to government. Afterwards government would receive large amount of dividends, which would be used for the purpose of welfare policy,[7] and would need not issue bonds any more. However Ouchi expects that this policy causes wages and production costs to be up, because life of labour would improve. In addition, according to him,

> It would be impossible for firms to obtain profits more than a certain extent by means of defeating small firms and concentrating. Then, the only way for firms is to reduce capital accumulation or to reduce dividends to stocks otherwise (1927, 674).

For this reason, revenue of governments would decrease, and it would depend on public debt again. However, in this argument there are some unreliable points. First, if there happens technological innovation, wage and production costs need not rise. Second, even if production costs would be up, domestic or foreign markets may extend wider. So, there is no necessity for profit of decreasing.

The third criticism by Ouchi is about the quality of state depending deficit[8]. He says that in order to survive crisis in modern capitalist society state needs fund, which must be collected through tax or public debt. In his view, the contradiction of capitalist society consists in the fact that tax cannot be enough for state to

[7] Goldscheid called the situation where by government spending the welfare of people is accomplished *"Menschenökonomie"* (humaneconomy). This is an ethical word. In order to understand Goldscheid's fiscal sociology, it is necessary to examine the meaning of this word. But for the subject of this paper, it would be enough to know that this word roughly means welfare of people. As for the relationship between public policy and "*Menschenökonomie*", see Goldscheid (1926, 167-171).

[8] As for following remarks, see Ouchi (1927, 675-677).

spend on increasing public demands. Public debt is therefore useful to avoid this crisis. Thus, he definitely says that the state which cannot owe public debt is powerless. We can easily see in this criticism his recognition that capitalist economy collapse inevitably, which was typical of Marxist.

As a whole, Ouchi's criticism, based on the standpoint of Marxism, pointed out the inadequacy of Goldscheid's proposal on fiscal reform. But nowadays, this criticism appears to be one-sided argument. We must investigate Goldscheid's work from other standpoints with more accurate and objective way. Of course, at that time, there were some scholars who did it. As was stated earlier, the mainstream of Japanese public finance had still conserved the traditional German public finance, when fiscal sociology was introduced. Next, we turn to view of "traditionalists".

It was Shichinosuke Yonehara that criticised Ouchi's view and also examined other thoughts of German fiscal sociologists. He defines fiscal sociology as a study on the function of public household, which is regulated by society and also regulates society.[9] From this viewpoint, he explains Goldscheid's thoughts and agrees with him on the necessity of reforming German public finance theory, which had not been based on reality but ethical fiction. He criticised Ouchi concerning that where state owns the bulk of share, the state could control wage or process. In addition, because of human economy domestic purchasing power could increase, so, the firms could maintain their former profits.[10]

On the other hand, he criticises Goldscheid from other points. First, he insisted that Goldscheid emphasised the political effect of public debt too much. That is to say, he pays attention rather on international competition of market as the reason why private capital controls government than public debt.

> Nowadays, when international conflict and competition escalate, state is naturally destined to protect private capital, to the extent that modern private capitalism remains. In the time of liberalism, private capital had immense market and could grow up with comparably less dependence on government. But once in monopolistic capitalism, we cannot expect capital growth and economic strength without help of state, because of largeness of firms and narrowness of market. Thus, the combination of state becomes extremely tight. If state does not protect private capital, it would fly to other country and national economy and government finance would collapse (1932, 394-395).

---

[9] See Yonehara (1932, 380). About this definition of fiscal sociology, Other Japanese sholars of public finance had already the same view as Yonehara.

[10] Yonehara (1932, 392-393). However, in order to make this argument meaningful, knowledge of macroeconomic analysis is no doubt necessary. In such detail, we cannot help feel the lack of analytical ability in Japanese economics or economists at that time.

Second, he criticises Goldscheid's proposal of nationalization. Namely, in spite of condemning traditional German public finance for being fiction, Goldscheid seems to have made another unrealistic concept "human economy", the key concept of his thought.

> The revenue of state after realization of national capitalism depends on prosperity of national economy. Therefore the interest of state is the same as the interest of private capital. Why should the needs of state be same as the needs of the masses? Why should the state do human economy? (...) There is nothing for it but to think that carrying human economy out after realization of state capitalism accompanies thought which makes state ethical. If so, he falls into fiction that he at first made effort to reject (1932, 399).

Yonehara (1933) also arranged other works of German fiscal sociologists subject to their research methods. In his view, there are two way of fiscal sociology. One is historical, and another is theoretical. According to him, H. Ritschl and H. Jecht belong to the former, and H. Sultan belongs to the latter[11]. After explaining Jecht's division of fiscal history, "conventional finance" and "rational finance", he criticizes Jecht for lacking fiscal-sociological content in spite of the purpose of his study. "I doubt whether Jecht's total system of thought has tinge of fiscal sociology. Especially, his explanation about the meaning of governmental finance is in the same way as the economic school" (1933, 402). Thus, he regards Jecht's thought rather "sociological history of finance" than fiscal sociology (1933, 402).

Next Yonehara (1933) refers to H. Sultan, who tried to create theoretical fiscal sociology. On the one hand Sultan crisicized Goldscheid of emphasizing only policy and neglecting theoretical side, on the other hand, regarded Jecht's method too philosophical, arguing that Jecht neglected political side of fiscal phenomenon.[12] Thus concerning the method of "Wissensoziologie" (sociology of knowledge), Sultan tried to grasp intuitively real existence and searched political moment that decides fiscal activity, especially in the field of taxation. Yonehara explains in detail Sultan's thought, referring his "Macht" (power) theory, in which there exist both potitical power and economic power interdependently decide circumstances of market. But Yonehara points out that as for taxation, which is main theme of Sultan's thought, he failed to describe how state revenue is decided politico-economically.

> His theory is made up more intensively on the field of market economy than field of public finance. The subject he tried to explain is nothing else capitalistic market economy, in which public finance is only one of the components and matters on its function (1933, 422).

---

[11] In this paper, Ritschul is not regarded as fiscal sociologist because he did not positively insist it. Thus in examination of Yonehara's view, his comment on Ritchl is not taken up.

[12] As for his criticism of Jecht, see Sultan (1932).

In this way, Yonehara understood precisely past German Sociology and added detailed criticism on each author. In spite of these efforts, however, he neither positively tried to give meaningful definition of fiscal sociology, nor showed something new method. It seems limit of his research.

After Yonehara other researchers of fiscal sociology appeared in Japan. Kakutaro Yamashita was one of the most dedicated promoters of this approach. Yamasita's research is characterized by his positive definition of fiscal sociology. He at first pointed out the necessity of reality in public finance, and insisted that social science should not be abstract study which pursue inevitable law in society, like method of natural science. From this point of view, he defines fiscal sociology as follows: "Fiscal sociology, thus, investigate the correlation between public household and society, on the really structural relation, and tries to elucidate public finance in its whole-social meaning" (1933-34, 56, 895). At this standpoint, Yamashita criticised former introducers of German fiscal sociology in Japan. For example, he regards Yonehara's understanding of Goldscheid too narrow for the reason that Goldscheid's study of relation between state and society seemed to be only a policy argument to him (1933-34, 56, 896). He also regards fiscal sociology as central field of public finance, thus, he insisted that it would rather better to use simply "public finance" than "fiscal sociology". However, on the other hand, Yamashita thought that it was difficult to unite theory to policy. "We emphasis that fiscal sociology as a science should be humble in problem of value judgment" (1933-34, 56, 892). He dedicated himself to the methodology of fiscal sociology, examining epistemology that discussed by Jecht and Sultan. In the end, he insisted that fiscal sociology should be studied socially, rejecting methods of natural science, and should be studied historically, that is to say, without neglecting its historical character.

> However, the limit of his research is in the fact that he did not apply his epistemologically deepened method in real problem of governmental finance in Japan or any other countries after all. His careful treatment of fiscal sociology ironically prevented his research from proceeding further to real fiscal problems.

Bunshichi Ohata has been seen as the most representative researcher of fiscal sociology in Japan before the World War II. He surveyed the various thoughts of German Public Finance theories and the thoughts of fiscal sociology in very comprehensive manner and tried to apply the sociological method to describing the history of western public finance (Ohata, 1930, 1934, 1939). His contribution is most significant in the explanation of the relationship between the taxation and the development of modern states in Europe (1934, 167-246). His attempt in an enormous amount of work, however, described only the history of fiscal history in Europe and cannot be seen to have succeeded to abstract the characteristics of the relationship between state and society, appearing in the fiscal conditions. Later his work was influenced by the thoughts of welfare economists, e.g. A. C. Pigou and E. A. Seligman, making his position at last ambiguous in the history of public finance theory.

In the end of this section, we take up the research by Motokazu Kimura, Which seems nowadays most important because he translated fully Schumpeter's *Die Krise des Steuerstaats* (the Crisis of Fiscal State) at first into Japanese and explained its meaning as regards the relation between Historical School and German public finance.

In his comments on fiscal sociology, he recognized the important difference between above two fields (Kimura, 1951). As for the former, "Historical School struggled in order to create economics which maintains theoretical character and satisfies the needs of nationals. (...) Consideration to theory always restricted its economics, disturbed and worried its principle (1951, 14). On the contrary, "for public finance, recognition of law had only subsidiary meaning because it deals with economy of state, in which state is a performer" (1951, 15). The last sentence seems to mean that German public finance regarded economic controllability of government as important. Therefore German public finance created a large-scaled field, in which many other subjects, e. g. ethics, law, accounts, etc, are included and state is expected to behave supremely to arbitrate interests of many different groups in society. But this magnificent system broke down when the historical conditions in which governments could really behave as such changed. He writes, "German public finance was essentially an 'economy of state'. Thus when economic and social organization are disturbed and supreme role of state becomes rejected, this system necessarily confront with its limit. That is to say, 'economy of state' does not matter but 'economy and state'" (1951, 17). Significance of Goldscheid, pioneer of fiscal sociology, exists in this point.

However Kimura appreciate rather Schumpeter than Goldscheid, for the reason that Schumpeter more carefully dealt with the relation between state and society, namely, analysed objectively, contrary to Goldscheid, and historically how tax state was formed concerning social condition. The importance of tax state has been already pointed out by Kimura. Therefore we can say Kimura's research leads directly leads to present study of fiscal sociology.

We have examined thoughts about fiscal sociology of Japanese scholars so far. As is easily seen in table 1, most of all works concentrates during 1920's and 30's, shortly after original works of German fiscal sociology. It can also be said that Japanese study of fiscal sociology rapidly decayed after World War II. From this point, Kimura's and Yamashita's works are exceptional. We must proceed further to inquire why this sudden change happened in Japanese public finance.

4 Specialities in Japanese Public Finance and Fiscal Affairs

As we have seen in previous sections, German fiscal sociology exactly influenced Japanese public finance theory. Among corresponding Japanese literature, there are remarkable researches, which understood deeply and correctly German originals and criticised them essentially. However, this Japanese literature at last ended in introduction, explanation, agreement and criticism. In other words, it lacked concrete proposal for Japanese fiscal matter. Moreover, Japanese research of fiscal sociology declined after World War II. Why have fiscal sociology remained in minor position in Japan? For this problem, at first we must know circumstance of public finance after World War II in Japan.

Like Germany, nay, more rapidly than Germany, American and English economics flowed in Japan. Also in the field of public finance, the one as applied economics occupied main position. Especially R. A. Musgrave's *The Theory of Public Finance* (1959) became one of the most authoritative textbooks in public finance because of its theoretical firmness and comprehensiveness.

However, concerning the influence of Anglo-Saxon economics, this change was fit for German case too. Nevertheless, in Germany, study of decision-making about fiscal policy which did not depend on modern economic theory remained after World War II.[14] Thus special Japanese reason should be considered.

It is well known that after World War II Marxian economics have been very influential in Japanese economics until recently. In the field of public finance, a characteristic thought of Marxian economists appeared. It tried to explain each fiscal phenomenon by reducing it to special development-stage of capitalism.[15] Of course Japanese Marxian economists regarded history as important, but because of that reason, they often placed fiscal events in its own historical context compulsorily. Therefore their real analysis had to become incomplete, and barren conflicts often happened among them about interpretation of economic or fiscal events. Under the environment, fiscal sociology had lost influential power, and post-war successor has never appeared until recently in Japan.

In addition, we must refer to the economic and fiscal situation in Japan after the introduction of fiscal sociology. Since modern fiscal system was established in Japan in last half of the 19th century, serious problems of public debt have little

---

[14] Of course in fiscal sociology, there exists postwar literature, e.g. Mann (1959). In addition, we can mention another approach "Finanzpsychologie" (fiscal psychology). See Hansmeyer and Mackscheidt (1977).

[15] This thought originated from Uno (1936). According to him, fiscal affairs in each time shows the character of the policy of state which corresponds with each development-stage of capitalism. He is to be said the founder of postwar Marxian public finance in Japan.

emerged, except for Russo-Japanese War in the beginning of 20th century. In case of World War I, indeed Japan participated, but the active area of Japanese army was restricted to eastern Asia, so the then military expenditure of Japan was extremely smaller than European countries. In World War II Japan issued largest amount of public debts, by which military expenditure was financed. But the bulk of this debt was accepted by central bank of Japan, and about the rest, accepted by private sector, redemption was postponed after the war. In addition, shortly after the war, hyperinflation lessened the value of this public debt. On the other hand, during the time when Japan accomplished remarkably high economic growth e.g. 1950's and 60's, government need not issue public debt in the general account (ipan-kaikei)[16] because of plentiful tax revenue.[17] But after 1970's these blessed economic condition disappeared and afterwards Japanese governments came to worry dealing with public debt, the expenditure for which has been large part of public expenditure.

Why does the historical condition relate to Japanese fiscal sociology? Originally fiscal sociology was born with need for measures against fiscal crisis. Indeed both Goldscheid and Schumpeter struggled with the enormous amount of public debt in their home country, Austria.[18] That is why their literature could receive large public concern. On the contrary, fiscal sociology did not receive much attention in Japan, where the fiscal condition was not so serious until 1980's.

5 Recent Trend Concerning Fiscal Sociology

As is stated at the beginning of this paper, doubt about modern economics is the background of recent re-examination of fiscal sociology. Especially in Japanese case, this trend relates to serious problem of public debt since 1990's. In this last section we briefly examine recent research which surveyed and arranged litera-

---

[16] Japanese central government has some accounts. The other accounts except for general account are called special accout (tokubetsu-kaikei). Both are considered in the National Diet. But the general account is most important because most of all national tax revenue is transferred to it, and the budget of it shows outline of policy.

[17] In Japanese fiscal law (Zaisei-Hou), there is an article which principally prohibits to issue public debt in the general account, Art.4. But this admits exception, in case of public investment or case which National Diet admits with legislation of specified duration. Therefore, it seems that this law did not play so important role for Japanese independency on public debt after the war. That is to say, rapid economic growth seems to be main reason.

[18] It is well known that Goldscheid proposed drastic measures to cure fiscal crisis in Austria, that is to say, nationalization by transferring stocks. But Schumpeter, in *Die Krise der Steuerstaat* (The Crisis of Tax State), dealt with how to solve the problem of public debt in Austria, besides detailed analysis of European tax history (Schumpeter, 1951). In this book he insisted one-time property tax, contrary to Goldscheid (1951, 101-103).

ture until recently from the viewpoint regarding fiscal sociology as anti-economic.

In addition, remarkable research and proposal by Japanese economists for public deficit is taken up.

According to DeWit (1999), fiscal sociology is defined generally "anti-economics". From this standpoint he classifies many publications concerning public household or taxation by methods, most of which were written about United States. On his view the fiscal sociology in United Stated after World War II were at first divided into two main approaches, Marxian, e. g. J. O'Connor (1973) and pluralistic, R. A. Musgrave (1980). The former regarded state as instrument of the ruling class, and the latter criticised the former to be partial. DeWit insists further, that under the influence of institutionalism new approach appeared, e.g. neo-Weberian fiscal sociology, social learning approach, institutional fiscal sociology since 1980's.

In this way, he regards many researches by political scientist and sociologist as fiscal sociology besides economists. Most of them did not refer to original German fiscal sociologist, e.g. Goldscheid and Schumpeter. On the contrary, they did not use the word "fiscal sociology" at all in their literature except for the case of O'Connor or Musgrave. Indeed it is not *sine qua non* for being fiscal sociologist whether they knew original German fiscal sociology. Only whether their researches belong to the field which classifier regards as fiscal sociology, is important. However, regarding fiscal sociology as only "anti-economics" seems to lead to losing sight of the meaning German fiscal sociology had.

For example, Thelen and Steinmo (1992), political scientists and classified by DeWit as "historical institutional fiscal sociologist" (1999, 271), described their thought which was different from "rational institutionalist"[19] as follows: "Rational choice and historical institutionalism diverge rather sharply on the issue of preference formation. While rational choice deals with preferences at the level of assumptions, historical institutionalists take the question of how individuals and groups define their self-interest as problematical. Rational choice institutionalists in effect "bracket" the issue of preference formation theoretically (...). This is quite different from historical institutionalists, who argue that not just the *strategies* but also the *goals* actors pursue are shaped by the institutional context" (1992, 8).

[19] According to Thelen and Steinmo (1992), scholars of "rational choice theory" includes D.C. North, one of representatives in new institutinalism of economics. Therefore it is clear that their criticism faces to new institutionalism throughout both economics and politics, which attempts to explain institutions as results of rational behavior of individual.

It is quite agreeable that preference itself, which "rational choice institutionalist" places as starting point of their analysis, is influenced by then institutional contexts. However, it seems impossible to research and analyse real fiscal phenomena without any assumptions of individuals or groups. Indeed original fiscal sociologists criticised former German public finance of its "fictinalism of state". But they did not reject to create "ideal types" in order to grasp fiscal affairs as interactive domain of economy and politics.[20] Not to reject model building but to propose more real and suitable model explaining fiscal matters is needed. If not so, we are likely to repeat "description without theory", in which Historical School fell.

As for recent economic and fiscal crisis in Japan, Naohiko Jinno, Masaru Kaneko, and some researchers in connection with them energetically propose reform agenda with criticising economics or public finance so far. There are many books and articles of them on this theme. But in this paper we will briefly summarize their thoughts taking up a few books which seems to explain them well. In addition, we examine and make comment on it from the viewpoint of fiscal sociology.

As the motive of their research, they points out that modern economics is not effective for analysing Japanese problem of fiscal deficit. For example, Jinno and Kaneko (2000) wrote that neither Keynesian policy nor anti-Keynesian policy, e.g. monetarist, supply-side economist etc, could improve Japanese economic situation. According to them, the reason is that "the character of this long-term depression is different from the one occurring in normal business cycle" (2000, 11). They ascribe the failure of recent Japanese macroeconomic policy to Japanese financial system. That is to say, because of large amount of bad loans mostly lent to construction industry, banking prefer to buy public bonds rather than lend to private sector. On the other hand, public investment as fiscal policy has little ripple effect because construction industries appropriate its earnings for paying back to banking. This vicious circle prevents funds from flowing into other private sector (2000, 16-18). In addition, ineffective public investment also caused much debt to local government in Japan because both central and local government has usually shared cost of public investment.[21]

---

[20] As was already shown, Sultan proposed a unique politico-economic model as premise for his research on state revenue. Although his model is primitive and rough, he clearly seems to have direction for theory applicable throughout history.

[21] In Japanese administration, it is mostly local governments that directly supplies public services to people. Central government usually subsidizes local governments in order that they could carry out service programme planed by central government. This is the reason why Japanese intergovernmental transfer is largest among developed countries.

Jinno and Kaneko argues that the mainstream of modern economics cannot solve these problems which originated from special Japanese institutions, and appeal that drastic institutional change is needed in order to improve Japanese economic situation. They expect Fiscal sociology to support their argument because it regards history and institutions, which have had relatively lower position in modern economics, as important.

Jinno and Kaneko proposed following plans. As for public debt, they put forward making a new account which integrate all governmental assets and debts existing in various accounts out of public sight. Main purpose of this new account is to prevent public debt from accumulating more. In their argument, it is

> a policy not increasing public deficit any more, in addition, not repaying soon. That is to say, it makes condition like in a sense 'freezing debt', and repays public debt in long-range without time-limit. The keywords of this reform is 'independence and sustainability' (2000, 42).

They call it "debt-managing state".

It is in respect of intergovernmental fiscal relation that is also important in their argument. They propose exhaustive decentralization, in which local governments are mainly responsible for welfare policies expected to be more important in future. They points out economic globalisation as the ground of their argument. According to them, globalisation causes capital to move quickly through countries, and makes governments unable to impose enough tax for redistributional policy. Thus, they think that the role of local government becomes important.[22] For the purpose of decentralization, they argue that central government should cede part of its taxes, e.g. income tax and consumption tax, to local governments. Under this condition, the main role of central government is guaranteeing minimum fund of local governments to carry out their own welfare programme.[23]

In this way Jinno and Kaneko's argument could be summed up to "three welfare government" proposal.[24] The first is central government, which is responsible for intergovernmental fiscal co-ordination and repayment of governmental debt. The second is social security fund, which provides public pension and benefit of

---

[22] As for discussion on relation between globalisation and role of governments, see Jinno (1999, 274-275).

[23] As stated earlier, there is large amount of intergovernmental transfer in Japan. But the bulk of it consists of various grants, the use of which is strictly limited by central government. Their proposal, on the contrary, means that central government does not make any restriction of subsidies to local governments.

[24] As for their proposal "three welfare state, see Jinno (1999, 284-289), Jinno and Kaneko (2000, 51-53).

public medical insurance. The third is local government, which has a role of supplying welfare service to residents.

Concerning the relation to fiscal sociology, Jinno and Kaneko's argument has a few interesting characters. First, their argument resembles Goldscheid's at the point that they criticize existing economics and public finance. In the case of Goldscheid, the object of criticism are German historical school and German public finance, and for Jinno and Kaneko, modern economics, above all, neoclassical economics and public finance which is based on such economics come into question. Second, they also discussed how to do with large amount of public debt in their country, like Goldscheid and Schumpeter.

Above all, it is very interesting that they also proposed one-time property tax by central government in case of emergent need of repayment.[25] Analysing their argument in detail, it becomes clear that the reason why they emphasise the need of fiscal sociology is that they regard these days as turning point of economy and society. "As Schumpeter argues, at a turning point when economic or social crisis emerges, fiscal condition necessarily falls into crisis, and 'crisis of tax state' emerges. We propose debt-managing government as 'the third way' because we regard this fiscal crisis, so large as to be 'bankrupt', as 'crisis of tax state'" (Jinno and Kaneko, 2000, 100).

They contributed remarkably to Japanese fiscal sociology, as regards there have been no concrete policy proposal from this field in Japan. However, their notable research has some logical problems by reason that it entirely inquires economic and fiscal reform. Firstly, it seems that their argument on economic and fiscal condition in Japan could not be criticism to modern economics itself. Criticising economics only in respect of policy would face a refutation that the way of applying the economics is worse. In case of criticising Keynesian or monetarist macroeconomics, it is necessary to prove with strict real analysis that their models are false. More important, is that the social condition in Japan is different from condition in the west, which have been the base of modern economic theory. It is necessary for fiscal sociologist to investigate whether the reason of the failure of the Japanese economic policy based on the "mainstream economics" is a special characteristic of social condition in Japan. In order to make their proposal more persuasive, original politico-economic theory would be needed.

---

[25] See Jinno (2000, 137-141).

6 Conclusion

As we have seen so far, though fiscal sociology is paid attention again recently, we have to say that it is still in the process of development to become a powerful analytical tool to reinforce existing public finance. Above all, if we know that the discussion to take fiscal sociology into consideration emerges in a country where economic and fiscal condition confronts with serious crisis, like Japan, the "fiscal sociology" seems as if a keyword in fiscal crisis. Exactly any sort of social science has to be always influenced by society because it is studied inside the society which is object. And a moment for a social science to develop consists in needs to solve some social problem. Therefore every social science is inseparably related to practice. However, in order that it could become an exact social science, it must have objectified and rigorous theory. As stated at first in this paper, it is meaningful to research fiscal sociology in the time when existing economics or public finance has lost its reliability. As a premise of the research, we have to arrange it theoretically. It has been a necessary task since the time when fiscal sociology began.

References

Backhaus, J. G. (1994), "Die Kategorie des Steuerstaats und die moderne Finanzwissenschaft" In H. Rieter (ed.), *Studien zur Entwicklung der ökonomischen Theorie*, vol. 13, Berlin: Dunker & Humblot.

Backhaus, J. G. (1997), "The Tax State: From Schmoller and Wagner to Schumpeter", In J. Backhaus (ed.), *Essays on Social Security and Taxation*, Marburg: Metropolis-Verlag.

DeWit, A. (1999), "The Main Currents of Contemporary Fiscal Sociology", (in Japanese), In Oshima, M., Jinno, N., and Kaneko, M. (eds.), *Confronting Fiscal Problems in Japan*, Tokyo: Yachiyo Shuppan.

Goldscheid, R. (1926), "Staat, öffentlicher Haushalt und Gesellschaft. Wesen und Aufgabe der Finanzwissenschaft vom Standpunkte der Soziologie" In W. Gerloff and F. Meisel (eds.) *Handbuch der Finanzwissenschaft*, vol.1, Tübingen: Mohr.

Fujii, T. (1998), "The Japanese social policy school: its formation and breakup" In S. Sugihara and T. Tanaka (eds.), *Economic Thought and Modernization in Japan*, Cheltenham, UK: Edward Elgar.

Hansmeyer, K. and Mackscheidt, K. (1977), "Finanzpsychology" In F. Neumark (ed.) *Handbuch der Finanzwissenschaft* vol. 1, 3rd ed., Tübingen: Mohr.

Hodgson, G. M. (1999), *Evolution and Institutions*, Cheltenham, UK: Edward Elgar.

International Monetary Fund (2001), *World Economic Outlook: December2001*, Washington, D. C.: International Monetary Fund.

Ito, H. (1935), *The Structure and Formation of theory on tax principle*, Tokyo: Chikurashobo.

Jecht, H. (1928), *Wesen und Formen der Finanzwissenschaft* Jena: Verlag von Gustav Fischer.

Jinno, N. (1999), "Three Welfare Regimes and Public Burden", (in Japanese), In N. Jinno and M. Kaneko (eds.), *Proposals for a "Welfare Regime"*, Tokyo: Iwanamishoten.

Jinno, N. and Kaneko, M. (2000), *Preventing Fiscal Breakdown*, (in Japanese), Tokyo: Iwanamishoten.

Kimura, M. (1949), *Public Finance-development of its subject*, Tokyo: Shunjusha.

Kimura, M. (1951), "A Statement of Fiscal Sociology", (in Japanese), in Schumpeter, J.A. *The Crisis of Fiscal State*, Tokyo: Keisoshobo.

Mann, F. K. (1959), *Finanztheorie und Finanzsoziologie* Göttingen: Vandenhoeck & Ruprecht.

Musgrave, R. A. (1959), *The Theory of Public Finance*, NY, McGraw-Hill.

Musgrave, R. A. (1980), "Theories of Fiscal Crisis", In H. J. Aaron and M. J. Boskin (eds.) *The Economics of Taxation*, Washington, D. C.: Brookings Institution.

O'Connor, J. (1973), *The Fiscal Crisis of the State*, New York: St. Martin's Press.

Ohata, B. (1930), *Social Public Finance*, Tokyo: Teiyushuppan.

Ohata, B. (1934), *Tax State*, Tokyo: Yuhikaku.

Ohata, B. (1939), *Introduction of Public Finance*, Tokyo: Yuhikaku.

Ouchi, H. (1927), Fiscal Sociology: Goldscheid's Critique on Public Finance, (in Japanese) *Journal of Economics* The University of Tokyo, 6, 633□679.

Schumpeter, J. A. (1951), *The Crisis of Tax State*, (German original, 1918, in Japanese), Tokyo: Keisoshobo.

Sultan, H. (1932), "Ueber die Aufgaben der Finanzsoziologie" *Vierteljahrschrift für Sozial- und Wirtschaftsgeschichte*, 25, 38-53.

Thelen, K. and Steinmo, S. (1992), "Historical Institutionalism in Comparative Politics" In S. Steinmo and K. Thelen (eds.) *Structuring Politics –Historical Institutionalism in comparative analysis*, New York: Cambridge University Press.

Uno, K. (1936), *Economic Policy*, Tokyo: Kobundo.

Yamashita, K. (1933-34), The Meaning and Way of "Fiscal Sociology", (in Japanese), *Journal of Economics and Business Administration* Kobe University, 56,886-904, 57, 91-110.

Yamashita, K (1962), *Study of Fiscal Sociology*, Tokyo: Toyokeizaishinposha.

Yonehara, S. (1932), Goldscheid's Fiscal Thought and Critique, (in Japanese) *Economic Studies* Kyushu University, 2, 377-403.

Yonehara, S. (1933), Recent Tendency of Fiscal Sociology, (in Japanese) *Economic Studies* Kyushu University, 3, 383-424.

Goldscheid's "Menschenökonomie" from A Modern Economic Perspective

Norio Sasaki
Associate Professor of Public Finance
Graduate School of Economics and Management
Tohoku University
Kawauchi, Aobaku,
Sendai 980-8576
Japan
Fon: ++81-22-217-6276
sasaki@econ.tohoku.ac.jp

Abstract: Although R. Goldscheid is quite famous as the creator of Fiscal Sociology, he was admired mainly for his sharp criticism of the public finance theory in Germany at that time and the proposal of a drastic solution for the increasing public debt, namely, *Unternehmerstaat* (owner state). In other words, comparatively little attention seems to have been paid to his basic view of the modern economy so far. In spite of the importance of the concept, *Menschenökonomie*, in which Goldscheid thought human labor can be used to best efficiency, there is a crucial logical leap between this concept and his fiscal views because of introducing a Marxian view of the modern state to the latter directly. Considering the recent changing situation of economics, to reevaluate the *Menschenökonomie* and to apply the reevaluation to the fiscal theory seem meaningful because of its sociobiological character.

Keywords: Fiscal sociology, Human Capital Theory.

JEL codes: B1, B2.

Introduction

The general valuation on Rudolf Goldscheid is of course as a founder of the "Finanzsoziologie" (fiscal sociology), in which interdependency of public finance and society is especially emphasized as a key-concept for analyzing all fiscal phenomena. In addition, Goldscheid argued strongly in his polemic article, "Staat, öffentlicher Haushalt und Gesellschaft: Wesen und Aufgabe der Finanzwissenschaft vom Standpunkte der Soziologie", which contributed more to make his name known, the exploitation of the state by the private sector and the necessity for drastic transfer of power and property from the financial sector to the government. Because of Goldscheid's challenging articles, the sociological approach to analyzing fiscal phenomena of modern states became widespread in the age between two world wars, as J. Schumpeter's *Die Krise des Steuerstaats* became a representative work in this field.

It was very unfortunate for this new hopeful approach, that the center of study of public finance moved to the United States after World War II, as other fields of modern economics, and the old-fashioned public finance theory did not interest the economist. However, the decline of fiscal sociology was not only due to this environmental reason, but also to a theoretical shortcoming. For example, Goldscheid's view of the decision making structure of the modern states was too simple to describe the various fiscal phenomena emerging from the reality of democracy in developed countries.

> There is much to be said for the Marxist tradition of emphasizing the importance of social groups, rather than isolated individuals, as forces that determine fiscal change. But it is incorrect and misleading to formulate the issue in terms of a two-class capital-labor model. While it is not surprising that this dichotomy dominates Marxist fiscal sociology, the outcome is unfortunate because the two-class model, whatever its strength or weakness for general social analysis, is inappropriate for interpreting fiscal conflict. Closer consideration of the fiscal processes, especially in its modern setting, shows that many grouping must be considered and that most of them cut across the Marxist class division. Moreover, the groupings interact, so that few problems can be understood correctly as bilateral conflicts.[1]

If we examine only the fiscal aspects of Goldscheid's articles, his theory might seem to be one of the examples of the failure of the reform proposal from the perspective of Marxism. However, Goldscheid's fiscal theory and his proposal are only a small part of his economic thinking, which originally dealt with the "human being", that is to say, how a human being grows up in the economy, what is the necessary condition of the normal development of a human being. In our view, there is a crucial logical leap between his earlier study of "*Menschenökonomie*" (human economy) and the later study of public finance. Therefore, the denial of his fiscal argument does not necessarily lessen the worth in his view on *Menschenökonomie*. Moreover, concerning the recent development of evolutionary economics and neo-institutional economics, both of which pursue the more precise description of economic entities with consideration of the behavioral character of each person, Goldscheid's approach to human nature is much more interesting because he was conscious of the latest development of the evolutionary theory at that time and he tried to explain the state, which has not been well described by recent theories of evolutionary or neo-institutional economics.

---

[1] Musgrave (1986), p. 181.

In this paper, we introduce his concept of *Menschenökonomie* briefly, and discuss the difference of the concept from the original Marxian thought. After that, we consider why his explanation of modern states resulted in failure in spite of the innovative idea of his former works. Last, we compare Goldscheid's views with one of the most successful concepts in economics for analyzing the character of individual behavior, *human capital*, established by Gary S. Becker, and consider the effectiveness of *Menschenökonomie*, introducing a new formulation of the labor value theory.

1 The Concept and Application of the *Menschenökonomie*

As a radical sociologist, much influenced by the "sociobiology" at that time, Goldscheid opposed strongly the Multhusian demographic theory and Darwinian evolutionary theory, and argued his ideal type of economy, based on the labor-value theory, which has ethical character. The contents of these books show that his thought of *Menschenökonomie* became more detailed and more policy-oriented.

Entwicklungswerttheorie, Entwicklungsökonomie, Menschenökonomie (1908)

Höherentwicklung und Menschenökonomie, Grundlegung der Soziologie (1911)

Grundfragen des Menschenschicksals, Gesammelte Aufsätze (1919)

Although his discussion of the *Menschenökonomie* dealt with many topics, in which there is no small number of faults or contradictions, we can sum up the concept throughout these books; the most ultimate problem in modern economy is "waste of labor". According to Goldscheid, the human society develops when people can use their labor power to more intellectual work as a whole. Therefore, "if they would come to the bright idea of using one of Rembrandt's pictures as fuel, the destruction of the value would become obvious, because the effect of using the goods reaches far beyond the adequate purpose."[2] For Goldscheid, using labor power for simple and mechanic work is nothing else but "devaluation".

Because of the misuse of human labor, it is necessary to develop an adequate "amortization policy" for labor power, according to Goldscheid. The method of amortization has a close relationship to the biological features of human life.

> Therefore, the proportion of the amortization is subject to the principle of the insurance calculation. It must be large enough, as well as the construction- the function-, the decay- and the reproduction expense of the labor power to obtain full compensa-

[2] Goldscheid (1908), p. 84.

> tion; the young phase, which is not yet productive, as well as the older phase of the labor power, which is less, or no more productive, must be paid from the proportion of the amortization.[3]

From his normative argument of the human-amortization, some social policies for the *Menschenökonomie* can be induced. Adequate amortization makes total added value of the production, namely *Mehrwert* (surplus value), larger. In order to realize it, ranges of the possible working ages in individual life should be extended. Goldscheid judged that this policy could not be achieved within private firms, so the government must carry them out instead with an education policy, in which the young should learn enough skills for future labor, rather than work from the beginning. In addition to that, Goldscheid argued that the labor of women should be especially protected because they have the important role of reproducing the human itself.

These policy agenda, which were produced from Goldscheid's unique view of the social biology and surplus value theory, was called *Biotechnik*. The economic implication of the agenda can be summed up as increasing labor productivity.

> What contributes to the method of making the economy and humanity only two sides of the same thing and identical, is to reach the maximum of the productivity through the synthesis of the strictest factuality and purest humanity.[4]

2 Goldscheid's Failure of Connecting Theories

Although it is well known that Goldscheid was one of the Marxists, this important normative proposition of Goldscheid's thoughts, increasing productivity, does not exist in the original Marxian economic theory. In fact, Marx only argued that the value of commodities is determined by input of labor power, which is homogeneous in all workers.[5] This difference in view of the modern economy between Goldscheid and Marx suggests inevitable divergence of the view of the state. In the former Goldscheid's theory we have seen, that there is no evidence that connects to discussions of drastic change of the regime. The state is rather necessary for the reform of the private economy under which many workers suffer from severe labor environments and unreasonably low wages. Contrary to that, Marx thought that the regime must be demolished because the state is controlled by the very capitalists who cause the misery in society.

---

[3] Goldscheid (1911), p. 580.
[4] Goldscheid (1976), p.287.
[5] Although Marx admitted the existence of skilled labor, he thought that the skill is obtained by buying former education services, which needed the other labor of teachers.

Therefore, it became clear that Goldscheid made a serious and crucial mistake by simply bringing Marx's dichotomy of the components in society, namely capital and labor, and his view of "class state" into his innovative sociobiological thought. In his later articles dealing with public finance, his desire to realize *Menschenökonomie* directly resulted in the famous proposal of transferring the private property to the public sector. However, if he had not been so influenced by Marx's exploitation theory, he would not have needed to argue for the drastic reform of the state, but he could instead have stated more realistic and effective labor policies by the state. As a matter of fact Goldscheid's proposal of *Unternehmerstaat* (owner state) has many inadequacies in terms of efficiency. It is unavoidable to admit that he did not take into account the possibility of the state to become a huge monopoly firm. In spite of having similar idealistic view of the modern society, F. Oppenheimer had already recognized that the decision-making of the modern state must exercised by many political actors, whose interests are quite different.[6] Unfortunately, Goldscheid's contempt for the political reality made his fiscal argument more widely known than his socioeconomic theory!

3 Comparison to Human Capital Theory

Although there are several faults in Goldscheid's state theory and fiscal view, we can clearly argue that his former theory of *Menschenökonomie* need not necessarily be understood in connection with his later thoughts, but can survive independently. In other words, if we try to incorporate his views into modern economics, we must restart at the point of *Menschenökonomie*.

By referring to the "productivity of labor" or "amortization of human labor", Goldscheid's thought can be regarded as human capital theories. These were brilliantly developed after World War II mainly in the United States and are now in the middle of mainstream economics. It is notable that the theory of human capital was developed with much referring to the modern sociobiology.[7] However, there are many differences between Goldscheid's original thought and the current human capital theory, established by G. Becker and T. Schultz. Bröckling (2003) reviews both ideas from the viewpoint of social philosophy, with a deep concern for the recent distinct developments in biotechnology. Based on this summary, we discuss what meaning these differences have.

First of all, the theory of *Menschenökonomie* is based on the labor-value theory, which gives the highest place to "production" or "productivity" of the whole

---

[6] About Oppenheimer's thought of the character of modern states, see Oppenheimer (1907).
[7] As a good example, see Becker (1976).

economy, whereas the human capital theory regards the "utility" as the most important purpose of individuals. Second,

> whereas Goldscheid distinctly understood his project as 'normative economics', the humancapital theorists insist on the descriptive character in their researches. They do not question how people should form their individualistic trade and social living economically, but impute that they always do it.[8]

Third, although both thoughts have interests in sociobiology, the methods of analyzing are quite different. Goldscheid strongly insisted "vitalism" as an analytical principle and rejected taking "mechanistic views" for theorizing the actions of people, whereas the individual is described as a utility- maximizer by the "rational choice mechanism" in the human capital theory.

Taking it into account that economics was too undeveloped to describe much complex human action, it was quite natural that Goldscheid could not take an analytically strict approach of socio-economics with regard to the human activity as biological phenomena. However, it is worth noticing that the directions of both approaches are totally opposite. Goldscheid struggled to make economics more similar to biology, whereas the human capital theorists try to bring the economic approach into other academic fields, including sociology or biology. There is an advantage in taking a more interdisciplinary approach, if one academic field faces difficulties in explaining phenomena in the field. In fact, there are many arguments of the confidence of the human capital approaches in explaining the various social activities of human. Potts (2000) wrote

> Reciprocal exchange and the division of labor no longer seem to be the dominant factors in the economic explanation of marriage. As such, I suggest that Becker's exchange and field-based theory does not provide a suitable ongoing basis for the analysis of the dynamics of the marriage institution.[9]

From the viewpoint of "ecological economics" in Mayumi (2001),

> G. S. Becker extended the neoclassical utility maximizing approach to endogenous preferences, including personal and social capital. According to Becker, this extended utility function remains the same over time and, for different individuals, includes addictive, social, advertising capital as arguments. However, Becker and other neoclassical analysts do not seriously consider the issue of relevant choices of the axioms underlying utility theory...[10]

Considering these criticism to the human capital theory, human preference and behavior should be understood in relationship to environmental factors. That is to say, the taste or utility structure of people is rather influenced by social envi-

---

[8] Bröckling (2003), p. 17.
[9] Potts (2000), p.148.
[10] Mayumi(2001) p. 142n.

ronment, than influence to it. In spite of some shortages, Goldscheid's *Menschenökonomie* can be worth being reevaluated because it had originally the sociobiological character, which recent hopeful fields of economics, especially evolutionary economics, should incorporate as an imposrtant factor.

4 Reinterpretation of the *Menschenökonomie* in Modern Economics

In the last section of this paper, we will discuss the possibility of reviving Goldscheid's thoughts on modern economic theories. As we have already shown, the most evident indicator of the *Menschenökonomie* is "maximum of labor productivity". However, this proposition cannot be reduced from the labor value theory Goldscheid himself depended on. Then, was Goldscheid's thought born to be hopeless contradiction? Fortunately, there is a quite unique study of labor value theory using modern economics, namely *Marx's Economics*, by Michio Morishima. We sum up his views on labor value theory.

It is well known that Marx's labor value theory can be described in a simple equation of matrices. In this model the value of each commodity is determined by the input of labor to produce one unit of each commodity and the technical relationship of how other commodities are needed to produce one unit of each commodity. However this model needs the strong assumption that each commodity is produced in only one sector, as the input-output analysis established by W. Leontief. If a joint production technique exists in the model, a negative value, which is contradictory to the labor value theory, can appear in the value equations. Morishima (1973) solved this difficult problem by introducing inequalities in the matrices model, which is similar to the equilibrium growth model established by von Neumann (1945). Under the model the renewed values of "composite commodities" are the solutions of linear programming in the model, which minimizes the total amount of labor input. In addition, the programming is dual to another programming that maximizes the net outputs.[11] Morishima wrote on the implication of the new value-determinant system,

> It will be seen that the values determined by the inequality system are non-negative and play the role of shadow prices in economics which maximize the productivity of labor by utilizing labor efficiently. In the capitalist mode of production where the price-guided (or profit guided) choice of techniques prevails, equilibrium prices determined competitively are different from values except in certain very special cases, but the values may still have some normative relevance in capitalist economies, because they enable us to find those techniques by the use of which the amount of labor needed to produce given amounts of commodities can be minimized.[12]

[11] About this linear programming model, see Morishima (1973), pp. 184-186.
[12] Morishima (1973), p. 180.

In this system, the values of commodities are determined simultaneously with the prices. Although this result contradicts with the traditional thought of Marx's economics, "independency of values from the prices", the model enables the value theory to revive in the co-determinant system. Therefore the normative meaning of Goldscheid's *Menschenökonomie* is found in Morishima's version of the value theory. It is a further problem, how the activity of the government should be placed in the modern interpretation of Goldscheid's thought.

References

Becker, G. (1976), "Altruism, Egoism, and Genetic Fitness: Economics and Sociobiology, *Journal of Economic Literature*, 14, 817-26.

Bröckling, U. (2003), "Menschenökonomie, Humankapital: Eine Kritik der Biopolitischen Ökonomie" *Mittelweg*, 36, 3-22.

Fujibayashi, K. (1941), "Rudolf Goldscheid no Ningen Keizaigaku ni Tsuite" (On Rudolf Goldscheid's "Human Economy"), *Mita Gakkai Zassi*, 35, 507-529.

Goldscheid, R. (1908), *Entwiclungswerttheorie, Entwicklungsökonomie, Menschenökonomie*, Leipzig: Werner Klinkhardt.

Goldscheid, R. (1911), *Höherentwicklung und Menschenökonomie*, Leipzig: Werner Klinkhardt.

Goldscheid, R. (1976), "Staat, öffentlicher Haushalt und Gesellschaft: Wesen und Aufgabe der Finanzwissenschaft vom Standpukte der Soziologie" In R. Hickel (1976) (ed.) *Rudolf Goldscheid, Joseph Schumpeter: DieFinanzkrise des Steuerstaates, Beiträge zur politischen Ökonomie der Staatsfinenzen*, Frankfurt am Mein: Suhrkamp Verlag.

Mayumi, K. (2001), *The Origins of Ecological Economics: The bioeconomics of Georgescu-Roegen*, New York: Routledge.

Morishima, M. (1972), *Marx's Economics: A Dual Theory of Value and Growth*, Cambridge: Cambridge University Press.

Musgrave, R. (1986), "Theories of Fiscal Crisis: An Essay in Fiscal Sociology" *Public Finance in a Democratic Society: Collected Papers of Richard A. Musgrave*, Wheatscheaf Books.

Neumann, J. von (1945), "A Model of General Economic Equilibrium" *Review of Economic Studies*, 13, 1-9.

Oppenheimer, F. (1907), *Der Staat*, Frankfurt am Main: Ruttern und Loening.

Potts, J. (2000), *The New Evolutionary Microeconomics: Complexity, Competence and Adaptive Behaviour*, Cheltenham: Edward Elgar.

Otto Veit and Subsequent Developments of Tax Morality

Enrico Schöbel
Krupp Chair in Public Finance and Fiscal Sociology
University of Erfurt
Nordhäuser Str. 63
Lecture Building 1, Room 120
99089 Erfurt
Germany
Fon: ++49-361-737-4554
Fax: ++49-361-737-4559
enrico.schoebel@uni-erfurt.de

Abstract: Besides monitoring and threatening taxpayers with penalties, the cultivation of their attitudes towards taxation is a topic of immediate interest. The importance of tax morality, meaning taxpayers' honesty in taxation, has been confirmed in current research. However, this is nothing new. In 1927 the economist and sociologist Otto Veit published a fiscal sociological study on this very topic.

Veit suggests an extensive economic approach of studying tax morality which is thoroughly based on philosophical and contemporary sociological concepts. In his approach, tax morality is an endogenous variable which depends on the behaviour of the individuals concerned. These individuals are tax legislators, tax administrators, and taxpayers. Tax morality is influenced not only by the technical design of a tax system and by law enforcement, e.g. monitoring, whistle blowing, and punishment, but also by social, political, and cultural factors.

In this article, Veit and his work on tax morality are presented. Firstly, Veit will be introduced as a fiscal sociologist. Then, his approach of studying tax morality and its philosophical and sociological foundation will be explained. Finally, conformity with Schmölders' approach in the 1950s and 1960s and with very current research on tax morality will be demonstrated. It is the basic message of this article that some of Veit's ideas are of immediate relevance and worth making use of.

Keywords: Fiscal sociology, tax morality, tax compliance, tax evasion.

JEL codes: B 31, B 41, H 26, P16.

1 Introduction

Otto Veit (1898-1984) is a well known monetary theorist and practitioner, who considerably contributed to the establishment of the German monetary system after World War II.[5] Beyond monetary theory and policy, he was interested in examining the social, political, and cultural influence of institutions such as money, monetary system, and fiscal system, and, vice versa, the influence of society, policy, and culture on institutions. His work clearly stands in the tradition of fiscal sociology and is based on his extensive knowledge of classical and contemporary philosophical literature. In 1927 he wrote his fiscal sociological study on the elements of tax morality.[6] Understanding tax morality is not only a very prominent fiscal sociological issue, *"im besten Sinne ein gesellschaftliches, ein finanzsoziologisches Problem"*, as Veit states,[7] but it is also a very current issue which is attracting more and more interest in fiscal policy as well as in theoretical economic research.

In January 2004 the German Government proposed a law to strengthen measures against moonlighting activities. The German shadow economy has been prospering, especially in the building industry, but also in other businesses. Moonlighting goes along with tax evasion. This means that individuals evade their contributions to the public household. More and more people could be encouraged to do the same. Therefore, the German government planned to change the judgement of moonlighting activities in a way that would have brought higher penalties. However, the public discussion was concentrated on the fact that the state would plan to control private households to find out if a person is paid for helping in the household. Then, the government shortly afterwards rejected the idea that private households should be threatened with controls and higher penalties. The question seems not only to be what a relevant amount of tax evasion is, but also how the threat of allegation and control could influence honest taxpayers, possibly taking away their intrinsic motivation to pay taxes. Instead of promoting denunciation, treating taxpayers with trust and respect may cultivate tax morality.[8] Bruno Frey points out that "Deterrence policy based on monitoring, and threat of punishment, is able to raise the tax revenue" but may cause a "reduction in tax morale" and "crowd out the sense of civic virtue".[9] A society of whistle blowers can not enable trust and civic virtue. Besides deterrence, preserving tax morality is a very important issue. However, the conventional

[5] Gutowski et al. (1974), p. 5.
[6] Veit (1927), pp. 317 ff.
[7] Veit (1927), p. 349.
[8] Feld and Frey (2002), pp. 91 ff., and Slemrod (2002), pp. 8 ff.
[9] Frey (1997), p. 113.

economies of crime model regarding tax evasion developed by Allingham and Sandmo and published in 1972 is restricted to monitoring and punishment.[10]

In the 1980s and 1990s some empirical economists came to the conclusion that taxpayers actually evade less than predicted by the conventional expected utility approach.[11] Some individuals will not evade taxes even if the probability of detection is zero. Therefore, the question has to be raised, why people comply and pay taxes. Tax evasion is obviously not only determined by the tax rate, the earned income, the penalty rate, and the probability of detection, as assumed by Allingham and Sandmo.[12] Beyond the conventional expected utility approach other factors like taxpayers' perception of the state, taxpayers' perception of public good provision, and the structure of the tax system are influential. Some authors have started to explain tax honesty by moral behaviour.[13] The impact of tax morality has been shown in current research.[14]

However, this is nothing new. In 1927 Otto Veit examined tax morality as a fiscal sociological issue and provided some basic ideas which are of immediate interest.[15] In 1932 Günter Schmölders goes on from Veit's study.[16] In an essay on tax morality and tax burden he takes up Veit's ideas and carries on his analysis. After world war two, in the 1950s, Günter Schmölders initiated empirical fiscal psychological research on tax morality. Veit and Schmölders were friends and in contact for many decades.[17]

Herbert Sultan, a leading fiscal sociologist who is well-known for his systematization of sociological public finance,[18] commends Veit's article from 1932 as being an excellent fiscal sociological study.[19] Agreeing with Veit and referring to Franz Meisel,[20] Fritz Karl Mann,[21] and others, he points out that it seems to be hasty to analyze taxpayers' behaviour towards taxation by generally supposing defence against taxation, "*Es scheint mir ein wenig voreilig, die "Reaktionen*

---

10 Allingham and Sandmo (1972), pp. 323 ff.

11 See Alm, McClelland, and Schulze (1992), pp. 21 ff., Pommerehne and Frey (1992), pp. 4 ff., Dubin and Wilde (1988), pp. 61 ff., Graetz and Wilde (1985), pp. 355 ff., Skinner and Slemrod (1985), pp. 347 f.

12 Allingham and Sandmo (1972), pp. 323 ff. A survey article is written by Andreoni, Erard, and Feinstein (1998), pp. 818 ff.

13 See Erard and Feinstein (1994), pp. 70 ff., and Spicer and Lundstedt (1976), pp. 295 ff.

14 See Beckmann (2003), p. 74, Frey and Feld (2002), pp. 11 ff., Beckmann (2001), p. 22, Torgler (2001a), pp. 146 ff.

15 Veit (1927), pp. 317 ff.

16 Schmölders (1932).

17 Solf (1988), p. 45.

18 Koch (1981), pp. 98 f.

19 Sultan (1932), p. 110.

20 Meisel (1911) and Meisel (1925).

21 Mann (1923), pp. 497 ff.

der Zensiten" von vornherein unter der Kategorie der "Steuerabwehr" zu analysieren."[22] In this sense, Schmölders recommends in his essay cultivation of a trustful relation between state and its citizens "*das Vertrauensverhältnis zwischen dem Staat und seinen Bürgern gerade im Hinblick auf Steuerbelastung und Steuerverwendung innerlich zu festigen*" besides other measures.[23]

2 Otto Veit (1898-1984) as an Important Fiscal Sociologist

Otto Veit (1898-1984) is an important representative of fiscal sociology. He was an Economist as well as a sociologist. Moreover, he had a thorough knowledge of classical and contemporary philosophical literature.

Veit was born in Frankfurt am Main but grew up in his grandparents' house in Berlin.[24] His grandfather James Hardy was the founder of the private bank Hardy. In the 1920s Veit studied in Frankfurt am Main where Wilhelm Gerloff was one of his academic teachers. Gerloff worked in the fields of monetary theory, public finance, and sociology, i.e. the sociology of money.[25] He published the "Handbuch der Finanzwissenschaft" together with Franz Meisel. Both encouraged Veit's fiscal sociological study on the elements of tax morality which appeared in the prestigious "Zeitschrift für die gesamte Staatswissenschaft", one of the oldest journals in political economy. The journal was founded in 1844 and still exists under the name of "Journal of Institutional and Theoretical Economics" (JITE).

Gerloff was also Veit's dissertation supervisor. Veit wrote his dissertation thesis on mining as a source of public income published in 1927.[26] His second book published in 1932 dealt with sentiments and rationality in the economy. It was encouraged by Max Weber's research on social relations and social groups, e.g. nations.[27] As Sultan points out, Veit's fiscal-sociological study on the elements of tax morality is based on Max Weber though he does not quote him.[28] Veit wrote further books on the tragedy of the technical age and on the future of gold, money and currency.[29] In 1927 he went back from Frankfurt am Main to Berlin and had several jobs and later became an economic adviser of the private bank Hardy. Besides this, in 1933 he was engaged in negotiations towards habilitation

---

22 Sultan (1931), p. 11.
23 Schmölders (1932), p. 13.
24 Solf (1988), p. 21.
25 Neumark (1954), pp. 741 f.
26 Der Bergbau als staatliche Finanzquelle (Dissertation, Frankfurt am Main, 1927).
27 Veit (1932), p. 12.
28 Sultan (1932), pp. 110 ff.
29 Die Tragik des technischen Zeitalters – Mensch und Maschine im 19. Jahrhundert (Berlin, 1935), Die Zukunft des Goldes: eine Abhandlung über Geld und Währung (Berlin, 1937)

with B. Harms and Walter Eucken but negotiations failed due to political reasons. He was not allowed to teach. However, Eucken invited him to Freiburg several times.[30]

During World War II Veit was not allowed to publish. He prepared the manuscript of a sociological book on the flight from freedom which is thoroughly philosophically founded and prepared his later habilitation thesis on the liquidity theory of money. In his book on the flight from freedom Veit refers to Aristoteles, Thomas Aquinus, and Immanuel Kant.[31] His phenomenological sociological method is based on the work of the philosopher Edmund Husserl.[32] The famous German writer Thomas Mann who was in contact with Veit commented that 'flight from freedom' is a good title for a good book.[33] He agrees with Veit that individuals are ambivalent. In a free society individuals strive after binding.[34] In an essay he explains this phenomenon by applying Gossen's first and second law.[35] Ambivalence is again the central message in his later book on the sociology of freedom which is a revision of his earlier book on the flight from reality, and in his last book on the ambivalence of individual and world published three years before he died.[36] Solf comments that book the quintessence of his historical-sociological and culture-sociological thinking.[37]

However, most of Veit's books, and articles deal with monetary theory and policy, for example monetary system, and monetary reform.[38] These books were frequently cited in German books on monetary theory and policy, by writers such as Albrecht Forstmann, Ernst Dürr, Dieter Duwendag et al., Otmar Issing, Peter Schaal, and Manfred Borchert,[39] but not in the English literature. In 1948

---

[30] Solf (1988), p. 23.
[31] Solf (1988), p. 19.
[32] Solf (1988), pp. 58 f.
[33] Solf (1988), p. 55.
[34] See also: Veit (1960/61), pp. 83 ff.
[35] Veit (1961), pp. 520 ff.
[36] Veit (1947), Veit (1957), and Ambivalenz von Mensch und Welt (Frankfurt am Main, 1981). Moreover, he wrote a book on the Christian-Jewish coexistence (Christlich-jüdische Koexistenz, Frankfurt am Main, 1st ed. 1965, 2nd ed. 1971).
[37] Solf (1988), p. 131.
[38] Deutsche Geldpolitik (Frankfurt am Main, 1950), Die veränderte Währungspolitik und ihre Folgen (Frankfurt am Main, 1957), Der Wert unseres Geldes (Frankfurt am Main, 1958), Reale Theorie des Geldes (Tübingen, 1966), Währungspolitik als Kunst des Unmöglichen (Frankfurt am Main, 1968), Grundriß der Währungspolitik (Frankfurt am Main, 1st ed. 1961, 3rd ed. 1969).
[39] Forstmann, Albrecht: Volkswirtschaftliche Theorie des Geldes, Zweiter Band (Berlin, 1955), Dürr, Ernst (ed.): Geld- und Bankpolitik (Köln, Berlin, 1969), Duwendag, Dieter, et al.: Geldtheorie und Geldpolitik (Köln, 1974) Issing, Otmar: Einführung in die Geldtheorie (10th ed., München, 1995), Issing, Otmar: Einführung in die Geldpolitik (6th ed., München, 1996), Schaal, Peter: Geldtheorie und Geldpolitik (4th ed., München, Wien, 1998), and Bor-

Otto Veit's habilitation thesis on the liquidity theory of money was published.[40] He develops an economic approach to liquidity which goes beyond the existing management concept. Besides John R. Hicks, Roland N. McKean, Heinrich Rittershausen, Günter Schmölders, Wolfgang Stützel, Ernst Dürr, and others, Veit aims at extending John Maynard Keynes' definition of liquidity beyond money. In his concept of liquidity, money becomes a good among all the other goods which all have a certain but not the same degree of liquidity on a scale. Liquidity is not only held in expectation of advantageous transactions but also for social prestige. In his opinion, and thereby he follows Gerloff, money is determined by society.[41] Veit's monetary work has a thorough psychological and sociological background. When Bismarck calls policy an art of the possible, Veit calls monetary policy an art of the impossible due to the conflicting aims of monetary policy.[42] He states that there is a connection between economic and sociological explanation concerning particular monetary phenomena, for instance index-thinking, inflation, and so on.[43] Since the end of World War II public opinion has been oriented in currency indices, although these concepts were largely criticized in the 19th century. The index-thinking became a matter of course though indices indicate only the average purchasing power.[44]

After World War II the American forces brought Otto Veit from Berlin to Wiesbaden near Frankfurt am Main. In 1946 he became the managing director of the public state bank Nassauische Landesbank in Wiesbaden,[45] where he lived with his second wife until he died. From 1947 to 1952 he was the president of the Regional Central Bank of the German state Hessen. In this position he strongly influenced the monetary reform in Germany after the World War II. In 1948 he became an extraordinary and later in 1952 a full Professor at the University of Frankfurt am Main when he got the Chair for Sciences of the State, especially Monetary and Banking Policy. At the same time he became the director of the "Institut für das Kreditwesen", a banking institute at the University of Frankfurt, and an adviser in Ludwig Erhard's federal ministry of economics. In the latter position he regularly met Fritz Neumark who was also in the advisory board. Both came in contact during Gerloff's seminar when Neumark was an assistant at the University of Frankfurt am Main.[46] Later Neumark and Veit were members of the "Frankfurter Gesellschaft für Handel, Industrie und Wissenschaft". From 1948 onwards Veit was in the board on the German central bank. He co-

---

chert, Manfred: Geld und Kredit: Einführung in die Geldtheorie und Geldpolitik (8th ed., München, Wien, 2003).

[40] Veit (1948).

[41] Solf (1988), p. 77.

[42] Veit (1968), pp. 11 and 80 ff.

[43] Veit (1968), pp. 83 ff.

[44] Veit (1954), pp. 61 f., and Veit (1968), p. 84.

[45] Solf (1988), p. 26.

[46] Solf (1988), pp. 35 f.

operated with Hermann Josef Abs and Otto Pfleiderer.[47] Both were also members of the German central bank board. Furthermore, he was in continuous contact with Sir Karl R. Popper in the "Mont Pélerin Society",[48] and in continuous contact with Günter Schmölders who taught in München.[49] Both met for the first time in Berlin, and later in Frankfurt am Main and Wiesbaden at the "Reichsverband Deutscher Banken", then in the Regional Central Bank of the German state Hessen, and in the advisory board on the ministry of economics. Schmölders' and Veit's research have some eyecatching parallels which will be demonstrated below.

Otto Veit was one of the so called Ordo-liberals[50] who advocated the conception of a social market economy. He frequently cooperated with Walter Eucken, Wilhelm Röpke, and Alexander Rüstow, men who were searching for a post-war-order oriented in the classical philosophical concept of ordo. The symbolic word ordo stands for an ideal metaphysical economic and social order and legitimacy comparable with the natural law in jurisprudence.[51] The notion of ordo is rooted in the Scholasticism. Later, Thomas Aquinus, Immanuel Kant, Max Weber, and others dealt with ordo and natural law.[52] The reference to a naturally given law exemplifies the search for an order as a new point of orientation in a period of heavy social and political change. Natural law was a major subject in Veit's analyses throughout his whole life and main topic of several publications.[53] In his opinion an individual's inner moral rules and legitimacy are a reflection of a metaphysical order.[54] For him it is possible for positive law, provided by the state, to violate rules of natural law and therewith equity.[55] The question of ordo and the concept and function of the state are linked, however, ordo is an optimal order which can not be reached by a state. Veit's social-psychological analysis of the individual and the collective is based on Franz Oppenheimer's writings.[56] Additionally, Veit refers to Sigmund Freud's "Tiefenpsychologie", to Georg Simmel's sociological analysis, to Nietzsche,[57] and he is an expert in Goethe's writings.[58]

---

[47] Solf (1988), pp. 47 ff.
[48] Solf (1988), p. 42.
[49] Solf (1988), p. 45.
[50] Solf (1988), p. 27.
[51] Veit (1953), pp. 5 f.
[52] Veit (1953), pp. 7 ff.
[53] Solf (1988), p. 24.
[54] Solf (1988), pp. 103 f.
[55] Veit (1953), pp. 20 ff.
[56] Solf (1988), p. 66.
[57] Veit (1955), pp. 14 ff, and Veit (1961), pp. 522 ff.
[58] Solf (1988), p. 103, and Veit's last book Ambivalenz von Mensch und Welt (Frankfurt am Main, 1981).

3 The Scope of Veit's Fiscal Sociological Study on the Elements of Tax Morality

In his article on the elements of tax morality Veit aims at connecting economic, sociological, and psychological research to explain the existence or non-existence of tax morality. He recommends establishing fiscal sociology as a particular research method and invigorates the methodological discussion when he refers to Rudolf Goldscheid who suggests that public finance issues should be examined from a sociological point of view. Veit quotes Goldscheid's contribution to the "Handbuch der Finanzwissenschaft" edited by Franz Meisel and his doctoral supervisor Wilhelm Gerloff.[59] Following Goldscheid's suggestion, Veit bridges tax morality, technical factors of taxation, and social effects, to explain what influences an individual's decision to comply or not to comply with taxation. Thereby, he identifies tax morality as a fiscal sociological issue,[60] making it clear that besides a fiscal sociological method there is a particular fiscal sociological field of research. In his survey article on fiscal sociology Fritz Karl Mann also makes this distinction.[61] Beyond that, Mann distinguishes between two types of fiscal sociological methods, analyzing the impact of social, legal, political, and cultural circumstances on fiscal institutions on the one hand and examining how society, law, and public policy are influenced by fiscal institutions on the other hand.[62] In a later systematizing article he recommends a separation of public finance into the three divisions: fiscal theory, fiscal policy and fiscal sociology.[63]

4 Veit's Approach of Tax Morality and its Philosophical and Sociological Roots

Veit's study on the elements of tax morality is based on Franz Meisel who analyzed the impact of tax law enforcement on tax morality. Meisel wrote a book about the morality of the Prussian income tax assessment.[64] In another book he compares British and German income tax.[65] Veit goes beyond Meisel when he explains that moral behaviour is not only determined by tax law design and enforcement ("*Steuertechnik*"), but has also a psychological and social foundation. Therefore, a fiscal sociological study should analyze the behaviour of the indi-

[59] Goldscheid (1926), pp. 146 ff.
[60] Veit (1927), p. 349.
[61] Mann (1961), p. 642.
[62] Mann (1961), pp. 644 ff.
[63] Mann (1972), pp. 1 ff.
[64] Meisel (1911).
[65] Meisel (1925)

viduals who are involved in the taxation process.[66] The concerned individuals can be separated into three groups: tax legislators, tax administrators, and taxpayers. Whereas the moral behaviour of tax legislators and tax administrators is termed "tax ethics", the moral behaviour of the taxpayers is named "tax morality". Veit defines tax morality as the taxpayers' behaviour towards taxation ("*das Steuerhandeln der Leistungsverpflichteten*") and the taxpayers' moral attitudes towards taxation, "*Demnach soll also auch hier nur die moralische Einstellung der Steuerpflichtigen zu den ihnen als solchen auferlegten Handlungen mit dem Wort Steuermoral gemeint sein*".[67] Synonymously, he speaks of an individual's tax moral consciousness ("*Ausbildung eines steuermoralischen Bewußtseins*").[68] Following this definition, tax morality is a subjective value judgement based on individual decisions. Besides this, Veit speaks of a tax morality postulate. Taxpayers who honestly pay their taxes fulfil the postulate of tax morality completely. Tax morality stands for the duty of honest tax payment, "*erfülle genauestens deine Pflicht als steuerzahlender Staatsbürger*".[69] Veit defines tax morality as a subjective value judgement and at the same time as a behaviour postulate. This ambiguity runs through the whole study and makes it difficult to understand.

Declaring tax morality as being the duty of honest tax payment means that taxpayers bear a certain responsibility. Veit concludes that the degree of tax morality is indicated by the extent of tax payment. In his opinion the so defined tax morality is objective and measurable in form of the financial result of taxation.[70] Unfortunately, he does not discuss the problems of quantifying hidden tax bases. However, Herbert Sultan points out that this may be an object of a quantitative analysis.[71] By defining tax morality a behaviour postulate, Veit tries to establish a counterpart to the ethical principles of taxation which he names tax ethics.[72] Normative tax ethics determine what financial result ought to be reached in the fiscal budget, whereas tax morality indicates what financial result is actually reached.

The discussion of normative principles of taxation has a long tradition in economic literature. Adam Smith, who is mentioned by Veit,[73] identified four maxims.[74] Individuals ought to contribute in proportion to their respective ability. Taxation should be certain and convenient. The administrative costs of taxation

[66] Veit (1927), p. 318.
[67] Veit (1927), p. 319.
[68] Veit (1927), p. 328.
[69] Veit (1927), pp. 322 f.
[70] Veit (1927), p. 323.
[71] Sultan (1932), p. 129.
[72] Sultan (1932), p. 110.
[73] Veit (1927), p. 321.
[74] Smith (1993), pp. 451 ff.

should be as low as possible. The discussion was continued by many authors, for instance David Ricardo, Fritz Karl Mann, and Adolf Wagner. However, Veit also mentions authors, such as Emil Sax, Walther Lotz, Wilhelm Gerloff, and Alfred Amonn, who criticise such a normative analysis in general. Nevertheless, the most extensive systematization of tax principles, containing 18 principles, was created by Veit's colleague and friend Fritz Neumark more than 40 years after Veit's article on tax morality was published.[75]

Veit demonstrates the existence of a link between both the tax morality postulate regarding taxpayers and the postulates for ethical taxation concerning tax legislators and tax administrators. Furthermore, he shows that both are linked to the question of what the function of the state is ("*die Beziehung zwischen Steuerethik (in der Gesetzgebung) und Steuermoral ist hergestellt; den Generalnenner schafft die jeweilige Theorie von Wesen und Rechtfertigung des Staates*").[76] Veit mentions different concepts of the state ("*Staatsauffassung*") by Charles Montesquieu, Georg Friedrich Wilhelm Hegel, and Adolf Wagner,[77] and points out that the more responsibility the state has to bear (e.g. social responsibility as required by Adolf Wagner), the more important is requiring tax moral behaviour. In Veit's opinion fulfilling the postulate of tax morality is threatened if taxation does not correspond with the ethical principles of taxation. Therefore, he lays emphasis on considering these principles. The existence of such principles should be stated by fiscal sociological research.[78] However, as the long tradition of searching for such principles shows, it is very difficult to identify such generally accepted meta-rules. Veit stresses the temporary and regional peculiarities. Moreover, not every tax rule or action of a tax administrator can be argued with reference to general principles.

Veit does not quote Max Weber in his study on tax morality, however, Sultan hints at this source.[79] Sultan quotes Weber's "Wirtschaft und Gesellschaft".[80] In his approach of a political sociology, Max Weber distinguishes between *Verantwortungsethik* which stands for a thinking considering responsibility and *Gesinnungsethik* which means a way of thinking as a matter of course not in terms of result. In his lecture on politics as a calling ("Politik als Beruf") which was published as an essay in 1919, Weber stresses this distinction.[81] Veit in his study does not speak of *Verantwortungsethik* and *Gesinnungsethik* but obviously knows Weber's approach and transfers it to the phenomenon of tax morality. Later, in the 'flight from freedom' he explains the philosophical sources of

---

[75] Neumark (1970), pp. 44 ff.
[76] Veit (1927), p. 328.
[77] Veit (1927), p. 329.
[78] Veit (1927), p. 322.
[79] Sultan (1932), pp. 96 f. and 110 ff.
[80] Sultan (1932), p. 99.
[81] Weber (1919), pp. 237 ff.

Verantwortungsethik and *Gesinnungsethik* and distinguishes between both.[82] In his book on the sociology of freedom, Veit again explains this antinomy and quotes the second edition of Max Weber's "Politik als Beruf" which was published in 1926.[83]

In that essay Weber points out that ethical behaviour can be oriented either in particular sentiments, e.g. Christian conviction, or in a feeling of responsibility regarding the consequences of such behaviour.[84] Both maxims are conflicting. Philosophers name it an antinomy. For example, the way to do anything could be in conflict with a Christian conviction though the purpose of the behaviour does not conflict. Christian conviction would refuse to go such a way. The consequences are born by God. However, a good result must not result from good behaviour and bad behaviour must not lead to a bad result. The opposite often occurs. Max Weber emphasizes that individuals are oriented in both principles.[85] He points out that politicians should know this paradox and act in consideration of their responsibility.[86]

Sultan states that politicians are oriented towards ethical responsibility, although the political outcome is of course a compromise among the holders of political power regarding the function of the state.[87] Besides politicians there are other groups who have political power. In a footnote he emphasizes that bureaucrats, e.g. in a revenue office, have in fact political power based on their specialized knowledge and, therefore, can get in conflict with other holders of political power.[88] Sultan demonstrates that tax ethics (considering ethical principles of taxation) is a question of *Verantwortungsethik*.[89] In his book on the flight from freedom Veit explains that such a responsibility could be in regard of the history which was a postulate by philosophers from the ancient Greek Stoics up to the Enlightenment.[90] But he qualifies that an extreme realization is unrealistic.

Though Veit does not quote Max Weber in his article on tax morality, his analysis is, nevertheless, obviously based on the antinomy of *Verantwortungsethik* and *Gesinnungsethik*. Veit distinguishes between tax morality on the one side and subjective willingness to pay on the other side. Sultan appreciates Veit's application to the phenomenon of tax morality.[91] He explains that tax morality is

[82] Veit (1947), p. 341.
[83] Veit (1957), p. 256.
[84] Weber (1919), pp. 237 ff.
[85] Weber (1919), p. 250.
[86] Weber (1919), p. 247.
[87] Sultan (1932), p. 104.
[88] Sultan (1932), p. 100.
[89] Sultan (1932), p. 110.
[90] Veit (1947), pp. 327 ff.
[91] Sultan (1932), p. 110.

a counterpart of tax ethics which denotes *Verantwortungsethik* whereas subjective willingness to pay taxes is a counterpart of *Gesinnungsethik*. Taxpayers are more or less oriented in both.

Veit defines the willingness to pay taxes as the individual psychological disposition to comply voluntarily with the tax duty.[92] If taxpayers are willing to pay taxes the request for tax morality can be reached. In his essay on tax morality and tax burden, which appeared in 1932 and is largely based on Veit's essay, Schmölders also distinguishes between tax morality and subjective or individual willingness to pay taxes.[93] With the latter he means the taxpayers' psychic attitude as well as Veit. However, in his later extensive empirical studies on the issue in the 1950s and 1960s, Schmölders brings both together when he defines tax morality as the taxpayers' moral attitudes towards taxation.

Veit emphasizes that subjective willingness can be substituted by tax law design and enforcement ("*technische Mittel der Finanzverwaltung*"), for instance threat with penalties, pressure, a particular method of tax assessment and so on.[94] In Schmölders' opinion individual willingness to pay taxes is the most important component of tax morality.[95] Veit explains that contrary to tax morality, individual willingness to pay taxes is subjective and can not be measured. By the assumption that taxpayers are generally willing to pay taxes, Veit goes beyond Franz Meisel and Fritz Karl Mann who suppose that taxpayers basically tend to protest.[96] This is remarkable in consideration of recent work on the topic. The conventional expected utility model of tax evasion by Allingham and Sandmo is even more restricted.[97] Only law enforcement in form of monitoring and punishment is considered but not the design of a tax system and other factors. However, current research on tax compliance is shedding more and more light on further influential factors to explain honesty in taxation.

The message that willingness to pay taxes could be substituted by tax law enforcement could be misunderstood by the reader of Veit's article. Therefore, Sultan points out that measures of tax law enforcement can not raise tax morality to the level of 100 percent fulfilment of what was required by responsibility oriented tax ethics.[98]

---

[92] Veit (1927), p. 323.
[93] Schmölders (1932), p. 6.
[94] Veit (1927), pp. 323 and 334 ff.
[95] Schmölders (1932), p. 7.
[96] Meisel (1911), Meisel (1925), and Mann (1923), pp. 497 ff.
[97] Allingham and Sandmo (1972), pp. 323 ff.
[98] Sultan (1932), p. 111.

Individuals may follow other moral rules which they set by themselves autonomously. Thus, Veit differentiates between the normative tax morality postulate on the one hand and the taxpayer's individual moral code on the other hand.[99] Then, he shows existing conflicts between an individual set of moral principles and the tax morality postulate. He points out that, surprisingly, even persons who strongly conform individual moral principles violate tax morality but he does not offer proof for the hypothesis empirically.[100] As Veit remarks, tax morality differs from individual moral principles more than other principles of civic behaviour. In contrast to other forms of social behaviour, reaching tax morality is **not** guaranteed by individual moral principles. Veit points out that there is a particular tax morality besides private and business morality. Schmölders comments that existence of a particular tax morality is a finding of recent date.[101]

However contrary to Veit, Schmölders in the 1960s, as well as later authors, such as Erard, Feinstein, Frey, Feld, Torgler, and others, do not speak of a behaviour postulate but define it taxpayers' attitudes towards taxation which means a subjective value judgement of a group or all taxpayers (e.g. Schmölders, 1960) or of individuals (e.g. Frey, Feld, Torgler). They do not distinguish between a tax morality postulate and a subjective willingness to pay taxes. Frey, Feld, and Torgler, for instance, define tax morality as the intrinsic motivation to pay taxes which is equivalent to subjective willingness to pay taxes".[102] Interestingly, in his book on the sociology of freedom (published in 1957), Veit mentions such an approach as one of two extremes of the antinomy. He refers to Immanuel Kant's theory of the will ("*Willenstheorie*").[103] In Kant's opinion morality is provided by the pure will. The opposite extreme occurs when behaviour is ethically not accepted but the result. However, Sultan supports Veit's distinction between tax morality and willingness because tax morality is determined by many factors besides subjective willingness to pay taxes, e. g. by social group dependence ("*Bedingungen der Gruppenlage*"), tax law enforcement ("*Steuertechnik*") and the use of the tax yield ("*Steuerverwendung*").[104] Sultan emphasizes that social group dependence "*Bedingungen der Gruppenlage*" is of great importance.

---

[99] Veit (1927), p. 323.
[100] Veit (1927), pp. 324 f.
[101] Schmölders (1932), pp. 4 f.
[102] Frey and Feld (2002), pp. 6 f., and Torgler (2003b) pp. 5 and 12.
[103] Veit (1957), p. 257.
[104] Sultan (1931), pp. 12 ff.

5 Veit's Analysis of Social, Political, and Cultural Impacts on Tax Morality

An individual's subjective value judgement is not provided in isolation but in a particular political, cultural, and social environment.[105] Individuals belong to social groups. Therefore, it is necessary to analyze how subjective attitudes towards taxation are influenced due to a taxpayer's dependence on different social groups. Sultan emphasizes that these social circumstances are of great importance: "*Die "Bedingungen der Gruppenlage" ... sind von großer Bedeutung für die Steuermoral*".[106] By analyzing group dependence Veit is again encouraged by Max Weber who examined social relations and social groups, for instance nations. In his book on sentiments and rationality in the economy published in 1932, Veit commends Weber's sociological research a grandiose analysis.[107]

In his study on tax morality, Veit points out that the society is hardly interested in the "tax honest behaviour" of an individual.[108] Public opinion even tolerates tax evasion. Therefore, social pressure is missing. However, Veit remarks that such an analysis of social influences is always related to a particular time and a particular geographical region. Veit states that in Germany after the First World War it is socially accepted that a tax evader glorifies himself and boasts of his successful tax cheating. In Veit's point of view such a social acceptance of tax evasion corresponds with lenient judgement of tax evasion by tax legislators and tax administrators. How good morality and law can guarantee any social behaviour depends on the legislator and the society. Both influence the individual order of moral precedence. However, he does not prove his findings empirically.

Veit goes back to David Hume (but does not quote him) by describing a strong social pressure within small groups.[109] Veit states that a tax evader is honest to his friend because of social pressure but cheats the tax authorities due to the missing reciprocity. The importance of reciprocity among individuals is also emphasized by Adam Smith. In the "Theory of Moral Sentiments" he names retaliation "the great law which is dictated to us by nature".[110] Veit does not quote him but obviously conforms with that insight. He reminds the reader that taxation is not connected with a claim to receive anything.[111] By definition taxes are payments without return. In his opinion the missing return is one of the most important reasons for a weak tax morality.[112] Nevertheless, Veit explains that

[105] Veit (1947), pp. 332 f.
[106] Sultan (1931), p. 12.
[107] Veit (1932), p. 12.
[108] Veit (1927), p. 324.
[109] Veit (1927), pp. 325 ff.
[110] Smith (2002), p. 96.
[111] Veit (1927), p. 323.
[112] Veit (1927), p. 328.

not only the design of the tax system has an impact on tax morality but also the fact if taxpayers can influence fiscal policy, especially taxation and public spending, by voting.[113] Besides group size, Veit explains that an individual's tax morality is influenced by the subjective valuation of financial contributions or services addressed to the state, by the taxpayer's affiliation to a particular social class, and by the taxpayer's type of profession.[114]

In consideration of the fact that an individual's tax morality depends on the technical form of taxation, law enforcement, penalties, and so on, as well as on political, social, and cultural factors, Veit makes some suggestions as to how tax morality can be increased. He explains four different ways: the distribution of the tax burden (equity of taxation and public spending), tax administration (convenience, penalties, and whistle blowing), civic education (or moral suasion) and social pressure, e.g. publishing the amount of taxes which a person paid.[115]

Veit's basic message is that the problem of tax morality is a very prominent fiscal sociological issue,[116] which means that beyond examining fiscal institutions political, social, and cultural influences toward tax compliance is necessary.

6 Schmölders'Aanalysis of Tax Morality in the 1950s and 1960s

As already mentioned, Günter Schmölders and Otto Veit met for the first time in Berlin in the later 1920s and then saw each other frequently in Frankfurt am Main and Wiesbaden in the "Reichsverband Deutscher Banken". After world war two they met frequently in the Regional Central Bank of the German state Hessen and in the advisory board on the ministry of economics.[117] Schmölders follows Veit's approach of tax morality as an endogenous variable which is influenced by many factors. He wrote an essay on tax morality and tax burden which appeared in the "Vierteljahresschrift für Steuer- und Finanzrecht" in 1932, and in the same year it was published by Carl Heymanns in Berlin as an extended separate print.[118] It was already mentioned above that this essay, which appeared five years after Veit's article on the elements of tax morality, is largely based on Veit's study. However, a reception of their early studies on tax morality is missing in the English economic literature.

[113] Veit (1927), p. 341.
[114] Veit (1927), pp. 332 ff.
[115] Veit (1927), pp. 339 ff.
[116] Veit (1927), p. 349.
[117] Solf (1988), p. 45.
[118] Schmölders (1932), p. 2.

In his essay, Schmölders explains several factors which influence tax morality. These factors are the tax burden, the distribution of tax burden, the ways in which the state makes use of the tax yield ("*Art der Verwendung des Steueraufkommens*"), the marginal tax rate, and psychological causes of individual willingness.[119] As Veit, Schmölders identifies the existence of a particular tax morality which differs from private and business morality. In his opinion this peculiarity of tax morality is caused by the compulsory character of tax laws, missing claims to be received on any return, missing reciprocity (anonymity of the tax claiming counterpart), taxpayers' feeling of fascination when evading tax rules comparable with doing sports, taxpayers' agreement with the state, and taxpayers' exemption of equity and effectiveness in taxation.[120] He says that taxpayers' agreement with the state and taxpayers' exemption of equity and effectiveness in taxation determine an individual's willingness to pay taxes besides tax morality. As a consequence, he suggests some policy measures which directly influence subjective willingness to pay taxes to increase tax morality. He suggests reduction of public budgets, distribution of tax burden, and enhancement of transparency, equity, and effectiveness in taxation.[121] He adds that it matters which territorial authority in a federal system imposes taxes. Moreover, he recommends cultivating a trust relation between authorities and taxpayers, for example by founding taxpayers' associations.

After World War II, in the 1950s, Schmölders initiated research on economic behaviour ("*ökonomische Verhaltensforschung*") that considers psychological, biological, sociological, anthropological, philological, and historical research.[122] In a later essay he refers to Immanuel Kant's philosophical anthropology ("*philosophische Anthropologie in pragmatischer Hinsicht*").[123] Such a science of economic behaviour should examine economic relevance of continuities in human behaviour. The idea to search for continuities in economic behaviour is based on the concepts of German Historical School, e.g. Gustav Schmoller, and, as a consequence of German Historical School, old institutional economics, e.g. Thorstein B. Veblen.[124] Schmoller and other representatives of the German Historical School encouraged to find out economic regularities by analyzing history. Schmölders' academic teachers in Tübingen, for instance Herbert von Beckerath, made him familiar with Schmoller's approach.[125] Schmölders was of the opinion that examining tax morality is an important field for an application of his concept of "*Ökonomische Verhaltensforschung*".[126] He initiated the so

[119] Schmölders (1932), pp. 3, 4, 9, and 10.
[120] Schmölders (1932), pp. 5 ff.
[121] Schmölders (1932), pp. 11 ff.
[122] Schmölders (1953), p. 205.
[123] Schmölders (1957), p. 40.
[124] Schmölders (1953), pp. 213 ff. and 222.
[125] Schmölders (1960a), p. 155.
[126] Schmölders (1953), p. 226.

called Cologne School of Fiscal Psychology, a very extensive fiscal social-psychological research programme including empirical research, and investigates in analyzing tax morality.[127]

In the same way as Veit, Schmölders examines tax morality as a dependent variable which is influenced by many factors. However, he does not speak of a behaviour postulate. In his work in the 1960s he does not explicitly distinguish between tax morality and subjective willingness to pay taxes as he did it following Veit in his essay in 1932. He brings both together when he speaks of tax morality as a value judgement of a group or all taxpayers but not of a single taxpayer as for example Frey and Torgler do it later. Schmölders emphasizes the relevance of social groups, social relations, moral suasion, direct voting, taxpayers' perception of the state and the use of the tax yield, besides the impact of tax rate, tax law enforcement, and threat with penalties.[128] Again, he speaks of a particular tax morality which differs from private and business morality.[129] Moreover, Schmölders encouraged three dissertation theses on the behaviour of taxpayers, on jurisdiction regarding tax evasion, and on tax mentality.[130] Beyond the behaviour of tax legislators and taxpayers, like Veit,[131] Schmölders states that analysis of the tax administrators' behaviour is missing but necessary, and also refers to Max Weber's sociological research on that field.[132]

Schmölders knows and appreciates Veit's work. He not only mentions Veit's 1927 article on the elements of tax morality in the list of literature to his book on the irrationalities of the public economy,[133] but also engages in research on monetary theory and monetary policy, writing for example a book on money and credit and the problems of economic policy published in 1938.[134] Veit's book on the future of gold, money, and currency was published one year earlier.[135] Furthermore, Schmölders wrote an article on the liquidity theory of money.[136] Veit published his book on the same topic twelve years earlier.[137]

---

[127] Schmölders (1960a).
[128] Schmölders (1953), pp. 226 ff.
[129] Schmölders (1953), p. 233.
[130] Holtgrewe, Karl-Georg: Der Steuerwiderstand Das Verhalten der Steuerpflichtigen im Lichte der modernen Psychologie (Berlin, 1954), Peres, Wolfgang: Die Steuerhinterziehung im Spiegel der Rechtsprechung (Berlin, 1963), and Tretter, Bertram: Die Steuermentalität (Berlin, 1974).
[131] Veit (1927), p. 318.
[132] Schmölders (1953), p. 236.
[133] Schmölders (1960a), p. 158.
[134] Schmölders (1938).
[135] Veit (1937).
[136] Schmölders (1960b), pp. 346 ff.
[137] Veit (1948).

In his book on the irrationalities of the public economy which was published in 1960, Schmölders defines tax morality the attitudes of a group or of all taxpayers towards taxation which means according the question how good tax liabilities should be fulfilled.[138] Tax morality is anchored in the tax mentality which means taxpayers' consciousness concerning taxes and state.[139] In his questionnaire study participants were asked about tax mentality, tax burden, tax perception, fairness of taxation and associations concerning tax. He came to the result that the taxpayers' attitudes toward taxation depend on sex, age, education, job and social status.[140] Schmölders corresponds with Veit by concluding that tax evasion had become socially accepted and explains this by the compulsory character of taxation, by the anonymity of the state, and by the missing reciprocity. In his opinion the tax attitude is best expressed in the approval or disapproval of tax offences.[141] Schmölders concludes that tax offences are not a question of opportunity, but rather there is a direct relationship between the consciousness concerning the state, the attitudes regarding taxation, the feeling of a burden, and tax morality.[142]

Frey regrets that Schmölders has not been considered in the English economic literature.[143] However, in their field experimental study "On legal sanctions" published in 1967 and often quoted since that,[144] Schwartz and Orleans refer to Schmölders' article on "Fiscal Psychology: A new branch of public finance" which appeared in the renowned National Tax Journal.[145] Moreover, Alan Lewis who was encouraged by Schmölders' research, investigates tax mentality in the United Kingdom by the use of survey and questionnaire method.[146] One of his interesting findings is that "Generally taxpayers do not equate their tax contributions with services received".[147]

In 1997 and 1999 the Office for Empirical Research on Social Economics which was founded by Schmölders in 1957 provided extended repetitions of his early questionnaire studies.[148] Both repetitions were encouraged by the Taxpayers' Association of the German State Nordrhein-Westfalen.[149] The comparison of the

[138] Schmölders (1960a), pp. 97 f.
[139] Schmölders (1960a), p. 69.
[140] Schmölders (1960a), p. 74.
[141] Schmölders (1960a), pp. 100 f.
[142] Schmölders (1960a), pp. 110 f.
[143] Frey (1994), p. 108.
[144] Schwartz and Orleans (1967), p. 283.
[145] Schmölders (1959), pp. 340 ff.
[146] Lewis (1982), pp. 5 ff., Lewis (1979), pp. 245 ff.
[147] Lewis (1979), p. 255.
[148] Forschungsstelle für empirische Sozialökonomik (Prof. Dr. G. Schmölders) e.V. (August 1997), and Forschungsstelle für empirische Sozialökonomik e.V. (November 1999).
[149] Bund der Steuerzahler Nordrhein-Westfalen e.V., Schillerstraße 14, 40237 Düsseldorf, Germany.

1958 and 1997 studies shows an increasing feeling of burden.[150] Furthermore, in a 1997 survey, 74% of the participants answered that tax honesty is not rewarded by anybody, a majority feel that tax laws are unfair and 80% of the participants do not see a fair adjustment between the poor and the rich.[151] For example, less than one third of the asked persons do not think that value-added tax evasion and non-declaration of extra income means a serious tax offence. This shows the bad tax morality in form of approval or disapproval of tax evasion.[152] However, the number of persons who see value-added tax evasion as a serious tax offence increased by 50% between 1977 and 1997. Moreover, some legal tax avoidance strategies are now being criticised more and more. Therefore, it is difficult to speak of decreasing tax morality.[153] But tax morality decreases if seemingly tax reforms only complicate the tax system.[154]

Recent research on the question of what determines tax morality shows that some of Veit's and Schmölders' ideas of an extensive approach of tax compliance considering technical factors of the tax system, punishment, and so on as well as social, political, and cultural aspects, are still relevant and of immediate interest.

7 Recent Research Following the Approach of Endogenously Determined Tax Morality

In the 1990s some authors extended the conventional expected utility approach beyond Allingham and Sandmo[155] to fill the gap between theoretical and empirical findings with tax morality as a further determinant. For example, Erard and Feinstein incorporate tax morality and misperception of audit probabilities to explain honesty in taxation.[156] In their model the feelings of guilt and shame are realizations of tax morality. Guilt and shame are exogenously given determinants which influence the individual's decision. In contrast to Erard and Feinstein's extension of the conventional expected utility model, in Veit's point of view tax morality is a dependent variable which is determined by technical factors of taxation as well as by psychological and social factors.[157] Tax morality becomes an endogenous variable. Such an extensive approach of tax morality points to the basic idea of fiscal sociology which aims at examining how fiscal

[150] Forschungsstelle für empirische Sozialökonomik (1997), p. 17.
[151] Forschungsstelle für empirische Sozialökonomik (1997), pp. 18-20.
[152] Forschungsstelle für empirische Sozialökonomik (1997), p. 23.
[153] Forschungsstelle für empirische Sozialökonomik (1997), pp. 25 f.
[154] Forschungsstelle für empirische Sozialökonomik (1997), p. 27.
[155] Allingham and Sandmo (1972), pp. 323 ff.
[156] Erard and Feinstein (1994), pp. 70 ff.
[157] Veit (1927), p. 339.

institutions influence and are influenced by the law, political decisions, social behaviour, and culture.[158] Veit's extensive approach of tax morality is, therefore, a very remarkable work. However, Erard and Feinstein mention that, contrary to their model, the feeling of guilt may depend on the audit frequency.[159] This additional remark supports Veit's and Schmölders' concept that tax morality is a dependent variable and influenced by many factors.

In the 1980s, 1990s, and very recently, some economists, for example Pommerehne, Frey, Feld, and Torgler, have a conforming idea of an extensive approach in which tax morality is a variable endogenously determined by political, social, and cultural impacts. However, contrary to Veit, they do not speak of a behaviour postulate but define tax morality the taxpayers' or a taxpayer's attitudes towards taxation which means a subjective value judgement. Synonymously, they speak of willingness to pay taxes. Frey, Feld, and Torgler, for instance, define tax morality as the intrinsic motivation to pay taxes which is equivalent to subjective willingness to pay taxes".[160] In contrast to Veit, they do not distinguish between tax morality postulate and subjective willingness based on Max Weber's distinction between *Verantwortungsethik* and Gesinnungsethik, but follow Immanuel Kant's theory of the will ("*Willenstheorie*") where morality is provided by the pure will.

Pommerehne summarizes numerous questionnaire and experimental studies,[161] and from these sources concludes that besides the technical design of taxation and tax law enforcement (penalizing, accountability, whistle blowing), other factors are relevant to avoid annoying taxpayers, for instance fairness in taxation, tax burden at the margin, excessive regulation, and subjective perception of tax burden and public good provision.[162] Therefore, direct voting and fiscal federalism should be invigorated, and the fiscal competencies of the state constitutionally ought to be restricted. He advocates developing a theory of tax morality. Tax morality should be genuinely integrated into the economic theory of tax evasion. This recommendation is exactly the course that Frey, Feld, and Torgler follow.

Pommerehne, Hart, and Frey[163], as well as Torgler[164], for example, examine the impact of voting and political system on tax morality. The impact of influencing fiscal policy by voting was emphasized by Veit and Schmölders.[165] Frey states

[158] Mann (1961), pp. 645 f.
[159] Erard and Feinstein (1994), p. 75.
[160] Frey and Feld (2002), pp. 6 f., and Torgler (2003b), pp. 5 and 12.
[161] Pommerehne (1985), pp. 1165 ff.
[162] Pommerehne (1985), pp. 1178 f.
[163] Pommerehne, Hart, and Frey (1993), pp. 3 ff.
[164] Torgler (2002), pp. 5 ff., and Torgler (2003b), pp. 212 ff.
[165] Veit (1927), p. 341, and Schmölders (1953), pp. 226 ff.

that on the one side deterrence may raise tax revenue, while on the other side decreasing tax morality.[166] Feld and Frey point out that instead of promoting whistle blowing, treating taxpayers with trust and respect may cultivate tax morality.[167] They emphasize the importance of a respectful treatment of taxpayers by the tax authorities and assume a psychological tax contract between both. The tax authorities should support and avoid breaching it. In Swiss cantons the degree of a respectful treatment of taxpayers by the tax authorities corresponds with the kind of democratic system. Torgler analyzes data from World Values Survey and concludes that there is a strong influence of trust in a government on tax morality.[168] Also by the use of data from World Values Survey, Slemrod confirms that taxpayers' honesty conforms with non-government related trustworthiness in a country.[169] Furthermore, Torgler analyses cultural impact on tax morality by an East-West German comparison after German reunification,[170] and by a comparison of different European countries.[171] Moreover, he confirms Schwartz and Orleans' result,[172] that moral suasion or moral appeal influences honesty in taxation.[173] Veit recommends moral suasion as a useful policy instrument to increase tax morality.

8 Summary

In his article, Otto Veit lays down an extensive fiscal sociological concept of studying tax morality. In his approach, tax morality is an endogenous variable which is determined by tax law design and tax law enforcement as well as by social, political, and cultural factors. Therefore, he encourages research to find out how tax legislators, tax administrators and taxpayers behave. Veit analyzes not only the impact of deterrence, penalizing, and whistle blowing but also the impact of a general understanding of what the function of the state is, the impact of relations to social groups (related to a particular time and particular geographical region), and the impact of taxpayers' voting on fiscal policy. From this, he concludes policy implications. He identifies four different ways to increase tax morality: the distribution of tax burden (equity of taxation and public spending), tax law enforcement (convenience, penalties, and whistle blowing), civic education (or moral suasion) and social pressure, e.g. publishing the amount of taxes which a person paid.

---

166 Frey (1997), p. 113.
167 Feld and Frey (2002), pp. 91 ff.
168 Torgler (2001b), pp. 9 ff.
169 Slemrod (2002), pp. 18 ff.
170 Torgler (2003a), pp. 508 ff., and Torgler (2003b), pp. 432 ff.
171 Torgler (2003b), pp. 456 ff.
172 Schwartz and Orleans (1967), pp. 274 ff.
173 Torgler (2003b), pp. 566 ff.

Current authors do not separate tax morality and subjective willingness to pay taxes, referring to Max Weber's distinction between *Verantwortungsethik* and *Gesinnungsethik*, but follow Immanuel Kant's idea that morality is provided by the pure will. However, Veit's analysis of social, political, and cultural influences on tax morality besides tax law design and enforcement, was extensively continued by Schmölders. Such an extensive economic approach of endogenously determined tax morality is of immediate interest in current economic literature and necessary to explain honesty and dishonesty in taxation.

References

Allingham, Michael G., and Sandmo, Agnar (1972), Income tax evasion: a theoretical analysis, in: *Journal of Public Economics*, Vol. 1, pp. 323-338.

Alm, James; McClelland, Gary H.; Schulze, William D. (1992), Why do people pay taxes?, in: *Journal of Public Economics*, Bd. 48, S. 21-38.

Andreoni, James, Erard, Brian, and Feinstein, Jonathan (1998), Tax compliance, in: *Journal of Economic Literature*, Vol. 36, pp. 818-860.

Beckmann, Klaus (2001), Steuerhinterziehung, begrenzte Rationalität und Referenzabhängigkeit: Theorie und experimentelle Evidenz, *Passauer Diskussionspapiere*, Diskussionsbeitrag Nr. V-24-01, Volkswirtschaftliche Reihe, Passau.

Beckmann, Klaus (2003), *Steuerhinterziehung – Individuelle Entscheidungen und Finanzpolitische Konsequenzen*, Tübingen.

Dubin, Jeffrey A., and Wilde, Louis L. (1988), An empirical analysis of federal income tax auditing and compliance, in: *National Tax Journal*, Vol. 41, pp. 61-74.

Erard, Brian, and Feinstein, Jonathan S. (1994), The role of moral sentiments and audit perceptions in tax compliance, in: *Public Finance*, Vol. 49, pp. 70-89.

Feld, Lars P., and Frey, Bruno S. (2002), Trust breeds trust: How taxpayers are treated, in: *Economics of Governance*, Vol. 3, pp. 87-99.

Forschungsstelle für empirische Sozialökonomik (Prof. Dr. G. Schmölders) e.V. (August 1997), *Steuermentalität und Steuermoral der bundesdeutschen Bevölkerung und deren Einstellungen zur Steuerreform 1997*, Köln.

Forschungsstelle für empirische Sozialökonomik e.V. (November 1999), *Steuermentalität, Steuermoral und Einstellungen zur Steuerreform 1999*, Köln.

Frey, Bruno S. (1994), Ökonomie und Psychologie: Die wirtschaftswissenschaftliche Perspektive, in: Smekal, Christian; Theurl, Engelbert (eds.), *Stand und Entwicklung der Finanzpsychologie*, Baden-Baden, pp. 107-120.

Frey, Bruno S. (1997), *Not just for the money: An economic theory of personal motivation*, Cheltenham, Brookfield.

Frey, Bruno S., and Feld, Lars P. (2002), Deterrence and morale in taxation: An empirical analysis, CESifo working paper no. 760, category 1: *Public Finance*, August 2002.

Goldscheid, Rudolf (1926), Staat, öffentlicher Haushalt und Gesellschaft. Wesen und Aufgabe der Finanzwissenschaft vom Standpunkte der Soziologie., in: Gerloff, Wilhelm, and Meisel, Franz (eds.), *Handbuch der Finanzwissenschaft*, Vol. 1, Tübingen, pp. 146-184.

Graetz, Michael J., and Wilde, Louis L. (1985), The economics of tax compliance: Fact and fantasy, in: *National Tax Journal*, Vol. 38, pp. 355-363.

Gutowski, Armin, et al. (1974), *Währungsstabilität in einer integrierten Welt – Beiträge zur Geldtheorie und Geldpolitik – Festgabe für Otto Veit*, Stuttgart et al., 1974.

Koch, Woldemar (1981), Finanzsoziologie, in: Albers, Willi (ed.), *Handwörterbuch der Wirtschaftswissenschaft*, Vol. 3, pp. 97-106.

Lewis, Alan (1979), An empirical assessment of tax mentality, in: *Public Finance*, Vol. 34, pp. 445-257.

Lewis, Alan (1982), *The psychology of taxation*, Oxford.

Mann, Fritz Karl (1923), Die Grundformen der Steuerabwehr, in: *Jahrbücher für Nationalökonomie und Statistik*, Vol. 120 (III. Folge, Vol. 65), pp.497-523.

Mann, Fritz Karl (1961), Finanzsoziologie, in: Beckerath, Erwin von, et al. (eds.) *Handwörterbuch der Sozialwissenschaften*, zugleich Neuauflage des Handwörterbuchs der Staatswissenschaften, Vol. 3, Stuttgart, Tübingen, Göttingen.

Mann, Fritz Karl (1972), Die drei Finanzwissenschaften, in: *Finanzarchiv*, Neue Folge, Vol. 30, pp. 1-13.

Meisel, Franz (1911), *Moral und Technik bei der Veranlagung der preußischen Einkommenssteuer*, Leipzig.

Meisel, Franz (1925), *Britische und deutsche Einkommensteuer*, Tübingen.

Neumark, Fritz (1954), Wilhelm Gerloff, in: *Zeitschrift für die gesamte Staatswissenschaft*, Vol. 110, pp. 740-744.

Neumark, Fritz (1970), *Grundsätze gerechter und ökonomisch rationaler Steuerpolitik*, Tübingen.

Pommerehne, Werner W. (1985), Was wissen wir eigentlich über Steuerhinterziehung?, in: *Rivista internazionale di scienze economiche e commerciali*, pubblica Universitá Commerciale Luigi Bocconi Milano, Vol. 32, S. 1155-1186.

Pommerehne, Werner W., and Frey, Bruno S. (1992), The effects of tax administration on tax morale, *discussion paper* no. B 9204, Department of Economics, University of Saarland, Saarbrücken, July 1992.

Pommerehne, Werner W., Hart, Albert, and Frey, Bruno S. (1993), Tax morale, tax evasion and the choice of policy instruments in different political systems, *discussion paper* no. B 9301, Department of Economics, University of Saarland, Saarbrücken, August 1993.

Schmölders, Günter (1932), Steuermoral und Steuerbelastung, Erweiterter Sonderabdruck aus Heft 1, 1932, der *Vierteljahreschrift für Steuer- und Finanzrecht*, Carl Heymanns Verlag: Berlin.

Schmölders, Günter (1938), *Geld und Kredit, Probleme der Wirtschaftspolitik*, Leipzig.

Schmölders, Günter (1953), Ökonomische Verhaltensforschung, in: *Ordo, Jahrbuch für die Ordnung von Wirtschaft und Gesellschaft*, Vol. 5, pp. 203-244.

Schmölders, Günter (1957), Ökonomische Verhaltensforschung, in: Fritz Baade, *Gesamtdeutschland und die Integration Europas*, Günter Schmölders, Ökonomische Verhaltensforschung, Arbeitsgemeinschaft für Forschung des Landes Nordrhein-Westfalen, Heft 71, Köln and Opladen, pp. 39-69.

Schmölders, Günter (1959), Fiscal psychology: A new branch of public finance, in: National *Tax Journal*, Vol. 12, pp. 340 ff.

Schmölders, Günter (1960a), *Das Irrationale in der öffentlichen Finanzwirtschaft - Probleme der Finanzpsychologie*, Hamburg.

Schmölders, Günter (1960b), The liquidity theory of money, in: *Kyklos*, Vol. 13, pp. 346-360.

Schwartz, Richard D., and Orleans, Sonya (1967), On legal sanctions, in: The University of Chicago Law Review, Vol. 34, pp. 274-300.

Skinner, Jonathan, and Slemrod, Joel (1985), An economic perspective on tax evasion, in: *National Tax Journal*, Vol. 38, pp. 345-353.

Slemrod, Joel (2002), Trust in public finance, National Bureau of Economic Research (NBER) *working paper* 9187, http://www.nber.org/papers/w9187.

Smith, Adam (1993), *An inquiry into the nature and causes of the wealth of nations* (first published in 1776), ed. by Kathryn Sutherland, Oxford, New York.

Smith, Adam (2002), *The Theory of Moral Sentiments* (first published in 1759), ed. by Knud Haakonssen, Cambridge.

Solf, Heinz (1988), Otto Veit – ein Ordoliberaler, *Neue Würzburger Studien zur Soziologie*, Vol. 12, Würzburg.

Spicer, Michael W., and Lundstedt, S. B. (1976) Understanding Tax Evasion, in: *Public Finance*, Vol. 31, pp. 295-305.

Sultan, Herbert (1931), *Art und Mass der Prognose der Steuerwirkungen*, Antrittsvorlesung am 18. Juli 1931, Recht und Staat in Geschichte und Gegenwart – Eine Sammlung von Vorträgen und Schriften aus dem Gebiet der gesamten Staatswissenschaften, Vol. 86, Tübingen.

Sultan, Herbert (1932), *Die Staatseinnahmen – Versuch einer soziologischen Finanztheorie als Teil einer Theorie der politischen Ökonomie*, Tübingen.

Torgler, Benno (2001a), Is tax evasion never justifiable?, in: *Journal of public finance and public choice*, Vol. 20, pp.143-167.

Torgler, Benno (2001b), *Tax morale and institutions*, Wirtschaftswissenschaftliches Zentrum (WWZ) der Universität Basel discussion paper 02/07.

Torgler, Benno (2002), Direct democracy matters: Tax morale and political participation, *WWZ-Discussion Paper* 02/05, July 2002.

Torgler, Benno (2003a), Does culture matter? Tax morale in an East-West-German comparison, in: *FinanzArchiv*, Vol. 59, pp. 504-528.

Torgler, Benno (2003b), *Tax Morale: Theory and empirical analysis of tax compliance*, Dissertation der Universität Basel zur Erlangung der Würde eines Doktors der Staatswissenschaften.

Veit, Otto (1927), Grundlagen der Steuermoral – Eine finanzsoziologische Studie, in: *Zeitschrift für die gesamte Staatswissenschaft*, Vol. 83, pp. 317-349.

Veit, Otto (1932), *Gefühl und Vernunft in der Wirtschaft*, Berlin.

Veit, Otto (1937), *Die Zukunft des Goldes: eine Abhandlung über Geld und Währung*, Berlin.

Veit, Otto (1947), *Die Flucht vor der Freiheit – Versuch zur geschichtsphilosophischen Aufhellung der Kulturkrise*, Frankfurt am Main.

Veit, Otto (1948), *Volkswirtschaftliche Theorie der Liquidität*, Frankfurt am Main.

Veit, Otto (1953), Ordo und Ordnung - Versuch einer Synthese, in: *Ordo, Jahrbuch für die Ordnung von Wirtschaft und Gesellschaft*, Vol. 5, pp. 3-47.

Veit, Otto (1954), Pecunia in ordine rerum, in: *Ordo, Jahrbuch für die Ordnung von Wirtschaft und Gesellschaft*, Vol. 6, pp. 39-77.

Veit, Otto (1955), Offenbarung des Menschen im Kollektiv, in: *Zeitschrift für Politik, Neue Folge*, Vol. 2, pp. 12-27.

Veit, Otto (1957), *Soziologie der Freiheit*, Frankfurt am Main.

Veit, Otto (1960/61), Freiheit in einer zerrissenen Welt – Acht Thesen zum Schisma der Welt, in: *Ordo, Jahrbuch für die Ordnung von Wirtschaft und Gesellschaft*, Vol. 12, pp. 77-102.

Veit, Otto (1961), Menschliches zum Problem des Fortschritts, in: *Offene Welt*, 1961, pp. 518-530.

Veit, Otto (1968), *Währungspolitik als Kunst des Unmöglichen*, Frankfurt am Main.

Weber, Max (1919), Politik als Beruf, in: Baier, Horst et al. (eds.) (1992), Max Weber Gesamtausgabe, Abt. 1, *Reden und Schriften*, Vol. 17, Wissenschaft als Beruf: 1917/1919 [u.a.], ed. by Mommsen, Wolfgang, J., and Schluchter, Wolfgang, Tübingen, pp. 157-252.

Justi's Moral Economics and his System of Taxation (1766)

Helge Peukert
University Lecturer
Krupp Chair in Public Finance and Fiscal Sociology
University of Erfurt
Nordhäuser Str. 63
99089 Erfurt
Germany
Fon: ++49-361-737-4553
Fax: ++49-361-737-4559
helge.peukert@uni-erfurt.de

Abstract: First, the originality of the cameralist approach which crosscuts modern understandings of fundamental paradigmatic differences is pointed out. Second, the background of Justi's ethical, non-materialist utopia without greed and luxury in his moral-philosophical writings is presented. Third, Justi's *System des Finanzwesens* is analyzed. Besides his first best system of a Platonic republic his proposal to introduce an educational Veblen tax to fundamentally revolutionize society and his third best tax system with the four main taxes of demesnes (auctioning), regalia (run by the state), *Akzisen* (which he in principle rejected) and his prime tax on profits are presented.

Keywords: Cameralism, fiscal sociology, moral economics, taxation.

JEL codes: B, B3, H, P, Z1.

Introduction

Not only from a history of economic thought perspective is cameralism a challenge for deeply ingrained habits of thought and preconceptions. Today we are accustomed to polarize an individualist, economic rational, spontaneous evolution, market efficiency perspective on the one hand and a holist, rule following, conscious design and political reform orientation on the other hand (Rutherford (1996)). For cameralists the market mechanisms did not prevail or lead to an overall equilibrium - public rules and regulations were warranted. This contrasts with liberalism. But against a more collective or socialist approach the cameralists put the rational individual with absolute rights as a normative ideal in the center of their considerations.

But against liberalism, in cameralism the state was an active mover and collective entrepreneur to modernize society from above with the objective normative commitment to overall individual felicity. Cameralism was rooted in the metaphysical thinking of German (idealist) philosophy. Therefore, it was indifferent to the surging natural science ideal and hostile to empirical utilitarianism as the British variant of enlightenment. Explicitly anticlerical, with a strong emphasis on equality cameralism rejected privileges in principle. A concern for the social question and an engagement for the poorer strata of society opposed them to the conservative powers, especially the church and the nobility. Finally, for fascist ideologies cameralism was not attractive because, whilst it urged the need for a strong state, it did not posit an organic state ideal or concept of society (Rath (1939/1940) with much sympathy for the *völkische* ideal). Furthermore, cameralists viewed peace as an important practical and ethical value.[1] Power politics or the so-called realist school in international relations was incompatible with the peaceful attitude of the cameralists (Jenetzky (1978, pp. 9-10)).

Consequently, posterity mostly ignored the cameralist paradigm of thought and its economic policy proposals.[2] An extreme case is the reception of Justi's oeuvre which has been ignored, downgraded (Roscher (1874, pp. 444-536)), instrumentalized (Hasbach (1891, p. 185)) or discussed very superficially (Frensdorff (1970), Schumpeter (1965, pp. 228-232), Bödeker (1985), Baum (1988, pp. 146-155), and most handbook articles on Justi). Besides the discussion of some very specialized topics in Justi (Jaeger (1910) and Borscheid (1989)), only two publications, Obert (1992) on Justi's political philosophy, and the profound study by Klein (1961) on Justi's economic policy proposals (the overview of Marchet (1885, part III. 1), may also be mentioned here), offer deeper insight into Justi's thought.

It is interesting to note that the economic-political literature mostly keeps silence on two intriguing aspects of cameralism in general and Justi in particular which are the subject of the following investigation: his moral economics, including his utopian ideals and his peculiar tax system[3] - and the interrelation between them.

---

[1] For example, Justi strongly rejects chauvinist feelings of general superiority and tries to show the value of other cultures and social systems, e.g. of the Incas and the Chinese. "Though their national pride may be widespread amongst all nations, we Europeans pursue this conceit to a far higher degree than any other nation on earth" (1762, p. 3; this and the following quotations of Justi's works into English are our translations; many thanks to Mark Peacock for assistance with the translations).

[2] Cameralism is discussed e.g. in Tribe (1988) and (1995), but see the critique of Lluch (1997) who points out that the influence of cameralism outside the Germanic world was considerable in terms of translations and the reception of their ideas.

[3] Justi's thinking on public finance is discussed in Klein (1952), Grimmig (1949), Schmidt (1937), Wysocki (1982), and Jenetzky (1978) in some detail. Nevertheless a precise overview of Justi's tax proposals is still missing in the literature.

The utopian vision in cameralist thought has been discussed by Zielenziger (1914, pp. 263-277) for the case of J.J. Becher who holds a communist-utopian, or a communist prime-Christian ideal of a non-materialist, egalitarian society. Against Roscher he shows that this ideal was not only an old-age phenomenon in Becher but a constant concern. For Zielenziger, Becher was realist enough not to put his ideal too vehemently at the forefront. Zielenziger interprets it as the ambivalent mixture of the ideals of the stationary middle ages in a period of transition to the dynamic modern times. "As a moral philosopher he [Becher] rejects what he endorses as politician" (1914, p. 269, our translation). But it has to be mentioned that for most cameralists the above mentioned search for individual felicity was meant in the sense of stoic perfection of the soul and does not only reflect a minor influence of their classical Greek-Roman tradition but represents a building-block of their intellectual design and paradigm. Its ignorance must lead to a misunderstanding of most cameralists's basic vision. In the following we will first discuss Justi's moral-philosophical writings and then turn to his tax proposals.[4]

1 Justi's Moral-Philosophical Writings

In this section we will analyze Justi's moral and philosophical early writings which are delineated in Justi (1760-1761; see also Bollnow (1941)). As a starting point we can summarize his critique of Leibniz with the remark that he simply puts the Christian dualism of a world of bodies and souls, i.e. an ideal versus a material world against Leibniz' pantheistic or objective idealist approach (see the quotes in Bollnow (1941, especially p. 387)). Nevertheless, Justi shares Leibniz′ metaphysical endeavor to understand the world in full and to believe in its meaningfulness and in a rational explanation of the existence of evil.

Man in fact can be malicious, i.e. he can have "a desire to act against the laws" (1760, vol. 2, p. 335).[5] The reason of this is the finiteness of man. The meaning of the free will is to lead man to felicity *(Glückseligkeit)* (1760, vol. 2, p. 312). Man naturally tries to reach felicity but his actions in this direction depend on insight. "The more highly developed our reason, the more freely are we resolved to act in accordance with that which is truely good" (1760, vol. 2, p. 423).[6] But as a finite being, man has only limited reason and is limited by more or less compulsive and irrational affections (1760, vol. 2, pp. 423f.). The state is necessary because today human beings lost their innocence and ignorance but have

[4] We will leave out an analysis of his fables (see Peukert (2002, part two)).
[5] "eine Begierde, den Gesetzen zuwider zu handeln".
[6] "(J)e höher die Vernunft ist, desto freyer determiniren wir uns zu dem wahren Guten".

not the full capacities of reason at their disposal. They are in an intermediate position.

The final orientation of human beings is the state of perfection, the communal felicity is the ultimate goal of the republic. Realistically, Justi sees self-love as the dominant force in human behavior and that man wants to be happy (1760, vol. 1, pp. 84, and 239). Self-love has been implanted by the creator to increase the will to live (and e.g. not to commit suicide) and to generate curiosity (1760, vol. 1, pp. 38, and 84). For Justi, virtue and vice result thereof. A fictitious and a real happiness or felicity must be distinguished. He underlines that "true felicity consists in a permanent complacency and pleasure of the soul ... Felicity is the condition of lasting joy" (1760, vol. 1, p. 29, and vol. 2, p. 409).[7] Stoic persistence is put against timely goods and sensory impressions. We should have dignified notions of our soul.

> When we harbor dignified notions of our soul as an immortal and non-material entity ... such that we must seek felicity in this spiritual essence alone, it is thus easily apprehended that such felicity consist in the tranquility and contentment of our souls (1760, vol. 1, p. 54).[8]

Dignified notions are opposed to the sensory everyday life. "It is most certain that the final aim of our existence consist not in the pursuit of our daily bread" (1760, vol. 1, p. 133).[9]

To transcend this level of simple procurement, we need reason to fight our passions.

> Reason alone conduces to the complacency of our souls. We must be sensible. We must establish in ourselves the rule of reason over our passions and desires. This supremacy is more felicituous by far than the gleaming throne of the loftiest monarch, for we attain therewith the complacency of our souls, the true felicity, which neither crown nor scepter can bring about (1760, vol. 1, p. 65).[10]

---

[7] "die wahrhafte Glückseeligkeit in einer beständigen Zufriedenheit und Vergnügen der Seele bestehet ... Glückseligkeit ist der Stand einer dauerhaften Freude."

[8] "(W)enn wir würdige Begriffe von unsrer Seele als einem unsterblichen und unkörperlichen Wesen haben ... daß wir die Glückseeligkeit allein bey diesem geistigen Wesen suchen müssen. Es ist dannenhero ganz leicht begreiflich, daß diese Glückseligkeit lediglich in der Ruhe und Zufriedenheit unsrer Seelen bestehe".

[9] "Es ist sehr gewiß, daß die Sorgen der Nahrung nicht den Endzweck unsres Seyns ausmachen".

[10] "Die Vernunft ist es allein, die die Zufriedenheit unsrer Seelen befördert. Wir müssen klug werden. Wir müssen in uns selbst ein Reich über unsre Leidenschaften und Begierden errichten. Diese Herrschaft ist weit glücklicher als der schimmernde Thron der höchsten Monarchen. Sie verschaft uns die Zufriedenheit unsrer Seelen, die wahrhaftige Glückseeligkeit, welche Kron und Zepter zu wirken nicht vermögen".

Felicity consists in the fulfillment of the ethical duties and the stoic insight: "Calmness paves the way to the real felicity of man, i.e. the contentment of the soul ... The tranquility of our souls, the true and highest felicity of our life is the inseparable companion of all virtues" (1760, vol. 2, p. 206, and vol. 1, p. 120).[11] He also strongly supports the Christian ethics of compassion and help for others. "To those in need we must hasten in help so far as such is within our power. We must endeavor to save the victims of persecution and oppression" (1760, vol. 1, p. 142).[12]

This stoic-ascetic view does not lead Justi to the classical Greek and Roman non-political privatism of the quiet stoic soul. Instead, as we will see in the next paragraphs, Justi engages in public discourse and politics for the common good and communal felicity instead of utilitarian-individual happiness. "We live in the present and it is in the present that we must observe our obligations and live in accord with the final aim of our existence" (1760, vol. 1, p. 148).[13] As we see, Justi also rejects a virtuous life in the distant future. "Since our soul, the most distinguished part of us is intended for a better and eternal life, there is nothing which better conduces to true felicity than that which improves and perfects the soul" (1760, vol. 1, p. 185).[14] Justi's writings have the function to bring practical policy closer to his stoic-Christian-humanist ideal which coincides with our potential as reasonable communal beings. The great force to meliorate the state of things is good education, for the leading strata by means of intelligent and insightful books and articles, but it should begin at the most elementary level.

> Those who work in public schools should be chosen from the most educated, witty, and intelligent men. Every village school master should be a true teacher of morals and good conduct when the general welfare of the people and of each state is concerned (1760, vol. 1, p. 50).[15]

---

[11] "Die Gelassenheit bahnt den Weg zur wahren Glückseligkeit der Menschen, nämlich zu der Zufriedenheit der Seele ... Die Ruhe unserer Seelen, die wahrhaftige und höchste Glückseligkeit unseres Lebens ist die unzertrennliche Begleiterin aller Tugenden".

[12] "Wir müssen den Nothleidenden, soviel in unsern Kräften ist, mit der That zu Hilfe eilen. Wir müssen die Verfolgten und Unterdrückten zu retten suchen".

[13] "Gegenwärtig leben wir, und gegenwärtig müssen wir unsre Schuldigkeit beobachten, und dem Endzweck unsers Seyns gemäß leben".

[14] "(D)enn da unser Geist, als der vornehmste Theil von uns, zu einem ewigen und bessern Leben bestimmt ist: so kann nichts unsre wahre Glückseligkeit befördern, als was denselben bessert und vollkommen macht".

[15] "Diejenigen so in öffentlichen Schulen arbeiten, solten billig aus den gelehrtesten, witzigsten und klügsten Männern bestehen, und ein jeder Dorfschulmeister solte ein wahrhaftiger Sittenlehrer seyn, wenn man die allgemeine Wohlfahrth der Menschen und eines jeden Staats ins besondere, recht vor Augen haben wollte".

2 Traces of the Good Society and Moral Economics in Justi's *System des Finanzwesens*

The *System des Finanzwesens* (1766) is largely identical with parts of *Die Natur und das Wesen der Staaten* (1760) and of the *Staatswirtschaft* (1755).[16] The advantages of social assistance lead to the establishment of the state. The state is the result of reason and insight, a primary social drive does not exist (§ 1), only self-love plus reason. The civic society is grounded on mutual advantage, a central authority is needed for defense (§ 2) but should not impede the natural liberty of the citizens. The beginning of Justi´s book does not show real traces of the moral-philosophical basis mentioned above. It sounds very individualistic. He holds a position which is neither in conformity with Hobbes (bad human nature-authoritarian state) nor with Rousseau's social human nature. Neither does he share Shaftesbury's social and friendly image of man, nor Mandeville's private vices-public benefit philosophy (just the opposite: private vices are the major enemy for public benefit). The sovereign has a functional and serving role for society. It is not clear if Justi holds any natural contract approach here, he sometimes refers to a silent acceptance ("stillschweigende Einwilligung", (1766, p. 347); see also §§ 677, 689 and 690). The moral dimension of the book lies in the fact that it is addressed to the sovereign (see the preface) with the intention to change his behavior. He should not go for war and he has to know exactly his country (§§ 14-15).[17]

The sovereign should be engaged to supersede defects and hindrances and guarantee that things are in the right proportion (§17). The most blessed and felicitous circumstances for a state are:

> an increase in the country's relative wealth and the state's revenues (both of which grow increasingly as the population and the productive classes expand); a growth in population in and of itself; the flourishing of the country's productive classes; and a vibrant circulation of currency. These are the blessed and most happiest circumstances for a state (1766, p. 261).[18]

---

[16] See also the excellent translation of a part of book four on the principles of taxation by Monroe (1927, pp. 379-399). Justi (1970/1762) coincides with Justi (1766, §§ 687ff.). We will not compare Justi's *System des Finanzwesens* with other writings, e.g. Justi (1969/1782); see Schefold ((ed.) 1993).

[17] "The ruler must know to the full both his country with respect to size, position, natural conditions and fertility, and also the inhabitants with regard to their number, skills, talents, genius, customs, predilections, and passions."
"Der Regent muß demnach sein Land nach seiner Größe, Lage, natürlichen Beschaffenheit und Fruchtbarkeit, so wohl als die darinnen befindlichen Einwohner nach ihrer Menge, Fähigkeiten, Geschicklichkeiten, Genie, Sitten, Neigungen, und Leidenschaften vollkommen kennen"(1766, p. 6).

[18] "Die Vermehrung des relativen Reichthums im Lande, und der Einkünfte des Staates, die durch die größere Bevölkerung und das Aufnehmen des Nahrungsstandes immer mehr an-

We find no sentence in Justi that this procurement is partly achieved by the use of some market mechanisms. This is not to say that Justi was not well aware of the functioning of the price mechanism (see e.g. § 642). An integral duty of the ruler and the state is to care for old age and health by means of an insurance system (§ 575).

The sovereign has to procure communal felicity, he is not free to act how he likes. Thrift and frugality should be his basic orientations what expenditures are concerned. At the end, he will be judged by god and therefore should pay attention (§ 19). Justi especially castigates the lust for power (§ 23, one reason why an unbound monarchy should be rejected, see § 717) and again and again wars.[19] The sovereign should especially pay attention to the dimensions of security, welfare and an economic developmental perspective.[20] The most important argument in the book is the thesis of the harmony of interest between the ruler and the rest of society (see esp. § 623). In the short run, the ruler may have a decent live and find grandeur in conspicuous (also public, see § 49) consumption and ostentation by increasing the level of taxes, etc. But in the longer run this will impoverish the country, reduce the stream of revenues and a hostile military takeover becomes possible (§§ 37-41; on tariffs see e.g. § 126).

One example is the negative long-run consequence of the manipulation of the currency (see also his detailed discussion in §§ 593ff. which cannot be discussed here). For Justi, honesty is the best policy.[21] The freedom to act, the increase and not the loss of the substance of private property and means should prevail. As a side-effect, otherwise wealthy people would simply leave the country (§ 42). An

---

wachsen, die Vergrößerung der Bevölkerung an sich selbst, der blühende auswärtige Handel, der Flor des Nahrungsstandes im Lande, und eine lebhaftige Circulation sind die gesegnetesten und glücklichsten Umstände vor einen Staat".

[19] "The nations have enthroned rulers over them not in an attempt to find felicity through feats of daring but in order to further their welfare through trusted and orderly undertakings." "Die Völker haben Regenten über sich gesetzet, nicht durch kühne Wagestücke ihre Glückseligkeit zu suchen, sondern ihre Wohlfahrth durch sichere und ordentliche Wege zu befördern" (1766, p. 13).

[20] "That which most of all furthers the contentment of subjects or security, wealth, increase in production, and the circulation of money should always be of priority in his use of the state's wealth." "Dasjenige, was das vergnügte Leben der Unterthanen, oder die Sicherheit, den Reichthum, das Aufnehmen des Nahrungs-Standes und die Circulation des Geldes am meisten befördert, hat bey ihm in dem Gebrauche des Staatsvermögens allemal den Vorzug" (1766, p. 12). He makes clear that "true wealth rests solely on the surplus of all kinds of goods which reduce scarcity and enhance the comfort of life."
"dieser wahre Reichthum lediglich auf dem Überfluß aller Arten von Güthern zur Notdurft und Bequemlichkeit des Lebens beruhet" (1766, pp. 258-259).

[21] "The driving forces of honor, honesty and the love for one's native country." "(D)ie Triebfedern der Ehre, der Redlichkeit und der Liebe des Vaterlandes" (1766, p. 28). "Nothing is so important as good faith". "Nichts ist so nothwendig als Treu und Glaube" (1766, p. 305).

increase in revenue should be due to an increase in economic activities. The state is maybe the most important institution for all cameralists, at the same time they defend the *citoyen* against all but a moderate confiscation of his income, wealth and property. This combination may be a fascinating inspiration for a present-day practical concept of *Staatswissenschaften*.

Justi systematically tries to convince the ruler to reduce the time preference rate and to enlarge the decision horizon by the use of reason. His books have also to be seen as exercises in the art of rhetoric; the secondary literature often lamented on the not straight to the point way of Justi's writings. But rhetoric needs time and some repetition to convince. He focuses on the second best society and does not mention the good society according to his Christian-stoic ideal up till now. But besides practical knowledge, the ethical dimension also in the sense of the lower time preference rate and the broad horizon is a necessary and elementary prerequisite for a good society, a government, and the cameralists (§§ 61ff.).[22] If necessary they have to oppose the rulers because most of them do not have the common good in mind (§ 62). An important aspect of Justi's work is his realism with respect to the weights of passions and reason in human behavior. But in contrast to e.g. public choice he does not legitimate behavior as immutable in contrast with the common felicity but he castigates it with a moderate belief in education and the power of arguments. Maybe, the fine-tuning of his major arguments have often been misunderstood as long and unimportant *Ausschreiberei* (hack writing), but in our view they elicit a well-organized intellectual architecture.

If we ask who Justi's present-day opponents may be adversaries we may point at new institutional economists and public choice approaches. For them

> the analytical unit ... is the utility maximizing individual ... Following the pessimistic tradition of liberalism the prevalence of self-interest is assumed. Where fraud pays, it will happen - in politics, the economy, and in private life. *Opportunism is predominant* (Richter (1998, pp. 326, and 342), our translation).

Besides innate opportunism, in the tradition of the new economic history a trade-off between private wealth accumulation and ethical behavior is assumed. North

> suggests that the trade-off between wealth and these other values is a negatively sloped function ... where the price one pays for expressing one's own ideology, or norms or preferences is extremely high, they will account much less for human behavior (North (1996, p. 22)).

[22] "We recall that a real cameralist must be first and foremost an upright and honest man." "(W)ir erinnern, daß ein ächter Cameralist vor allen Dingen ein redlicher und rechtschaffender Mann sein müsse" (1766, p. 29).

For North, the common good is in no one's interest or utility function. At the end we read his admission that

> (i)t is hard - maybe impossible - to model such a polity with wealth-maximizing actors unconstrained by other considerations. It is no accident that economic models of the policy developed in the public choice literature make the state into something like the Mafia - or, to employ its terminology, a leviathan. The state then becomes nothing more than a machine to redistribute wealth and income ... no one at this stage in our knowledge knows how to create such an entity [an efficient state]. Indeed with a strictly wealth-maximizing behavioral assumption it is hard even to create such a model abstractly (North (1996, pp. 140, and 59)).

Justi started with a different behavioral assumption and he developed such a model from a theoretical background with practical economic policy implications.

At the beginning of the first main part of the *System* Justi presents a universal-historical stage theory of development which contrasts with his decay thesis mentioned above and which can also be found in the writings of other social scientists in his century (e.g. A. Smith) and later. Surprisingly, he argues that simple modes of production go hand in hand with a restricted degree of reasoning, culture and a state-like organization of society. A general upgrading of economic performance, political organization, reason, good customs and culture takes place. The stages are hunting, cattle-breeding, agriculture, and finally manufacture.[23]

From one stage to the next, more and more rules and regulations become necessary because more and more conflicts naturally arise. The stages are regarded as a universal law of history. The driving force from one stage to the next is not a new mode of production which challenges, provokes or develops a new level of reason(ing) (Marx), but knowledge and higher cognitive levels drive needs.[24]

---

[23] "Thus, the forms of living and means of subsistence amongst all nations could not, in their beginnings, be but bad ... With the growth of knowledge, herdsmen emerged from populations of hunters and fishermen. With a growth in the power of reason, the art of husbandry developed from that of herding ... With the full development of reason there emerged artisans, manufacturers artists and merchants. This is the universal history of all people on earth." " (S)o haben die Lebensarten und Unterhaltungs-Mittel bey allen Völkern, in ihrem ersten Ursprunge, nicht anders als schlecht seyn können. ... Aus Völkern von Jägern und Fischern werden durch die wachsende Erkenntniß Viehhirten. Aus Völkern von Viehhirten werden bey zunehmendem Verstande Ackersleute ... [Sie] werden endlich bey völlig entwickelten Verstande zugleich Handwerksleute, Fabricanten, Künstler und Kaufleute. Dieses ist die allgemeine Geschichte aller Völker des Erdbodens" (1766, p. 48).

[24] "The needs of a nation always multiply along with the growth in its knowledge. Hence, the greater the enlargement and enlightenment of a nation's power of reason, the more will it become acquainted with the multifarious commodities and conveniences of live and the more will it witness a demand for that which was previously unknown to it."

Here Justi does not translate convenience with laziness, he seems to be an outright positive modernist. But his old skepticism comes back when he adds that convenience probably misleads rulers to luxurious exuberance and extravagance. The result will be exaggerated taxes (§ 99). His deep sympathy for an egalitarian, simple, ethical and virtuous communal life becomes more pronounced in the following paragraphs where he describes the ideal communities of Sparta and especially the Peruvian empire (esp. § 105; his rosy picture does not coincide with our present knowledge of the Peruvian empire, see Peukert 1993).[25] A bunch of paragraphs on the so-called *Plus-Machen* follow (detrimental ways to increase the state's revenues, see §§ 162-186).

We can note that in this part of the book his positive upgrading and his decadence thesis coexist side by side.[26] We see an ambivalent dialectics in Justi's view on history: on the one hand the increase of reason is adequate for man to develop his distinguishing potential, on the other hand the side-effect is an increasing need for comfort and ostentation which is detrimental to virtue. Another interpretation could be that Justi had an antagonistic dual model in mind

---

"Die Bedürfnisse eines Volkes vermehren sich allemal nach dem Wachsthum seiner Erkenntniß. Je mehr also der Verstand eines Volkes erweitert und aufgekläret wird; je mehr werden sie tausenderley Bequemlichkeiten des Lebens kennen lernen, und ein Verlangen darnach bezeugen, wovon sie vorher nichts wußten" (1766, p. 51).

25 "There was absolute equality amongst all subjects; superiority in ability and virtue alone held out the prospect of advantage over others. All men worked in united effort for the common good ... Everyone lived happily and contented, and nobody felt the burning passion of ambition and avarice which cause so much evil in the world ... None was poor or wretched else he were so for illness or crime, and of these were but few because the main source of all vice, money, did not exist."
"Alle Unterthanen waren hier auf das vollkommenste einander gleich; nur die Aussicht über andere, die man durch seine Fähigkeit und Tugend erlangte, gab hier einen Vorzug. Alles arbeitete hier mit vereinigten Bemühungen zum gemeinschaftlichen Besten ... Alles lebte hier glücklich und vergnügt. Niemand fühlte hier die brennenden Begierden der Ehrsucht und des Geldgeitzes, die so viel Böses in der Welt verursachen ... Hier war kein armer, kein elender Mensch, der es nicht durch Krankheit oder Verbrechen war; und auch diese letztern waren überaus selten; weil hier die Hauptquelle aller Laster, das Geld, nicht vorhanden war" (1766, p. 55).

26 This conflict also becomes manifest in another respect. In general Justi is liberal vis-à-vis comsumption patterns, he gives relatively few normative comments. On the other hand we read: "It is easily seen that the shipping of a country cannot be left to itself. Profit-seeking and foolish passions could lead to an export of the most indispensable needs and to an import of those goods which serve nothing but vanity and lavishness."
"Man siehet leicht, daß die Schiffahrt eines Volkes nicht sich selbst überlassen werden kann. Die Gewinnsucht und die thörichten Begierden der Menschen könnten die im Lande unentbehrlichsten Bedürfnisse ausführen, und dargegen nichts als unnütze zu der Eitelkeit und Üppigkeit dienende Waaren in das Land bringen" (1766, p. 211).
He also often speaks of imaginary needs ("eingebildete Bedürfnisse", 1766, p. 359; see also § 708).

which coexist in a contradictory way side by side and express his position as a transitory figure between the Middle Ages and modernity. It is at least irritating that he sometimes argues in favor of taxes because otherwise the majority of people would have enough to live and would follow their natural laziness, taxes can therefore have the function to put an end to their dullness (§ 724). In Justi's opinion this detrimental situation prevailed in agricultural Germany in the 1660s (§ 728). But he is neither an anti-agricultural mercantilist nor a one-sided physiocrat (see e.g. § 816). It is also surprising that at the end of the book Justi is not critical vis-à-vis lotteries as a revenue generating device for the state (§§ 1017 ff., esp. § 1028).[27]

Before analyzing Justi's financial theory and policy in the next section, we will highlight a characteristic feature of his approach: the opinion that pure reason alone can help us to formulate a detailed tax system without contradictions and trade-offs and which always conforms with the essence *(das Wesen)* of taxes, contributions, etc.[28] As we know today there is no such system as the natural first best tax system without trade-offs (e.g. transparency vs. justice). We further know that every system depends on peculiar tax political ideals (Mann 1937). When he comes back to discuss realistic reforms at his time he opts for the abolition of feudal dependencies and statute labor *(Frondienste)* not only because it contradicts human freedom but also from a practical point of view: these services will not be done efficiently because the subjects have no motivation to do good work (§ 195, see also § 239 on the motivation of tenants, and § 249 on the indolence of public servants). We can observe here that Justi holds a third model of man besides his reason and passion models: the self-interest, (neo)classical *homo oeconomicus* model of man also plays a (limited) role in his practical considerations on economic institutions. The prevailing model in reality is the passion-driven man.[29] The self-interest of man is also an argument for him why e.g. the jurisdiction should not be leased to tenants. They will exploit their position as the law giving institution and oppress involved subjects (§ 241; compare also the reasons against the leasing of the regalia in § 275).

---

[27] See also his remarkable generosity vis-à-vis opulence and exuberance, e.g. in Justi (1970/1761a, pp. 73-92).

[28] "Common sense alone shows that duties should be levied for no other reason than this." "Die gesunde Vernunft giebt von selbst an die Hand, daß die Abgaben auf keinem andern, als diesem Grunde gelegt werden sollte" (1766, p. 853). Maybe this belief in the capacity of reason is the only somewhat unrealistic view in Justi. But it coincides with the modernist belief in undistorted reason which was questioned only much later by a post-modernist worldview.

[29] "People are only very rarely good housekeepers of their fortunes. They are either squanderers or misers."
"Alle Menschen sind mit ihrem eigenen Vermögen überaus selten vernünftige Haushälter. Sie sind entweder Verschwender, oder Geitzige" (1766, p. 358). This especially holds for the sovereign (§ 692).

The next example of Justi's stoic view of the good society can be found at the beginning of his introduction to taxes. It is underlined that a state with high expenses need not be in a happier situation then with less expenses and the same holds for individual happiness.[30] The real necessary goods and services are by nature rather limited.[31] The distinction between real and imagined needs shows up again.[32] According to his pragmatic approach (he even made proposals how to organize the excise tax(es) *(Akzise)* despite his fundamental rejection of it) also the level of expenses can be checked in modern republics with developed needs and aspirations (the civil army of Switzerland is an example).[33]

Taxes should not be paid in barter but in money. But money impedes the realization of equality and for Justi it is the evil *per se.*[34]Justi's criticism could hardly be formulated stronger, he even calls into question his view of the progression of reason. He also discusses the first best tax system in which the people would be

---

[30] "To assert that a state which lives in grandeur is happier than a more frugal one is to assert nothing more than that a private person is none the happier because he spends more."
"Allein, daß ein Staat, der vielen Aufwandt macht, deshalb glücklicher ist, als ein anderer, der nur wenig aufwendet, - das ist eben so wenig zu behaupten, als eine Privatperson deshalb nicht glücklicher ist, weil sie viel aufwendet" (1766, p. 355).

[31] "The true necessities and conveniences of nature are of little scope for such states as well as such persons."
"Die wahren Nothdurften und Bequemlichkeiten der Natur, haben sowohl bey denen Staaten, als bey denen Menschen, gar keinen weiten Umfang" (1766, p. 355).

[32] "Vanity and excess seduce them into thinking up thousands of imaginary needs which, were they to be punished therewith, would not add to their happiness."
"Die Eitelkeit und die Üppigkeit verleiten sie, daß sie sich tausend eingebildete Bedürfnisse ersinnen, ohne daß sie deshalb glücklicher werden, wenn sie mit allen ihren eingebildeten Bedürfnissen versehen sind" (1766, p. 354-355).

[33] "Even without neglect of welfare and in the depth of a lavish and extravagant century, the costs of running a state can be met with moderate expense."
"Allein, auch ohne Außerachtsetzung des Wohlstandes und mitten in einem üppigen und verschwenderischen Jahrhundert lassen sich die Kosten zu Unterhaltung des Staates mit gar mäßigem Aufwand bestreiten" (1766, p. 355).

[34] "Seeing as families are neither of equal industry or skill and further do not face the same expenses, there will always be families which accumulate money and others which are in need and must sell their property. Where the invention of gold and silver or a general measure of the value of all things has been of salutary significance to the human race is a very big question, one which I would dare not answer affirmatively. One can rather look upon this invention as the source of all evil and misfortune in the world. It is naturally the primeval essence of evil."
"Da die Familien weder gleichen Fleiß und Geschicklichkeit haben, noch gleichen Aufwandt machen; so würde es allemal Familien geben, die Geld sammleten, und andere, die in Noth wären, und ihr Eigenthum verkaufen müßten. Allein ob die Erfindung des Goldes und Silbers zu einem allgemeinen Werth aller Dinge dem menschlichen Geschlechte in der That heilsam gewesen ist, das ist eine sehr große Frage, die ich niemals zu bejahen mir getrauen werde. Man kann diese Erfindung vielmehr als die Quelle alles Bösen und alles Unglücks in der Welt ansehen. Das ist eigentlich das böse Urwesen" (1766, p. 366).

guided by virtue (his platonic republic). But this first best republic is unrealistic and it is therefore not pursued further by Justi (§ 405). The second best tax reform would consist in a tax which uses ambition and the need for opulence to transform human preferences in the longer run. As far as we know, this tax reform has not been noticed in the secondary literature with the exception of the brief remark by Scheer (1998, p. 174). Therefore, it will be cited more fully here.

> In light of the depraved states of today - which manifest not a single one of those noble and effectual forces of the old societies but which instead avail themselves of ambition and excess - I have only one proposal to make: a clear and simple regulative concerning taxes and duties ... A state must divide its population into eight or 10 classes and determine for each an ever greater level of duties. Rank, ostentation and other sorts of waste and excess may only be permitted if a particular class in the population pays the state a greater sum in the form of duties than the others ... Each would endeavor to put itself in a position of being able to pay more duties ... This general regulative would be quite appropriate to the corrupt nature of today's bourgeois constitutions which honor nothing but wealth (1766, pp. 405-406).[35]

We will leave out the further details of this Veblen tax (Veblen (1991/1899)) and only point out the educational motive of the tax.

> A large part of humanity would begin to think reasonably and philosophically; they would not seek advantage in trivialities but in virtue and true desert. Thus would Europe prepare herself for the great change of which all states are in need (1766, p. 406).[36]

But Justi is realist enough to see that even this second best proposal was too far ahead of his time, "and thus it will long remain necessary that taxes and duties be levied on the particular items and objects of people, or immovable goods, of

---

[35] "Vor unsere heutigen im Grunde verderbten Staaten, welche nicht eine einzige von denen edlen und wirksamen Triebfedern der alten bürgerlichen Gesellschaften aufzuweisen wissen, sondern welche einen übelverstandnen Ehrgeiz, und die Üppigkeit statt aller anderen Triebfedern gebrauchen, weiß ich nur einen einzigen Weg, ein leichtes und einfaches Regulativ vor die Steuern und Abgaben an die Hand zu geben ... Ein Staat müßte nämlich sein Volk in acht oder 10 Classen eintheilen, vor jede Classe immer größere Abgaben bestimmen, den Rang, die Kleiderpracht und andere Arten der Verschwendung und der Üppigkeit nur nach der Maaße zulassen, als eine Classe des Volkes dem Staate mehr Abgaben entrichtete, als die andern ... ein jeder würde sich bestreben, durch seinen Fleiß und Geschicklichkeit sich in den Stand zu setzen, größere Abgaben entrichten zu können ... Dieses allgemeine Regulativ wäre der verderbten Natur unserer heutigen bürgerlichen Verfassungen ... die nichts, als den Reichthum ehren".

[36] "Ein großer Theil der Menschen würden vernünftig und philosophisch zu denken anfangen, und ihren Vorzug nicht in dem Äußerlichen, sondern in der Tugend und in wahren Verdiensten suchen; und dadurch würde Europa zu der großen Veränderung vorbereitet werden, welche alle Staaten so sehr nöthig haben".

consumption and of trade"(1766, p. 406).[37] Therefore, most of the text deals with a reform of the tax system. But his cameralist tax proposals which are in the center of the - mostly very general and imprecise - secondary literature and which will be discussed in the next part of our analysis are only the third best solution and transitory for Justi. We hope, that our brief analysis has demonstrated that Justi's understanding of a good society and a moral economy not only lurked in the background but that he explicitly thought about an alternative tax system with an educational single tax to transform the basis of economy and society. Justi always comes back to his critique of the rotten situation and the very questionable motivational orientations of the people, rulers, and states at his time (§ 878, 880, etc.). Even Switzerland may be on the wrong track, his great ideal is again Greek and Roman antiquity (for a more realist evaluation of these good old times see Peukert (1992)).

3 Justi' Proposals for a Third-Best Tax System in his *System des Finanzwesens*

As the title already indicates, Justi tries to develop a *system* of public finance. In the preface he mentions "und endlich habe ich es gewaget, diese Wissenschaft in einem größern System ausführlich abzuhandeln". Public finance is the "große Quelle fast aller Mittel zur Wohlfahrt der Staaten" (p. X). The book is dedicated to Frederic the Second. In fact, the systematic and concrete proposals coincide to some degree with the Prussian tax system of his time, but he also deviates in important respects.[38] The book was originally published in 1766 when cameralism was ascending.[39]

"Die klassische Finanzwissenschaft ... beginnt auf der Basis des Wolffschen Gesamtsystems, mit Johann Heinrich Gottlob von Justi" (Backhaus (2001, p. 8)). Some years earlier Müllensiefen had already stated: "Sowohl durch die Erhebung dieses Gegenstandes zum wissenschaftlichen Erkenntnisobjekt, als auch durch die methodische Analysierung des Begriffes bezeichnet man ihn mit Recht als den Begründer der deutschen Finanzwissenschaft" ((1928, p. 27); in the same vein see e.g. Schmidt (1937, p. 19), and Jenetzky (1978, pp. 102-103)).

[37] "und folglich wird es noch lange Zeit nöthig bleiben, daß man die Steuern und Abgaben auf die besonderen Gegenstände der Personen, der unbeweglichen Güter, der Consumption und der Gewerbe legt".

[38] For a short comparison see Klein (1961, pp. 178-189), and Wysocki (1982).

[39] For a comparison of Justi and the cameralist literature on finance see - as mentioned - especially Jenetzky (1978). It should be pointed out however, that his discussion of Justi is not always correct (see e.g. (1978, p. 92)).

Schmidt underlines that Justi was the first who identified public finance as a distinct and separate object of knowledge, that his analysis strongly depends on his cameralist economics, that he aimed at practical financial politics and that he did not develop a theory of public finance in the modern sense (1937, p. 33).

The long introduction on general principles of public finance with fifty pages reiterates the function of public finance for the attainment of the general happiness and welfare of the community. The science of police (*Polizey-Wissenschaft*, see § 9) deals with the creation of wealth for the state. It depends on the flourishing of production and commerce. Wealth *(Vermögen)* also comprises abilities and capabilities of the members of society, i.e. their human capital. The second branch of government is the cameral or financial science which deals with the reasonable and wise use of the wealth of society (§ 10). Both (police and finance) are interdependent. Justi does not clearly differentiate between the wealth of society at large and the wealth of the state. As already mentioned above, the most important characteristics of a reasonable ruler and a good cameralist are moral integrity, practical knowledge, abstract intelligence and wisdom. The good cameralist should also - besides imagination, and diligence - be independent in his judgments (see § 68 on his uncompromising attitude). Justi discusses in his introduction character traits in an ethical perspective. A good ruler should not be engaged too much in warfare, luxury and short-termism (e.g. high taxes which impede growth).

The passions should be controlled by reason and morals. Justi's book is an educational tract with an Aristotelian understanding of politics and society which would not be found in modern textbooks on public finance. He formulates a principle (the criterion of conformity with happiness) and some basic rules to specify his educational devices. The first rule says that the wealth of the state should be generated by the least harmful way with regard to the wealth of the people. This includes the recognition of the economic principle in public expenses and in the administration of public enterprises (§ 39). His general message is "daß man erst säen soll, ehe man ärndten kann" (§ 40). Therefore, freedom to act and the capability to increase commerce and production should not be hindered by the state. In conformity with the first, the second rule states that the substance of wealth should not be reduced by taxes etc. The third rule decrees that the expenditures of the state depend on its revenue *(Einkünfte)* and not vice versa (§ 45).

The fourth rule states that the expenditure should be made in conformity with the final aims of the state in mind. He differentiates necessary (e.g. internal and external security), useful (e.g. measures to increase the productive potential of society) and acceptable *(wohlanständige)* expenditures (e.g. costs for the moderate luxury of the ruler and his entourage). Expenditures of the first category are e.g. more valuable than those of the second, but in general expenditures should be wisely distributed among these three categories and for no other reason. The fifth rule praises order: all expenditures should be documented and considered together. No conflicts should arise between expenditures and revenues of the state (§ 50). Justi's rules have been an inspiration for many in the years after its publication. In our view, their essential point is the general spirit and not their systematic character. For Justi, the rules were self-evident and followed naturally from his basic principle. As in the stability pact of the Maastricht treaty he supports a balanced budget idea and moderate taxes, but in opposition to the Maastricht treaty revenue should direct expenditures and not the other way round.[40]

The first book deals with state revenue in a general way. In a historical perspective, he delineates a stage theory (hunters and gatherers, cattle breeding, etc.) in which economic, social, legal, cultural and financial aspects are intertwined. Public finance systems depend on the general stage of development, but also on the stylist peculiarities of society and economy, e.g. in a system dominated by trade, taxes on consumption goods should dominate over taxes on immovable goods (§ 103). Further, financial systems depend on the governmental governance structure. He notes e.g. the empirical fact that in monarchies and in contrast to democracies very often high taxes can be found due to the greedy aspirations of the monarch (§ 110). He also stresses some reasonable empirical rules of thump, that e.g. in early manufacturing systems and even in highly developed agricultural systems taxes are usually levied not in barter but in money (§ 105). The introduction to book one demonstrates the historical-sociological embeddedness of Justi's approach. It may be classified under the rubric of fiscal sociology.

Justi then turns to more modern economic systems. Profit *(Gewinnst)* should be taxed (§§ 119ff.) but in such a way that an agreeable life is still possible and that the substance of income and wealth will not be reduced (income and wealth were not really distinguished by Justi). Profit is defined by him as the advantage, for example the sales price of a product, after the deduction of all costs and efforts (§ 794). A just proportion should be taxed (§ 120) but Justi leaves open what he exactly meant (e.g. a proportional or progressive tax). This demonstrates that Justi was only at the beginning of a systematic approach to differentiate taxes and their structure. Instead, he criticizes the high level of the *Akzise* on consumption goods (§ 121). Justi was also against the *Akzise* in general which played an ascending role in the realized tax systems of his time. It corre-

---

[40] "If the ruler has little revenue, it is natural that he abstain from many measures salutary to the welfare of the state."
"Wenn der Regent wenig Einkünfte hat, so ist es natürlich, daß er viele heilsame Anstalten zu der Wohlfahrt des Staates unterlassen muß" (p. 65).

sponds in many respects to the modern excise tax but it usually lacked a systematic character. For example, in Saxony in the 17th century, the *Akzise* was levied on the consumption on foreign and domestic products, in towns and at the countryside, on town real estates, on the turnover of business enterprises and on purchase and exchange activities of commodities (for the development and multifold differences the brief summary in Nathan (1923)).

Justi gives examples of goods with an excise tax rate between 12 per cent and 20 per cent.

> Nothing but a higher price of the means of living can result thereupon, which is not always a sign that there is much money in the country. It is though obvious that the higher price does not weigh heavily on the poor subjects alone; it is also disadvantageous to the productive class and, in particular, to foreign trade (§121).[41]

The citation shows that for Justi moral and competitive arguments go hand in hand and do not exclude each other. In a later paragraph he generalizes the argument that high taxes or tariffs produce a short-term gain in terms of money but discourage the longer-run productive basis from which the tariffs and taxes can be drawn (§ 126).

Without further taxonomic sophistication he states that immovable goods and land should be taxed according to their size and quality. For movable goods and objects the taxation of profit could be focused on (1) the goods themselves in their potential to yield a surplus, or (2) the final products, or (3) the materials necessary for their production or (4) the number of employees could be considered as the tax base. Surprisingly, he opts primarily for the third and fourth solutions and against the first two as the tax base

> because that will hinder the commencement of commerce and the entire productive class as well as the freedom of the subjects. Furthermore, for the purpose of such a regulative, countless cameral activities and still more higher and lower officials are required to ensure the avoidance of fraud amongst subjects and tax collectors (p. 64).[42]

---

[41] "Daraus kann nun nichts anders als ein hoher Preis der Lebens-Mittel entstehen, der folglich nicht allemal ein Kennzeichen ist, daß viel Geld im Lande ist. Dennoch ist es offenbar, daß der hohe Preiß der Lebens-Mittel nicht allein die armen Unterthanen sehr drücket, sondern auch dem Aufnehmen des Nahrungsstandes, und besonders den ausländischen Commercien sehr nachtheilig ist".

[42] "weil dadurch das Aufnehmen der Commercien und des gesammten Nahrungs-Standes, sowohl als die vernünftige Freyheit der Unterthanen gar sehr gehindert und eingeschränket wird. Ueberdieß werden zu einem solchen Regulativ unzählige Cammeral-Geschäffte, eine überaus große Aufsicht, um den Betrug der Unterthanen und der Einnahme-Bedienten zu vermeiden, und ungleich mehr höhere und geringere Bedienten erfordert"

Justi combines the arguments that a taxation on final products and inputs hinders commerce and production, severely restricts the liberty of citizens, provokes fraud and comes with substantial control costs. It seems at least an open question for us if his arguments are convincing or not in this case.

On the one hand Justi believes in economic progress in the private economic sector. On the other hand he supports active developmental programs by the government as a main function of the state's expenditures.

> This is primarily a matter of cultivating the land in barren, arid and scarcely inhabited areas. An insightful cameralist has to turn his attention to two matters, namely the removal of the hindrance and the making of such an area suitable for cultivation and thereupon he must occupy the area with new inhabitants (p. 71).[43]

Another source of revenue are the demesnes which are partly identical with state farms. In Prussia they also included buildings and e.g. castles, public swimming baths and mineral springs (see the condensed overview in Fauser 1926). In Justi´s view, an increase of this source of state revenue is necessary. For reasons of efficiency, they should be auctioned and rented out because this seems to be the most efficient way (§ 143). The demesnes should be increased and their quality improved. Therefore, he proposed the introduction of inspectors who check the auctioned demesnes. They are entitled to set standards and enforce improvements.

The last main type of fiscal revenue are the regalia (on the more than 400 regalia in former Germany and their often unsystematic character see Troeltsch (1901)). Their total amount should also be increased but only by an enlargement of existing enterprises or the launching of new enterprises in regions where they have not yet existed. He especially mentions the mail service and canal, forestry, salt and harbor regalia. For Justi they should be limited to seven regalia in four areas. The product prices should be reasonable and the state should not create artificial monopolies and the revenue motive should never dominate. A reasonable price is the price charged at major foreign markets, in so far as the supply and demand conditions in the respective countries are not too different (§§ 149-152). To underline the cautious approach for levying taxes he finishes this part of the book with a further, longer, harsh criticism of the *Plus-Macherei,* i.e. the aspiration to increase taxes and tariffs without considering the happiness of the people (pp. 83-94).

---

[43] "Hierunter ist nun vornehmlich die Anbauung und Cultivirung des Landes, in seinen öden, unfruchtbaren und wenig bewohnten Gegenden zu rechnen; und ein verständiger Cameralist hat hier zwey Augenmerke vor sich zu nehmen, nämlich die die vorseyende Hinderniß zu heben, und eine solche Gegend urbar, oder zur Anbauung geschickt zu machen, sodann aber dieselbe mit neuen Einwohnern zu besetzen".

In the following, Justi discusses the different taxes in detail. In the relatively short second book on the demesne, Justi first criticizes the view that they belong to the sovereign and should never be transformed into peasant holdings. Just the opposite should be done in his view: relatively small holdings (about 60 acres are his ideal, see § 193) should be auctioned for about six years (§ 247). "The more moderate the size of peasant holdings, the greater the industry which their owners can and will expend cultivating their property" (p. 100).[44] He strongly rejects socage for its negative motivational impacts. The reason for auctioning has also to do with the motivational aspects of a public-bureaucratic compared with a part-time privatized institutional setting. "A tenant, whose advantage prevails therein, is far more attentive to the collection of taxes than the manorial officials and the landlords" (p. 121).[45]

He also opts for trying out different practical procedures, including a system with hereditary leasehold and the cost-free building of houses and handing over of cattle to attract new and poor peasants according to the mercantilist-cameralist economic development ideal (§§ 199-202). We see again the interesting combination of a relatively modern image of man (opportunist behavior) and institutional mechanisms (auctioning) with the idea that the public sphere and the state plays an important economic role.

Justi considers the revenue of demesnes to be less important compared with the ascending importance of taxes and duties (§ 205). He also takes into consideration a certain tax multiplier effect by an increase of economic activities and population.

> The increase in population which results unerringly from the cultivation of state farms by the subjects will enlarge the state's revenue from excise, tariffs and other duties on consumption far more than a future increase in the revenue of the demesnes (p. 105).[46]

Nevertheless, not all demesnes should be auctioned off to have a buffer for the uncertain future (§ 228). His moderate and balanced view also becomes evident when he pleads against the inclusion of the judicial power in the auctioning process because the tenant would exploit his power vis-à-vis his subjects (§ 241). The presupposition of self-interest and greedy passions takes him to the support of public judicial institutions. Finally, another aspect of his sophisticated

---

[44] "Je mäßiger die Bauer-Güther sind, desto mehr Fleiß können und werden ihre Besitzer an die Cultur ihrer Grundstücke anwenden".

[45] "Ein Pächter, dessen eigener Vortheil darunter vorwaltet, ist auch auch auf die Eintreibung der Zinsen ... viel aufmerksamer, als die Wirthschafts-Bedienten des Landesherrn".

[46] "Die vergrößerte Bevölkerung, welche durch die Bebauung der Domainen mit Unterthanen so unfehlbar erfolget, wird ihre Einkünfte in denen Accisen, Zöllen und andern durch den Verbrauch der Waaren entstehenden Abgaben gewiß weit mehr vergrößern, als die künftige Vermehrung der Domanial Einkünfte nicht gethan haben würde".

public-private partnership with auctions is the introduction of an economic inspector who formulates in advance obligatory improvements of the demesnes which must be pursued by the tenant and which are written into the leasing contract (§ 254).

The long third book on the regalia with more then two hundred pages starts with a definition. Regalia are royal rights which can generate revenue (see his definition in § 266). Right at the beginning he castigates the fact that rulers in the past tried to introduce more and more regalia. For Justi the legitimacy of regalia strictly depends on clearly defined characteristics, i.e. they should not be owned privately, and, to make them serve the common good, strong regulatory intervention by the state is necessary.

> ...because the use of these things, to which belong the seas, lakes, large rivers and roads, must be communal. The second reason concerns the incompatibility between the extension of ownership in factors like forests, wild animals and fisheries and the goals of private property. The third reason consists in fact that the use of these things does not take place on the surface of the land (as is primarily the case with immobile private property); whence follows that the demarcation of property boundaries below the earth's surface cannot follow the demarcations on the surface (p. 138).[47]

He includes minerals, salt, mining etc. and in his more general list the mail service and the currency are regalia. The generation of revenue should never be the central motive for introducing regalia and the revenue must be limited, otherwise it would impede growth and commerce (§ 281).

In Justi's opinion the regalia should never be auctioned but run by the state. The reasons are twofold, first no great cultivating effort is needed and second and more important, e.g. in mining and salt factories an overexploitation by the auctioneers would ensue (§§ 275-276). The only exception to the non-auction rule may be fishing and hunting regalia (§ 278).

It is interesting to note that Justi does not really argue about his two central points: which are natural regalia according to his definition and should they be auctioned or not. It is at least an open question if salt and the mail service are natural regalia. Further, it is surprising that for Justi the demesnes can be auc-

[47] "... weil der Gebrauch dieser Dinge allen Unterthanen gemein seyn muß; und von dieser Art sind die Meere, Seen, großen Flüsse und Landstraßen. Die zweite Ursache kömmt darauf an, daß das Eigenthum davon eine so weitläuftige Erstreckung erfordert, die mit dem Endzwecke des Privat-Eigenthums nicht übereinstimmet; und hierunter sind die großen Wälder, die wilden Thiere und die wilde Fischerey begriffen. Die dritte Ursache endlich bestehet darinnen, daß der Gebrauch dieser Dinge nicht auf die Oberfläche der Erde ankömmt, als welche zu dem unbeweglichen Privat-Eigenthumevornehmlich gewidmet ist weshalb auch das Eigenthum nicht nach den Gränzen bestimmt werden kann, die auf die Oberfläche der Erde eingeführet sind".

tioned and the regalia cannot because in the case of demesnes a high degree of cultivating effort is warranted and for demesnes Justi sees no problem in the strong public influence by the public jurisdiction and the target plans of the economic inspectors. In the case of the regalia, the regulatory necessity is raised as an argument against auctioning. It should be mentioned that Justi's reasoning is absolutely independent of recent public goods arguments because the existence of regalia presupposes that revenue can be generated. So the non-exclusion rule does not hold for them.

In the next section he discusses the specific regalia in detail. In the case of mining he argues that private property does not refer to underground objects (§ 519). In fishery the main problem is over-fishing. In the case of the roads he argues that the state has to make sure that comfort, convenience, security and an interrelated system of roads are essential for the growth of the economy (§ 288). His main argument for a state run system is the network character and the interlocking of roads. He extends this argument to the water regalia (§ 402). Those who benefit should pay the regalia (§ 429), including foreigners who have to pay a tariff. As mentioned, in general, the regalia should be low, but strictly enforced (§ 312).

Justi leaves open, if it would be ideal if all the costs should be carried by the users. His positive externalities arguments imply that this could hardly signify an ideal constellation. What tariffs are concerned a strong mercantilist argument creeps in. The export of raw materials like wood should be forbidden (§ 472). Imports which are also produced in the home country and luxury goods should get a tariff between 15 per cent and 20 per cent, non-essential foodstuffs which are not produced in the country should have a 5-6 per cent tariff. Mercantilist reasoning (see e.g. § 527) and his criticism of luxury consumption also holds in the case of seafaring.

> It can easily be seen that shipping cannot be left to itself. Profit-seeking and the foolish desires of the people could lead to an export of the most indispensable goods and would bring nothing but useless goods into the country which would only serve vanity and excess (p. 211).[48]

It is interesting that Justi only takes into consideration arguments against a strict mercantilist policy with regard to tariffs on goods which pass through the country. He argues that high tariffs would eventually provoke retribution and create a

[48] "Man siehet leicht, daß die Schiffahrt eines Volkes nicht sich selbst überlassen werden kann. Die Gewinnsucht und die thörichten Begierden der Menschen könnten die im Lande unentbehrlichsten Bedürfnisse ausführen, und dargegen nichts als unnütze zu der Eitelkeit und Ueppigkeit dienende Waaren in das Land bringen".

bad atmosphere between the countries which will complicate the own export activities. But Justi does not generalize this objection.

For Justi, the currency must be under the control of the state to prevent fraud and the counterfeiting of coins. He does not hold a Carl Mengerian spontaneous order explanation of the emergence of money. He tells a conscious decision story in which money is consciously introduced by the communities, their innovative deliberations were based on intelligent reasoning (§ 598). He holds a metallist bias. The face value of coins should always represent the exchange value of gold and silver as commodities (§ 624). He strongly criticizes fraud in this respect for moral (general trust), long-run self-interest (increase in transaction costs and deterioration of commerce and trade), and social reasons (§ 642: a value depreciated currency increases prices, and e.g. workers have fixed income contracts). Only coins which solely circulate in the country should be minted without full coverage to generate revenue.

Book four deals with taxes and contributions. The introduction once again delineates his general philosophy of restraint and moderation, his view of man, the aforementioned first best Platonic republic, his critique of luxury and exaggerated ostentation of the rulers, the necessity of economic growth, etc. Justi integrates sociological, political science (§§ 706ff. discuss the relationship between types of government and tax systems), anthropological and other aspects.[49] With regard to taxes he states that in principle demesnes and regalia should cover the financial needs of the state. But there are natural ups and downs. He exceptionally and strongly attacks Montesquieu who argued that the greater the liberty of the citizens the more revenue generated by the state is necessary (§ 715). He strictly defends his up and down view of revenues in the long-run course of social and economic development. A necessary condition that taxes and contributions will not increase without limit is the yearly vote of the population on the taxes. All taxes should be included in the voting decision so that taxes which were valid in the past can always be abolished or diminished later (§ 678).

Justi strongly rejects poll taxes, mainly for psychological reasons (§§ 759ff.); they are only compatible with despotic regimes and maybe with monarchies. Class, rank and dignity taxes are only compatible with monarchies (§ 779).

The first important tax which is applicable in all governmental systems is the tax on immovable property.

---

[49] We will not discuss his ideas concerning the division of taxes between the estates *(Landstände)* and the central government and we will not follow his changes of mind (see e.g. § 676).

> The freedom of human actions, the trustworthiness of the subjects, and the well-being of agriculture and commerce do not suffer. A just equality and proportion can be maintained; and this reason for the tax is absolutely sure and unmistakable (p. 431).[50]

Practicality, justice, freedom and economic growth are Justi's arguments for the tax. The tax includes fields, meadow, vineyards, wood, and other plots of land. He does not have a modern tax in kind in mind because only the profit should be taxed. For practical reasons, houses should be split up into the categories small, middle and large, land in the categories of good, average and inferior quality (§§ 793-794). With respect to e.g. fields the average yearly yield should be determined. Next the seed and the average own consumption of the producing unit will be deducted. One sixth of the remaining profit will be taxed (§ 796). With respect to houses, the yield for renting is the basis and 50 per cent is deducted as construction (or maintenance) costs. The present exchange value of the plot of land is in his opinion too volatile and depends on too many tax irrelevant circumstances.

The taxes on consumption *(Akzise),* which largely correspond to recent excise taxes, are strongly rejected by Justi (§ 826). He understands that in the process of deliberate reductions in domestic tariffs and the fact that some trades in towns did pay almost no taxes the *Akzise* became more popular and important (§ 824). In his view the *Akzise* impedes the flourishing of trade and production. Second it restricts the liberty of the people. This has to do with the specific way how the *Akzise* was raised at his time: when people and goods crossed local borders, so that people's belongings were controlled and registered. Third the *Akzise* is against social justice, because some productive groups can increase their prices as a reaction to the *Akzise* and some others cannot (§ 829). Fourth, a lot of expensive control is necessary to counteract circumvention (§ 830). But Justi accepts the fact of the existence of the excise tax and makes some proposals how to organize it in accordance with his mercantilist stance (§ 833).

At the end of his major four tax categories comes the sales tax as his prime tax which did not exist in reality as Justi proposed it (§ 854). His tax coincides with present sales taxes (e.g. the German business tax) but not with income taxes. Workers who only earn an income do not have to pay any personal taxes. It may best be described as a profit tax because only a part of the profit *(Gewinnst)* of a business enterprise should be taxed. For Justi it is an evident consequence of clear reasoning that profit should primarily be taxed because profits can only be made under the protection of the state (§ 853). But also private wealth cannot be

---

[50] "Die vernünftige Freyheit der menschlichen Handlungen, der Credit der Unterthanen, und das Aufnehmen des Nahrungsstandes und der Commercien leidet hierbei nichts. Es kann hierbey eine gerechte Gleichheit und Proportion beobachtet werden; und dieser Grund der Steuer ist ganz sicher und unbetrüglich".

accumulated without the protection of the state and Justi rejects a wealth tax so that his point seems not very convincing.

Profit will be calculated on average to reduce information costs but also to protect the private sphere of the citizen. The drawing up of tables are a necessary precondition. In commercial firms the calculation of profit is easy: the price of the products in the country are know, the tariff registers inform about the import prices. If the sales price is compared with them, and a certain amount for freight and tariffs is deducted, the profit of the merchant results. The tax base should be the average profit rate of different trades. In the case of producing and selling economic units like bakeries the price of machines and other input factors (like grain) must be included in the tables and calculations. After the calculation of the yearly average profit, two third will be deducted as the costs of housekeeping. The tax is 25 per cent on the remaining third part. So the computation starts with the total receipts, minus costs, minus housekeeping, and the 25per cent tax on the remaining third part. The total receipts of the trades are computed by the tables which divide the trades according to their location in small, medium and big cities (e.g. in a big city on average 2000 shoes are sold annually, in a small town only 500). Another factor of correction refers to the size of the enterprises. For a sales clerk *(Ladendiener)* half of the profit tax must be paid, and one fourth for each apprentice and journeyman (§§ 855-862).

For Justi, this tax would *not* limit freedom, restrict the easiness of travel, depress trade and commerce, provoke fraudulent behavior (the number of employees e.g. can be easily monitored), and entail anti-social consequences like the *Akzise* (§ 864). The prices of the end-products would be lower compared with a tax system based on the *Akzise* and insofar his system is also considered to be conducive for exports (§ 870). In the next short section, Justi confirms his negation of a wealth tax (§ 894).[51]

The final book six discusses exceptional revenues in cases of emergencies like war. Emergency situations should be reduced to a minimum (e.g. no unnecessary warfare) and if possible, no special revenues should be generated (§ 975). If necessary, the state could rely on credits for some time but he should never frustrate the trust of the citizens. In general, the credits should be sold by subscriptions to domestic citizens. But if this would be only possible in the case of two or three per cent higher interest rates on bonds, compared with the lending of money in a foreign country the state should be oriented to the cheaper foreign source (§ 996).

---

[51] We will leave out the less interesting book five on the accidental revenues (§§ 899-971).

4 Conclusion

In this paper we first pointed out the originality of the cameralist approach which crosscuts modern understandings of fundamental paradigmatic differences. The background of Justi's ethical, non-materialist utopia without greed and luxury can be found in his moral-philosophical writings where a Christian dualism, the control of the passions by reason and a stoic state of perfection is put forward. We then found traces of his view of the good society in his *System des Finanzwesens,* including critical remarks on the destructive role of money and his proposal to introduce an educational Veblen tax to fundamentally revolutionize society. We further analyzed his proposal for a third best tax system with the four main taxes of demesnes (auctioning), regalia (run by the state), *Akzisen* (which he in principle rejected) and his prime tax on profits.

In general, his writings have the aim to change the time preference rate and enlarge the horizon of reflection. His special concerns are the level of reasoning of the rulers, relatively low taxes and a balanced budget in a mixed economy where state regulation, intervention and public property on the one hand and free enterprise and private property on the other hand are balanced. His *System des Finanzwesens* is not only one of the first systematic accounts on the way to a modern tax system. It also transgresses a financial sociological approach in the narrower sense because Justi integrated political, social, cultural, economic, ethical and moral considerations. State, economy and society were regarded as an integrated whole which can be arranged according to the results of practical political reasoning, good sense and moral insight. In so far his early concept of cameralism represents a prime and high-grade example of the emerging concept of *Staatswissenschaften.*

References

Backhaus, J. (2001), *Alte oder neue Finanzwissenschaft?* Inaugural lecture, Erfurt.

Baum, D. (1988), *Bürokratie und Sozialpolitik,* Berlin: Duncker und Humblot.

Bödeker, H.E. (1985), "Das staatswisschenschaftliche Fächersystem im 18. Jahrhundert." In R. Vierhaus, (ed.), *Wissenschaften im Zeitalter der Aufklärung,* Göttingen, Vandenhoeck und Ruprecht.

Bollnow, O.F. (1941), "Die philosophischen Grundlagen der Staats- und Wirtschaftslehren bei J.H. Justi." *Finanzarchiv* 8, 381-402.

Borscheid, P. (1989), "Die Anfänge der landwirtschaftlichen Versicherung in Deutschland." *Zeitschrift für Agrargeschichte und Agrarsoziologie* 37, 37-55.

Fauser, K. (1926), "Domänen." In L. Elster et al., (eds.), *Handwörterbuch der Staatswissenschaften,* Jena, Fischer.

Frensdorff, F. (1970), *Über das Leben und die Schriften des Nationalökonomen J.H.G. von Justi.* Glashütten i.T.: Auvermann.

Grimmig, J. (1949), *Johann Heinrich Gottlieb von Justi und Joseph von Sonnenfels als Finanzwissenschaftler.* s. l.: Huber.

Habermas, J. (1984), *Theory of Communicative Action,* Boston: Allyn and Bacon.

Hasbach, W. (1891), *Untersuchungen über Adam Smith und die Entwicklung der politischen Ökonomie.* Leipzig: Duncker und Humblot.

Jaeger, A. (1910), *Vergleichende Darstellung der Ansichten von R. Price und J.H.G. v. Justi über Staatsschuldentilgung,* Diessen: Huber.

Jenetzky, J. (1978), *System und Entwicklung des materiellen Steuerrechts in der wissenschaftlichen Literatur des Kameralismus von 16880-1840,* Berlin: Duncker und Humblot.

Justi, J.H.G. (1977/1762), *Ausführliche Abhandlung von denen Steuern und Abgaben,* Wiesbaden: Gabler.

Justi, J.H.G. (1762), *Vergleichungen der Europäischen mit den asiatischen und andern vermeintlich barbarischen Regierungen,* 3 Vols., Berlin: Rüdiger.

Justi, J.H.G. (1759), *Fabeln und Erzählungen von Thieren und sehr alten längst verrosteten Zeiten, bey deren Lesung man ganz sanft und süß wird einschlafen können,* Cologne: Altona.

Justi, J.H.G. (1970/1761a, 1761b and 1764), *Gesammelte politische und Finanz-Schriften,* 3 Vols, Aalen: Scientia.

Justi, J.H.G. (1969/1782). *Grundsätze der Policeywissenschaft,* Frankfurt: Auvermann.

Justi, J.H.G. (1766), *System des Finanzwesens,* Halle: Renger.

Justi, J.H.G. (1760/1761), *Moralische und philosophische Schriften,* 3 Vols., Berlin: Rüdigers.

Klein, E. (1961), "Johann Heinrich Gottlieb Justi und die preußische Staatswirtschaft." *Vierteljahrschrift für Sozial- und Wirtschaftsgeschichte* 48, 145-202.

Klein, E. (1952), *Johann Heinrich Gottlieb von Justi. Ein Beitrag zur Abhängigkeit der cameralistischen Theorie von der staatswissenschaftlichen Praxis,* s. l.: Huber.

Lluch, E. (1997), "Cameralism beyond the Germanic world: A note on Tribe." *History of Economic Ideas* 5, 85-99.

Mann, F.K. (1937), *Steuerpolitische Ideale,* Jena: Fischer.

Marchet, G. (1885), *Studien über die Entwickelung der Verwaltungslehre in Deutschland,* München: Oldenbourg.

Monroe, A.E. (1927), *Early Economic Thought,* Cambridge, MA: Harvard University Press.

Müllensiefen, K.P. (1928), *Die deutsche Finanzwissenschaft von 1716-1830,* Giessen: Wenger.

Nathan, O. (1932), "Akzise." In L. Elster et al., (eds.), *Handwörterbuch der Staatswissenschaften,* Vol. 1, Jena: Fischer.

North, D.C. (1996), *Institutions, institutional change and economic performance,* Cambridge, MA: Cambridge University Press.

Obert, M. (1992), *Die naturrechtliche "politische Metaphysik" des Johann Heinrich Gottlob von Justi (1717-1771),* Frankfurt: Lang.

Peukert, H. (1993), *Wirtschaftssystem und -stil der Wildbeuter und früher Landwirtschaftsgesellschaften,* Publication of the research project "Wirtschaftssysteme im historischen Vergleich," No. 8, Frankfurt: Mimeo.

Peukert, H. (1992), *Das klassische griechische Wirtschaftssystem und der Wirtschaftsstil unter besonderer Berücksichtigung des Geld- und Bankwesens,* Publication of the research project "Wirtschaftssysteme im historischen Vergleich," No. 7, Frankfurt: Mimeo.

Peukert, H. (2002), "Justi's concept of moral economics and the good society." In J. Backhaus, (ed.), *Johann Heinrich Gottlob von Justi,* Marburg, Metropolis, forthcoming.

Rath, K.W. (1939/1940), “Staat und Staatswirtschaft im kameralistischen Denken.“ *Finanzarchiv* 7, 75-99.

Richter, R. (1998), “Neue Institutionenökonomik: Ideen und Möglichkeiten.“ In G. Krause-Junk, (ed.), *Steuersysteme der Zukunft*, Berlin, Duncker und Humblot.

Roscher, W. (1874), *Geschichte der National-Oekonomik in Deutschland*, Munich: Oldenbourg.

Rösch-Wanner, B. (1993), *J.H.G. von Justi als Literat*, Frankfurt: Lang.

Rutherford, M. (1996). *Institutions in economics*, Cambridge, MA: Cambridge University Press.

Scheer, C. (1998), “Steuerpolitische Ideale — gestern und morgen.“ In G. Krause-Junk, (ed.), *Steuersysteme der Zukunft*, Berlin, Duncker und Humblot.

Schefold, B. (ed.). (1993), *J.H.G. von Justis "Grundsätze der Policey-Wissenschaft"*, Vademecum, Düsseldorf: Verlag Wirtschaft und Finanzen.

Schmidt, A. (1937), *Die Entstehung eines Eigensystems der Finanzwissenschaft*, Offenbach.

Schumpeter, J.A. (1965), *Geschichte der ökonomischen Analyse*, Vol. 1, Göttingen: Vandenhoeck und Ruprecht.

Tribe, K. (1988), *Governing Economy*, Cambridge, MA: Cambridge University Press.

Tribe, K. (1995), *Strategies of Economic Order*, Cambridge, MA: Cambridge University Press.

Troeltsch, W. (1901), “Regalien.“ In J. Conrad et al., (eds.), *Handwörterbuch der Staatswissenschaften*, Vol. 6, Jena, Fischer.

Veblen, T. (1991/1899), *The Theory of the Leisure Class*, Fairfield, NJ: Kelley.

Wysocki, J. (1982), “Zur kameralistischen Theorie der Besteuerung von Grund und Vermögen unter Bezug auf die Reform Josephs II.“ In F. Neumark, (ed.), *Studien zur Entwicklung der ökonomischen Theorie II*, Berlin, Duncker und Humblot.

Zielenziger, K. (1914), *Die alten deutschen Kameralisten*, Jena: Fischer.

Fritz Karl Mann (1883-1979)

Helge Peukert
University Lecturer
Krupp Chair in Public Finance and Fiscal Sociology
University of Erfurt
Nordhäuser Str. 63
99089 Erfurt
Germany
Fon: ++49-361-737-4553
Fax: ++49-361-737-4559
helge.peukert@uni-erfurt.de

Abstract: The text deals with F. K. Mann's approach of fiscal sociology. First, his biography is presented. Second, his book on tax policy ideals is discussed critically. Third, three conceptual elements of his fiscal approach are extracted from major writings of Mann. Fourth, the relationship between fiscal theory and sociology is analyzed. Finally it is asked which of his writings, ideas and concepts stand the test of time.

Keywords: Fiscal sociology, Historical School, fiscal theory and history.

JEL Codes: P 16, B 31, B 41.

1 Introduction

Besides Sultan, Ritschl and Jecht (Köllner 1987), Mann can be considered as the most important German theorist of fiscal sociology in the second half of the last century (Koch 1981, p. 99). Despite elements of fiscal sociology in the classics (e.g. Smith and Ricardo) and before (e.g. Montesquieu), elements of fiscal sociology play a major in the works of the three German system builders of fiscal theory: Stein, Schäffle and Wagner (Jecht 1961), but also e.g. in Marx and later in M. Weber. Especially the German historical school was germane to the more broader interrelations and dependencies of the fiscal system. In this context, the word fiscal sociology comprises much more than a sociological perspective in the modern narrower sense. According to Mann, fiscal sociology encompasses the social component of the fiscal system and the fiscal component of society (see his summary and discussion in Mann 1961, especially p. 644).

Mann belongs to the German speaking more historical-social tradition of economics mentioned above which did not fulfill its promises: Schmollers fiscal history has never been written and marginal approaches (Sax) were a first opposing orientation. A quick look in recent volumes of the major German journal, the *Finanzarchiv* (see the *festschrift* for Mann in volume 23, 1963, pp. 1ff.), shows that the economization of fiscal theory dominates the field today. Mann would have preferred another focus and he developed some tools for the sociological complement besides pure fiscal economics. Fiscal sociology as a separate field of research was "invented" in Germany after World War I in the Goldscheid-Schumpeter debate. At this time Mann was in his early thirties. It can be stated that his relevant contributions on fiscal sociology started to be published at the end of the 1920s and the early 1930s. After World War II and in the second half of his lifetime, he focused on fiscal sociology as a separate field of research because in his view the fiscal phenomena cannot be understood from economic, jurisdictional or technical aspects only. In so far he belonged to the second generation of explicit fiscal sociologists. Against the prevailing methodological individualism he stressed the macro and structural perspective with strong hermeneutical elements. His basic premise is that

> the economy is not an isolated entity, but similar to other social organisms like nations the church and the state. Therefore, the economy is embedded in the larger society, and depends on many other influences. So the economy is interwoven into so many dependencies that it cannot be explained by itself (1923b, p. 11; our translations).

Therefore, the social economist should study the basics of law, economics, philosophy, logic, geography, and even have elementary knowledge of e.g. forestry, the natural sciences and biology (1923b, pp. 21-23).

2 Biography

Mann was born in Berlin (10.12.1883) and he died with 95 years in Washington D.C. (14.9.1979). He was married and had four children (for Mann's biography and further references see Weinhard 1999). He had to leave Germany in 1935 due to the second wave of dismissals and he became professor at the catholic American University in Washington D.C. Mann was Jewish, his father was a successful entrepreneur who co-founded a joint stock company in Berlin which dealt with varnish, oil and rust protection colors. The son was member of the supervisory board and he published an article on the subject which proves his practical and empirical sense (Mann 1913/14).

Since 1902 he studied law and economics in Freiburg, Munich, and Berlin. Among his teachers in law were H. Brunner, O. v. Gierke, and J. Kohler, in economics G. Schmoller, A. Wagner, M. Sering, and L. Brentano. But he also participated in lectures on philosophy (Rickert, Simmel), art history (Wölfflin), and antique lyrics (Wilamowitz-Moellendorff). He finished his first examination in jurisprudence in 1905, one year later followed his Ph.D. in law (Dr. iuris utr.) in Göttingen on the pledge of drafts (Mann 1906). In 1907, after the military service he definitively left the Prussian judicial service and studied languages in London and history, philosophy and economics in Berlin and Paris, including archival studies. His interest in the history of the economic ideas of the 16th – 18th century led in 1913 to the subject of his second dissertation (Dr. phil.) on the economic and tax policy of marshal Vauban. Schmoller and Sehring were his supervisors. In 1914, with a much extended version (Mann 1914), he became the *venia legendi* in economics in Kiel. Not later than his habilitation demonstrates Mann's peculiarities of research and thinking. His contribution is not only a dry history of economic thought exercise of Vauban's Dixme Royale (a direct tax). It also compares critically physiocracy and mercantilism as socially embedded theories. Mann criticizes mercantilism but he also highlights strong points in mercantilist thought; he does not share A. Smith's simplified version and critique. He also discusses Vauban's tax proposals and policy from the background of a necessarily complex tax system and he stresses the importance of the sociological-historical conditions of the realization of a tax system (see the summary in Hansmeyer and Mackscheidt 1988, pp. 17ff.).

After the outbreak of WW I Mann went as a reserve officer to the Western front and then to Romania. He wrote two books on the Romanian war economy and its money problems in 1918/19 in the sprit of descriptive geography, and in 1918 he was a delegate of the peace talks in Bukarest. Besides a short interim in Breslau, he lectured on fiscal theory, and history of economic thought at the University of Kiel where he became professor in 1920. In 1922 he was offered a chair at Königsberg and he became director of the institute of the East-German Economy (1926b). In 1926 he was offered the first modern chair in fiscal economics in Cologne. It should be mentioned that Mann had already published a bunch of articles on strictly economic and fiscal problems (1926c), e.g. his report on tax shifting which correctly summarizes the knowledge of his time (Mann 1926a), but also on the principles of taxation, etc.

A specific trait of Mann's thinking can be found in these publications: an empirical (see his comparative study on the German fiscal system and development before and after WW I in [1929a]) and historical sense of the complexities and interrelations of cause and effect in the real economic world. This may be one of the reasons why we seldom find sharpened hypotheses in his writings. The economic policy conclusion is for him that historical arrangements should only be changed if it is really necessary and he warned against easy recipes.

> My analysis makes clear that every economic agent who is buying or selling in the exchange economy is able to shift taxes ... so we must also check carefully the direct taxes and in how the shifting of these taxes will lead to unwelcome burdens and relief ... how sensitive all cells of the economic organism may react to a new tax and to which degree disturbances of economic equilibrium may take place until the final acceptance of the tax ... [Therefore], *the historically given tax constitution always deserves the primacy over change* (1926a, p. 300).

Mann also lectured on business cycles and crises, economic sociology, the reparation problem, money and currency, etc. and founded the institute of international fiscal economics. In his years in Cologne he published the books which founded the so-called Cologne school of fiscal economics (Mann 1929b, 1930, 1937). Mann held the skeptical and historical-complex view of fiscal phenomena until his last publications, where he e.g. criticized more formalized concepts (1978b, pp. 75-90), especially those of equal sacrifice and he guesses that behind formalism often prejudices and personal political preferences are hidden (Mann 1972b). Until his last years he also underlined the double aspect of all phenomena and e.g. policy measures. It should be stressed "that investment grants have a subjective, an objective, a social psychological and a quantitative impact" (Mann 1963, p. 38; see also his discussion of the resistance of 'common sense' against compensatory fiscal policy on pp. 23-24).

With the help of E.R.A. Seligman and financial assistance of the Rockefeller foundation and after his forced retirement, Mann could emigrate to the US and worked at the American University on the assumption to be able to return more sooner than later. He lost his chair in Germany due to the canceled privileges of the front fighters. In 1941 the secret police informed the University of Cologne: "The Jew Prof. Dr. Fritz Karl Israel Mann ... was denaturalized due to the 11. Verordnung zum Reichsbürgergesetz, dated 25.11.1941" (cited in Hansmeyer and Mackscheidt 1988, p. 16). As a man in his sixties the start in a new environment was not easy for him and the first years were also characterized by financial bottlenecks. Mann became a US citizen, in 1945 he founded an Institute on Federal Taxes, and in 1956 he retired. 1943/44 he was an expert on economic questions for the War Department. After the war he liked to be guest professor at Cologne University, he received two honor Ph.D. (Frankfurt, Tübingen), and the German high order of merit (*Großes Bundesverdienstkreuz)*, he was an honorary member of the German Sociological Association (*Deutsche Gesellschaft für Soziologie)* and member of e.g. the Herder Society *(Herder Gesellschaft)* in Riga. In the 23 years after his retirement he did not only publish and edit Schumpeter's "History of Economic Thought" (Mann 1963a) and "Das Wesen des Geldes" [The Essence of Money] (Mann 1970, where he stresses Schumpeter's methodological open-mindedness and in our view correctly points out some substantial inconsistencies). He also published a history of fiscal theory (Mann 1977) and wrote many articles on fiscal theory (see the references), economic country studies (1963) in an empirical-historical-theoretical setting and a final conclusion and summary on fiscal theory (Mann 1978b, the book is mainly a compilation of ideas of earlier articles).

As Weinhard (who arranged the register of Schumpeter's book on money, see Mann 1970, p. XXVII) mentions in his excellent short biography, Mann was a wanderer between Europe and the US (1999, p. 414). Mann never returned to Europe after WW II "because he wanted to pay back his thanks and duty to the American people by his work in the United States until his last hour" (Hansmeyer and Mackscheidt 1988, p. 16). But in a certain sense he never left Europe. In an introduction he remarks, "that I have continued my fiscal economic work in my former orientation after the move to the United States" (1959, p. V). This may explain why Mann never gained much influence in the US (Hagemann 2002, pp. 89-92.) but the more valuable are his writings for those who consider a fiscal sociology a necessary aspect in the multifaceted rainbow of the social sciences (Krull 1980). His biography shows that he has never chosen the easy way (he e.g. rejected the offer of C.L. v. Bar to write a habilitation in law in 1906) and that he was an interdisciplinary personality deep down.

3 Tax Policy Ideals

Mann's book on tax policy ideals can be considered as his most important book, at least what today's reception is concerned. An early article on tax sociology can be seen as a preparatory groundwork where he calls the question: in how far does the social structure influence the tax system as belonging to the field of a sociological tax theory (1934, p. 282). As he underlines in the preface of the book, his aim is not a general history of economic thought and the delineation of tax theories and systems. In a comparative and ideal-type manner he wants to present the underlying ideals, and wishes which are often hidden and implicit at their time, in a secular perspective (1600-1935). He will not focus on the logical reasoning of the relevant authors, but with reference to Pareto's residue and derivation concept, he wants to highlight the practical aims, which are driven by instincts, interests and passions (1937, p. VI; curiously, the preface is dated Spring 1937, Cologne). The reader may feel a certain ambiguity between his reference to the Pareto model on the one hand and his statement of a relatively autonomous sphere of symbols and ideas which are a separate driving force of real economic and financial developments. At any rate, the ideals of yesterday are not only forgone thoughts but they may also encapsulate more general human hopes and needs and are therefore not ossified thought systems of the past.

In the first part the ideals of absolutism and its background (the importance of war and emulation, the feudal arbitrariness, the autarky principle, etc.) are presented. From the principle that the prince is god's representative on earth, the unlimited rights of the prince vis-à-vis his subjects, e.g. by the confiscation of property by taxes, could be deduced (1937, p. 16). Mann explains that state and economy have neither been divided in theory nor in absolutist practice in the 17th century and we can speak of a planned economy which was the model of later mercantilist thought. Mann shows that in the 16th – 18th century taxes were not regarded as normal but as an exception or even an anomaly.

> In the foreground stood the state political principle, that governing was a private matter of the ruler and that he consequently had to finance the financial needs of the state by his personal income ... In the corporative state the king was only the largest owner of the land. His usual income came ... primarily from the yields of his land, secondly form domains, forestry, regalia, and the selling of public functions (1937, p. 39).

Mann cites many sources and he convincingly demonstrates the interlocking of the state and the economy, the influence of state philosophies, interest groups and their powers and the tax ideals, their contradictions and opposition (e.g. by Locke), as well as the profound difference to our understanding of taxes as a regular phenomenon.

He also goes into details, e.g. in his discussion of the early excise tax (*Akzise,* mainly but not only an excise duty) which became instantaneously an ideal and a general problem-solver. The rational arguments are still raised today: the direct taxes did not suffice, excise duties have the advantage of being almost imperceptible, technical easiness, it deprives luxuries consumption, it has a social element, because the indirect taxes must be paid by everybody including the clergy and the nobility. Mann shows how especially these two interest groups tried to counteract a general excise tax.

Mann clearly differentiates from this debate the emerging ideal of a natural order. He goes back to Greek and Roman theories and forth to Grotius, Hobbes and Locke. But how could a natural system of taxation be deduced? Besides organic theories individualist theories of tax justice were elaborated, based on the general equivalence principle which evolved in many directions, e.g. the idea of insurance. But what was the general good for which taxes can be levied regularly: peace, life, other services, or property, and in the latter case: should rich people pay more or less and progressively or linear? A more or less direct consequence of arguments of justice was a new preference for direct taxes.

> Only the tax was just which corresponded in its amount to the individual advantage or at least the reciprocal part of the costs. This was the meaning ... of the analogy to the free exchange economy ... [At best] it could depend on property, yields, or income (1937, p. 124).

But besides ideal also material factors play a role.

> Irrespective how large we consider the influence of ideal factors: We should not overlook that the prevailing tendencies were also favored by external influences. We think primarily at the innumerable series of big wars ... times of war were the trailblazers of general direct taxation (1937, p. 125; see also p. 143).

Next, Mann discusses the classical maxims and argues that A. Smith's four principles are not new and not really well explained and that the classical contribution is in so far a non-event (for his obvious dislike of the classical and neoclassical school see also 1977, pp. 81-93, and 1978b, part 1 under the heading of ideologies and illusions). A really new era was reached with the idea of an ideal single tax which cannot only be found in the physiocratic literature, but e.g. also in Locke. One motive was transparency and the countervailing of arbitrariness.

Fiscal liberalism or classicism (Smith, Say, Ricardo) is a major system with a simple tax ideal which Mann describes in a rather critical way.

> The unity of classical fiscal theory depended on its bondage to political economy ... Who for once had accepted the idealization of the free exchange economy and the insufficient classical concept of productivity was already caught in chains. At least he had to accept the *negative* program: Limitation of state expenditure, renunciation of state property and enterprises, and "minimalization" of taxes ... Taxing is like a market process. The state protects the citizen and his property, the citizen pays a price for this. Taxation without a public return is theft (1937, pp. 202 and 209; see the resume on p. 221).

Mann argues that Smith did not support a general income tax (1937, p. 225) and that the liberals first vehemently opposed it (1937, pp. 230ff.), one reason being the disclosure of sensible personal information, but for practical reasons they later opportunistically adopted the income tax (1937, pp. 240ff.) and reified it as good and just (assisted e.g. by the socialists). It is very interesting to follow Mann in his description of the arguments pro and con for a proportional or progressive income tax (1937, pp. 262ff.) which very much resemble the recent debates on the tax scale system.

A completely different outlook was purported by the romantics who were yearning for a tax free society, among them the early E. Sax. The next system is the socialist ideal with a natural tendency property taxes and the relative disregard of e.g. Marx vis-à-vis tax questions, but revitalized by the writings of Goldscheid. The social reform movement and the social democrats argued against all indirect taxes and in favor of a (first: single) progressive income tax. The so-called socialists of the chair, especially A. Wagner, asked for a strong state and the influence of social concerns as a separate and important variable in the tax structure.

The book ends with the ideal of the authoritarian state (Stahl) in an organic frame of reference. Tax policy is seen as executor of the general political will, the social element plays a role and the tax system is interpreted as a factor for an enhancement of the productivity of the whole system. It is not so clear if the author does not imply that the tax policy of e.g. fascist Germany is up to day or not. In the epilogue of the second edition he states that with these changes:

> changes the *meaning* of fiscal theory in toto. The fiscal center of the country (not only of the state and not only in authoritarian, communist or fascist countries of the recent time) enlarges as the economic center of the country; or to put it ... in a purely economic comparison: The functions of fiscal policy are "economized". (1978a, pp. 365-366)

4 Three Conceptual Elements for Fiscal Analysis

In his early book on "Die Staatswirtschaft unserer Zeit" [The state economy of out time] (1930) Mann tries to describe the changes in the relationship between the state, the economy and the fiscal system with three conceptual observations. In the preface he notices that many people feel that we live in an age of transition. The only point they agree upon is

> that the great idea of a free societal order which helps to develop all capabilities. It saw in the constant surmounting of former achievements the ethical and customary final purpose and tried therefore to support the individual in fight and competition. But it belongs to a bygone phase of societal development (1930, preface).

In our view, this statement is not obvious and underlines Mann's more collectivity oriented view.

The first thesis consists in the description of the transition form the share system *(Anteilsystem)* to the control system *(Kontrollsystem)*. The centralized system of communist Russia did not (yet) materialize, nor the collapse of the tax state nor will the old liberal capitalist state survive. Instead we observe a new mixed system, the control system. An observable fact is the increase of the financial needs of the state after WW I (1930, p. 4) which now held between one third or one fourth of the gross national product in the 1930s, including the parafiscal entities. This changes the structural role of the state because it now importantly influences the economy not only from the income side but also what the expenditure part are concerned. It should be noted that Mann correctly interpreted the trend of an increasing share of the state (see the data in Nowotny 1999, ch. 6).

Two new problem areas are connected with the control system. The first is an implicit and autonomous trend of an accelerating increase of the share due to

> the increasing frictional resistance which our capitalist economic system produces; the will to power of established bureaucracies; the mass psychological adaptation to public care which only allows an increase but nor a reduction ... Because the motive to withdraw taxes increases with the degree of interventions the state cannot withhold to check the firms and their accounting; even though ... the costs of the necessary number of public servants will be immense. So the public economic sector is driven to take over plan economic functions for fiscal reasons (1930, pp. 14-15).

Mann's prediction was correct and it demonstrates his multifaceted viewpoint, including psychological, sociological, public choice etc. arguments. The strong point in his argument is that he is not as one-sided as e.g. public choice, i.e. he holds the adequate level of complexity or variety facing a complex phenomenon (Hayek). But he also saw a counteracting tendency to stop the increasing share. But Mann asks, how can parliaments for "reasons of humanity" not increase expenditures? Therefore, a limited right of parliaments and a special role of the finance minister to insulate him from these claims will be established, becoming a neutral power dubbed financial dictatorship by K. Schmitt (1930, p. 15; see for the respective institutional arrangement in present-day Germany Nowotny 1999, ch. 9).

When these breaks do not work there is only one way out: "The fusion of the exchange economy and the public economy and with it the end of an independent fiscal economic order as such" (1930, p. 15). It is not clear if Mann considers this development as inevitable or desirable (at least the above mentioned frictions and resistance, are a more or less objective influence). The second point is the coexistence of the share and the control system which leads to capital movements in favor of the share system. This undermines the output performance of countries with a control system and leads to even higher tax burdens (1930, p. 16). We may leave open if Mann's prediction was a common hunch of the literature at his time, but the problems in the recent tax debate in Germany in the year 2002 are adequately depicted by Mann's two problems.

The second trend is the increase of the parafiscal entities (Mann calls them die *hilfsfiskalische Verzweigung,* 1930, pp. 17ff., or *intermediäre Finanzgewalten,* see already 1929a, pp. 75ff.) as an almost universal tendency of more advanced economies (a long-term trend which Mann correctly identifies, for Germany see Nowotny 1999, ch. 20). He also includes the fascist *Stato Corporativo* which is discussed without qualifications. Mann argues that it is not surprising that specialized agencies are established and the state only holds some control rights. All judicial differences notwithstanding, this means an increase of the sphere of the state but the principle of delegation is chosen because of

> the organizational superiority of middle sized units ... further the exemption of resistance which will result due to the reemergence of the dispute on the "agenda" and "non-agenda" of the state ... further the half darkness in which the strongest fiscal po-

> litical achievements flourish ... a state who has problems to get further credit can get additional credit by the detour of the new economic subjects ... Finally the parliamentary rights can be broken by the creation of semi public authorities (1930, pp. 18-19).

Once again we may ask if Mann holds this development for inevitable or desirable. In our view a clear evaluation as part of every good scientific research is missing. At the end of the chapter Mann criticized theories of the pluralist state (the state as one organization among others, like the church, parties, families, etc.). With respect to these groups the state should not have a relationship of duties and fidelity.

> As far as the unity of the state becomes problematic in social life, not only the precondition of all ethical and judicial norms is missing as *Carl Schmitt* describes it; also the state economy would cease to exist to the degree that it seps back into the front of the other singular economies (1930, pp. 27-28).

We will only hint at the fact that Schmitt and his state philosophy was also a favorite of many early intellectual sympathizers with the German Nazi movement (see also Mann's friendly interpretation of the policy of the first fascist Italian finance minister, de'Stefani, 1930, pp. 32-33, and later in 1977, p. 95). At least we find a certain double bind in Mann: on the one hand he describes the reasons of the growing importance of the state and the parafiscal entities in a rather critical or negative way, on the other hand he more or less implicitly holds an authoritarian ideal of the state.

The third trend Mann identified refers to the rationalization according to economic principles *(Ökonomisierung)* of fiscal policy. It has now a social function, it has to influence the business cycle etc. and looses its relative autonomy.

> *On the one hand* fiscal policy does not represent an independent system of means, which should secure the balance of the public household ... fiscal policy becomes a technique to fulfill economic goals. – *On the other hand* it becomes obvious that fiscal policy gets an increasing importance; consequently, the fiscal center gets more and more economic aims. This double tendency can best be described as the *"economization of fiscal policy"* ... The business cycle policy of the pubic authorities is a new symptom for the endeavor of *the fiscal center to enlarge and become the economic center as such* (1930, pp. 38 and 41).

In other terms, Mann describes the functional enlargement which has been described by Musgrave as the functions of allocation, distribution and stabilization. These changes will also alter the view of the state and lead to

> the insight that in a higher degree as earlier the state creates the preconditions of cultural life ... that his destiny is the common destiny. This will lead to a feeling of unity and will initiate a stronger self-consciousness of the state (1930, p. 45).

In this context also belongs another article (first published in 1947) which distinguishes three economic functions of taxes: the distributive, the regulative (deliberate influence on allocation) and the traditional fiscal function (1956, pp. 52-66).

5 Fiscal Theory and Fiscal Sociology

In the following we will discuss Mann's articles which are collected in Mann (1959). The first deals with methodology and the debate on method in fiscal theory. The article is a plea for methodological pluralism (in the same vein Mann 1958/59). The author distinguishes the older autonomous cameralist view of production according to need *(Bedarfsdeckung)*, the classical view of fiscal theory as part of the economic system and circulation (Smith, Say, Ricardo) as an enlarged price theory, and the third institutionalist view which includes other spheres of social life. He does not share Schmölder's approach because "deep psychology is essentially individual psychology, whereas changes in the fiscal economic realm are to be explained by the behavior of social groups" (1959, p. 12). He describes the debate of the second, the microstatic model, in a relatively neutral manner, only once he talks about the *Angst* psychosis of liberalism against higher taxes and the breakdown of the system (1956, p. 29). In more recent times the Keynesian macrostatic model was a new turning point which Mann describes in another article (1956, pp. 36-51) without any personal assessment. But in another contribution Mann is explicit and castigates the Keynesian approach as lacking dynamic and historical elements; in so far the new macro models dismiss the strong points of the older German systems, especially those of members of the historical school (Mann 1954/55, pp. 231-232). Besides Keynesianism, fiscal sociology is another newcomer. It has two functions:

> On the on hand it should make research on the *fiscal component* of society, on the other hand of the *social component* of the fiscal economic realm ... The first task refers to the active function, the second the passive function of the fiscal economy (1956, p. 28).

The first component was often described as the genuine, the second as the non genuine fiscal sociology (Mann 1951, p. 131), a valuation which he later gave up (1978b, p. 135).

While not coining the term, for Mann A. Schäffle is the conceptual founder of fiscal sociology (Mann 1932, p. 50). Mann tries to motivate for a sociological fiscal approach in the following way.

> Did not an intense interplay exist between societal living conditions and the fiscal economy? Wasn't fiscal policy dependent on the social needs, social behavior and the structure of society to such a high degree that the public household has often been celebrated as one of the best "mirrors of society?" ... The "sociological place" of fiscal systems had to be determined. For this purpose for example the question posed peripherally by Max Weber should be answered: which type of political power systems typically gives birth to specific duties like fees, specific excise taxes, and direct taxes. The fights about tax burdens and exemptions between social classes, income and professional groups (Schäffle), have been fought in parliaments, public gatherings, and in the press. They could be interpreted as the sociological frame in which the economic fights on taxes, like tax shifting, tax compensating behavior, redemption, and tax evasion took place (1956, p. 28).

The different approaches (fiscal economics, Keynesianism, etc.) can only partly explain and describe the fiscal and economic reality. Which approach should be applied also depends on the research question. Rejecting the often used dichotomies of pure vs. descriptive and ideal vs. real types he concludes: "Therefore all methods need mutual confirmation and if necessary corrections and enlargements" 1956, p. 35). Mann's methodological deliberations are sympathetic but from a theoretical point of view somewhat unsatisfactory. The article is mainly descriptive and repeats the debates. Deeper methodological considerations and references to the literature cannot be found. A long lasting methodological principle of Mann seems to be his strict distinction between science and economic policy, objectivity and values.

> Such a behavior is often self-denying: like the doctor who has made his diagnosis and who should now conceal the adequate medicine! But the choice of economic political remedies always depend on the personal political world view: on the values which we consider important in this or that sphere of live ... That is why economic policy objectives should never aspire to be research with the highest degree of objectivity (1926c, p. 42).

It is questionable if we can justify a field of research with reference to specific questions because it is not evident that e.g. the tax fights in parliament can best be described in a sociological manner and not in a microstatic (public choice) model. Further, Mann gives no hint what the principles or the paradigm of such a sociological approach would be (for the same state of the art in later years see Mann 1972a, and 1978b, pp. 129-141). He only mentions that it descends from sociology like fiscal theory from economics and therefore rests on specific premises and a particular methodology (1978b, p. 141). Also the distinction between fiscal sociology and economic sociology is somewhat fluid (Mann 1951, pp. 132-133). He rejects Goldscheid's dictum that fiscal sociology is the key field of research of sociology in general (Mann 1951, p. 134). Would the analysis of the tax fights at A. Smith's time be described in a different way compared with Smith's own extended and well informed analysis or not (Smith 1976/1776, II, pp. 341ff.)? Maybe it is impossible because too many factors intervene so that clear-cut hypotheses cannot be formulated. "The role of the fiscal component depends on too many factors to make a general prognosis possible" (1956, p. 30). But maybe the function of science is not to generate hypotheses. These questions must be answered in a methodological discourse. It is missing in Mann's deliberations.

This is not to say that Mann did not know the sophisticated debates on method in Germany before the war, see e.g. his critique of H. Jecht's *Wesen und Formen der Finanzwirtschaft* [Essence and form of fiscal theory] (Jena, 1928) where he correctly criticizes some aspects of Jecht's over-sophisticated ideas but where his own standpoint is missing. In later articles, Mann adds comparative fiscal political theory as a separate field besides fiscal economics and fiscal sociology.

> In so far as these investigations [social stratification, political parties, education] refer to political motivations or that their results should be used practically for political decisions, it refers to the independent branch which may be called "fiscal policy." (1971, p. 7, see also 1977, p. 97, and 1978b, pp. 130-134).

It may be asked why we should not also e.g. add fiscal jurisprudence theory. In an early article Mann criticized those who pleaded for a tax sociology "without asking for the precise subject, limits and procedures" (1934, p. 281). Maybe he is guilty here for the same verdict.

All this criticisms notwithstanding: In 1933 Mann wrote an article on the sociology of the fiscal policy decision process (Mann 1933) which formulated an interesting research agenda. We will leave open it was wise in 1933 to publish an article on the insufficiencies of the democratic decision making process (in the same vain see already Mann 1929a, pp. 118-123) with some populist antidemocratic flavor (e.g. 1933, pp. 716 and 730). In a certain sense Mann formulates many insights which can also be found in public choice. But the influencing factors that he identifies are broader: public opinion, the constitution, the voting system, the personal interests of the parliamentarians (power, income, prestige), the parties and their organizations, the party programs, general public ideologies, relevant social group interests, the capturing of public servants and institutions, friendly agreements, the fact of necessary compromises in plural systems, strong and lasting public bureaucracies. Mann considered his article on "Economics of fiscal decisions in a pluralistic society" as a "counterpart" (1964, p. 513, fn. 1) but the general message is the same he pinpoints in how far "institutional trends of a pluralistic society may impede or prevent rational fiscal decisions" (1964, p. 532). Nevertheless, he tries to keep a certain balance in his judgement.

> Pluralism, therefore, will be neither enthusiastically praised nor idealized as the most desirable form of social organization, nor considered as a sort of utopian scheme nor,

> inversely, blamed as a form of oligarchy leading to dictatorship, or as a cause of social instability and as dangerous and incurable social disease (1964, p. 524).

He explicitly criticizes Downs ("I hesitate to approve this primitive compass of fiscal behavior", 1964, p. 521).

The text also shows Mann's skepticism against multiple aims in fiscal systems.

> Fiscal policies ... also serve a variety of economic, social and cultural ends. They are instrumental in controlling the money market, in stemming the tides of inflation and deflation ... and in lessening social tensions. We may wonder, of course, whether fiscal policies are sufficiently flexible to serve several masters equally well and whether, by being a Jack-of-all-trades, they may lack rationality and result in waste of public funds and in inefficiency of governmental action ... the basic functions of Treasuries to finance public activities and to provide for balanced budgets (1964, p. 513).

A further article on the dual-debt system as a method of financing government corporations, first published in English in the *Journal of Political Economy* in 1947 (volume 55, pp. 39-56; one of the very few major journal articles of Mann; see also his article on the government corporation as a tool of foreign policy, 1956, pp. 124-141) exemplifies in an almost completely descriptive manner Mann´s theses concerning the parafiscal entities (1956, pp. 67-94). But now he holds a more Anglo-Saxon vista and underlines the multifold shortcomings of easier financing by these corporations. The same stance can be found in the following article on the socialization of risks (1956, pp. 95-111, first published in 1945) of farmers, companies, workers, etc. which he compares with a bacillus which deeply infected the economy (1956, p. 110-111).

A further article on the sociology of taxation (1956, pp. 112-123, first published in 1943) points out three ways in how far taxes can influence social life: "1. By changing socially unwanted human behavior; 2. By regulating the economic power of social groups and classes and 3. By fighting the social abuses of capitalism" (1956, p. 113). Taxes can enlarge and reduce social differentiation and income disparities. "At all times the ruling class has used the state power to increase its own well-being and to strengthen its economic position" (1956, p. 117).

The last article of the book under consideration here is an interesting example how a sociological approach can be applied. Mann analyzes the fiscal component of revolutions (1956, pp. 142-162, first published in 1947). In the first part Mann shows that fiscal policy may have a conservative influence on the social structure.

> The conservative influence hardly needs any illustration. Under no form of government has the ruling class withhold the temptation to use a considerable amount of pub-

> lic expenditures to fortify its economic position and to eternalize its political supremacy (1956, p. 143).

Mann gives numerous more or less obvious examples like nepotism *(Amtspatronage)*, the activities in semi-public enterprises, etc. But fiscal factors and systems can also have revolutionary consequences and impacts. Mann discusses the literature and casts some doubts on the often quickly stated influence of the taxes on revolutionary developments. One example is the French revolution and he criticizes H. Taine, Tocqueville, and others. The same holds in his view for the glorious revolution. But they were never missing as a factor of influence and in the case of the British colonies he holds "that the fiscal political conflict which was caused by the Boston Tea Party had caused the revolution" (1956, p. 155). After discussing the situation in Greek antiquity, his general conclusion is "that the influence of fiscal factors on political and social upheavals should be evaluated with great caution" (1956, p. 160). Apparently, more general and precise lessons cannot be drawn from history in a sociological perspective. The reader may conceive this as a little bit frustrating. Does this depend on the archeology of the field of fiscal sociology or does it depend on the personality of our researcher? Does the characterization Schäffle's also apply to Mann?

> He never wrote ... a fiscal sociology or another work which deserves the name ... Has he not been ... a deep digging researcher? Can we combine a single lasting result, a single lasting fruitful interpretation with his name? (Mann 1932, pp. 11 and 76).

6 Conclusion

Our overview will have shown that Mann often wrote articles without developing a really clear and distinctive point of view (see e.g. 1968). Sometimes he even formulated more or less unfounded critiques (in 1973 e.g. on the social market economy). But Mann is nevertheless an important precursor for a modern research agenda of fiscal sociology.

In the words of Neumark we may summarize his achievement:

> Your scientific oeuvre shows a surprising extent and an impressive range and scope ... The specificity of your researches seems for me to consist in the way how you combine theoretical and empirical-historical knowledge and how you furthermore pay attention to the often undeservedly neglected sociological aspects of fiscal sociological thinking and acting (1963, p. 1).

References

Secondary literature:

Hagemann, H. (2002), "Zur Emigration deutschsprachiger Finanzwissenschaftler nach 1933 nach 1933". *Die Rolle des Staates in der Ökonomie - Finanzwissenschaftliche Perspektiven: Festschrift für Otto Roloff zum 65. Geburtstag*, Hg. I. Barens and M. Pickhardt. Marburg: Metropolis, 85-116.
Hansmeyer, K.-H. and Mackscheidt, K. (1988), "Fritz Karl Mann (1883-1979)". Henning, F.-W. (ed.). *Kölner Volkswirte und Sozialwissenschaftler*. Köln, Pp. 15-38.
Jecht, H. (1961), "Finanzwissenschaft". Beckerath, E. et al. (eds.). *Handwörterbuch der Sozialwissenschaften*. Vol. 3. Stuttgart, Pp. 707-722.
Koch, W. (1981), "Finanzsoziologie". Albers, W. et al. (eds.). *Handwörterbuch der Wirtschaftswissenschaft*. Vol. 3. Stuttgart, Pp. 97-106.
Köllner, L. (1987), "Bemerkungen zur Finanzsoziologie heute". *Jahrbücher für Nationalökonomie und Statistik*, 203 , 26-42.
Krull, Ch. (1980), "Fritz Karl Mann". *Finanzarchiv*, 38, 1-3.
Neumark, F. (1963), "Vorwort". *Finanzarchiv*, 23 (1963), 1-2.
Nowotny, E. (1999), *Der öffentliche Sektor*. 4th ed. Berlin: Springer.
Smith, A. (1976), *An inquiry into the nature and causes of the wealth of nations*. Chicago: , Phoenix Books.
Weinhard, K. (1999), "Mann, Fritz Karl". Hagemann, H. and Krohn, C.-D. (eds.). *Biographisches Handbuch der deutschsprachigen wirtschaftswisenschaftlichen Emigration nach 1933*. Vol. 2. Munich, Pp. 410-415.

Mann's Early Writings:

Mann, F.K. (1913/14), "Über den Standort der chemischen und der Farbenindustrie". *Farbenzeitung*, 19, 1609-1612.
Mann, F.K. (1919), "Der Umbau der deutschen Reichsfinanzverfassung". *Die deutsche Nation*, 1 (1919/1), 1-8.
Mann, F.K. (1919), "Der Reichsbankrott". *Die deutsche Nation*, 1 (1919/5), 1-5.
Mann, F.K. (1922/24), "Besteuerung und Volkswirtschaft". *Schmollers Jahrbuch*, 46 (1922), 773-783, and 47 (1924), 301-308.
Mann, F.K. "Die Grundformen der Steuerabwehr". Jahrbücher für Nationalökonomie und Statistik, 120 (1923), 491-523.
Mann, F.K. (1925), "Reichsnotopfer". *Handwörterbuch der Staatswissenschaften*. 4th ed. Pp. 1222-1224.
Mann, F.K. (1926), "Zur Frage der steuerlichen Lastenverteilung". *Jahrbücher für Nationalökonomie und Statistik*, 123 (1926c), 30-40.

Dissertation:

1. Mann, F.K. (1906), *Die Verpfändung eines Wechsels durch Einigung und Übergabe des indossierten Papiers: Ein Beitrag zur Theorie des Wechselaktes*. Göttingen.
2. Mann, F.K (1913), *Die Volkswirtschafts- und Steuerpolitik des Marschall Vauban*.

Habilitation:

Mann, F.K. (1914), *Der Marschall Vauban und die Volkswirtschaftslehre des Absolutismus: Eine Kritik des Merkantilsystems.* Munich.
Mann, F.K. (1926a), "Wesen und allgemeiner Verlauf der Steuerüberwälzung". Boese, F. (ed.). *Krisis der Weltwirtschaft. Übervölkerung Westeuropas. Steuerüberwälzung.* Munich, Pp. 275-300.
Mann, F.K. (1926b), *Ostdeutsche Wirtschaftsforschung.* Jena.
Mann, F.K. (1929a), *Deutsche Finanzwirtschaft.* Jena.
Mann, F.K. (1929b), "Vom Wesen der Finanzwirtschaft". *Jahrbücher für Nationalökonomie und Statistik*, 131, 33-49.
Mann, F.K. (1930), Die Staatswirtschaft unserer Zeit: Eine Einführung. Jena.
Mann, F.K. (1932), "Albert Schäffle als Wirtschafts- und Finanzsoziologe". Mann, F.K. (ed.). Gründer der Soziologie. Jena, Pp. 11-78.
Mann, F.K. (1933), "Zur Soziologie der finanzpolitischen Entscheidung". Schmollers Jahrbuch, 57, 705-730.
Mann, F.K. (1934), "Beiträge zur Steuersoziologie". Finanzarchiv, 2, 281-314.
Mann, F.K. (1937), *Steuerpolitische Ideale: Vergleichende Studien zur Geschichte der ökonomischen und politischen Ideen und ihres Wirkens in der öffentlichen Meinung 1600-1935.* Jena.
Mann, F.K. (1951), "Vom Beruf der Finanzsoziologie". Specht, G. (ed.). *Soziologische Forschung in unserer Zeit.* Köln, Pp. 130-134.
Mann, F.K. (1954/55), "Die Staatswirtschaftslehre unserer Zeit". *Finanzarchiv*, 15, 212-232.
Mann, F.K. (1956/57), "Volkswirtschaftliche Analyse und Institutionalismus in der Finanzwissenschaft". *Finanzarchiv*, 17, 451-467.
Mann, F,K. (1958/59),"Die Finanzwirtschaft als Modell und als System". *Finanzarchiv*, 19, 25-45.
Mann, F.K. (1959), *Finanztheorie und Finanzsoziologie.* Göttingen.
Mann, F.K. (1961), "Finanzsoziologie". Beckerath, E. et al. (eds.). *Handwörterbuch der Sozialwissenschaften.* Vol. 3. Stuttgart, Pp. 642-648.
Mann, F.K. (1963a), "Vorwort". Schumpeter, J.A. *Geschichte der ökonomischen Analyse.* Göttingen, Pp. V-VII.
Mann, F.K. (1963b), *Die konjunktur- und finanzpolitische Lage der Vereinigten Staaten von Amerika.* Berlin.
Mann, F.K. (1964), "Economics of fiscal decisions in a pluralist society". Kloten, N. et al. (eds.). *Systeme und Methoden in den Wirtschafts- und Sozialwissenschaften.* Tübingen, Pp. 513-532.
Mann, F.K. (1970), "Einführung des Herausgebers". Schumpeter, J.A. *Das Wesen des Geldes.* Göttingen, Pp. VII-XXVII.
Mann, F.K. (1971), "Die drei Finanzwissenschaften". *Finanzarchiv*, 30, 1-13.
Mann, F.K. (1972a), "Finanzsoziologie". Bernsdorf, W. (ed.). *Wörterbuch der Soziologie.* Vol. 1. Frankfurt, Pp. 241-245.
Mann, F.K. (1972b), "Der interpersonale und der strukturelle Ausgleich der Steuerlast". *Zeitschrift für Wirtschafts- und Sozialwisssenschaften*, 92, 393-403.
Mann, F.K. (1976), "Adam Smith: The heir and the ancestor". *Zeitschrift für die gesamte Staatswirtschaft*, 132, 683-690.
Mann, F.K. (1977), "Abriß einer Geschichte der Finanzwissenschaft". Albers, W. et al. (eds.). *Handbuch der Finanzwissenschaft.* Vol. 1. Tübingen, Pp. 77-98.
Mann, F.K. (1978a), "Nachwort zum Neudruck". Mann, F.K. *Steuerpolitische Ideale.* 2nd ed. Stuttgart, Pp. 365-367.

Mann, F.K. (1978b), *Der Sinn der Finanzwirtschaft*. Tübingen.

Critical Remarks on Joseph E. Stiglitz: *Economics of the Public Sector* (3rd ed., New York: Norton, 2000)

Helge Peukert
University Lecturer
Krupp Chair in Public Finance and Fiscal Sociology
University of Erfurt
Nordhäuser Str. 63
99105 Erfurt
Germany
Fon: ++49-361-737-4553
Fax: ++49-361-737-4559
helge.peukert@uni-erfurt.de

Abstract: Since the award of the Nobel price, Stiglitz is one of the best known economists. This paper comments on the general approach and on some selected topics of Joseph E. Stiglitz' *Economics of the Public Sector* which has a conservative-liberal stance. Its main arguments are contrasted with those of Stiglitz' "Globalization and its discontents" (2003).

Keywords: Fiscal sociology, public sector.

JEL codes: B, B3, H, P, Z1.

1 Introduction

Since the award of the Nobel price, Stiglitz is one of the best known economists of the world. He is the Joan Kenney Professor of Economics at Stanford University and a senior fellow at the Hoover Institute. He served as chairman of President Clinton's Council of Economic Advisors and then as chief economist of the World Bank. Before, he worked at the faculties of Yale, Princeton, Oxford, etc. Besides the theory of economic regulation, major theoretical contributions were made in the theory of market failure due to imperfect and asymmetric information. Like e.g. Akerlof and Krugman he belongs to the group of top modern economists who operate outside the neoclassical framework in portions of their work. Nevertheless, he belongs to the mainstream (also in the sense of academic success) and does not define himself as a heterodox economist (see the excellent survey by D. Colander: "The death of neoclassical economics," *Journal of the History of Economic Thought*, 22, 2000, pp. 127-143, especially p. 137).

His non-mainstream leanings became more explicit in his later publication *Globalization and its discontents* (New York: Norton, 2002; see the critical discussion of the book by K. Basu: "Globalization and the politics of international finance: The Stiglitz verdict," *Journal of Economic Literature,* 41, 2003, pp. 885-899). He strongly criticizes the policy of international organizations, in particular the IMF. For Stiglitz, the economic policy of the IMF is based on a dogma of bad economics (the simple belief in a free exchange economy), ideology and partial interests. The book is used as a gold mine in the anti-globalization movement and the book itself illustrates the fact of globalization: Wherever the reviewer had a look in a shop window, Stiglitz' book was already there.

At first sight, Stiglitz' book on the public sector also seems to be *the* valuable reference for lectures and seminars held in the spirit of non-dogmatic, mildly heterodox economics. In the following we try to make clear why we have not chosen his book and have preferred a less well known German textbook in introductory courses at the University of Erfurt, despite the general preference for English written textbooks due to the international orientation of that university. We will not comment the entire book but concentrate on some selected topics.

2 A Closer Look

On the front page a lighthouse is reproduced and the reviewer spontaneously asked himself, if this signifies the superior elucidating light which the author sheds on the public sector, if it is an example for natural public goods or if it highlights Coase's empirical argument that what seems at first sight to be a public good (the lightning of a lighthouse) was in fact delivered by private institutions. Therefore, we started reading the book with ambiguous curiosity.

The first page begins with the author's copyright. It underlines how important intellectual private property rights seem to be in the world of wisdom and knowledge. "Copyright ... by Joseph E. Stiglitz, the Trustee of Edward Hannaway Stiglitz Trust, the Trustee of Julia Hannaway Stiglitz Trust and the Trustee of the Trust for the Benefit of Joseph E. Stiglitz' Children". So many trust interests seem to be involved here that the reviewer personally loses some trust in the intellectual purity of Stiglitz' motives. Was the author's intention to write a bestseller and sell his name as a trademark or did he want to deliver a scientific introduction or can he do both at once?

In the preface the author first puts himself in the limelight (member of the President's Council, a two pages list with very important economists he talked with, etc.). An impressive compilation of all foreign editions comes next. It may be mentioned that the German translation and revision of the second American edition by B. Schönfelder (*Finanzwissenschaft*, Munich: Oldenbourg, 1989) closely follows the English version. But it contains some revisions due to e.g. the different tax systems in Germany and the US. It has minor extensions (at least compared with the third English edition), for example on Rawl's philosophy (1989, pp. 80-81). But it also entails a bunch of mistakes, e.g. with respect to the translation of key economic terms.

In the substantial part of the preface he points out: (1.) The book follows the unique perspective of a public sector economist; (2.) It is written for a low undergraduate level; (3.) It can significantly help to improve practical public policy; (4.) It seeks to find the appropriate balance between the public and private sector (complementarity); (5.) It tries to look at the world in an impartial manner; (6.) It wants to depict the unintended consequences of political action; (7.) The questions of the book will stretch from "What should be the role of the government?" (p. XIX), to "Should education be publicly provided?" (p. XX). Stiglitz holds that "a clear delineation between the analysis of the consequences of any policy and the value judgements associated with assessing the desirability of the policy" is possible and warranted (p. XX). In the following sentence he underlines the frequent uncertainty about the outcomes of certain policies. Stiglitz argues conventionally when he defines the role of the economist to cure "a lack of widespread understanding of basic economic issues" (p. XX).

He seems to believe that an economist can really answer e.g. the above mentioned question on education in a neutral manner (or others, e.g. on national defense). His realistic remarks on frequent uncertainty on causes and effects puts into perspective his claim for objectivity. In the following, the reader sometimes has the feeling of a wishy-washy due to his on the one/on the other side undecidedness. Stiglitz does not offer a more precise account where he exactly stands in the economic policy debates. He only makes a general remark on Clinton's endeavor to "reinvent government" (p. XX), without explaining what this means (see the sparse general description on pp. 198-199; on 'reinventing prisons' see pp. 208-209). From the most abstract level he often quickly changes to the policy debates of his days.

In the brief introduction to part one some basic questions are asked, e.g. "What should the government do?" He continues, "(t)o answer these questions, we must begin by understanding what the government does today" (p. 1). The implicit inductive methodology of this statement does not orient the following exposition because in chapter one a deductive reasoning prevails (market failure approach, etc.) before chapter two describes the public sector of the US in detail. In the first chapter the fact of mixed economies in advanced western countries in general and a stronger role of the government in European countries in particular is mentioned. A history of economic thought passage follows where interventionism and laissez-faire are contrasted. "Smith argued that the economy was led, as if by an invisible hand, to produce what was desired and in the best possible way" (p. 6). We have shown elsewhere that this statement does not correctly describe Smith's viewpoint (H. Peukert: "Adam Smith's invisible hand", *Festschrift für G. Meijer*, ed. J. Backhaus, 2003).

Stiglitz may argue that the book is only an elementary introduction, but this modest aim notwithstanding, he does no service to the reader in wrongly summarizing Smith who mentions about 80 cases for necessary interventions, including the fixing of the interest rate at a low level. A large part of *The Wealth of Nations,* book five "Of the revenue of the sovereign or commonwealth", is dedicated to the state and its activities. Stiglitz' summary, "(t)here is now widespread agreement that markets and private enterprises are at the heart of a successful economy, but that government plays an important role as a complement to the market", is a rather conservative statement and close to the laissez faire doctrine. He does not consider the market as a social institution but as a more or less automatic independent mechanism upon which the state intervenes. He repeats the image of a core (the market) and an intervening agent from outside (periphery), the state.

If two things are really complementary this distinction does not make sense and he seems to pay tribute to the conservative-liberal stance of American mainstream economists and the public opinion. In fact, modern markets like the stock exchange are themselves the result of an instituted process, i.e. laws, customs, etc. The best example is the US in which after the Civil War the government played a major developmental role and - contrary to the liberal image - applied a tough protectionist economic policy with e.g. high tariffs for imports. These historical facts are excluded from Stiglitz' stylized descriptions which contradict the underlying liberal-conservative ideology of the book. Stiglitz' setting the stage also contradicts somewhat his own insights not only in his recent critique of the IMF (see below) but also his older criticism of the big bang transition strategies in former socialist countries (see his book *Whither socialism?,* 4th print., Cambridge [Mass.]: MIT Press, 1997), where the establishment of markets was at the heart of the reform policies and the accompanying institutions came next.

The author continues to briefly describe the changing attitudes vis-à-vis the government (the Great Depression, Keynes, Johnson's war on poverty, etc.). In our view, these historical underpinnings are worthwhile, but the author only concentrates on the American example. It would be much more interesting to write a really comparative and internationally oriented book, including e.g. Canada, Europe etc. so that the horizon of students is really enlarged. Further, the methodological or theoretical status of historical facts is not clear: Do we gain major insights by history or not, does he follow an inductive or a deductive methodology. More general: Does the public economist have a special theoretical toolbox or not?

In Stiglitz' description state interventions lead to a catastrophe, the farm programs, the fight against homelessness and poverty, all failed more or less (p. 8). In his important introduction in which the theoretical field of the following is elaborated the author argues only *ex negativo*: Because the state mostly failed, if action is considered necessary, "greater care must be taken in the appropriate design of government programs" (p. 8). It is hard to believe that the state always did wrong in the history of the US. It is surprising that the public sector is introduced with an array of examples where it failed. Why didn't Stiglitz introduce the public sector with a positive example and deduce from this the importance of appropriate design? Why does he not mention that markets themselves are created and structured by hundreds of laws which all have e.g. impacts on distribution (e.g. labor legislation, accounting rules for firms, etc.). These orienting rules are therefore not neutral and should not be taken for granted. The superficial distinction between the market and the state stipulates a neutral operation of the laws of the market into which the state politically interferes and distorts the distributive process by taxation and welfare programs. His first more detailed example (in blue color, pp. 8-9) is the absolute failure of rent control in New York.

He lists four reasons of government failure before the concept of market failures shows up in the textbook: limited information, limited control over private market responses, limited control over bureaucracy, limitations imposed by political processes. The section concludes with Friedman's dictum "that the government should be restrained from attempting to remedy alleged or demonstrable deficiencies in markets" (p. 10). So the book starts with a negative bias against the public sector. This may correspond to the American mind in the years 1999/2000 but in a textbook it provokes the impression that the author follows an opportunist ideology. In usual micro textbooks for example the exposition starts with a simple supply and demand schedule with the clearing of the market and the equilibrium price. In an ideal type fashion first the efficiency and positive performance is highlighted and then the specifications (conditions for a Pareto optimum, etc.) follow. Why has an inverse strategy been chosen for the public sector?

In our view it is absolutely in order to write a book with a framing assumption, for example that the state should be reduced to a certain minimum if theoretical reasons and the underlying assumptions, for example a public choice approach, are presented (see for example the refreshing open-mindedness in C. B. Blankart: *Öffentliche Finanzen in der Demokratie*, 4th ed., Munich: Vahlen, 2001). But Stiglitz only presents some descriptive empirical facts and hums and haws before he simply sets his final conclusions. He concedes that the market is efficient only under fairly restrictive assumptions but he concludes that

> the recognition of the limitations of government implies that government should direct its energies only at those areas in which market failures are most significant *and* where there is evidence that government intervention can make a significant difference. Among American economists today, the dominant [and his own] view is that *limited* government intervention could alleviate (but not solve) the worst problems (p. 10).

This is compatible with the concept of a minimal state à la Noszick (restriction to the most obvious failures, intervention must make a significant difference, etc.). His claim to achieve a balance between the public and the private sector is a misnomer, his motto in fact is ′the most market and the least state as possible.′ So Stiglitz does not favor a really complementary view nor does he follow e.g. a historical methodology or a case to case view (the mixture always depends on the circumstances).

He does not reinvent government but adopts to the ideological position (minimize the government) which is quickly forgotten in economic policy when it comes to practical policy (see e.g. the recent conservative-liberal support for Bush′s protectionist and interventionist policies). The wishy-washy aspect consists e.g. in the fact that in his catalogue on the function of the state we also find "maintaining full employment" (p. 10). With an accompanying Nairu argument this obvious contradiction can surely be solved. Up till now, the student only knows Stiglitz' mainstream preference. What else has he learned? Maybe that a public economist deals with his subject in a somewhat fuzzy way.

His four government failures can almost equally be applied to market processes: Limited or ambiguous information (and accompanying herd behavior) e.g. in financial markets, limited control over the bureaucracy in multinational corporations, and the fact that "representatives have incentives to act for the benefit of special interest groups" (p. 10), e.g. the Enron management. It can be argued that we face similar problems in markets and in the public sphere. Either the author can show theoretically that these problems are in principle more pending in the public sphere or he must use a case to case method, i.e. depending on the problem at hand and the special circumstances a decision pro market or state must be made or he can argue that most important are the design problems to improve an institution's efficiency, be it the state or the market. The strong pro market bias has no theoretical foundation in Stiglitz' book.

In the following, he proclaims the emergence of a new consensus, highlighted by the initiatives of deregulation and privatization. Again the author is arguing from the political economic situation when the book was written. He also makes some advertising: "The Clinton administration sought a balance ..." (p. 11). Only at the end of the paragraph the author pretends to give a balanced picture, discussing the extreme case of the privatization of enriching uranium. "To many, this privatization appeared to be a case of the ideology of privatization gone amok – government had lost the sense of balance between the private and public sector required to make a mixed economy work" (p. 13). At the end, the author does not give any further hint how the balance should look like in principle.

On three pages the question what or who is the government is described in a very general, brief and unoriginal way (elections, certain rights of compulsion, etc.). The following part on thinking like a public sector economist starts with the orthodox description of the production possibilities schedule and the four questions: what, how etc. is to produced (pp. 14-16). The introductory statement, that economists study scarcity is far from evident because in the formal definition it buys the view of the non-satiability of wants. Alternative definitions like Polanyi's "collective satisfaction of material needs" are not mentioned (see K. Polanyi: *The livelihood of man,* New York: Academic Press, 1977).

The author thinks about the public sector in terms of consumer good markets when he states, "just as some individuals like chocolate ice cream and some like vanilla ice cream, some individuals get greater enjoyment out of public parks than do others" (p. 15). Aspects like fairness do not play a role or make a difference, only consumption goods in the narrow sense seem to interest Stiglitz' citizens. The author does not know the concept of a public ethos of public servants, he supports the public choice view that different policies are good for different people, a common good for society does not exist (p. 16). This is a very dismal picture for a public sector economist. But Stiglitz does not believe this 'interest only' stylization. In flat contradiction he plays the role of the distinguished intellectual scientist in his book on globalization (mentioned above) who argues from a common interest standpoint beyond and against ideologies and partial interests.

Maybe his textbook reflects the degeneration of the American public spirit (see R.D. Putnam: *Bowling Alone*, New York: Simon and Schuster, 2001). A formal four stage decision model (describing, analyzing, evaluating, interpreting) and an apologia of model building follows. The only substantial point is that economists should always emphasize the importance of economic incentives (p. 18). Further in a rather traditional way the author makes the distinction between normative and positive economics. The author puts it in a cost-benefit framework. His example with the tax on beer and the insight that the increase in the beer price reduces car accidents is nice but the author nevertheless falls into the objectivity trap because it depends on our subjective evaluations e.g. what should be considered as cost (only car accidents, or also family problems, etc.).

It is also surprising to read that Buchanan "has focused on *describing* the impact of political processes on social choices" (p. 20). Buchanan would not have won the Nobel price if he had only neutrally described and had not presented a very specific interpretation of political processes. In contrast, Musgrave's three branches (allocation, stabilization and distribution) are mentioned but Stiglitz does not discuss and criticize openly his approach of a public economist in a democratic society. Again he chooses the formal defense line that the three branches cannot be compartmentalized but are intertwined, a fact that Musgrave would never have doubted. Instead, Musgrave have reproached to Stiglitz' book that he subjects the three autonomous functions of the public sector to the problem of allocation. The first chapter ends with a hint at the disagreements among economists over values and the insight in alleged trade-offs between efficiency and equality, employment and inflation. But the author claims that a clear distinctive line between normative and positive can be drawn and that he is able to describe the major views of these debates in a detached way (p. 22).

The second chapter offers a mere description of the public sector in the US plus his skeptical bias against the state. The chapter starts with eight lines on those who opine that the public sector is too large. References of Friedman and Nozick are given. Two lines follow with the remark that the opposite opinion exists as well, this time without a reference. The author distinguishes four types of government activity (production, regulation, purchase, and redistribution) and describes different types of taxes, etc. He briefly underlines the importance of the provision of a legal system. Unfortunately this part is absolutely unconnected to the other chapters, especially to chapters one and three, where the markets are framed as more or less automatic mechanisms. The methodological problem is that Stiglitz chooses the simplified neoclassical model but that for a public sector economist maybe the institutionalist perspective is more adequate.

For example, J. Commons (see his *The legal foundations of capitalism*, Madison: University of Wisconsin, 1968 [1924]) sought to develop a realistic analysis of economic interactions based on empirical observation, a historical and evolutionary understanding and anthropological and sociological insights. He used a fivefold concept of market transactions including a sovereign authority, future considerations, material scarcity, efficiency and working rules (laws and customs). But Stiglitz prefers to use the traditional neoclassical framework as the core element. His description is almost exclusively concentrated on the US. The most important trends are pointed out (growing influence of the public sector, most importantly social insurance, income tax as the principal source, dwindling of corporate taxes). But the chapter is written without any intellectual zeal or an original organizing principle.

The first 50 pages of the book offer the preference of the author, i.e. his skepticism vis-á-vis the state, and some historical and empirical data. The reader has not got much bread to become an elucidated public economist. With great expectations he starts reading part two. But the second part begins with the traditional fundamentals of welfare economics, completely uncoupled to the previous descriptive chapter. In the introduction he argues that if the markets were efficient, there would only be a very limited role for government (p. 53). This can be doubted: people may prefer a non-market nexus even if markets work well. People may want spheres in their live world in which the cash nexus does not play the organizing role. With this introduction in part two Stiglitz testifies his market fundamentalism. He starts with Smith's metaphor of the invisible hand. Again in a very simplistic way he states that Smith argued that the pursuit of private interest fosters the public interest. We cannot delve into the Smith debate here but we will only mention the fact that the sentence which Stiglitz quotes on page 56 begins with the words "(b)y preferring the support of domestic to that of foreign industry, he intends only his own security." Playfully, Smith picks up arguments of the mercantilists (for a full exposition of the context see our article on Smith's invisible hand mentioned above).

The following combination of mercantilism and the establishment of colonies is far besides the point (for the core ideas of mercantilism see H. Peukert: "Mercantilism", *Founders of Modern Economics*, ed. J. Backhaus, in print). It is annoying to read that "Smith argued that it was not necessary to rely on government or on any moral sentiments to do good. The public interest, he maintained, is served when each individual simply does what is in his own self-interest" (p. 56). This statement is flatly contradicted by Smith's long chapter on the state. The infusion of public economists with such a history of economic thought nonsense background does not qualify the book. His conclusion that there "is widespread consensus among economists that competitive forces do lead to a high degree of efficiency" (p. 57) is contradicted by his own view of international financial markets in which psychology and volatile herd behavior plays a major disturbing role (see below) and his research on information asymmetries (see e.g. J. E. Stiglitz and A. Weiss: "Credit rationing in markets with imperfect information", *American Economic Review*, 71, 1981, pp. 393-410).

After this caricature of the history of economic thought and the alleged consensus he continues with the exposition of the concept of welfare economics and Pareto efficiency. Traditional micro follows, or better: a superficial version of it. For the beginner it is impossible to understand the two theorems because they are not theoretically developed but only stated (p. 60). In the preface to part two he underlines that only under specific idealized conditions a competitive economy is efficient. In chapter three he mentions some restrictions (e.g. full information, p. 61) but he evades a discussion of the full list. "The first theorem tells us that if the economy is competitive (and satisfies certain other conditions), it is Pareto efficient" (p. 60). In footnote two on page 61 we read that "(t)here are also a number of technical assumptions." That's all.

Stiglitz does not and cannot fully specify all necessary conditions because it would become evident that in reality markets which fulfill the Pareto conditions do not exist. Stiglitz uses the heuristic tool of microeconomics to justify an economic policy prejudice. When he states that the second fundamental theorem "thus provides a major justification for reliance on the market mechanism" (p. 61) he commits what A. N. Whitehead called the 'fallacy of misplaced concreteness'. This is simply bad economics. Further, Stiglitz does not explain to the reader how the statements that indifference curves are not cardinal measures and that in problem seven (p. 75) indifference curves with cardinal numbers show up can be reconciled. We will leave it to the reader to evaluate if our public economics student has now got a clearer understanding of his role after page 75 and the rudimentary knowledge of Pareto efficiency.

Chapter four deals with market failure. Stiglitz first points out that property rights and contracts must be enforced. "In some societies, land is held in common; anyone can graze their cattle and sheep on it. Since no one has the property right to the land, no one has an incentive to ensure that there is no overgrazing" (p. 77). He repeats the story of the tragedy of the commons. Private property is offered as the only reasonable alternative. Unfortunately, he does not mention that for thousands of years socially shared norms controlled and regulated overgrazing successfully (see E. Ostrom: *Governing the commons*, Cambridge: Cambridge University Press, 2002). He seems to believe that the problem can only be solved with markets and private property because then "the benefits of such improvements are reflected in the market price of the property" (p. 77). It is surprising that the chapter on market failure gives the market three cheers at the beginning. He then comes to the classical cases of imperfect competition and public goods, his prime example is national defense.

Interestingly lighthouses are mentioned as examples for pure public goods (non-rivalry and almost non-excludability, see also page 128). Stiglitz does not recognize the historical-empirical examples of Coase that lighthouses could and were run by private institutions. This example highlights the problem that it is almost impossible to define a public good by its alleged intrinsic characteristics. Even for defense a (semi-)private solution is not totally unrealistic. In addition, he describes incomplete markets (insurance and capital markets in particular), externalities, information failures (very poorly described on page 82), and finally unemployment and inflation as examples for macroeconomic disturbances. Unfortunately, Stiglitz does not tell the reader how markets work in general in the real world (we only have the unrealistic neoclassical model in chapter three).So the reader does not know how important the failures are (in his view). At the end of the chapter, he discusses income distribution and merit goods. The chapter as a whole seems to be written by a different author (compare page XXIII) compared with the previous ones because the anti-public bias is missing.

The conclusion of the chapter is that if markets are imperfect and do not lead to a Pareto optimal result, the state should intervene. But he adds two qualifications. "First, it has to be shown that there is, at least in principle, some way of intervening in the market to make someone better off without making anyone worse off, that is, making a *Pareto improvement*" (p. 89). This is a surprising remark, first because it implies that we can really measure the utility of all economic agents involved, again we see the problem of misplaced concreteness lurking in the background. Second, it is almost logically impossible that no one is worse off in cases of remedying market failures: The monopolist looses his monopoly rent, the producer looses profit when he has to pay for the externality he produces, etc.

Stiglitz' argument leads the market failure-public function approach into absurdity. So at the end he comes back to his anti-public attitude and finishes the chapter with the remark that often programs justified in terms of market failure are simply rhetoric (p. 90). But the opposite may also be true: So many arguments (Pareto principle, bureaucracy, information costs, etc, which are scattered on pages 87-90) can be piled up that together they serve to legitimize a do-nothing attitude in the face of obviously disfunctional market or anti-market (monopoly) processes. At the end the author once again does not hold the alleged balance.

Chapter five tackles the delicate problem of efficiency and equity. For Stiglitz there is no doubt at all that there "is a **trade-off** between efficiency ... and equity" (p. 94). He does not give any reason for this stipulation and puts it in an all or nothing context: oranges are taken from Robinson and given to Friday but some oranges will be lost due to this distributive procedure. He does not put the general argument in a realistic economic context of present-day societies. Instead he constructs a diagram with utilities, possibility curves, and social indifference curves signifying social preferences for utilities of Robinson and Friday. His elaboration boils down to a rudimentary introduction into the concepts of marginal utility, etc. With the objectively neutral looking concept of decreasing marginal utility he derives formally that transfers are costly. But he also smuggles in the most primitive and conservative argument against redistribution which is at least very helpful for people on the sunny side of society.

It must be underlined that Stiglitz presents the following argument without any qualification; it is the only substantial remark beyond the abstract Robinson-Friday curves. "Social welfare functions can be thought of as a tool economists use to summarize assumptions about society's attitudes toward different distributions of income and welfare" (p. 99). They are presented as realist tools for empirical decisions of the public economist. There is no doubt, that something like Figure 5.5 (a social indifference curve with combinations of different group utilities among which society is indifferent), has never been constructed by a serious economist with the claim to depict something in the real world.

"In our society, the way we transfer resources from one group (say, the rich) to another (say the poor) is by taxing the rich and subsidizing the poor" (p. 98). This is the method with the slash-hammer. A public economist should know that e.g. labor legislation, zoning laws etc. also influences distribution. He continues:

> The way we do that normally interferes with economic efficiency. The rich may work less hard than they would otherwise, because they reap only a fraction of the returns to their effort; while the poor may work less hard because by working harder, they may lose eligibility for benefits (p. 98).

Complex societal and economic problems are reduced to a primitive utilitarian laymen psychology. No hint is given to e.g. the discussion of the Asian miracle where the argument plays a role that greater equality is good for economic development and that great inequality reduces the developmental prospectus of countries (this is at least a main argument in chapter four in Stiglitz 2002). But the major aim of the book seems to be to infuse young economists with the ideology of the great trade-off and the explicit message that the state should better not intervene and the public sector be minimized.

Next, a primitive version of utilitarianism and Rawl's position are contrasted. It is not to ask for misplaced sophistication in a textbook when we mention that it is pure nonsense to summarize Rawls argument with the following words: "(S)ociety is better off if you improve the his [the worst-off individual's] welfare but gains nothing from improving the welfare of others. There is, in his view, no trade-off" (p. 102). Surprisingly, the author adds some caveats. Stiglitz notes that in this chapter the assumption is made that we can compare levels of utility of groups or individuals cardinally, but that "many economists believe this interpersonal comparisons cannot be made in any meaningful way" (p. 103).

After having learned the exercise of defining utility possibility curves, individual and social indifference curves, budget constraints, and finally admiring the tangency between social indifference and utility possibilities curves, the exhausted reader is informed that "(u)nfortunately ... few policy changes are Pareto improvements, and hence without making interpersonal comparisons of welfare, economists have little to say regarding policy" (p. 104). This is the admonition that all the curve drawing is good for almost nothing and a well-intentioned young student will be disappointed. But maybe this is the silent lesson: Reduce your good intentions and your aspiration level, do not believe in the common good and that something can be changed, take a know- and (almost) do-nothing attitude and understand that this exercise is not *Economics of the Public Sector* but *Economics against the public sector*. For Stiglitz, society does not even exist. In a Thatcherite manner he explains: "Society consists of many individuals; but society itself does not have preferences" (p. 104).

In the rest of the chapter the author presents a wild mixture of realism and theoretical opportunism. He first states that "(i)n practice, government officials do not derive utility possibilities schedules, nor do they write down social welfare functions" (p. 104). But then he continues that they first try to measure the net benefits and second try to find out if it is a Pareto improvement or not. "*Efficiency* is measured by simply summing the gains or losses for each individual ... *Equity* is measured by looking at some overall measure of inequality in society" (p. 105). So statistics is the solution and willingness to pay studies are the tool to measure benefits. In a complicated way he explains with numerical examples how a (compensated) demand curve can be derived. He does not give one sentence to the fact that it is almost impossible to realistically draw a compensated demand curve based on willing to pay inquiries not to mention the preference camouflage, which is highlighted in chapter six where he discusses the free rider problem, i.e. the incentive not to reveal the full value of a good or service (p. 135). "Even if individuals were asked directly what their preferences are, would they truthfully and meaningfully reveal them?" (p. 157). Good question! In addition, he does not mention the framing effects of the respective inquiries. Equity can be measured (e.g. by a poverty index) but how shall we compare it numerically with efficiency, if we accept the alleged trade-off?

This problem is hinted at in the last sentences under the rubric of the use of weights. Three assumptions are mentioned which are helpful for weighting: diminishing marginal utility (the layman psychologist's principle which is correctly put into question, see G. Becker et al.), different individuals have the same relation between utility and income (a strong assumption), and society is concerned with total utility (but why should society buy this unsophisticated utilitarian philosophy?). The last sentence of the chapter leaves the student with a question mark. "While each of these assumptions may be questioned, we can think of these procedures as simply a convenient way to summarize data that decision makers often find helpful" (p. 117). It is not clear what the author wants to say: how can assumptions be a convenient way to summarize data? With this final nonsense sentence the author admits that we are facing sad remains.

Part three deals with public expenditure theory. Chapter six distinguishes public and private goods in the usual way. Three methods of rationing publicly provided goods (user charges, uniform provision and queuing) are described with their advantages and disadvantages in an objective way. Unfortunately, a part on efficiency conditions for public goods follows, collective demand curves are derived and the optimality conditions are describes in detail. "Pure public goods are efficiently supplied when the sum of the marginal rates of substitution (over all individuals) is equal to the marginal rate of transformation" (p. 141, in italics). At least in one instance the author points out that efficiency considerations and questions of distribution cannot be separated.

> (O)ne cannot separate out efficiency considerations in the supply of public goods from distributional considerations. Any change in the distribution of income, say, brought about by a change in the income tax structure, will thus be accompanied by corresponding changes in the efficient levels of public-goods production (p. 147).

This is correct insight which might have been taken into consideration in the chapter on efficiency and equity. The chapter ends with the recognition of an efficient government as a public good but in a few lines only trivialities are presented. "If the government is able to become more efficient and reduce taxes without reducing the level of government services, everyone benefits" (p. 149). Is this all what a public economist has to say?

Chapter seven repeats the well-know arsenal of public choice. First without any caveat the glory of the market is highlighted. "Indeed, one of the central results of modern welfare economics, as we pointed out in Chapter 3, is that in a competitive economy, the resulting resource allocations are efficient. Decisions about resource allocations in the public sector are made in quite a different manner ... there is no comparable effective way that individuals can express their views about the desirability of one public good versus another" (p. 157). By and large the following analysis is a deficiency analysis of the public sector. It does not come to the author's mind that there may exist a different logic for vanilla and e.g. the decision making process of the educational system. In one sentence it is noted that votes are intended to represent the interests of the constituents. Then a great fuss is made on the voting paradox and some pages are filled Arrow's impossibility theorem. The author does not ask if it is very important in reality (in G. Tullock's opinion the answer is no) and his explanation of the property of single-peakedness is not very easy to follow for a freshman (pp. 166-167).

The author does not discuss the proposals to limit or prevent the voting paradox. Instead he underlines Buchanan's view of the self-interested individuals, Lindahl's approach (and the problem of revealing preferences), and a rather unimaginative diagram on Lindahl's solution (for a better exposition see e.g. D.

Brümmerhoff: *Finanzwissenschaft*, 8th ed., Munich: Oldenbourg, 2001, p. 127). The final conclusion is that "it appears that there is no perfect solution to the problem of collective decision-making in democratic societies" (p. 177). The end result of each chapter seems to be that the only thing a public economist learns is that no practical conclusions can be drawn when the traditional neo-classical economic tools (which may be adequate for the analysis of market processes) are used to analyze the public sector.

The author also briefly mentions the paradox that people vote at all. His only explanation is educational manipulation ("considerable time and energy are devoted to inculcating into our children notions of civic responsibility," p. 178), i.e. again an ad hoc psychological layman explanation. But he suddenly comes back to the main track, now focusing on the power of special interest groups. He is a dismal negativist who cannot imagine more altruistically oriented politicians or mechanisms which favor a somewhat altruistic behavior, well-knowing that "(e)ffective government depends on the quality of these public servants" (p. 179). In a blue collar comment (pp. 180-181) he doubts that social reforms to limit the amount of money that any organization can give to candidates or political parties can be successful. So the chapter once again ends with the message of economics against the public sector.

Under the heading "Public production and bureaucracy" chapter eight is concerned with the role of government in production, e.g. in the case of a natural monopoly. He also discusses alternatives (regulation and taxation) and the Demsetz/Stigler view to leave private monopolies for themselves. Again a major emphasis of the chapter is put on government inefficiencies. He hints at "shocking stories of government inefficiencies" (p. 198), and claims that "comparisons of costs of government and private firms engaged in similar activities tend to show substantially lower costs for private firms, whether in housing, garbage collection, bus transportation, ..." (p. 198). This statement is a somewhat incorrect extrapolation of the non-evident record of the data. Consequently, one page later he states, "some evidence shows that this need not be the case" (p. 199). The student reader will be a little bit perplexed.

In brackets he still mentions that eventually other components of public procurement are not or cannot measured in price comparisons, e.g. citizenship values. But the sources of inefficiency are identified in soft budget constraints (public enterprises not driven by the profit motive), civil service rules (high pay for good civil servants and job security), procurement and budgeting restrictions, and bureaucratic behavior (e.g. risk aversion). Unfortunately, the author does not really show why this is necessarily so in the public sector and in how far a difference between public and private corporations exists. He mentions in passing that the principal-agent problem of controlling managers also exists in private firms (p. 203) but this does not at all influence the main thrust of his reasoning. The chapter ends with the description of a growing consensus on the government's role in production. But the only sure points seem to be that the government should not be engaged in the production of private goods, that private firms should have an extended role in production, and that the government is in any case responsible for defense. "To what extent can government, by imitating the private sector - for instance, by making more extensive use of incentive pay - achieve comparable efficiencies?" (p. 209). It may be asked if the private sector and its logic should really be the only benchmark and ideal model for the public sector. Cannot the public sector find its own way of empowerment instead of copying the private sector (see R. Frank: *Choosing the right pond*, New York: Oxford University Press, 1986) and can't the public servants be motivated in a less self-interested way (see A. Etzioni: *The moral dimension*, New York: Free Press, 1988).

The reader is again left alone with a bunch of open questions. "Should prisons, welfare agencies, schools, or the production of the material to make nuclear bombs be privatized?" (p. 211). A rereading of the book after 9/11 shows how strongly the short-period *zeitgeist* rules the roost (in the quote especially the remark on the nuclear bombs!) when he finally states that the locus of controversy refers to services once thought to be part of the central provenance of government. The renationalization of services like the control at airports shows the changing emphasis.

Chapter nine deals with externalities and the environment. The text describes the problems and the solutions, e.g. fines and taxes, subsidies and marketable permits etc., in a non-biased way. Sometimes, the reader is left in the air, e.g. when the Coase theorem is described and the text continues that of course "the determination of who compensates whom makes a great deal of difference to the distributive implications of the externality" (p. 219). So, is the theorem finally correct or wrong? The interested reader gets no answer. Also the defense of the rejection to ratify the Kyoto protocol (unwillingness of the developing countries) by the US Congress can irritate the reader.

Instead of discussing chapter by chapter, in the following we will only highlight some points and then draw final conclusions. Chapter eleven presents the cost-benefit-analysis. The author mentions that e.g. the value of a human being varies in these analyses between 1 and 20 million dollar. It can be asked if e.g. the 'constructive method:' "What would the individual have earned had she remained alive?" (p. 280) is in conformity with human rights and the German Constitution. Also the strong disagreements on the concrete value of the discount rate (the differences are summarized on page 288) casts strong doubts on the alleged scientific objectivity of this procedure.

Chapter 13 on defense and technology has strong apologetic underpinnings. It justifies scientifically the American policy in the past arms race. "Game theory was used ... as the basis of the theory of deterrence, which underlay American defense strategy" (p. 335). Figure 13.2 applies the would-be precision of marginal analysis to the number of missiles. "The relevant question is ... how many extra kills we get from each additional missile. There may be sharply diminishing returns" (p. 334). Like other American textbooks, in the defense business a more is better philosophy prevails (with the typical Stiglitz caveats, see pages 337 and 775) in contrast to the curtailment arguments when the social question is dealt with. The author also supports the theory of the two-theater capability which easily can be enlarged to a multi-theater argument. "(P)otential enemies or troublemakers may wait until the United States is occupied with fighting in one theatre [a minimizing newspeech word] to start trouble in another" (p. 336). Is it funny or tragic to read that "even if Iraq had not engaged in biological warfare, the numerous maladies plaguing those returning from the Gulf War were a constant reminder of the threat of chemical weapons" (p. 338)? The description of the American attitude with respect to arms control agreements (pp. 337-338) is lamentable fairy tale (compare the irritating opposite view in e.g. Stiglitz' article *Bush braucht Widerstand* [Bush needs resistance] in *Süddeutsche Zeitung*, 29.09.2003, p. 2; for the historical facts see Ch. Johnson: *Blowback*, London: Time Warner, 2002).

The chapter on social insurance is descriptively interesting but one-sided. In the part on reforms only investing trust funds in equities and privatization are mentioned (pp. 377-378). The alternative of a broadening of the basis of those who have to pay into the social security system as it exists in the Switzerland is not mentioned at all (compare the recent debate in Germany on an encompassing citizen insurance). In the chapter on welfare programs a strong emphasis is put on distortions and with the typical Stiglitz relativity remark at the end (pp. 413-414).

The large part five deals with taxes. It has a remarkable slip of the tongue.

> Such forced transfers have been likened to theft, with one major difference: Transfers through the government wear the mantle of legality and respectability conferred upon them by the political process. When the political process in a country becomes detached form the citizenry and is used to transfer resources to the groups in power [a probable fact, especially according to chapter seven], the distinction between taxation and theft becomes blurred at best (pp. 451-452).

This is a peculiar way to introduce taxes in a textbook.

The underlying assumption in his discussion of taxes is that in "competitive markets, firms produce at the level where price equals marginal costs" (p. 484).

The author does not discuss for a second in how far this assumption holds in the real economic world. We agree with Stiglitz II who underlines: "Economic policy must be predicated not on an ideal world but on the world as it is. Politics must be designed not for how they might be implemented in an ideal world but for how they will be implemented in the world in which we live" (2002, p. 194). But maybe the negative message is the more important point here: the student learns to deduce from diagram 18.1 that a tax reduces output and increases prices (p. 485). Somewhere in the chapter on tax incidence in a brief paragraph the fact of oligopolies is mentioned: "There is no widely accepted theory of firm behavior in oligopoly, and so it is impossible to make any definite predictions about the incidence of taxation in this case" (p. 501). Full stop, and here he goes and continuous with partial equilibrium analysis. If reality does not allow easy conclusions, it deserves to be disregarded.

In chapter 19 taxation and economic efficiency and in chapter 20 optimal taxation are discussed. The author does not mention that the deadweight loss philosophy in these chapters depends on the assumption of fully competitive markets, firms as price takers, etc. The text does not convey the honest spirit of optimal taxation theorists who never forget to mention their limited relevance for practical economic policy. In the following, Stiglitz tries to support the view

> that interest income should be exempt from taxation ... *Whatever the government could do with a distortionary tax on producers, it could do better with a direct tax on consumers that maintained the economy on the production possibilities schedule* (pp. 567 and 569).

In chapter 21 he argues against the taxation of capital. To be able to do so, he constructs a "simple economy in which individuals own their own firm, investing their savings in capital, facing decisions on how much to save and invest" (p. 578). Without taking into account repercussions and restricting himself to the level of a single business firm (fallacy of composition?) it is almost tautological to show that a tax on capital is bad for investment. "In a closed economy, in equilibrium savings must equal investment. Thus, *in equilibrium* a policy which promotes savings must promote investment, and conversely" (p. 583). If the real economy ever was in a partial or total equilibrium does not seem to be an important question. The message counts: Don't tax the rich! He enumerates all important arguments for a consumption-based tax (pp. 579ff.), but he does not even mention one argument against it, e.g. that a neutral consumption tax must have a tax percentage increase of 25 per cent or more. Does Stiglitz assume that his self-interested economic agents will not have a strong incentive to circumvent the high final consumer prices and choose black market solutions?

Finally, in a pre-scientific way he tells the student that "(b)y borrowing, the government places the burden of reduced consumption on future generations"

(p. 783). Counter arguments are wiped away in few sentences, they have no scientific validity. That the underutilization of resources can be harmful and deficits can in principle stimulate the economy is mentioned on nine lines in a book with 823 pages.

3 Conclusions

Summarizing, we may formulate the following shortcomings of the book: (1.) It has an implicit conservative-liberal ideology without putting the normative cards explicitly on the table; (2.) The book applies the wrong methodology (formal neoclassical reasoning), and almost completely ignores sociological, historical and other aspects; (3.) The descriptive parts do not really convey framing knowledge and they are not comparative; (4.) The economic history and history of economic thought parts are more fairy tale than scientific elaborations in a nutshell; (5.) The author takes the necessary public institutions for granted which are necessary for the functioning of the private sector (antitrust policy, third party enforcement of contracts, etc.), he only mentions them peripherally, the market is construed as an objective, automatic mechanism into which the state interferes; (6.) Very often the diagrams are not well explained; (7.) The student has no applicable tool-box for decisions of the real world in the public sector at hand; (8.) The author shifts between the assumption that the neoclassical tool-box can be applied and the opposite view that this is not possible; (9.) The author has in fact written a book *Economics against the public sector* because a positive normative vision of the productive role of the state is missing; (10.) If we take into consideration his recent publications we have get a somewhat schizophrenic impression of a Stiglitz I (his textbook) and a critical Stiglitz II.

Stiglitz II castigates the Washington consensus and "market fundamentalist policies" (2002, p. 106), decisions should not be made "on the basis of what seemed a curious blend of ideology and bad economics, dogma that sometimes seemed to be thinly veiling special interests" (2002, p. 12). His reproach is that "(f)iscal austerity, privatization, and market liberalization were the three [only] pillars of Washington Consensus advice" (2002, p. 53). The same holds to a certain degree, besides the descriptive parts, for his textbook which is in most parts "based on a simplistic model of the market economy, the competitive equilibrium model in which Adam Smith's invisible hand works, and works perfectly" (2002, p. 74). Stiglitz II calls this attitude 'market fundamentalism.' Another aspect of market fundamentalism is its normative one-sidedness. "Stabilization is on the agenda; job creation is off. Taxation, and its adverse effects, are on the agenda; land reform is off" (2002, pp. 80-81). Further, it comprises a spontaneous order theorem, the "IMF simply assumed that markets arise quickly to meet every need, when in fact, many government activities arise because markets have *failed* to provide essential services" (2002, p. 55).

In his book on globalization he underlines the positive effects of state supported firms.

> While its neighbors, Singapore and Malaysia, had invited in multinational companies, South Korea had created its own enterprises. Through good products and aggressive marketing, South Korean companies had sold their goods around the world (2002, p. 102).

The closure of state enterprises "may leave a huge gap" (2002, p. 55).

Against the trickle-down hypothesis, i.e. that efficiency and growth will at the same time more or less solve the distributional problem, he now argues, "(t)rickle-down economics was never much more than just a belief, an article of faith" (2002, p. 78).

Ideal type markets like capital markets, can be unstable in principle due to the rational and irrational moods of the investors. He shares Keynes pessimism on the "often seemingly irrational changes in sentiment" (2002, p. 100).

Stiglitz should rewrite his textbook and start with a positive vision of the state and the public sector, following his own more recent intuition. The discount which must be paid to reality comes early enough. We need young students who are enthusiastic to become civil servants, who want to foster the common good and who find the dismal self-interested anti-public rhetoric boring and wrong, young motivated public sector economists who grasp the potential of a democratic, social, environmentally sound and efficient state which gives the citizen the realistic feeling of fairness and belonging.

> Government can, and has, played an essential role not only in mitigating these market failures but also in ensuring *social justice*. Market processes may, by themselves, leave many people with too few resources to survive. In countries that have been most successful, in the United States and in East Asia, government has performed these roles and performed them, for the most part, reasonably well. Governments provided a high-quality education to all and furnished much of the infrastructure – including the institutional infrastructure, such as the legal system, which is required for markets to work effectively. They regulated the financial sector, ensuring that capital markets worked more in the way that they were supposed to - hey provided a safety net for the poor. And they promoted technology, from telecommunications to agriculture to jet engines and radar. While there is a vigorous debate in the United States and elsewhere about what the *precise* role of government should be, there is broad agreement that government has a role in making any society, any economy, function efficiently- and humanely (2000, p. 218).

References

Basu, K. (2003), "Globalization and the politics of international finance: The Stiglitz verdict," *Journal of Economic Literature,* 41, pp. 885-899.
Blankart, C. B. (2001), *Öffentliche Finanzen in der Demokratie*, 4th ed., Munich: Vahlen.
Colander, D. (2000), "The death of neoclassical economics," *Journal of the History of Economic Thought*, 22, 2000, pp. 127-143.
Etzioni, A. (1988), *The moral dimension*, New York: Free Press.
Frank, R. (1986), *Choosing the right pond*, New York: Oxford University Press.
Ostrom, E. (2002), *Governing the commons*, Cambridge: Cambridge University Press.
Peukert, H. (2003), "Adam Smith's invisible hand", In: *Economic Policy in an Orderly Framework: Festschrift für G. Meijer*, ed. J. Backhaus, Münster: Lit-Verlag.
Putnam, R.D. (2001), *Bowling Alone*, New York: Simon and Schuster.
Stiglitz, J.E and A. Weiss (1982), "Credit rationing in markets with imperfect information", *American Economic Review,* 71, pp. 393-410).
Stiglitz, J.E. (1997), *Whither Socialism?,* 4th print., Cambridge [Mass.]: MIT Press.
Stiglitz, J.E. (2000), *Economics of the Public Sector*, 3rd ed., New York: Norton.

Finanzsoziologie

Herausgegeben von Jürgen G. Backhaus

Band 1 Jürgen G. Backhaus (ed.): Essays on Fiscal Sociology. 2005.

www.peterlang.de

www.ingramcontent.com/pod-product-compliance
Ingram Content Group UK Ltd.
Pitfield, Milton Keynes, MK11 3LW, UK
UKHW020121290926
15471UKWH00003B/214

9 783631 399675